Cosmopolitan Desires

FLASHPOINTS

The FlashPoints series is devoted to books that consider literature beyond strictly national and disciplinary frameworks, and that are distinguished both by their historical grounding and by their theoretical and conceptual strength. Our books engage theory without losing touch with history and work historically without falling into uncritical positivism. FlashPoints aims for a broad audience within the humanities and the social sciences concerned with moments of cultural emergence and transformation. In a Benjaminian mode, FlashPoints is interested in how literature contributes to forming new constellations of culture and history and in how such formations function critically and politically in the present. Series titles are available online at http://escholarship.org/uc/flashpoints.

1. *On Pain of Speech: Fantasies of the First Order and the Literary Rant,* Dina Al-Kassim
2. *Moses and Multiculturalism,* Barbara Johnson, with a foreword by Barbara Rietveld
3. *The Cosmic Time of Empire: Modern Britain and World Literature,* Adam Barrows
4. *Poetry in Pieces: César Vallejo and Lyric Modernity,* Michelle Clayton
5. *Disarming Words: Empire and the Seductions of Translation in Egypt,* Shaden M. Tageldin
6. *Wings for Our Courage: Gender, Erudition, and Republican Thought,* Stephanie H. Jed
7. *The Cultural Return,* Susan Hegeman
8. *English Heart, Hindi Heartland: The Political Life of Literature in India,* Rashmi Sadana
9. *The Cylinder: Kinematics of the Nineteenth Century,* Helmut Müller-Sievers
10. *Polymorphous Domesticities: Pets, Bodies, and Desire in Four Modern Writers,* Juliana Schiesari
11. *Flesh and Fish Blood: Postcolonialism, Translation, and the Vernacular,* S. Shankar
12. *The Fear of French Negroes: Transcolonial Collaboration in the Revolutionary Americas,* Sara E. Johnson
13. *Figurative Inquisitions: Conversion, Torture, and Truth in the Luso-Hispanic Atlantic,* Erin Graff Zivin
14. *Cosmopolitan Desires: Global Modernity and World Literature in Latin America,* Mariano Siskind
15. *Fiction Beyond Secularism,* Justin Neuman

Cosmopolitan Desires

Global Modernity and World Literature in Latin America

Mariano Siskind

NORTHWESTERN UNIVERSITY PRESS | EVANSTON, ILLINOIS

THIS BOOK IS MADE POSSIBLE BY A COLLABORATIVE GRANT
FROM THE ANDREW W. MELLON FOUNDATION.

Northwestern University Press
www.nupress.northwestern.edu

Digital Printing
ISBN 978-0-8101-2990-0

Library of Congress Cataloging-in-Publication Data

Siskind, Mariano, 1972– author.
Cosmopolitan desires : global modernity and world literature in Latin America / Mariano Siskind.
pages cm. — (FlashPoints)
ISBN 978-0-8101-2990-0 (pbk. : alk. paper)
1. Latin American literature—20th century—History and criticism. 2. Modernism (Literature)—Latin America. 3. Cosmopolitanism in literature. I. Title. II. Series: FlashPoints (Evanston, Ill.)
PQ7081.S58 2014
860.998—dc23

2014001057

Para Analía Ivanier
son tantos tus sueños que ves el cielo

Contents

Acknowledgments

I wrote this book between 2007 and 2012, and during those five eventful years I incurred many debts of gratitude. Sylvia Molloy is my favorite cosmopolitan intellectual. Learning from her at New York University was a privilege that has shaped my work profoundly, and I continue to consider myself her student. I am deeply grateful to Diana Sorensen and Doris Sommer for going above and beyond the call of duty to support my research and teaching at Harvard. I benefited enormously from Diana's insightful comments on the first draft of chapter 1, particularly regarding the materiality of literary networks, and I have learned a great deal from Doris's incisive questions on the role of Caribbean and Jewish dislocations in chapters 2 and 5. From the moment I met him, David Damrosch has treated me with unparalleled kindness, encouraging my research on cosmopolitanism, inviting me to take part in American Comparative Literature Association panels, and including my work in anthologies. Michelle Clayton, who is one of the most generous scholars of the North Atlantic rim, took an interest in this book even before it was finished; in addition to her thoughtful comments on several chapters, I want to thank her for making my *Cosmopolitan Desires* part of the Flashpoints series of the Modern Languages Initiative and for taking care of the manuscript as if it were her own. Graciela Montaldo and Chris Bush read the entire manuscript and made extremely useful comments on its general structure and on global modernisms at the exact moment when I was beginning to rewrite numerous sections. Luis Fernández Cifuentes took me under his wing from my first days at Harvard, providing priceless advice when I most needed it. I am incredibly fortunate to work with colleagues who have always made me feel at home at the Department of Romance Languages and Literatures. Thanks to Mary Gaylord, Luis Girón Negrón, Virginie Greene, Christie McDonald, Susan Suleiman, Francesco Erspamer, Jeffrey Schnapp, Brad Epps, José Rabasa, Tom Conley, Janet Beizer, Nicolau Sevcenko, Joaquim Coelho, Alice Jardine, and Verena Andermatt Conley, and also to Mike Holmes, Kathy Coviello, Katherine Killough, Susan Fuerst, Frannie Lindsay, and Walter Hryshko. I am particularly grateful to my junior colleagues with whom I have shared the trenches during all these years, Mylène Priam, Sylvaine Guyot, Sergio Delgado, Daniel Aguirre, and Giuliana Minghelli, and to Johanna Liander, Adriana Gutiérrez, María Luisa Parra, Clemence Jouët-Pastré, and Stacy Katz for their warmth and collegiality.

Among the many friends who have contributed to this book, I especially want to thank Alejandra Uslenghi, Gonzalo Aguilar, and Alejandra Laera for their lucidity as readers and for being ever-present for almost two decades. Writing books, organizing panels, presenting papers, and imagining future collaborations are all the more enjoyable when done in the company of friends and colleagues like Erin Graff Zivin, Héctor Hoyos, Guillermina de Ferrari, César Domínguez, Víctor Goldgel, Martín Gaspar, Ximena Briceño, Nirvana Tanoukhi, Heather Cleary, Rebecca Walkowitz, Jing Tsu, Javier Uriarte, Florencia Garramuño, Ernesto Livon-Grossman, Emily Maguire, Nina Gerassi-Navarro, Nathalie Bouzaglo, Víctor Vich, Javier Guerrero, Fernando Degiovanni, Gabriela Nouzeilles, Lena Burgos-Lafuente, Martín Bergel, and Gabriel Giorgi. I am also extremely grateful to María Teresa Gramuglio, Beatriz Sarlo, Carlos Altamirano, and Nancy Ruttenburg for supporting this project in its preliminary and later stages, but also for their unwavering friendship.

I was able to conduct archival research in the United States and Latin America thanks to two travel fellowships from the David Rockefeller Center for Latin American Studies at Harvard and a Faculty of Arts and Sciences Research Enabling Grant. I have learned a great deal about this book from my co-panelists and audiences at numerous conferences and invited lectures where I have presented draft portions of this project. I would like to express particular appreciation to Homi Bhabha for inviting me to speak at Harvard's Mahindra Humanities Center; to Franco Moretti, Margaret Cohen, and Nancy Ruttenburg for welcoming me at Stanford's

Center for the Study of the Novel; to Hernán Feldman for his intellectual hospitality at Emory University; to Florencia Garramuño for fruitful discussions of the ideas underlying this book at the Foro de Crítica Cultural at Universidad de San Andrés; and, finally, to Martín Bergel, Alejandra Laera, Adrián Gorelik, Lila Caimari, and Hugo Vezzetti for a heated and interesting debate at the Instituto Dr. Emilio Ravignani at the Universidad de Buenos Aires. Early versions of chapter 1 and chapter 2 appeared in *Comparative Literature* (Fall 2010, 62.4) and *The Cambridge History of Postcolonial Literature* (2012), respectively. I thank Duke University Press and Cambridge University Press for permission to reprint them in revised form. I would like to express deep gratitude to George Rowe and Ato Quayson, editors of those publications, for their help and encouragement with these two chapters. The anonymous referees at Northwestern University Press provided invaluable criticism and helpful suggestions. I have tried out many of the hypotheses of this book in undergraduate and graduate seminars at Harvard, and I want to thank my students for many precious conversations. Among the participants in these seminars, I would like to acknowledge Rosario Hubert, Lotte Buiting, Carlos Varón González, Anna White-Nockleby, and Ernest Hartwell.

I am deeply grateful to my loving friends in Buenos Aires, New York, Chicago, Washington, D.C., Paris, and Australia, whose faces and voices are constantly with me over e-mail, Skype, and cell phones, and occasionally even face to face: Gabriel Schvarstein, Martín Moya, Juan Saadia, Mariano Polack, Mariano Kulish, Carmen Güiraldes, Martín Kohan, Carolina Lutenberg, Ernesto Semán, Claudio Benzecry, Lorelei El Jaber, and Sergio Chejfec. I thank each of them.

But above all, I want to thank my family for their unconditional affection and support. Raquel and Hugo, in-laws *extraordinaire*, my dear sister Luli and her family in Santiago de Chile, my adoring parents, Rosalba and Horacio, and my grandfather, Bernardo Smulevici, who passed on to me his love of literature and storytelling (directly and through my mother): I could never adequately thank them for oh so many ways of loving and caring for me. Finally, I thank my beloved, beautiful sons, Valentín and Bruno, who every day rescue me from myself and take me to our shared universe of Beatles songs, movies, soccer rituals, and picture books (from *Gorilita* to *Gruffalo*!). This book is dedicated to the love of my life, Analía Ivanier, not because I could not have written this book without her, but for everything, everything else.

Cosmopolitan Desires

Introduction

In Latin America (as in other global peripheries), critical and aesthetic cosmopolitan discourses shared a common epistemological structure that I call *deseo de mundo*, desire for the world. Cosmopolitan intellectuals invoked the world alternately as a signifier of abstract universality or a concrete and finite set of global trajectories traveled by writers and books. In either case, opening to the world permitted an escape from nationalist cultural formations and established a symbolic horizon for the realization of the translocal aesthetic potential of literature and cosmopolitan forms of subjectivation. I want to begin by reading the constitutive nature of these *desejos do mundo* and *deseos de mundo* in two particular and meaningful cosmopolitan imaginings of Latin American culture.

In 1900, the Brazilian politician, diplomat, and writer Joaquim Nabuco published a memoir, *Minha formação* (*My Formative Years*), describing his sentimental education as one of the most influential public intellectuals of the late Empire and early Republic. The historical importance of Nabuco's autobiography lies in his firsthand accounts of the abolition of slavery, the revolts and political maneuverings that led to the Empire's collapse, and his travels and encounters with notable literary and political figures. What interests me, however, is a remarkable section of the book titled "Atração do mundo" ("The Attraction of the World"), where Nabuco grounds his intellectual self-representation in a cosmopolitan discourse: "Minha curiosidade, o meu interesse, vae sempre para o ponto onde a acção do drama contemporâneo universal é mais complicada ou mais intensa. Sou antes um espectador do meu seculo do que do meu país; a peça é para mim a civilização, e se está representando em todos os theatros da humanidade, ligados hoje pelo telegrapho" (33–34) ("My curiosity or my interest always focuses on the most complicated or intense part of the action in the contemporary universal drama. I am more a spectator of my century than of my country. For me, the play is civilization, and it is staged in all great theaters of humanity, now connected by the telegraph"; 24). Silviano Santiago reads Nabuco's cosmopolitan declaration as a crucial milestone in a tradition that Antonio Candido has described as a "síntese de tendencias particularistas e universalistas" (12) ("synthesis of particularistic and universalist trends").[1] But instead of a dialectical synthesis of opposites, Santiago characterizes Nabuco's self-representation as that of a marginal witness to world affairs (thus his reliance on modern technologies of communication, like the telegraph), the sort of global mediation that shapes the peripheral position of Brazil and Latin America at the beginning of the twentieth century: "Morando em um país provinciano, [Nabuco] está distante do palco onde a grande peça se desenrola, mas dela pode ser espectador no conforto do lar em virtude dos meios de comunicação de massa modernos, no caso o telégrafo. A oposição entre país de origem e século, e a preferencia pela crise da representação [do Imperio] e não pela busca de identidade nacional da joven nação" (12–13) ("Living in a provincial country, [Nabuco] is far from the stage where the great play is being performed, but he can be a spectator from his comfortable location thanks to modern media like the telegraph. The opposition between country of origin and his times signifies his preference for the [Empire's] crisis of representation, to the detriment of his young country's search for national identity"). Nabuco admits that, despite their national significance, local politics bore him (33). He conceives of himself as a spectator, a world-historical witness, only to "a acção do drama contemporaneo universal" ("the action of contemporary universal drama") that takes place beyond the national stage, out there in the undetermined, universal realm of civilization—the discursive field where Nabuco grounds a cosmopolitan self-representation that relies on the radical opposition between the nation ("meu país") and humanity at large ("meu século," "drama contemporâneo universal," "os theatros da humanidade").

Half a century later in Buenos Aires, Jorge Luis Borges wrote a programmatic and polemical essay, "El escritor argentino y la tradición"

("The Argentine Writer and Tradition"). In that piece, written as a lecture in 1951 and revised and published in 1953, he examines the contingency and boundaries of the aesthetic tradition that should structure the Argentine literary imagination. He asks, "¿Cuál es la tradición argentina?" (272) ("What is Argentine tradition?"; 425), not because he seeks descriptive satisfaction, but rather in order to introduce his normative, radically universalist answer. However, before he articulates his cosmopolitan theory of the sources, institutions, and structures of signification of Argentine literature, he devotes his polemical energies to discrediting the prevailing responses to his question. His targets include predominant forms of particularistic localism (including the *criollista* avant-garde to which he had subscribed three decades earlier), the national populism of *Peronismo*'s cultural *dicta*, a meager proposal to rekindle a close relation with peninsular cultural traditions, and more generally, any foundationalist and essentialist conception of cultural identity. Beyond the essay's polemical pulse, Borges is concerned with providing an interpretative framework for the narrative universe he had been assembling since the mid-1930s, one that was frequently characterized as too abstract, lacking clear referents, and, most problematically, disregarding and radically reshaping the traditional motifs of national literature. By the end of the essay, this framework doubles as a forceful call on Argentine writers to disregard national determinations and produce a cosmopolitan literature: "Creo que nuestra tradición es toda la cultura occidental, y creo también que tenemos derecho a esa tradición, mayor que el que pueden tener los habitantes de una u otra nación occidental" (272) ("I believe that our tradition is the whole of Western culture, and I also believe that we have a right to this tradition, a greater right than that which the inhabitants of one Western nation or another may have"; 184), concluding, "Debemos pensar que nuestro patrimonio es el universo" (274) ("We must believe that the universe is our birthright"; 185).

In asserting Argentina's lateral geocultural positionality, Borges demarcates a field of transcultural relations structured around antagonistic links. This is clear in Beatriz Sarlo's characterization of Borges's cosmopolitanism as "la condición que hace posible una estrategia para la literatura argentina: inversamente, el reordenamiento de las tradiciones culturales nacionales lo habilita para cortar, elegir y recorrer desprejuiciadamente las literaturas extranjeras, en cuyo espacio se maneja con la soltura de un marginal que hace libre uso de todas las culturas. . . . Desde un margen, Borges logra que su literatura dialogue de igual a igual con la literatura occidental. Hace del margen una estética" (*Borges, un escritor* 16) ("a condition that allows him to invent a strategy for Argentine literature. Conversely, the reordering of national cultural traditions enables Borges to cut, select and reorder foreign literatures without preconceptions, asserting the liberty of those who are marginal to make free use of all cultures. . . . From the edge of the west, Borges achieves a literature that is related to foreign literature but not in any subordinate way"; *Borges, a Writer*, 5). The same antagonistic cosmopolitanism can be read in Sylvia Molloy's interpretation of Borges as a writer "tampering with the European archive." For her, Borges's cosmopolitanism is a disruption of "the authority of that archive (even as he relies on it)"; he "contaminates that archive (as he gives it new life) by inserting it in a new cultural landscape, in the 'outskirts' of Latin American literature. . . . To bring up Browning when speaking of Carriego invites readers to a new view of Carriego; but it also, inevitably, invites them to a new view of Browning" ("Lost in Translation" 17).

I believe—along with Sarlo and Molloy—that one should read the differential affirmation of a cosmopolitan and disruptive aesthetic identity not in terms of a particularistic cultural politics but as a strategic literary practice that forces its way into the realm of universality, denouncing both the hegemonic structures of Eurocentric forms of exclusion and nationalistic patterns of self-marginalization. In other words, it is a cosmopolitan attempt to undo the antagonistic structures of a world literary field organized around the notions of cultural difference that Latin American cosmopolitan writers perceive to be the source of their marginality, in order to stake a claim on Literature with a capital L—the imaginary, undifferentiated grounds of a cosmopolitan literature "free from constraint, whether nationalist or pedagogical" (Balderston 47), or, to borrow the words from the title of an essay by Juan José Saer, "una literatura sin atributos" (272) ("a literature without attributes").

These passages from Nabuco and Borges perform the point of departure of this book—a point of departure that will be reproduced, contested, and dislocated by the restless characters and objects convened there. Nabuco and Borges pose a horizontal, universal discursive field where they can represent their cosmopolitan subjectivity on equal terms with the metropolitan cultures whose hegemony their discourses try to undermine. I propose that this is an omnipotent fantasy (an imaginary scenario occupying the place of the real, according to Lacan), a strategic, voluntaristic fantasy that is nonetheless very effective in opening a cosmopolitan discursive space where it is possible to imagine a non-nationalistic, nonanthropocentric path to a modernization that is set against the horizon of abstract universality. I call this cosmopolitan discursive space the "world," and I trace and examine the ways in which Latin American literature has represented, invoked, challenged, and inhabited this imaginary space, this world defined as radically exterior to Latin America's cultural particularity.

Cosmopolitan Desires reads Latin American literary modernity as a global relation, a set of aesthetic procedures that mediate a broadened transcultural network of uneven cultural exchanges. It traces world-making discourses and physical displacements within comparative, translational, and displaced frames of legibility from the 1870s onwards: the globalization of the novel form during the second half of the nineteenth century and the *planetary novels* of the Argentine Eduardo Ladislao Holmberg and the French Jules Verne; the global dislocations of magical realism between the 1920s and the 1990s, from Franz Roh's coining of the term in Germany in 1925, to its Latin American reconceptualizations between the 1930s and the 1960s, to the postcolonial transformations the genre has experienced in Africa, South Asia, and eastern Europe since the 1970s; the production of a literary world construed both as a repository of universalist discourses and as a global web of real and imaginary itineraries in the context of *modernismo*, the heterogeneous and internally differentiated aesthetic formation that sought to renew Latin American culture from the 1880s to the early 1920s, from José Martí to Baldomero Sanín Cano; Rubén Darío's deliberate and sophisticated construction of French universality as a cosmopolitan horizon of modernization for Latin America between 1893 and 1905, the dates of his residences in Buenos Aires and Paris; and the crisis of Orientalist discourses in Enrique Gómez Carrillo's early twentieth-century travel writing, where his encounter with the cultural ambivalence of Eastern Jews destabilizes his notions of East and West.

I situate these cosmopolitan imaginaries and global mappings within current debates on the meaning, scope, and cultural geographies of world literature, debates where Latin America's participation (as a literary corpus, field of study, and place of enunciation) has been minimal.[2] In fact, the two-part structure of this book corresponds to the attempt to reconceptualize, in two different directions, the meaning of world literature in relation to the marginal specificity of the Latin American literary field. Because the book does not present a totalizing history of cosmopolitan discourses in the region, its structure is not chronological; rather, it responds to the theoretical logic of the reformulations of world literature that I put forth in each of the two parts.

By reframing the history of the novel and magical realism within global circuits of economic, cultural, and aesthetic exchange, Part One views world literature as the material production of a literary world that does not preexist the circulation of the texts and objects that makes its form visible. Part Two understands world literature as a universalist, modernizing, strategic discourse on the literatures of the world, whose structural presence in Latin America can be traced to the early 1880s. This world literature is crucial to the understanding of the cultural politics of *modernismo*, as well as the transcultural relations that constitute its meaning.[3] In reading the conceptual and historical specificity of a modernist world posed by cosmopolitan discourses from Latin America, Part Two relies on Part One's theorization of the global space that grounds them and ensures their cultural efficacy. The two parts intersect at the point where Latin American intellectuals and texts articulated the possibility of a cosmopolitan modernity, anxiously imagining a world that could accommodate their need to live in perfect synchrony with what they believed to be taking place elsewhere. Whether "elsewhere" was France, a general idea of North Atlantic and Mediterranean connections that they called "Europe" or "*Occidente*," or a vaguely defined space of conceptual universality dominated but not exhausted by European or Western culture, this signifier of exteriority was a blank screen upon which cosmopolitan writers projected their aesthetic desires and their longing to participate in the actualization of modernity, a historical task open to anyone with a modern aesthetic sensibility. During the extended period I study here, this tradition was admittedly minoritarian—especially when compared to the hegemony of nationalist and Latin Americanist modernizing imaginaries throughout the region—but the reconstruction of its discursivity remains crucial if we are to understand the "history of [our] vanishing present" (to invoke the subtitle of Gayatri Spivak's *A Critique of Postcolonial Reason*), a history made up of continuities and breaks with the past, as well as moments of translation, productive misreadings, and appropriations that inform the continued impact of a disjointed process of cultural globalization and Latin America's ambivalent place in it.

In the tradition formalized by Kant in his moral and political philosophy, cosmopolitanism is most often thought of as an ethical mandate to concern oneself with the good of others (Nussbaum), as an obligation to those who are beyond the people who are close to us like our kin or our compatriots (Appiah). Because cosmopolitanism is often conceptualized in rather abstract terms, the cultural and geopolitical obstacles that mediate the cosmopolitan subject's response to such universalist unconditional and disinterested demand tend to be overlooked. In fact, geopolitical particular determinations, libidinal drives, and obscured motives are constitutive of the kind of cosmopolitan agency I am interested in here. The hero of this book, if I may call him that, is a Latin American cosmopolitan intellectual (a distinctively male writer) who derives his specific cultural subjectivity from his marginal position of enunciation and from the certainty that this position has excluded him from the global unfolding of a modernity articulated outside a Latin American cultural field saturated with the nationalistic or peninsular signifiers that determine its backwardness.[4] In his second seminar, Lacan explains that "desire is a relation of being to lack. The lack is the lack of being properly speaking" (*Ego in Freud's Theory* 223). Following Lacan, in this book I depict the figure of a cosmopolitan marginal intellectual defined by both a constitutive lack, translated as a signifier of exclusion from the order of global modernity, and a longing for universal belonging and recognition that mediates his discursive practices and measures the libidinal investment that produces his imaginary cosmopolitan "body-ego" (Freud, *Ego* 31).[5]

However, the contradiction between the desire for universality and the marginal conditions of enunciation points to the anxiety and frustration of a split subject whose "impossible longing affirms [itself] as the limit of satisfaction" (Butler 187). But while these universal desires can never be satisfied, Latin American cosmopolitans can still constitute their intellectual identity through the omnipotent and voluntaristic representation of their imagined universality. According to Ernesto Laclau, "The universal is the symbol of a missing fullness," and he goes on to explain that "the universal is part of my identity in so far as I am penetrated by a constitutive lack—that is, in so far as my differential identity has failed in its process of constitution. The universal emerges out of the particular not as some principle underlying and explaining it, but as an incomplete horizon suturing a dislocated particular identity" (28). Laclau's account is useful to describe the formation of the cosmopolitan subjectivities that I conceptualize here. If the universal is the retrospective effect of a general process of cultural identification, in the case of cosmopolitan intellectuals dislocated by the symbolic order of nationalism, the universal appears as the negation of the local and the particular, which are perceived only in relation to their castrative potential. The world, in turn, is the signifier of the universal. So, on the one hand, cosmopolitanism (or, in the opposite scenario, nationalism) is a story that cosmopolitan subjects tell themselves to make sense of their traumatic experience of marginality in the order of global modernity. On the other, the signifier "world" that enables this fantasy exists only as the discursive instance that assures the imaginary fullness of a cultural-political identity that organizes its discourse around master signifiers of universal equality and justice. In other words: the world does not exist, or rather, it does not preexist the acts of imagining it, naming it, and acknowledging the ways in which it constitutes *my* cosmopolitanism.[6] Throughout this book, the "world" in world literature and ideas like "the production of the world" should be understood as the phantasmatic projection of cosmopolitan desires onto a variety of a priori undecidable geographical assemblages that may or may not coincide with the territoriality of existing conventional institutions of national or regional sovereignty. The "world," then, is the imaginary ground where Latin American cosmopolitan writers work through the traumatic aspects of the question of modernity, inscribing their modernist subjectivity in their universality.[7]

In the Latin American critical tradition, cosmopolitanism has been considered in terms different from the ones I develop here. Before the 1980s, the concept of cosmopolitanism was often used in reductive and superficial ways, a fundamental feature of three markedly different, homogeneous moments in a linear and teleological literary history: *modernismo*, the avant-garde, and the literary articulations of humanism. In cursory characterizations of the long historical arc of these three moments (1880s–1950s), cosmopolitanism was not a critical concept but a shorthand for supposedly elitist, denationalizing, apolitical, antipopular, uprooted, Francophile, queer, displaced, and mobile forces in the literary field. As I show in chapter 4, this notion of cosmopolitanism led the Uruguayan poet and essayist José Rodó to declare Darío the author of a "poesía enteramente antiamericanista" ("entirely anti-American poetry").

However, in the first half of the 1980s, there were a number of attempts to redefine cosmopolitanism, principally in relation to the avant-garde, but also in relation to *modernismo* (and even to the Boom and pre-Boom novels of the 1950s and '60s), as a form of particularized universalism, an inward importation of modern European literary tropes, vocabularies, and procedures where universalist desires were subsumed by the particularistic logic of differential (national or regional) identities. In other words, cosmopolitanism was viewed as the attempt to disrupt and transform a particular cultural field—usually replete with nationalistic signifiers—by translating the putative universality of modern and modernist metropolitan cultures into the vernacular languages and aesthetic traditions that make this appropriation polemical.

In "Sobre la vanguardia, Borges y el criollismo," an essay published in *Punto de Vista* in 1981, Beatriz Sarlo read the Argentine avant-garde magazine *Martín Fierro* and Borges's essays and poetry of the 1920s along these lines, as a "cosmopolitismo criollista" ("*criollista* cosmopolitanism"). She developed this view of vernacular cultural modernizations and particularized universalisms in several pieces: "Vanguardia y criollismo: La aventura de *Martín Fierro*" (1983, coauthored with Carlos Altamirano), *Una modernidad periférica* (1988), and *Borges, a Writer on the Edge* (1993). This dialectical conception of the relation between Latin America and Europe had been pioneered since the early 1960s by the Brazilian critic Antonio Candido, whose work was central to Sarlo's thinking. In a 1980 interview for *Punto de Vista*, Candido explained his view of the dialectical specificity of Brazilian and Latin American cultures:

> Una literatura [moderna] necesita que sus escritores experimenten la presencia de la nacionalidad: en el nivel de la función ideológica, la voluntad de ser nacional, de ser específico, es muy productiva. Si una de nuestras literaturas dijera: quiero ser europea, estaría perdida. El movimiento debe afirmar: nada tengo que ver con Europa, soy un escritor brasileño, canto al indio. Y lo canta efectivamente en estrofas italianas. O imitando la prosa poética de Chateaubriand. Lo que quisiera demostrar es que el proceso literario, en un mundo regido por la interdependencia de los pueblos, engloba tanto el punto de vista cosmopolita como el local. . . . Creo que debemos percibir un movimiento dialéctico, que se da en nuestra historia, entre lo local y lo universal. (9)

> A [modern] literature needs its writers to experience the presence of nationality: at the level of ideological function, the will to be national, to be specific, is very productive. If one of our literatures were to say: I want to be European, it would be lost. The movement should declare: I have nothing to do with Europe, I am a Brazilian writer, I sing in Indian. And in fact he sings it in Italian stanzas. Or imitating Chateaubriand's poetic prose. I want to demonstrate that the literary process, in a world governed by the interdependence of all peoples, includes the cosmopolitan point of view as

> much as the local. . . . I believe that we should perceive a dialectical movement, occurring in our history, between the local and the universal.

Jorge Schwartz's *Vanguardia y cosmopolitismo en la década del veinte: Oliverio Girondo y Oswald de Andrade* (*The Avant-Garde and Cosmopolitanism in the 1920s: Oliverio Girondo and Oswald de Andrade*) (1983), a classic comparative study of the Argentine and Brazilian avant-gardes, applied Candido's insights to Oswald de Andrade's anthropophagy: "La fórmula oswaldeana de la antropofagia, que apunta a la asimilación de lo extranjero para la producción y exportación de lo nacional . . . condensa con humor paródico la cuestión de la devoración de lo foráneo para la producción de una síntesis nacional" (103–04) ("The Oswaldian formula of anthropophagy, which calls for assimilating the foreign for the production and exportation of the national . . . condenses with parodic humor the question of devouring the foreign to produce a national synthesis"). For Schwartz, São Paulo—the organic home of Oswald de Andrade's avant-garde aesthetic practices—takes on a cosmopolitan character as a result of the dialectical relation between importation (of modern institutions and transnational capitals) and exportation (of national cultural forms and commodities such as coffee).[8] This attempt to mediate conflicting universal and local demands would gain traction in US and European humanities from the 1990s onward, in the context of postcolonial and post-Marxist reformulations of the cultural situatedness of marginal cosmopolitanisms (see, for example, Kwame Anthony Appiah on "rooted cosmopolitanism" [*Ethics of Identity*; *Cosmopolitanism*] and "cosmopolitan patriotism" ["Cosmopolitan Patriots"], Homi Bhabha on "vernacular cosmopolitanism" ["Unsatisfied"], and Toni Erskine on "embedded cosmopolitanism," among others).

Ángel Rama's characterization of cosmopolitanism as the flip side of transculturation in his notable *Transculturación narrativa en América Latina* (*Narrative Transculturation in Latin America*) (published in 1982, although he began to develop the idea in a 1974 essay) further complicates things. Rama borrowed the concept of transculturation from the Cuban anthropologist Fernando Ortiz in order to systematize an interpretation of Latin American novels from the 1950s and '60s that included Juan Rulfo's *Pedro Páramo*, João Guimarães Rosa's *Grande Sertão: Veredas* (*The Devil to Pay in the Backlands*), José María Arguedas's *Los ríos profundos* (*Deep Rivers*), and Gabriel

García Márquez's *Cien años de soledad* (*One Hundred Years of Solitude*). These novels can be characterized by their dialectical resolution of the contradiction between universality and particularity, between a modern universal desire to implode and overcome the narrative protocols of realism and regionalism and the use of local oral and popular traditions that constitute both their cultural content and their formal experimentation.[9] These *novelas transculturadoras* (transculturizing novels) produced a national-popular aesthetic form, a rhetoric and imaginary that political leadership could help to translate into actual social transformations. For Rama, transculturation is a critical concept that can mediate art and the revolutionary politics that intensified after the Cuban Revolution in 1959.

This ideological orientation of transculturation defines its opposition to Rama's understanding of cosmopolitanism as an elite literary practice marked by the imitation of well-established, metropolitan, experimental narrative practices, devoid of any political investment in the national-popular materials, voices, and images that might ground it in progressive politics (Rama's paradigmatic antitransculturizing cosmopolitan writer was Mario Vargas Llosa). It is significant that Rama recognizes a common modernizing anxiety in both transculturalizing *and* cosmopolitan narratives. Both interrogate the cultural hegemony of western European modern culture and the aesthetic or conceptual materials that bear the traces of Latin America's asymmetric social relation to them. Yet, while cosmopolitanism is the outward desire for inclusion within that hegemonic formation, transculturation attempts to disrupt the hegemonic nature of its modernist practices by introducing subaltern materials that determine its inward movement. That is, cosmopolitanism stresses the highly ideological, indeed imaginary, impulse to do away with or at least postpone Latin America's cultural difference in order to gain access to the perceived universality of the *hegemon*, universalizing Latin America's particularity even at the cost of erasing it. Transculturation instead emphasizes inward, local instances of appropriation, translation, and resignification of the hegemonic universal, thereby reproducing and reinforcing the process of cultural differentiation that produces Latin America's identity in particularistic terms. If cosmopolitan writers posit a Latin American aesthetic identity against the backdrop of the universality of Humanity, Culture, and Literature (with a capital H, C, and L), the *transculturadores* anchor their works' aesthetic identity in the manifest confidence that their narratives can liberate the political potential of the subaltern and the national-popular at the local, national, or regional level. Rama sees this difference as markedly ideological: apolitical, elitist and abstract universalism on one side, emancipatory, particularistic politics on the other.

I believe Rama's characterization of cosmopolitanism as the conservative and elitist Other of the emancipatory aesthetics of transculturation overlooks the complex tensions between inclusion and elitism, egalitarianism and political naïveté, in the cosmopolitan traditions that I trace here. If it is true that these marginal cosmopolitan desires are sustained by narcissistic and omnipotent fantasies about the openness and receptivity of the universal, it is also true that transculturizing discourses derive the libidinal force that sustains their politics from an investment in the redemptive power of literature that is hardly less symptomatic.

My interest in the production of a cultural and aesthetic discourse on the world as a horizon of signification comes from the desire to understand the historical grounds of cosmopolitan literary discourses whose aspirational and proleptic temporality cannot be subsumed under predominant nation-bound, identity-driven hermeneutics. In this sense, the return of world literature in the twenty-first century provides a set of productive frames of intelligibility that illuminate the transcultural and transhistorical seams of the imaginary and material processes from which modern Latin American literature emerged. They also reveal the historicity of current ethically inclined cosmopolitan discourses that seek to overwrite and redirect a process of globalization (understood as a preeminently economic phenomenon characterized by the hypercirculation of financial capital, the explosion of global trade and transnational outsourcing, generalized deregulation, and the decline of traditional institutions like unions) toward more just goals.[10] If, in the context of global unevenness that results from these combined processes, the inclusionary potential of this ethically inflected new world literature means that "it is the outliers that would most benefit from a new global forum" (Tsu 161), why has Latin American literary criticism largely failed to engage in these debates? As an attempt to inscribe Latin American literature in the world, and to interrogate the figurations of the world in Latin American literature, *Cosmopolitan Desires* answers Jing Tsu's challenge to world literary critics to produce an "expansive historicization of the geopolitical origins of [world literature's] gesture of hospitality" (161).

Regardless of the signifiers that name it, the obsession with the world as a way to overcome national determinations of literary signification has a long history. Before Johann Wolfgang Goethe conceptualized his own anxiety through *Weltliteratur*, the Abbé Prevost formulated the idea of "la République des lettres" in his *Journal étranger* (1754), and the Spanish Jesuit Juan Andrés devised a structure for its internal classification in his *Origen, progresos y estado actual de toda la literatura* (*Origin, Progress and Current State of All Literature*) (1806).[11] But it was Goethe, from 1827 to his death in 1832, who in conversations with his disciple Johann Peter Eckermann, as well as diary entries, correspondence, and aphorisms, gave world literature the conceptual substance that continues to define it. Recognizing the increase in translations and interactions between writers, Goethe urged writers to read beyond their national boundaries ("National literature has not much meaning nowadays: the epoch of world literature is at hand, and everyone must work to hasten its coming" [qtd. in Strich 349]), mitigating the restrictions "imposed by linguistically and politically drawn cultural borders" (Pizer 4). Goethe's *West-östlicher Divan* (*West-Easterly Divan*) (1819) reveals the aesthetic and philological channels that were being forged between western European national literary fields, as well as the connections between these channels and a totalized representation of Eastern languages and literatures that was only then being conceptually articulated. Martin Puchner explains that an *inter*-national market of translated texts resulted from this relation between writers and state-sponsored institutions (*Poetry* 50). Goethe believed that, within this sphere of cultural commerce, men of letters still derived their identity from national cultures that served as indivisible units of comparison: "The peculiarities of each nation are like its languages and coins, they make commerce easier, in fact they make it possible in the first place" (qtd. in Puchner, *Poetry* 50).

Goethe's description of world literature as an emerging field of literary exchanges organized around institutions and translating agents was fragmentary and unsystematic. And yet he set the parameters that continue to define our thinking about the transformations that aesthetic forms undergo when they cross cultural boundaries, as well as the anxiety of writers and critics who view their literary systems as confined and impoverished in their particularity because, as Arjun Appadurai has put it, "One man's imagined community is another man's political prison" (32).

Throughout the nineteenth and twentieth centuries, critics like Hugo Meltzel, George Brandes, Richard Moulton, Erich Auerbach, Werner P.

Friederich, René Étiemble, Fredric Jameson, and Sarah Lawall, among others, contributed to the material institutionalization of world literature, adding layers of complexity, historical specificity, and variability to world literature as an intellectual practice, corpus, and humanistic pedagogy (D'haen, chs. 3 and 4). Over the last two decades, new and varied formulations of the meaning, scope, organization, and urgent contemporaneity of world literature productively intersected discussions of the inherited, naturalized scales of inquiry that structured literary studies around nations (Tanoukhi; Dimock and Buell). Taking the acceleration of globalization as a condition of contemporary experience (Jameson, "New Literary History" 375), and responding to the demands of a new cultural landscape marked by "tensions between cultural homogenization and heterogenization" produced by uneven global flows of migrants, technology, finance, media, and ideology (Appadurai 32–36), a number of comparative literature scholars resurrected world literature.[12] Pascale Casanova's *La république mondiale des lettres* (*The World Republic of Letters*) (1998), Franco Moretti's "Conjectures on World Literature" (2000), and David Damrosch's *What Is World Literature?* (2003) were the most influential (but by no means the only) attempts to rethink the field's object of study in relation to a world that "has given rise to so many inhospitable acts of violence, so many prohibitions, so many exclusions" but that also represents "the positive condition and democratic pole of a desired globalization" (Derrida, "Globalization" 373–74).[13]

Much has been written on the competition between nations that binds the world literary field in Casanova's theory, and the role of Paris as its arbiter and center; on Moretti's notion of *distant reading* and his *law of literary evolution*; and on Damrosch's definition of world literature as a mode of reading texts that have traveled "beyond their culture of origin either in translation or in their original language" (*What Is World Literature?* 4). Though scrutiny of methodologies and key concepts is a worthy undertaking, what I believe is at stake in these theorizations is the conceptual structure that grounds their critical discourse: the world, not as a metaphorical aspiration to overcome the local and the national, but as a critical account of a transcultural space that can contain the cosmopolitan literary epistemologies and ethico-political interventions articulated by artists and critics.[14]

Casanova, who derives her theoretical model from Pierre Bourdieu's sociology of culture, views the world as a literary field of aesthetic and institutional relations defined by the regulating function of a Paris that bestows hierarchical relations and consecration on texts and authors from every corner of the globe, reproducing both the uneven relations that shape the field and a normative notion of aesthetic value. Similarly, Moretti sees the world as a relational system of literary circulation (emphasizing the novel as the paradigmatic global genre), organized according to Immanuel Wallerstein's world-systems theory into a core, a periphery, and a semiperiphery.[15] But if Casanova arranges the world around the transit of works and writers through Paris, therefore limiting the scope of participants in her field of socio-aesthetic relations, Moretti's world is the totality of the literary real, one that includes potentially every text ever written and even an imaginary repository of unknown texts (which he calls, citing Margaret Cohen, "the great unread") whose future discovery is presupposed. Although Moretti pays lip service to the empirical research necessary to collect these texts, he also relies on the abstract formulation of a totality whose universality is not grounded in any concrete formation. Moretti's world coincides with the universal *qua* universal and "refers not to the actual world but to the total enworldedness, or world-constituting force, of a system" (Hayot 31). Because this totality is inapprehensible from any particular context of enunciation—it can be appreciated only from an apparently Hegelian universal perspective of absolute distance—it requires a change in methodology from close reading to "distant reading." Finally, Damrosch's world is a relation of mobility; it is made visible by the circulation of texts through networks of translation and reception that the world literary critic must trace and reconstruct. For Damrosch, the world is not a system of forces, or the totality of the real, but a much more restricted and material set of literary displacements. As novels, poems, stories, and essays cross cultural and linguistic boundaries, they leave behind the traces that produce the world.[16]

I would like to draw two conclusions from these conceptions of the world that were useful to me in developing my hypothesis about the production of the world in Latin American literature. First, it is possible to think about world literature as a critical discourse whose specific contribution lies in positing contingent worlds that do not preexist the critical or aesthetic act that calls them into existence. Second, because its scale is invoked to disrupt the naturalization of the local, the particular, and the national, world literary discourse can be seen as a function of the impossibility of the idea of the world as a stable, sutured totality. The world in Latin American world literary discourse is a space constituted by an antagonism that prevents its realization as a given totality of literary texts always already comparable to one another because of a supposedly common ground. This book analyzes Latin America's place in the production of a global modernity shaped by an actually existing field of transcultural exchanges that supports the critical practices, aesthetic imaginaries, and universalizing fantasies of world literature. The focus on Latin America is an invitation to think about the differential specificity of marginal renderings of the world, vis-à-vis the worlds devised in metropolitan locations.[17] My point throughout the book is that marginal literatures (however we define the subaltern materiality of their marginalities) expose the hegemonic making of modernist global mappings. If hegemonic articulations of world literature (as in Casanova and Moretti) are concerned with singular aesthetic exchanges as fragments that point to the universal totality of the global, which can be represented only from the point of view of the epistemological self-certainty of hegemonic subject positions, the world literary figurations produced by Latin American cosmopolitan writers are strategic discourses oriented by their modernizing desires, a point Aguilar effectively makes in his *Episodios cosmopolitas*. These figurations allow us to work through the tension between the desire to join the global order of modernism and the anxiety provoked by the experience of exclusion and the anticipation of the exclusion to come.

As mentioned above, the relation between Part One and Part Two of this book is not historical but theoretical. If in Part Two I conceptualize *modernismo*'s *deseos de mundo*, in Part One I trace the material history of the global displacements that created the worlds where these desires circulate. In chapters 1 and 2, I define world literature as a process of global expansion, retraction, and dislocation of cultural and aesthetic institutions, practices, and values that determine the meaning of the world as a totality of meaning, very much in the sense that Karl Marx and Friedrich Engels described world literature as part of the globalization of capital in *The Communist Manifesto* (1847): "The need of a constantly expanding market for its products chases the bourgeoisie over the whole surface of the earth. It must nestle everywhere, settle everywhere, establish connections everywhere. . . . In place of the old local and national seclusion and self-sufficiency, we have intercourse in every direction, universal inter-dependence of nations. And as in material, so also in intellectual production. . . . National one-sidedness and narrow-mindedness become more and more impossible, and from the numerous national and local literatures, there arises a world literature"

("Manifesto" 476–77). World literature here stands for the material, dynamic formation of a global field of symbolic and material exchange, where Latin American writers and texts actively negotiate the terms of their participation in this world-historical process. With this general notion in mind, in chapter 1 I analyze the effective production of the world as a global totality of novelistic production, reception, and translation during the second half of the nineteenth century through readings of science fiction novels by Jules Verne and Eduardo Ladislao Holmberg. Written between 1863 and 1876, these novels reproduce and sustain the process of globalization through very different narrative strategies and from very different positions within a field of signification that they help to create. In chapter 2, I historicize the concrete, material displacements, appropriations, and resignifications that made magical realism a global genre from the 1920s to the 1990s, from Germany to France and Latin America, and from Latin America to eastern Europe, China, India, Turkey, Mozambique, Nigeria, the US South and Southwest, and back to Latin America, with a special emphasis on the circulation, translation, interpretation, and cultural reappropriations of *Cien años de soledad* (1967). In these first two chapters, I explore the different ways that marginal aesthetic forms alternatively reproduce, resist, and destabilize hegemonic totalizations of the world through scientific, antipositivistic, world literary, cosmopolitan, and postcolonial discourses.

In Part One I use science fiction and magical realist narratives to interrogate the formation of the world as a global field of literary exchanges during two markedly different historical periods of Latin American modernity. In Part Two I focus on a single period, the *modernista* moment in Latin American literature at the turn of the twentieth century. In this context, *world literature* designates, not the circulation of texts, but rather a critical discourse that collects the aesthetic materials from outside Latin America that enable a cosmopolitan modernization in the region, emancipating it from a cultural particularity that bears the marks of exclusion. Most *modernistas* were unaware of the specific term *Weltliteratur* (with the significant exceptions of Enrique Gómez Carrillo and Baldomero Sanín Cano, both of whom wrote about it), but they produced a meaningful and voluminous corpus on the literatures of the world. Although they represented this world of aesthetic signs as radically exterior to Latin America, it was not strange to them: it was a world of modernist aesthetics, a familiar, welcoming world eager to receive them.[18]

Along these lines, in chapter 3 I reconstruct a lost archive of *modernista* world literary discourses that have never been studied as an organized repository of *deseos de mundo*. Because many of these discourses are not contained in self-standing essays or poems but rather must be found in texts where the desire for universality coexists in a productive and unresolved tension with the particularistic goal of producing a differential Latin American identity, this chapter's main contribution is to assemble and analyze these texts as an archive, that is, as part of "a single corpus, in a system or a synchrony in which all elements articulate the unity of an ideal configuration" (Derrida, "Archive Fever" 10). I hope that the ambitious attempt to restore this archive with all its complexity and historical mutations justifies the unusual extension of this chapter. From José Martí, who issued the inaugural world literary call to Latin American writers in 1882, enjoining them to read "diverse literatures" from around the world, to Manuel González Prada, Manuel Gutiérrez Nájera, Pedro Emilio Coll, Enrique Gómez Carrillo, and Baldomero Sanín Cano, the objective of this chapter is to highlight a genealogy within *modernismo* of universalist writings on the world as the site of desire.

In the last two chapters of the book, I examine the scope of *modernismo*'s world mappings, as well as the construction and destabilization of French culture as the naturalized home of the universal, with Paris as its center. Chapter 4 reinterprets Rubén Darío's Francophilia, not as an aestheticist imposture, but as a discourse with the potential to constitute—in his universalist representation of France's cultural particularity—the horizon of his worldly imagination and the surface upon which he inscribes his Herculean will to organize, from Paris, a dispersed universe of modernist signifiers. The chapter asks: If Darío's is a French world, is it possible to speak with any rigor of his world literary discourse? And is there a world at all in Darío, or just the hegemony of a French culture that apprehends the globe as the site of its *mission civilisatrice*?

Chapter 5 presents the first methodical account of Gómez Carrillo's travels to a wide array of Eastern destinations between 1905 and 1912: the Maghreb, Egypt, the Levant, Turkey, Cyprus, Greece, Sri Lanka, Singapore, Korea, China, Japan, and Russia. As the most original and important travel writer of the turn of the century, Gómez Carrillo produced in his eastbound narratives a Latin American world that stretched well beyond Paris (although the French capital remained its structural center). For Latin American audiences, before the global circulation of *modernistas*, the world consisted of a handful of transatlantic routes; Gómez Carrillo's role in broadening his readers' world cannot be overestimated. Yet this larger world, unified by the modernist gaze, breaks down on several occasions. This chapter highlights moments when the Orientalist traveler recognizes the oppression and sorrow of an eastern European Jewry that interpellates his cosmopolitan ethical subjectivity in ways neither he nor the *modernista* literary field could have anticipated. In the second half of this chapter I argue that Gómez Carrillo's representation of Jews' exceptional status among a diverse cast of marginalized Oriental characters derives from his experience of the Dreyfus Affair in France. A committed *Dreyfusard*, Gómez Carrillo was the only *modernista* to live in Paris for the entire duration of the Affair (from 1894 and 1906), and he was the only Latin American intellectual to pay systematic attention to the Jewish captain's fate.

I want to conclude this introduction by acknowledging the challenges that an analysis of cosmopolitan imaginaries presents to a critic and researcher who imagines his or her task in cosmopolitan terms. During the period that I study here, cosmopolitan discourses and maneuvers were strategic, self-conscious, calculated attempts to take part in, contest, overwrite, and redirect the global hegemony of modern culture, in deliberate opposition to local forms of nationalistic, Hispanophile, or racially based hegemonies. These cosmopolitan self-representations required the dislocation of the Latin American intellectual's symbolic order, one constituted by a traumatic experience of crippling marginality that needed to be repressed. This triggered a process of cosmopolitan identification understood as the formation of a cosmopolitan ego based on an idealized self-image accompanied by an omnipotent sense of mastery and a promise of fullness: that is, a misrecognition (*méconnaissance*) that "characterize[s] the ego in all its structures" (Lacan, "Mirror Stage" 6). For Latin American cosmopolitans, the specific meaning of this misrecognition was determined by the Latin American writer's inability to fully inhabit the cosmopolitan subject position opened by a discourse enunciated from a marginal geocultural situation that was always already incommensurable with cosmopolitan modernization and universal justice. Cosmopolitanism, then, could be seen as an imaginary discourse (perhaps even a constellation of neurotic fantasies) that, although it fails to realize its maximalist universal purpose, nonetheless widens the margins of cultural and political agency and illuminates new meanings by reinscribing cultural particularities in larger, transcultural networks of signification. It is my hope that this book (product of my own cosmopolitan critical fantasies) will accomplish this same kind of cosmopolitan failure.

Cambridge, Massachusetts, September 2012

Part I

World Literature as a Global Relation, or The Material Production of Literary Worlds

CHAPTER I

The Globalization of the Novel and the Novelization of the Global

KANT AND THE GLOBAL NOVEL

In "Idea for a Universal History with a Cosmopolitan Purpose" (1784), Immanuel Kant lays out the historiographic parameters for a reconceptualization of human history that takes as its end the actualization of freedom in a cosmopolitan political formation that he imagines as a world-republic (*Weltrepublik*).[1] Kant articulates a shift from a conceptual universality of reason to its universal (general *and*, global) actualization in concrete cosmopolitan political and economic institutions. The discursive construction of the world as a global totality of rights and moral legality is, of course, a highly ideological operation that requires naturalizing the assumed universality of reason, when this universality in fact results from the hegemonic universalization of the cultural particularity of European modernity and its values and institutions. More importantly, Kant's discourse of globalization translates the abstract and philosophical concept of the universal into its concrete geopolitical realization in this *world-as-ethico/political-totality*. Kant's narrative of the global realization of freedom (which Hegel revised and historicized soon after, through the concept of "world history") both opens the interpretative horizon of globalization as the necessary spatial dimension of the project of modernity (in other words, the globalization of modern institutions and practices) and provides the epistemological structure for the economic, political, and military discourses of globalization that surround us today.

In addition to Kant's cosmopolitical narrative, I want to underscore an idea that, to my knowledge, has been overlooked by the many literary critics interested in the relation between literature and globalization. Toward the end of "Idea for a Universal History with a Cosmopolitan Purpose," Kant suggests that the novel could play an important role in the production of the discourses of globalization by imagining the world as a totality mediated by bourgeois/modern culture. He concludes that "it is admittedly a strange and at first sight absurd proposition to write a *history* according to an idea of how world events must develop if they are to conform to certain rational ends; it would seem that only a *novel* could result from such premises" (51–52).What I find striking about Kant's admission is his implicit disciplinary comparison between philosophical and novelistic discourses as he attempts to determine which is more adequate to tell the story of a modern world moving toward the global actualization of rational freedom. He is confident that, although the novel appears to be better suited to this task, it remains a philosopher's job. But even if Kant believes that the philosopher must *conceptualize* the process of globalization, his formulation concedes that the challenge of *imagining* the world as a reconciled totality of freedom could fall to the novel—the novel as the cultural formation that renders the historical process of globalization visible in the nineteenth century; the novel, or at least the imaginary potential of discourse contingently embodied in novel form, as a discursive latency that makes the process of globalization available for reading audiences to work through the transformations they are experiencing at home.[2]

During the second half of the nineteenth century, when bourgeois reason (through its economic, political, and cultural institutions) was believed to occupy every region of the planet, the novel produced privileged and efficient narratives of the global formation of a modern world. Because the novel was the hegemonic form of narrative imagination in the nineteenth century, and because of the aesthetic and political force of its social totalities, most novels dealing with distant places generated powerful images of the globalization of modern culture.[3] This is the unique nature of the relation between the novel and the historical process of globalization vis-à-vis modern philosophy: if philosophy conceptualized the transformation of the globe as the realization of a totality of freedom (as evidenced by Kant, Hegel, and Marx), the novel provided this philosophical concept with a set of images and imaginaries that elevated the fiction of ubiquitous modernization to a foundational myth.

I began with this Kantian account of the link between the novel and the global geographies of cosmopolitical imagination in order to address my discontent with some of the ways in which world literature (understood as both concept and critical and pedagogical practice) has been institutionalized in the North American and European humanities. As I explained in the Introduction, I believe the return of world literature has the theoretical and political potential to shake up the particularistic determinations that have reified and exhausted research agendas and institutional designs and to help us rethink aesthetic, cultural, and historical meaning as a transcultural relation, as movement and displacement, on varying and supplementary scales. World literature—when activated *with a cosmopolitan purpose* as *deseo de mundo*, or world-desire, desire for the world—could reveal the contingent sutures of cultural forms susceptible to being inscribed *out there*, in the world, against the immediacy of meaning as a function of the local, whether national or regional. Nowhere is this critical renewal needed more than in institutionally marginalized fields of study, saturated with particularistic emphasis and identitarian provincialism. The question is whether world literature, as a concept instantiated in concrete pedagogical, curricular, and research practices that tend to reproduce static and dehistoricized literary mappings that result from the aggregation of singular nation-bound texts, is in fact capable of achieving the cosmopolitan modernization that it needs in order to renew itself. That is, how can we produce a critical narrative on the literatures of the world and the hegemonic mediations that organize their spatial and temporal continuities and discontinuities?

In this chapter, I propose two complementary models—the globalization of the novel and the novelization of the global—to address these cosmopolitan critical anxieties and the consequent need to redefine world literature as the hegemonic process that produces contingent literary worlds. The first—*the globalization of the novel*—works not with particular textual formations but with the historical expansion of the novel form hand in hand with the colonial enterprise of western Europe. This concept sheds light on the historical and theoretical parameters that have been used to study both the historical spread of the novel from Europe to the peripheries and the constitution, at the end of the nineteenth and throughout the twentieth century, of a global system of production, reception, and translation of novels. The second model—*the novelization of the global*—focuses on the production of images of a globalized world as they are constructed in certain novels. I will read these figures, primarily, in novels by Jules Verne and a novel by Eduardo Ladislao Holmberg. As might be expected, these two writers create entirely different images of travelers spreading their discrete conceptions of modern culture throughout the world and beyond, reaching even into outer space. While Verne was a professional novelist working in France and surrounded by imperialist discourses and a reading public immersed in the state's *mission civilisatrice*, Holmberg was an amateur writer (whose principal occupation was in the medical and natural sciences) living in Buenos Aires, then a large village (*gran aldea*) on the threshold of becoming a city. Verne lived and breathed the experience of modernity; Holmberg's context was marked by the desire for that very modernity.[4] The point I want to make is that the particular geopolitical determinations that conditioned each writer produced dissimilar imaginaries of the global reach of their characters and plots. In Verne's novels, omnipotent, muscular characters (based on the *topos* of the *bourgeois conquérant*) travel adventurously, around the world and beyond: to the bottom of the sea, the center of the earth, the moon, the sun, and Mars. In Holmberg's *Viaje maravilloso del señor Nic-Nac al planeta Marte* (*The Marvelous Journey of Mr. Nic-Nac to the Planet Mars*) (1875), however, the social position of the Argentine (and Latin American) intellectual and political elite within the global economy of the discourse of adventure allows only for spiritual/immaterial/imaginary travel: Nic-Nac's body never leaves home, and only his soul (!) travels to Mars. I read these novels, which borrow from discourses of adventure, science fiction, and spiritism, in relation to the hegemonic protocols of realism in order to try to broaden the concept of representation as it pertains to the globalization of modernity.

Finally, I connect these interpretative models with what I deem to be the cultural politics of world literature and the critical and pedagogical practices derived from world literature. I also examine its underlying claim to address the cosmopolitan expectations in academic practices related to the production of a multicultural discourse about the world based on the respect for cultural difference. In other words, I ask whether world literature, as a concept and a practice, can become an effective cosmopolitan discourse in a context of extreme global inequality, and to what extent the globalization of the novel and the novelization of the global might preserve a horizon of universality for

cultural relations while accounting for the hegemonic links that determine them.

THE GLOBALIZATION OF THE NOVEL

During the eighteenth and nineteenth centuries, the novel traveled from Europe to Latin America, as well as other peripheries of the world, through the colonial and postcolonial channels of symbolic and material exchange.[5] Novels appealed to a Creole class torn by the contradiction between its cultural and economic attachment to Europe and its desire for political autonomy. To local elites, those narratives of subjective freedom contained the possibility of imagining and modeling identities independent from the colonial metropolis. In Latin America in particular, the consumption of novels offered the opportunity to grasp an experience of modernity that, for the most part, was not available to the reading Creole class in its everyday life, despite liberal aspirations that were beginning to be articulated as a political and cultural project.

Because of the kind of experiences that the novel afforded to readers in peripheral regions of the world, Latin American intellectuals immediately realized the important role that the consumption, production, and translation of novels could play in the process of sociocultural modernization. The Argentine Domingo F. Sarmiento was perhaps the most prominent writer and politician to propose that novels were an essential instrument for the modernization of Latin America. In *Facundo: Civilización y Barbarie* (*Facundo: Civilization and Barbarism*) (1845) he argued that Latin America could shed its premodern backwardness if it imposed civilized/modern (that is, European) cultural practices and institutions over its barbarian, natural state of being. Modernization was a process of conversion (forced or voluntary—and, in any case, violent) to be enacted by reproducing European modernity in Latin America. Immediately after the publication of *Facundo*, Sarmiento traveled to Europe, North Africa, and the United States. Walking through the streets of Paris, Sarmiento reflected: "Las ideas y modas de Francia, sus hombres y sus novelas, son hoy el modelo y la pauta de todas las otras naciones; y empiezo a creer que esto que nos seduce por todas partes, esto que creemos imitación, no es sino aquella aspiración de la índole humana a acercarse a un tipo de perfección, que está en ella misma y se desenvuelve más o menos según las circunstancias de cada pueblo" (138–39) ("The ideas and fashion of France, her

men and novels, are today the model and pattern for all other nations; I am starting to believe that this which seduces us in every way, this which we think is imitation, is nothing but the inherent human aspiration to be close to perfection that develops itself according to the circumstances of each nation").[6] Sarmiento defends a mimetic path to modernization by arguing that imitation is not the postcolonial condition of the periphery but, in a Platonic turn, an inherently human feature. And he does not hesitate to prescribe precisely which aspects of modern European culture should be imitated: namely, discourses (ideas and trends) and cultural institutions, with the novel being his only example.[7]

For Sarmiento, the importance of the novel as an effective modernizing institution that needs to be imported has been studied by a number of notable critics. In their analysis of Sarmiento's representation of his own intellectual education, Carlos Altamirano and Beatriz Sarlo explain Sarmiento's resort to European and North American "chains of books" (novels and autobiographies) in order to legitimize an autobiographical discourse, the place of authorship, and his modernizing aesthetico-political intervention ("Vida ejemplar" 126–27); Doris Sommer has argued that Sarmiento found in Fenimore Cooper's frontier novels (particularly, *The Last of the Mohicans* and *The Prairie*) "a formula for writing about America that took advantage of her originality and that should therefore be taken as a model of New World writing" (*Foundational Fictions* 55); David Viñas foregrounded the role of books (novels or not) in the actualization of modernity in the deserted landscape of barbaric cultural hegemony: "Si el exterior es peligroso, se le conjurará con el libro; si el exterior permanece desierto, habrá que poblarlo a través del libro. De donde se sigue que el territorio argentino sea presentido hacia 1850 como un Mercado potencial del libro: se hará mercado unificado y por lo tanto *país* mediante esa difusión" (17) ("If the exterior is dangerous, its threat will be averted with the book; if the exterior remains deserted, it will be populated through the book. On that account, the Argentine territory will be perceived around 1850 as a potential book market: it will become a unified market and, through the dissemination of books, a country"); and Ricardo Piglia analyzed Sarmiento's desire for literary autonomy (in the face of heteronymous determinations) in relation to Flaubert's discourse on the novel in his letters to Louis Colet (128–29). Recently, Alejandra Laera has unearthed and interpreted a rare journalistic piece by Sarmiento, "Las novelas" (1856), where he equates the degree of modernization of a given culture with the number of novels it consumes: "Caramelos y novelas andan juntos en el mundo, y la civilización de los pueblos se mide por el azúcar que consumen y las novelas que leen. ¿Para qué sirve el azúcar? Díganlo los pampas que no lo usan" (qtd. in Laera 9) ("Candy and novels go hand in hand in the world, and the culture of a nation can be measured by the amount of sugar they consume and the novels they read. What is sugar good for? Ask the Pampa Indians who don't use it"). Although sweetness can be considered a sign of gastronomic refinement or civilization, its value as an inscription in networks of modern consumption becomes especially clear, Sarmiento suggests, when juxtaposed to the sentimental and political education the novel provides—the novel as a universal measure of modernity.

Through processes of formal and thematic imitation, importation, translation, and adaptation, the institution of the novel put down roots in Latin America during the nineteenth century, and by the 1880s novelistic production and consumption had become well established (the same process took place, with minor temporal variations, in colonial Africa, Asia, and eastern and southern Europe).[8] Because of the global hegemony of modern European culture (produced and reproduced in colonial, postcolonial, and neocolonial links to its peripheries), the novel became the first universalized aesthetic form and institution of modernity.[9] It is important to bear in mind that the global preeminence of the novel form among discursive genres cannot be explained as the result of the universal human impulse to explain through narration: narration (or storytelling) and the novel (the historically determined cultural and aesthetic form described here) are in fact incommensurable cultural practices. The universality of the novel form was the historical outcome of the formation (through colonialism, trade, and promises of emancipation) of a world in which modern European culture was increasingly hegemonic, if not forcefully dominant. Wherever one looked for modern desires (the desires for self-determination, identity, material development, and progress), one found novels. One could thus define the novel as modern desire formally enclosed and regulated.

Was there (indeed, is there), however, a difference between the European novel and the Latin American novel, the Asian novel, the African novel, and so on? Well, yes and no. One can point to the diverse formal and thematic aspects of individual works (as I do in the next section, conceptualizing and analyzing the idea of *the novelization of the global*), whose difference was informed by, among other things, a geopolitically determined experience of the process of globalization of modern institutions, practices, and values. However, if one looks at the globalization of the novel form as a modern and modernizing institution, it becomes quite difficult to identify differences in terms of the institutional and political function of the novel in these different locations. In other words, the world system of novelistic production, consumption, and translation reinforces the dream of a global totality of modern freedom with Hegelian overtones—that is, a totality whose internal heterogeneity (the formal and thematic particularity of the Latin American or African or Asian novel vis-à-vis the European novel) is functional in creating the identity of the *global novel.* I insist that the globality of the novel form is the result of a historical process of global hegemony—the product of the universalization of its bourgeois and European particularity. In an interesting note in the *Prison Notebooks*, "Hegemony of Western Culture over the Whole World Culture," Gramsci uses the same category that he developed to analyze social formations within national scenarios to consider the processes of globalization as the world history of the West's hegemony over its cultural Others: "Even if one admits that other cultures have had an importance and a significance in the process of 'hierarchical' unification of world civilization (and this should certainly be admitted without question), they have had a universal value only in so far as they have become constituent elements of European culture, which is the only historically and concretely universal culture—in so far, that is, as they have contributed to the process of European thought and been assimilated to it" (416). In this quotation Gramsci is at his most Hegelian. He affirms that World Culture—the possibility of proposing the existence of a global cultural field—depends on the universal mediation of Europe. As global *hegemon*, European culture recognizes and incorporates the subaltern aesthetic norms, forms, and practices that are central to the cultures of its Others in order to form a world cultural field structured around the predominant nuclei that governed the appropriations that gave it form in the first place—a global cultural field whose universality and relatively stable homogeneity is the result of the hegemonic mediation of European or North Atlantic bourgeois/modern culture. Thus the periphery does not merely receive and absorb cultural mandates from the core on the basis of an international division of labor and trade balance that favors the development of the First World; on the contrary, core-periphery relations are culturally mediated by hegemonic production of consent in the margins of globalization.[10] This hegemonic cultural mediation can be read in the gap that separates the globalization of the novel and the novelization of the global—between capitalism's creation of "a world after its own image" (Marx and Engels 477) through the global expansion of its aesthetic and cultural institutions, and the local literary reappropriations and reinscriptions of that epochal process.

In this sense, and taking a cue from Gramsci's understanding of hegemony, the operation of universalization that constitutes the discursive basis for the globality of the novel should not be understood as an instance of the periphery's cultural subordination to the core. That is why I mention notions of "importation," "translation," and "adaptation," instead of thinking only in terms of "imitation," "implantation," or "imposition." The ideas of coercion and consent embedded in the concept of hegemony presuppose an active agency on the part of peripheral cultures in the enterprise of universalizing the novel. That is, in the nineteenth and early twentieth centuries, the representation of the particularity of European modernity and its institutions as universal was a project shared by intellectuals and practitioners both at the center and at the margins of a global discursive field that sanctioned the universality of the novel form.

It would be easy to dismiss the universalization of the novel as cultural form and modern institution simply as a function of colonialism, to see globalization *only* as a new name for the same old colonial relations. But this would be a mistake. Although the two processes overlap to some extent, the global expansion of modern institutions presupposes the universal realization of the promise of a political and cultural modernity, and—whether in the nineteenth century or today—the peripheries of the world have an intense desire for sociopolitical and cultural modernization (a desire represented in and by novels). In other words, the globalization of modernity and its institutions in the nineteenth century implied both the threat of (neo) colonial oppression and the promise of emancipation. Looking at this aporia through the deconstructive dictum that Derrida first formulated in "Plato's Pharmacy" about the double meaning of *pharmakon* as medicine and poison, one could say that globalization makes modernity (and novelistic difference) both possible and impossible in the margins of the universal.

INTERLUDE: GLOBALIZATION AND THE IMPOSSIBLE TOTALITY

The idea of a world produced as a cultural totality through the expansion of the European novel form is an optimistic but somewhat incomplete narrative of globalization, perhaps excessively Hegelian in its affirmation of an all-encompassing triumph of modernity. Hegel grounds his world-historical confidence in the necessary nature of the material mediation that forms the modern world-totality: for him, commerce, legal treaties, colonization, and war transform a global space made up of national difference and material unevenness into a self-reconciliated world of modern/bourgeois economic, legal, and cultural relations.[11] This narrative conceives of any resistance or opposition to the march of Spirit in the most remote corners of the planet in dialectical terms: that is, they contribute to its actualization. Resistance does not stand a chance in the face of world-historical forces that move forward, precisely, by overcoming (*Aufhebung*) opposition: "In contrast with this absolute right which [a world-historical nation] possesses as bearer of the present stage of the world spirit's development, the spirits of other nations are without rights, and they, like those whose epoch has passed, no longer count in world history. . . . [They] will perhaps lose [their] independence, or [they] may survive or eke out [their] existence as a particular state or group of states" (*Elements of the Philosophy of Right* 374, § 347).[12] Before moving on into the novelization of the global, I would like to interrogate this account of globalization's unwillingness to pay attention to local instances of resistance that cannot be subsumed as moments of its own dialectical resolution. The point is not to affirm the irreducibility of cultural difference or to make an empiricist and antitheoretical argument about the incommensurability of the social in its materiality and the critical models that try to apprehend it. Instead, I am interested in those (admittedly exceptional) places, practices, subjectivities, and natural barriers that defy, at least momentarily, their epistemological colonization by modern consciousness to prevent the suture of the world into a global totality. Through these challenges, they shed light on the fissures of the articulation of the discourse of modernity and the process of globalization. Here I will read an overlooked episode from the history of colonial failures, Antarctica's persistent rejection of the globalizing impetus of colonialization and property rights: Captain James Cook's several unsuccessful attempts, between 1772 and 1775, to conquer the Southern Continent.

The importance of his failures to incorporate Antarctica into the *discovered world* and the global cognitive mappings of colonial Europe resides in their power to underscore the ideological and hegemonic nature of the idea that there is a world that can be symbolized by an account of crisscrossing trajectories, cultural relations, and spatial signification.

In July of 1771, by the end of Captain Cook's first southern circumnavigation, every continent save one had been colonized or, at least, explored and charted to some extent—an accomplishment that was a prerequisite condition for later Kantian, Hegelian, and Marxian discourses of cosmopolitanism, world history, global capitalism, and universal revolt. The last redoubt that challenged and excited the minds of colonialists and explorers alike was *Terra Australis Incognita*. During his second circumnavigation, on August 2, 1773, Cook wrote in his journal:

> Having now crossed or got to the north of Captain Carteret's Track [near Tahiti], no discovery of importance can be made, some few islands is all that can be expected while I remain within the Tropical Seas. As I have now in this and my former Voyage crossed this Ocean from 40° South and upward it will hardly be denied but what I must have formed some judgment concerning the great object of my re-searches (viz) the Southern Continent. Circumstances seem to point out that there is none but this is too important a point to be left to conjenctor [*sic*], facts must determine it and these can only be had by visiting the remaining unexplored part of this Sea which will be the work of the remaining of this Voyage. (278)

The Royal Society's instructions to Cook were "to further discoveries towards the South Pole" (Edwards 221). Since Magellan's circumnavigation, the idea of a Great Southern Continent formed by a compound of barely charted territories that were believed to be the tips of an unknown continent—South Africa, Australia, Tasmania (or Van Diemen's Land), the New Hebrides, the Kerguelens, New Guinea, New Zealand, and Tierra del Fuego—had driven continued exploration of the South Seas. In 1772, Alexander Dalrymple, an important fellow of the Geography Division of the Royal Society, published a study speculating on the existence of a *Terra Australis Incognita* characterized by abundance: "The number of inhabitants in the southern continent is probably more than 50 million," a population of "greater extent than the whole civilized part of Asia, from Turkey to the eastern extreme of China. The scraps from this table would be sufficient to maintain power, dominion, and sovereignty of Britain, by employing its manufacturers and ships" (qtd. in Chapman 19–21). Dalrymple's imaginings (driven by the daunting myth of El Dorado that some located in the world's southernmost extreme) drove the Royal Society to sponsor Cook's second voyage, now with the specific aim of conquering these promising lands.

Cook was the right man for this world-historical task. An eighteenth-century Columbus-like figure, he had left his signature and planted Queen Anne's colonial flag on territories and islands throughout the South Pacific but had failed four times to reach the icy coasts of Antarctica. On his third unsuccessful attempt (January 30, 1774), Cook managed to go further south than anyone before him, achieving a latitude of 71°10'S. A year later, on his fourth and final attempt, with part of his crew very sick, he decided it was not worth the risk and turned around. He justified his decision in two journal entries dated February 6 and 21, 1775:

> The risk one runs in xploring [*sic*] a coast in these unknown and Icy Seas, is so very great, that I can be bold to say, that no man will ever venture farther than I have done and that the lands which may lie to the South will never be explored. Thick fogs, Snow storms, Intense Cold and every other thing that can render Navigation dangerous one has to encounter and these difficulties are greatly heightened by the enexpressable [*sic*] horrid aspect of the Country, a Country doomed by Nature never once to feel the warmth of the Suns rays, but to lie for ever buried under ever lasting snow and ice. The ports which may be on the Coast are in a manner wholly filled up with frozen snow of a vast thickness, but if any should so far be open as to admit a ship in, it is even dangerous to go in, for she runs a risk of being fixed there for ever, or coming out in an ice island. . . It would have been rashness in me to have risked all which had been done in the Voyage, in finding out and exploaring [*sic*] a Coast which when done would have answered no end whatever, or been of the least use either to Navigation or Geography or indeed any other Science. (412)

A country doomed by nature and unusable ports, a continent from which no benefit will ever be extracted: not only do Cook's empirical observations put an end to the mythical narratives of Antarctic cornucopias, but also and significantly, the portrayal of Antarctica as an unsurpassable obstacle irremediably modifies the image of the world as conquered/conquerable totality.[13] Cook's resignation both acknowledges the impossibility of knowing what is *incognito* about Antarctica and recognizes that the world as a whole is not knowable. Antarctica is doomed, but so is the very idea of a mappable, transparent world, as well as Cook's own self-representation. In the *Phenomenology of Spirit*, Hegel famously depicted Napoleon as History itself passing by on horseback: "At the forefront of all actions, including world-historical actions, are individuals as the subjectivities by which the substantial is actualized. . . . These individuals are the living expressions of the substantial deed of the world spirit and are thus immediately identical with it" (375, § 348).[14] Cook saw himself in the same light, at least until the disappointing moment when he saw that the ultimate world-historical mission was impossible: "I whose ambition leads me not only farther than any other man has been before me, but as far as I think it possible for a man to go, was not sorry at meeting with this interruption, as it in some measure relieved us from the dangers and hardships, inseparable with the navigation of the Southern Polar regions. Sence [*sic*] therefore we could not proceed one Inch farther south, no other reason need be assigned for our Tacking and stretching back to the North" (331). Dangers, hardships, and cursed scenery impose a radical limit to the possibility of discovering Antarctica and incorporating it into the world created by the globalization of modernity. The conclusion of the British seaman's *un-discovery* is rather obvious: Cook's globalizing agency was inadequate to actualize the world as a self-reconciled totality, and the world itself was not the transparent, immediately graspable terrain where such totalizing spatial imaginary could be effectively inscribed. The emphasis here is on the need for discursive mediations, a need that becomes apparent when a different kind of resistance arises to denaturalize the idea of globalization as a fait accompli rather than as a very effective displacement and reassemblage of geopolitical imaginaries.

This is, in fact, another way to explain the usefulness of the globalization of the novel and the novelization of the global, as an attempt to foreground the mediations that constitute the materiality of the worlds that are produced by literature. As such, these concepts allow for the articulation, within a critical agenda, of the cosmopolitan desire to inscribe the meaning of aesthetic forms in multiple contexts that include but transcend local, national, and regional determinations in search of an account of the true complexity of cultural and historical signification. In terms of the globalization of the novel, the exceptionality of Antarctica (its nondialectical negative exteriority that can be read in its continuous resistance to claims of national sovereignty and capitalist exploitation) highlights the hegemonic representation of the particularity of any sequence of aesthetic exchanges, appropriations, translations, and importations as the universality that grounds the totalizing horizon of the discourse of globalization.[15] It is precisely this impossibility—the inapprehensible nature of the world as a totality of meaning—that triggers the discursive figurations that I analyze below.

THE NOVELIZATION OF THE GLOBAL

The idea of the globalization of the novel explains the role that the novel form played in the global expansion of modern culture and its institutions in the nineteenth century. The crisscrossing trajectories of infinite exchanges, importations, translations, and adaptations of novels (what I term the global novel as cultural form) make visible the spatial extension and intensity of the process of globalization. However, this explicatory matrix does not provide any insight into the different textual devices, strategies, plots, or characters that can be found in the great variety of novels that gave specific content to the global novel as cultural form. It remains necessary, then, to account for not only the historical spread of a global form but also the narratives of globalization as a discursive figure produced by a subset of texts usually concerned with lands and peoples far removed from Europe. If the globalization of the novel looks at the world as a global cultural totality and makes sense of it as a system, the novelization of the global—the second and complementary way in which I conceptualize the idea of the global novel—traces the specific imaginaries of universalism that these novelistic texts forge, effective accounts of the global reach of modern forms of agency in terms of the production and reproduction of discourses of universal adventure, exploration, and colonial profit.

Jules Verne's novels make a productive case study of the novelization of the globe. If spatial meaning is always produced discursively (an idea Edward W. Said worked through with the notion of "imaginative geography"), or, to put it bluntly, if fiction is the way we apprehend, categorize, and represent the world, then Verne's novels can be said to have provided some of the most radical imaginaries of the transformation of the planet into a totality of modern culture and sociability, producing a textual surplus that goes beyond the typical reading of Verne as colonialist fiction.[16] The bourgeois characters in his novels travel across the five continents, remapping the world in an epistemology of adventure and exoticism: see, for example, *Cinq semaines en ballon* (*Five Weeks in a Balloon*) (1863); *Voyages et aventures du Capitaine Hatteras* (*The Voyages and Adventures of Captain Hatteras*) (1864–65); and *Le tour du monde en 80 jours* (*Around the World in 80 Days*) (1873). Verne even dares to send his characters beyond the surface of the earth into the unknown: to the moon in *De la Terre à la Lune* (*From the Earth to the Moon*) (1865) and *Autour de la Lune* (*Round the Moon*) (1870); to the sun in *Hector Sevandac* (1874–76); to the bottom of the sea in *Vingt mille lieues sous les mers* (*Twenty-Thousand Leagues under the Sea*) (1869–70); and to the center of the earth in *Voyage au centre de la Terre* (*Journey to the Center of the Earth*) (1864). In the closing paragraphs of *De la Terre à la Lune*, the omniscient narrator channels the pride and fear that J. T. Maston felt for his three friends in space: "Ils s'étaient mis en dehors de l'humanité en franchissant les limites imposées par Dieu aux créatures terrestres" (243) ("They had placed themselves beyond the pale of humanity by crossing the limits imposed by the Creator on his earthly creatures"; 140). In Verne's novels there are no limits to the dream of universal economic and political freedom: the utmost recondite corners of the universe expect the arrival of Verne's *bourgeois conquérants* (see Morazé). Contemporary readers saw their own *local* experience transformed in these novels into global adventures that underscored the intensity and excitement available to those willing to embrace their bourgeois subjectivity and explore its universalizing potential. Writing about sea voyages and their literary imaginaries in the eighteenth century, Margaret Cohen establishes the precedent of the relation between reading publics and the novelized adventure I'm addressing for the second half of the nineteenth century: "Occurring in an environment that few could access yet that affected the lives of so many, sea voyages piqued the curiosity of stay-at-home-audiences. As global ocean travels grew up together with the printing press, armchair sailors combed sea voyage literature, factual and fictional, for strange, surprising adventures as well as information about world-altering developments and events recounted in what was called 'news from the sea'" (657). Following

Cohen's clue, I propose to read these narratives of global adventure (whether at sea, in distant lands, or in outer space) not just as representations of the global but, perhaps more importantly, as a recreation, reinforcement, and reproduction of the possibility of the global adventure of the European economic and political elites.

The construction of images and imaginaries of globality, of the transformation of the earth, is a symbolic challenge too great for one novel. Therefore, it has to be reconstructed as a panorama, putting together pieces from much (if not all) of Verne's novelistic archive. Verne developed a variety of narrative strategies that permitted novels and their readers to imagine the earth (in fact, the entire universe) as a bourgeois playing field, ready and available for science, profit, and amusement.

First, all of Verne's novels involve travel of some sort; these journeys always feature at least one moment when the novel takes a step back to capture an image of space as a meaningful cultural totality. The eye's perception of the real is always fragmented, and organizing the successive fragments into a larger mental image is a complex psychological and intellectual operation, one that Kant theorizes conclusively in *The Critique of Judgment*. Only an imaginative discourse can produce an image inaccessible to empirical perception, such as the earth as a round significant whole. In *Autour de la Lune*, for example, Michel Ardan, a French astronaut on a three-man crew (the other two are American), looks out the small window of the rocket and exclaims: "Hein! Mes chers camarades, sera-ce assez curieux d'avoir la Terre pour la Lune, de la voir se lever à l'horizon, d'y reconnaître la configuration de ses continents, de se dire: là est l'Amérique, là est l'Europe; puis de la suivre lorsqu'elle va se perdre dan les rayons du Soleil!" (94) ("Ah! My dear comrades, it will be rather curious to have the earth for our moon, to see it rise on the horizon, to recognize the shapes of its continents, and to say to oneself, 'There is America, there is Europe,' then to follow it when it is about to lose itself in the sun's rays!"; *From the Earth* 192–93). Dr. Fergusson has this same bird's-eye view in *Cinq semaines en ballon*: "Alors l'Afrique offrira aux races nouvelles les trésors accumulés depuis des siècles en son sein. Ces climats fatals aux étrangers s'épureront par les assolements et les drainages; ces eaux éparses ser réuniront en un lit commun pour former une artère navigable. Et ce pays sur lequel nous planons, plus fertile, plus riche, plus vital que les autres, deviendra quelque grand royaume, où se produiront des découvertes plus étonnantes enconre que la vapeur et l'électricité" (88)

("Then, Africa will be there to offer to new races the treasures that for centuries have been accumulating in her breast. Those climates now so fatal to strangers will be purified by cultivation and by drainage of the soil, and those scattered water supplies will be gathered into one common bed to form an artery of navigation. Then, this country over which we are now passing, more fertile, richer, and fuller of vitality than the rest, will become some grand realm where more astonishing discoveries than steam and electricity will be brought to light"; *Five Weeks* 123). In addition to the clearly colonialist idea that Africa "will offer" its treasures to a new race of explorers, scientists, and colonialists, the view from afar and from above produces a clear hierarchy between the subject and the spatial (humanized) object of observation, producing a symbolic relation in which the object subordinates itself to the will of the subject. In their mappings (of planet Earth in the first example, of a continent in the second), Verne's novels represent space as an opportunity for exploration, adventure, and profit.[17]

Second, given the positivistic inclinations of the French cultural field during the second half of the nineteenth century, the effectiveness of an image of the world or universe as a homogeneous space that can be crisscrossed back and forth depends on its measurability. For example, the eighty days that Phileas Fogg gives himself to circle the earth in *Le tour du monde en 80 jours* signals the philosophical and scientific certainty that the earth can be apprehended in a predetermined amount of time. All that is required is a willful individual. Analogously, the journey in *De la Terre à la Lune* is expected to take exactly ninety-seven hours and twenty minutes, as the subtitle of the book indicates (*Trajet direct en 97 heures 20 minutes*) (*Direct in 97 Hours 20 Minutes*); in fact, obsessive preparation for the journey and the study of the scientific and economic variables occupy almost the entire novel, which ends right after the rocket is launched. In both cases, the possibility of measuring the course of the adventure with scientific precision reinforces the initial intuition that seizing the earth or the galaxy is entirely feasible.

Third, after having produced the images that trigger an imaginary of global availability, these novels represent the process of taking possession of these "vacant" spaces. Some of Verne's characters are straightforward representatives of state colonialism—for example, the members of the Gun Club in *Autour de la Lune*, who propose the exploration of outer space "pour prendre possession de la Lune 'au nom des États-Unis pour ajouter un quarantième état à l'Union! Pour coloniser les règions lunaires, pour les cultiver, pour les peupler, pour y transporter toutes les prodiges de l'art, de la science et de l'industrie. Pour civiliser les Sélénites" (63) ("to take possession of the moon in the name of the United States; to add a fortieth state to the Union; to colonize the lunar regions; to cultivate them, to people them, to transport thither all the prodigies of art, science and industry; to civilize the Selenites"; *From the Earth* 203). But that is not the only available path. A more interesting one is chosen by those characters who, rather than advance their colonial agenda in the name of the nation-state, act in the belief that they embody the enterprise of modernization. That is why Verne's novels are populated by bourgeois businessmen, politicians, professors, *patresfamilias*, scientists, and *bonvivants*—not only from France but from most of the other western European nations, not to mention the United States, Russia, and virtually any country that had a growing middle class at the time. The *bourgeoisification* of the world is the key to understanding the transnational dimension of the philosophical and literary conceptualization of the process of globalization, even in the nineteenth century—the desire to produce a homogeneous totality that would eventually coincide with the surface of the earth (and, in Verne, with the entire universe). That is why *De la Terre à la Lune*, perhaps the most striking novel within this corpus, closes with a sentence (spoken by J. T. Maston, the Gun Club secretary) that pays homage to the astronauts who venture into outer space in the name of bourgeois civilization: "A eux trois ils emportent dans l'espace toutes les ressources de l'art, de la science et de l'industrie. Avec cela on fait ce qu'on veut, et vous verrez qu'ils se tireront d'affaire!" (244) ("'Those three men,' said he, 'have carried into space all the resources of art, science, and industry. With that, one can do anything; and you will see that, some day, they will come out all right'"; *From the Earth* 140).

Jules Verne's novels are usually read as an intersection of science fiction and adventure. Without disputing these generic inscriptions, I would like to propose that, in order to foreground the political relation of his narratives with the globalization of modern institutions and practices, one needs to examine their connection to the realist novel's hegemonic protocols of representation. In other words, what happens if we think of Verne's novels as a form of oblique or, rather, virtual realism—as representation of the real of the bourgeoisie's technological potential, that is, reality not necessarily as it is but *as it could be*? Gilles Deleuze explains that virtuality is opposed not to the real but to actuality and to what he calls *the possible*: "The possible has no reality (although it may have an actuality); conversely the virtual is not actual, but as such possesses reality. . . . The possible is that which is 'realized' (or is not realized). . . . For the real is supposed to be in the image of the possible that it realizes. . . . And every possible is not realized, realization involves a limitation by which some possibles are supposed to be repulsed or thwarted, while others 'pass' into the real. The virtual, on the other hand, does not have to be realized" (Deleuze, *Bergsonism* 96–97).

Verne's novels have been conventionally read as having prophesied technologies that would be invented in the next century or having imagined new and hitherto inconceivable uses for the technology already available; in other words, they have been read in terms of Deleuze's notion of the possible. I identify the place of Verne's novels right on the edge of the realist novel's representational protocols: narratives of virtual worlds, virtual practices, and virtual viewpoints, whose efficacy lies in their ability to illuminate the world-historical globalizing agency of the bourgeoisie during the second half of the nineteenth century, precisely because that virtuality points to the potentiality of a desire for totalization constitutive of the historical subject in his novels, that can never be fully accomplished. In this sense, I believe Verne's novels account for the real of global modernity and of bourgeois social relations more productively than any realist novel could. Eric Hayot's recent programmatic book *On Literary Worlds* underscores the need to interpret the signifying forces emanating from the interval between a literary text and the extradiegetic world it points to, and theorizes the conditions of possibility for my proposal to read Verne as a writer of virtual realism. For Hayot, literature is always a relation to and theory of the lived world and advises an intense critical investment in "a work's degree of orientedness toward *the* world, the degree, that is, to which it responds or corresponds to the basic philosophical or social-world imperatives of its age, the normative sense of a 'real' or 'actual' world that bears some noncontinuous (and possibly oppositional) relation to the aesthetic. . . . An attention to the world-creating and world-relating dimensions of their work shows us what kinds of realism there are, opening up inside the field of realism" (44–46). The specific and historically determined tension between the continuities and discontinuities that articulate the diegetic and extradiegetic universes in Verne's novels, between the fictional and the actual, gives rise to an oblique realism that taps into the real of the global imaginaries of European modernity and thus represents the discursive conditions of globalization.[18] What Verne's singular realism represents, then, is not (not only, not necessarily) the concrete social formation of the middle classes at the turn of the century but the latent power of the ideology that sustains them.[19] This is the radical and productive ideological potential that the novelization of the global opens up for the late nineteenth-century novel: to imagine the world as a global space in which the novel, or rather the global novel, will inscribe itself.

THE LATIN AMERICAN NOVELIZATION OF THE GLOBAL

The globalization of the novel and the novelization of the global are not two parallel or alternative critical roads. The critic makes them intersect through comparative readings of novels produced or consumed at different points on an uneven global field of production, consumption, and translation, thus mapping the ubiquity of the novel form. In other words, to understand the relation between different aesthetic articulations of the novelization of the global at distant points of a global field (in this case, the material conditions of production of Verne's novels, on the one hand, and those of Eduardo Holmberg's *Viaje maravilloso del señor Nic-Nac al planeta Marte*, on the other), one needs to read diachronically the displacements of "outer-space novels" (the globalization of the novel) together with the actual figurations of the universe produced in each of these cultural locations (the novelization of the global).

Holmberg began publishing *Viaje maravilloso del Señor Nic-Nac al planeta Marte* as a serial in the Buenos Aires newspaper *El Nacional* in November of 1875. It tells the story of Nic-Nac, an aficionado of all kinds of scientific and pseudoscientific disciplines and gadgets, who makes an appointment with a doctor of spiritism who has just arrived from Europe: "Aquel espiritista se llama Friederich Seele, o si queréis su nombre en castellano, Federico Alma" (39) ("The spiritist's name was Friederich Seele, or if you want his name in Spanish, Frederick Soul").[20] Nic-Nac develops a "spiritual" crush on the doctor and convinces Seele to teach him the technique of transmigration or *transplanetation* ("transplanetación"), which consists of fasting for an extended period of time until the soul leaves the body to travel across the universe: "¿Y si ahora tuviera la idea de lanzar mi espíritu a visitar los planetas?" (43) ("How about launching my spirit to visit other planets now?"). After an eight-day fast, Nic-Nac collapses, and, as his soul leaves his body, he sees a doctor trying to resuscitate him. Soon after beginning his spiritual journey, Nic-Nac encounters Dr. Seele, who will be his guide on the voyage to Mars, a planet whose natural, sociopolitical, and cultural features turn out to resemble those of Argentina.[21] His spiritual adventure complete, Nic-Nac (or, rather, his soul) returns to his body in Buenos Aires.

The most interesting characteristic of Holmberg's book is its structure. The first-person narrative that tells Nic-Nac's story and authorizes his spiritual space travel is framed by two paratexts by the apocryphal editor of Nic-Nac's manuscript. In the "Introduction," this editor refers ironically to the general reading public's relationship to paranormal phenomena and narrates an encounter with two young men who read out loud newspaper headlines stating that Nic-Nac has been admitted to a hospital for mental patients. Moreover, people in the street do not seem to agree whether Nic-Nac's journey is real or imaginary, "unos negando el hecho, otros compadeciendo a su autor, algunos aceptando todas y cada una de las circunstancias del viaje" (30) ("some denying the truth of the event, others feeling sorry for the author, and some accepting every single detail of the circumstances of the trip"). Similarly, in the note that closes the novel, "El editor toma un momento la palabra" ("The Editor Briefly Takes the Floor"), the fictionalized editor blames its deficiencies on the insanity of its author, who has been diagnosed with "manía planetaria" (180) ("planetary mania"). "¿Pero quién es Nic-Nac? ¿Dónde está? ¡Ah! ¡En una casa de locos!" (179) ("But who is Nic-Nac? Where is he? Oh! In the loony bin!").

There are many things to contrast in Verne and Holmberg's novelization of the global (or, perhaps more accurately, of the universal or cosmic)—among them, the huge disparity in aesthetic quality (*Nic-Nac* is poorly written in both style and plot).[22] Rather than focus on their unequal literary value—explainable in terms of the talent of the novelists or the varying degrees of autonomy within the French and Argentine literary fields—I wish to concentrate on critical questions raised both by the immaterial nature of Nic-Nac's universal spiritual/imaginary journey and by the text's own ambiguity toward his first-person narrative. If in Verne's novels the universality of the traveling characters is determined by the fact that they take real trips with real consequences (within the plot)—that is, that they transcend their respective localities (France, the United States, or the earth at large) in order to materialize their aspirations by making the universe *theirs*—how should one read the imaginary or spiritual nature of Nic-Nac's journey to Mars? Or, to say it differently, how should one understand Nic-Nac's adventure to Mars when the universal predicate of his trip depends, not on leaving his country, but on leaving his own body?

Perhaps the most obvious possibility would be to interpret it in relation to Holmberg's marked interest in spiritism and paranormal phenomena, and his attempt to reconcile these practices with the hegemonic positivist creed—as many others were trying to do in both Latin America and Europe in the late nineteenth century.[23] However, Holmberg's intellectual curiosity about spiritism cannot account for the many differences between his novels and Verne's, nor does it explain the decision to narrate the trip as a spiritual/imaginary one. The imaginary nature of Nic-Nac's travel might be characterized as a novelistic option determined by the conditions of enunciation at the periphery, conditions that did not provide the symbolic and material resources available to Verne. Holmberg's choice could then be attributed to the marginality of a culture that lacked firsthand experience of the globalization of modernity. According to this line of thought, Holmberg represented a spiritual voyage because it was all that his marginal conditions of enunciation could afford. Nic-Nac's journey would thus also be inspired by a cosmopolitan desire to explore what lies beyond one's location, but a cosmopolitan drive of less consequence: a spiritual, immaterial cosmopolitanism aware of its limitations and impossibilities.

The assumptions behind these interpretations, however, are not historically accurate. Toward the end of the nineteenth century, Latin American elites were engaged in worldwide travels and exploration. And even if they were not involved in a world-historical transcultural imperialistic process, they did not lack experience of cultural and political hegemony, since they were engaged in an internal colonization that would soon lead to the consolidation of nation-states. Holmberg, moreover, could easily have written an account of an actual trip to Mars by an Argentine astronaut in the same way that Verne sent two Americans and a Frenchman to the moon. Verne's *De la Terre à la Lune* was published ten years before *Viaje maravilloso del señor Nic-Nac al planeta Marte*, and it seems highly likely that Holmberg, usually identified as the first Latin American author of science fiction (see A. Prieto), would have read Verne's novel before he wrote *Nic-Nac*.[24]

Why, then, did Holmberg write a novel about a galactic voyage made possible by transmigration and *transplanetation* instead of modern technology and science? Structural determinations (such as the lack of direct experience of technological modernity, or the cultural authorization of paranormal explanations) play only a limited role in a writer's creative decisions within the relative autonomy of the literary imagination. I want to suggest that there is no need to resort to subjective or objective explanations to explain the nature of Nic-Nac's spiritual voyage because the novel itself, in its paratexts, defines the main character's travel as a pathological adventure:

> No, Nic-Nac no es un loco furioso, es un loco tranquilo. Y es tan cierto lo que afirmamos, que basta abrir el libro de entradas de aquel establecimiento para leer una partida en la que consta que el señor Nic-Nac padece de una "*manía planetaria*." El director del establecimiento, hombre instruido y observador incansable, ha manifestado que Nic-Nac es un ente original, afable, un tanto instruido, al que se le pueden creer muchas de las cosas que dice, exceptuando, empero, los medios de los que se ha valido para transmigrar de la Tierra a Marte y de éste a aquélla. (179–80)
>
> No, Nic-Nac is not a raving lunatic, he is crazy but calm. We are certain about this, and the records of the establishment confirm it in an entry stating that Mr. Nic-Nac suffers from "*planetary mania*." The director of the establishment, a learned man and indefatigable observer, has declared that Nic-Nac is an original, affable, somewhat educated person; one can believe almost anything he says except his references to the means he may have used to transmigrate from Earth to Mars and back.

By stating that the main character suffers from "planetary mania," the *editor* returns Nic-Nac's experience to the scientific realm of psychiatric taxonomies, which deems *transplanetation* a mental illness and not the possibility of a journey through the universe. The *editor* sets the record straight: anyone aspiring to reach the stars should develop the necessary technology, just as the members of the Gun Club did in Verne's *De la Terre à la Lune*; paranormal sciences lead, not to the realization of universality, but instead to psychiatric confinement. At the end of the editor's note, the normative and instrumental relation to the world that had been broken by Nic-Nac's (delusional) first-person narrative has been restored, and the possibility of literary renderings of the universe as a totality of meaning depends upon aesthetic protocols à la Verne whose rational, technological, and instrumental symbolic health cannot be doubted.

Verne's novels produce effective images of the world as a totality of freedom mediated by modern social relations because they are confident about their place as novels (indeed as French novels) in the historical process of global expansion of bourgeois institutions, values, and practices. What, then, determines *Nic-Nac*'s Latin American "radical situational difference in the cultural production of meaning" (Jameson, "Brief Response" 26)? *Viaje maravilloso del señor Nic-Nac al planeta Marte* does not even attempt to imagine a world unified under the hegemony of modern social relations. Instead, it puts forth an alternative universalist imaginary that it then negates, as if the marginal conditions of production of universality allow only for the demarcation of the limits of its impossibility.

At a historical moment immediately prior to the inauguration of a new universalist horizon of Latin American culture that was marked by the discourse of *modernismo*, at a time when Latin American writers were primarily concerned with the exploration of the frontiers of their national or regional particularities (think of Ignacio Manuel Altamirano's *El Zarco*, Lucio V. Mansilla's *Una excursión a los indios ranqueles* [*An Expedition to the Ranquel Indians*], José Hernández's *Martín Fierro*, Francisco Moreno's *Viaje a la Patagonia austral* [*Journey to Southern Patagonia*], most of Ricardo Palma's *Tradiciones peruanas* [*Peruvian Traditions*], González Prada's first essays, and Machado de Assis's *Memórias póstumas de Brás Cubas* [*The Posthumous Memoirs of Brás Cubas*]), Holmberg's *Nic-Nac* posed questions about the novelization of the global and the universal that few others in the peripheries of the world seemed to be considering: Can my characters travel the way Verne's characters do? Can they produce images of a reconciled and available modern world with and through their displacements? Can they be identified as cosmopolitan, metropolitan, or colonial subjects, striving to inscribe themselves in the universal order of modernity? Verne's novels presuppose affirmative answers to these questions with their confident belief in their universal discursive nature. The "radical situational difference" (Jameson, "Brief Response" 26) of Holmberg's *Nic-Nac*—and any Latin American narrative being interrogated by questions better suited for a Dr. Fergusson, a Phileas Fogg, or a Michel Ardan—lies not in a hopeful affirmative response to those questions but in the recognition of a limit. It is this epistemological obstacle that might be taken to inform the conditions of enunciation from a marginal space, where the world-historical affirmation of a teleological discourse of globalization is coded as the "planetary mania" of a schizophrenic and the "spiritist fantasy" of a crude proto-novel that nevertheless anticipates the cosmopolitan aspirations of the discourse of *modernismo*.

A COSMOPOLITAN CRITIQUE OF WORLD LITERATURE

This chapter's twofold argument stems from a double critical anxiety. On the one hand, I am motivated by the question of the role of literature in general and the novel in particular in the contemporary production and reproduction of the discourses of globalization, and, at the same time, the ways in which those discourses determine the imaginaries and their forms in the novel. On the other hand, I am uneasy in the face of the reemergence in the context of US academic discourse of the concept of world literature as an attempt to address what I have been calling the global ubiquity of the novel as a genre and as a modern institution and thus the formation of a global field of production, consumption, translation, and displacement of novels. In this final part of the chapter, I would like to interrogate the critical practices, political implications, and picture of the global literary field presupposed by the concept of world literature.[25] I am not particularly interested in determining whether world literature is a tool meant to classify *world literary texts* and exclude others, whether it is a discipline and a way of reading (and thus the new paradigm for comparative literature), or whether it is the name of the historical formation of a space of symbolic exchange and circulation that exceeds particular national cultures; world literature entails, to a certain extent, all of these critical and pedagogical operations. Rather, I want to focus on the cultural and theoretical effects that the revival of the concept of world literature may have on the ways we conceptualize, imagine, and teach the transcultural making of the novel, but also of the spaces where novels are produced and consumed. My concern has to do with the potential of world literature (understood as the name of a field of study, a discipline, a pedagogical practice, a canon, and a cosmopolitan desire for transcendence of cultural particularity) to illuminate or obscure the global unfolding of the hegemonic formation of the literary institution—an uneven process that determines both the world literary status of certain texts and the discourse of world literature itself. In short, the problem I would like to examine here is whether world literature serves the cosmopolitan purpose that is supposed to be constitutive of its critical and pedagogical horizon.

Behind the *rentrée* of the concept of world literature lies a commendable political goal: to imprint a universalist inclination on a US educational system and cultural environment that has become increasingly chauvinistic and that is (appropriately) seen as a symbolic battlefield for the future of global citizenship. This aim of the new world literature, with which it is difficult to disagree, is very much in line with the radical and controversial proposal of a cosmopolitan education for American students that Martha Nussbaum put forth over a decade ago in "Patriotism and Cosmopolitanism":

> As students here grow up, is it sufficient for them to learn that they are above all citizens of the United States, but that they ought to respect the basic human rights of citizens of India, Bolivia, Nigeria, and Norway? Or should they, as I think—in addition to giving special attention to the history and current situation of their own nation—learn a good deal more than is frequently the case about the rest of the world in which they live, about India and Bolivia and Nigeria and Norway and their histories, problems, and comparative successes? Should they learn only that citizens of India have equal basic human rights, or should they also learn about the problems of hunger and pollution in India, and the implications of these problems for larger problems of global hunger and global ecology? Most important, should they be taught that they are above all citizens of the United States, or should they instead be taught that they are above all citizens of a world of human beings, and that, while they themselves happen to be situated in the United States, they have to share this world of human beings with the citizens of other countries? . . . I shall call [this second kind of education] cosmopolitan education. (6)

When understood as part of the larger project of a cosmopolitan education, the political worth of the concept of world literature becomes undeniable, especially when, as in the case of Nussbaum's proposal, the notion of cosmopolitanism takes the form of a desire for universal justice.[26] But is world literature capable of accomplishing this cosmopolitan goal, or, better yet, which conception of world literature, if any, could produce critical and pedagogical practices capable of accomplishing what Nussbaum proposes? Indeed, at least some discourses of world literature produce a canon of Global Great Books that tends to repeat itself in anthologies or on syllabi that too often reinforce romantic essentialisms (a remnant of Goethe's concept of *Weltliteratur*) according to which the Third World specializes in the production of hyperaestheticized national allegories that express their cultural particularities—for example, their frustrated dreams of modernity—while the metropolitan centers contribute true aesthetic innovations.[27]

Some of the most prominent comparatists have been working for a decade now to redefine world literature in relation to the heritage of postcolonial studies. This discursive articulation has managed, to some degree, to move the theory of world literature away from the two major threats that loom over the discipline. On the one hand, there is the postulation of world literature as an even playing field that makes possible an idealistic sense of parity among the literatures of the world—in other words, world literature as an equalizing discourse that rights the wrongs of cultural imperialism and/or economic globalization. On the other, there is an *expressive* logic according to which some works convey the historical or aesthetic experience of their cultures of origin and, therefore, become part of the corpus of a world literature composed of a plurality of global particularities.

In the critical discourses of Franco Moretti, Pascale Casanova, David Damrosch, Haun Saussy, Emily Apter, Shu-mei Shih, Wai Chee Dimock, Françoise Lionnet, and Martin Puchner, among others, world literature has already overcome the twin menaces of expressiveness and ideological blindness to the political determinations that shape the discipline, thus earning the *post-* prefix that indicates its inscription in a post–identity politics discursive field. Their world literatures are, indeed, post–world literary reshapings of the concept and have, for the most part, begun to transcend the first of the two dangers above.[28] In the work of each of these authors, the articulation of a world literature with postcolonial concerns, poststructuralist discourses on identity (national or otherwise), translational practices, and world-system theory results in an account of the global that takes into consideration the constitutive unevenness of social relations throughout the world or within a given cultural configuration (see also Bhabha, *Location* 12).[29] But this theoretical refashioning of the concept of world literature cannot modify (at least not soon enough) pedagogical practices that, as all of these theorists acknowledge, seem to lag behind in a romantic mood. A quick review of world literature syllabi and most anthologies shows that the logic of representation and expressiveness is still at work, especially when one considers the aesthetic features of those texts that have made it into the classroom and canon and the relation between these features and the imagined characteristics of the country or region that they stand for. As David Damrosch puts it, "In world literature, as if in some literary Miss Universe competition, an entire nation may be represented by a single author: Indonesia, the world's fifth-largest country and home of ancient and ongoing cultural traditions, is usually seen, if at all, in the person of Pramoedya Ananta Toer. Jorge Luis Borges and Julio Cortázar divide the honors for Mr. Argentina" ("World Literature" 44).[30] Even though anthologies of world literature have expanded their coverage enormously (see, for example, the recent Longman and Norton anthologies, edited by a group of scholars led by David Damrosch and Martin Puchner, respectively, both of which render truly global accounts of a significantly wider literary world), a great majority of the newly included texts—especially those that hail from peripheries of the Euro-American world—find a place in these new, pedagogically oriented world literary canons by virtue of a supposedly expressive relation between them and the cultural particularity of their origin.

A fitting case study of this institutional capture of the literatures of the world by a conservative world literary reason is the MLA series "Approaches to Teaching World Literature," whose importance lies in its symptomatic nature. In 2009 the series featured ninety-five titles; by 2010 it had reached one hundred volumes, and it has added thirty more titles since, though the percentual representation of languages and literary traditions remains the same. In terms of discursive heterogeneity the list does not follow the patterns of the postmulticultural global canon that is familiar in university classrooms across the United States (at least comparative literature classrooms). The overwhelming majority are nineteenth- and twentieth-century modernist works in English, along with a handful of the eighteenth-century British novels, a few classics (Homer, Euripides, Virgil and the Bible—all of them included in the list as foundational, Über-narratives), and several medieval and early modern canonical texts (Chaucer, Dante, Elizabethan theater and poetry, Molière). Frederick Douglass's slave narrative is the only entry that might at one time have been thought to stretch the limits of the literary institution. Moreover, although the series bears the name "Approaches to Teaching World Literature," there is only one text in a non-Western language (Japanese), not counting the Hebrew Bible, which I am considering grouped with the classics. Out of ninety-five titles, sixty-five are in different intonations of English, fourteen in French, three in Italian (Boccaccio, Dante, and—surprisingly—Collodi's *Pinocchio*), three in German (Goethe, Kafka, and Mann), three in Spanish (early modern Spanish drama, Cervantes, and García Márquez), three in classical Greek and Latin (Homer, Euripides, and Virgil), and one each in Russian (Tolstoy), Norwegian (Ibsen), Japanese (Murasaki Shikibu), and classical Hebrew (the Bible).[31]

In *What Is World Literature?*, Damrosch convincingly argues that the scope of world literature in the United States has changed dramatically over the last hundred years. If at the beginning of the twentieth century world literature anthologies and course syllabi "defined 'the world' unhesitatingly as the Western World" (124), Damrosch points out that during the 1990s several anthologies radically changed their approach to world literature, turning it into a truly global field that encompassed the whole world and historical stages that ranged from pre-1492 indigenous narratives from the Americas to postcolonial and postmodern literatures from every periphery of the Western world. But in spite of the expansion of the canon, the disparity between Damrosch and others' progress toward institutional disciplinary reform and the continued state of the discipline, as revealed by the MLA series, remains enormous. Given the institutional weight of the MLA, this series cannot be taken as the mere residual presence of an archaic conception of the field; on the contrary, it appears to reveal the actual pedagogical practice of world literature in most corners of the field of comparative literature, in striking contrast to the way that many progressive intellectuals theorize it.[32]

Apart from the production and reproduction of the global hegemony of English, the inclusion of the English and French works in the MLA list responds to a straightforward dynamic of canon reproduction, the constitutive grounds for institutionalization. The same logic seems to apply to the Bible, the Greco-Roman classics, Cervantes, Lope de Vega, Goethe, Tolstoy, Ibsen, Kafka, and Mann. The three remaining texts—the medieval *The Tale of Genji*, supposedly authored by Shikibu, García Márquez's *Cien años de soledad* (*One Hundred Years of Solitude*), and Achebe's *Things Fall Apart*—speak to underlying assumptions about what the margins of the West can contribute to the discursive field of world literature. Behind the choice of *The Tale of Genji*'s eleventh-century account of the misadventures of Japanese courtesans, *Things*

Fall Apart's 1958 history of colonial unrest in Africa, and *Cien años de soledad*'s 1967 magical realist genealogical allegory is a belief that these texts express the Japanese, African, and Latin American historical experiences. Each culture is thus reduced to a singular essentialized meaning: a traditional Japan that lives on in the West's imaginary, a tribal Africa that falls victim to the violent social restructuring of colonialism, and a Latin America forever doomed to political unrest and the premodern identity of private and public domains. The transformation of *Cien años de soledad* into a global best seller came to represent and express what a large portion of the world's literary public assumed to be the essence of Latin American culture and social history—a narrative metaphor for all of Latin America, not merely tropical South America, or Colombia, or Santa Marta. Thus the essentialist logic of expression can be read as (1) a romantic ideology that assumes that cultural particularity is contained most perfectly in the indivisible unity of fixed cultural localities (whether regional or national); and (2) a discourse of globalization based on the supposed coexistence of fixed regional identities and national institutional formations.

It goes without saying that none of the proponents of a *post–world literary* world literature would adopt this logic in the construction of syllabi, anthologies, and research agendas (and the making of this series would have been, perhaps, very different if it had been published under the auspices of the American Comparative Literature Association). But what might be an alternative—and presumably more adequate—method of determining the specific textual content for a critical and pedagogical *world literary* practice? In his "Conjectures on World Literature," Franco Moretti provides an abstract answer to this question. For him, as I have anticipated in the Introduction, world literature must live up to the universal promise implied in its name, and he proposes a shift from world literature to the literatures of the world—all of the literatures ever written anywhere in the world.[33] This new universal field would transform world literature into a necessarily collective enterprise with a very clear division of labor: on the ground floor, specialists produce knowledge about particular literatures through close readings of texts and cultural contexts; on the upper level or metadiscursive realm, über-comparatists such as Moretti trace, through what he calls "distant reading," universal trends and patterns that make visible the world system of literature as a global cultural totality. By proposing to read *everything*, Moretti avoids the danger of a world literature composed of texts that are chosen and isolated because of their supposed capacity to express and represent their national or regional cultures of origin. We would no longer have magical realism and *testimonio* standing for all of Latin America;

instead, we would have the entirety of the region's immensely heterogeneous aesthetic universe.[34] At the same time, as I state in the Introduction, Moretti's call to read everything relies on the abstract notion of an undetermined totality, and the world in his proposed world literature coincides with the universal *qua* universal; the textual corpus at stake obscures the concrete determinations that shape its aesthetic specificity, its boundaries, and its historicity.

Nonetheless, even if the constitutive threats of actually existing world literary practices were overcome, what I consider to be the most important question at the center of these world literary anxieties remains unanswered: Is world literature as a cosmopolitan project that articulates cultural difference in order to foster emancipatory goals even possible? Can a discourse about, and a pedagogy of, world literature produce *the planet* that Gayatri Spivak has proposed, a concept that assumes the responsibility to "overwrite the globe," as in "the gridwork of electronic capital . . . drawn by the requirements of Geographical Information Systems" (*Death* 72)?[35] This ethically normative dimension has marked the cultural and political urgency of world literature's historical task since Goethe: an aesthetic formation highlighted by the cosmopolitan demand to undermine, on a global scale, unjust social relations, whether colonial, warmongering, or generally oppressive. From this Goethean perspective, world literature gives aesthetic form to the cosmopolitan desire to overcome the restrictions and limitations of our own particular culture and our claustrophobic experience of it and to affirm the necessarily universal nature of the promise of cultural emancipation of the planet. World literature becomes, in short, a discourse with the potential to lead the way toward the realization of a global culture (as the dialectical negation of the one-sidedness of local particular cultures) capable of releasing the emancipatory potential of "culture." Damrosch notes that no one has stated these lofty goals more eloquently than René Wellek, whose article "The Crisis of Comparative Literature" (1959) proposed a discipline structured around *world literary* goals: "Comparative literature has the immense merit of combating the false isolation of national literary histories" (282–83). In the last paragraph, Wellek establishes the crucial role that such a critical discourse could play in the production of cosmopolitan values and thus in the actualization of the abstract construction of the universal subject imagined by the Enlightenment: "Once we grasp the nature of art and poetry, its victory over human mortality and destiny, its creation of a new world order of the imagination, national vanities will disappear. Man, universal man, man everywhere and at all time, in all his variety, emerges and literary scholarship ceases to be an antiquarian pastime, a calculus of national credits and debts and even a mapping of networks of relationships. Literary scholarship becomes an act of the imagination, like art itself, and thus a preserver and creator of the highest values of mankind" (295). While the cosmopolitan echoes of Wellek's discourse still seem relevant and even urgent in the context of raging inequalities fueled in part by a process of economic globalization, it is once again difficult to share his optimism about the humanistic potential of world literature. The problem I find with this genealogy of world literature (from Goethe to Wellek, and to many of the proponents of a renewed world literature today) is that it tends to see the literary world—*the world* of world literature—as a field where the different cultural singularities that otherwise define each other through violent cultural and economic antagonisms find a common discourse and enter into a dialogue that, supposedly, serves as a model for global political agency. Underlying this belief that humanistic world literature is capable of producing a reconciled world is an unshakable confidence in the redeeming power of culture.[36]

In this world literature, "informed by a sense of the implicit parity between literatures" (Trumpener 198) and represented as a Habermasian public sphere for global dialogue, what is lost is the opaqueness of cultural otherness and the intermittent failures of communication and global translation inherent in the hegemonic social relations that make up the aesthetic and cultural exchanges of world literature.[37] These exchanges entail the hegemonic formation of world literature's disciplinary discourse and object, and the necessary delimitation of what falls within and outside of world literature: what gets to be translated (and through what specific institutional articulations) and therefore reaches audiences (particularly in metropolitan academic centers) beyond the culture of origin of a given text.[38] Thus a critical reading of García Márquez's *Cien años de soledad* with a cosmopolitan purpose should not transform the novel into an allegorical sign of Latin America's cultural particularity, measuring its world literary worth in terms of its ability to represent the region, or, even worse, because of the exotic flavor it would add—with its characters ascending to heaven amid bedsheets—to the world literary canon. These usually complementary ways of arguing the paradoxical universality of *Cien años de soledad* depend on the (metropolitan) assumption that magical realism expresses something about the prerational constitution of Latin

American societies that escapes the modern realist representation. This assumption reifies a reductive and condescending perception of the complex aesthetic and political relations between Latin American aesthetics and the region's social structure. Sylvia Molloy lucidly explains this metropolitan fascination: "Magic realism is refulgent, amusing, and kitschy (Carmen Miranda's headdress; José Arcadio Buendía's tattooed penis)—but it doesn't happen, couldn't happen, here" ("Postcolonial Latin America" 375).

A cosmopolitan approach attentive to the hegemonic articulations at work in cultural formations would insist that the global status of García Márquez's novel has nothing to do with a supposedly privileged relation to its culture of origin and would instead investigate the material production of its globality. For example, it would ask questions about the globalization of magical realism through Africa, Southeast Asia, eastern Europe, and the Chicano Southwest of the United States: When was García Márquez translated in each of these locations? And how were his novels and short stories received? What existing local aesthetic traditions and social relations may have contributed to the transformation of magical realist narratives into a form of postcolonial interpellation (cf. Bhabha, "Introduction" 7)? How, and in what specific forms and instances, was magical realism appropriated and rewritten? Were the traces of these global appropriations of magical realism obscured, or were they acknowledged in order to produce cosmopolitan forms of affiliation? And, in turn, how did García Márquez and other Latin American proponents and practitioners of a magical realist aesthetic respond to the global echoes (cosmopolitan and postcolonial, but also metropolitan) of their discourse?[39] In the following chapter, I develop these questions further and trace the material trajectories of these magical realist translations, appropriations, and rewritings.

The twofold idea of the globalization of the novel and the novelization of the global that I have put forth here is an attempt to recharacterize the debate on world literature in relation to cosmopolitan goals, while also accounting for the process of universalization of novelistic writing, reading, and translation, and for the production of singular images and imaginaries of universality that reduplicate the global discursive horizon of modern literary practices in specific texts. Or to put it in slightly different terms: it is an attempt to apprehend the hegemonic making of the universality of world literature, while resisting the temptation to fall back on particularistic reaffirmations of national or regional cultural identities, and in fact preserving universality as the necessary horizon of cosmopolitan practices with an emancipatory purpose.[40]

In spite of their methodological differences, the most intelligent interventions in this debate agree on their views of world literature, not as a defined corpus, but as a way of reading, drawing connections, and imagining unexpected and transcultural contexts that may illuminate new modes of signification. In thinking about cosmopolitan discourses, I have come to understand world literature to fit the terms of the classical Marxist characterization of class as a social relation: that is, to see world literature as a relational concept and practice that depends on a cosmopolitan representation of its historical task of universal reparation. The model of the globalization of the novel and the novelization of the global, with its emphasis on historical processes on a global scale and the production of global imaginaries, allows us to see world literature as a cosmopolitan social relation, both a critical discourse and a concrete universal field of cultural exchanges constituted by asymmetrical structural forces disputing the meaning of the global. In other words, the globalization of the novel and the novelization of the global foreground the constitutive tension at the center of the discourse of world literature. This tension consists, on the one hand, of the cosmopolitan drive to represent a diverse globe as a reconciled multicultural totality and, on the other, of the equally cosmopolitan mandate to map the asymmetric interaction of hegemonic and subaltern cultural and economic forces that account for the historical formation of the unevenness of the globe. Our challenge is to acknowledge and rearticulate these complex cosmopolitan interpellations that point to opposing ways of symbolizing global differences in our pedagogical practices and our research agendas, assuming that it is impossible to embrace the normative side of cosmopolitan discourses such as world literature before accounting for the global hegemonic relations that shape them. The desires for commodities and discourses "of distant lands and climes" (Marx and Engels 477) that continue to constitute our cosmopolitan subjectivities are at once the symbolic ground on which we hope to inscribe an intellectual emancipatory practice and a domestication of the world that reproduces the hegemonic relations that world literature may or may not address.

CHAPTER 2

The Global Life of Genres and the Material Travels of Magical Realism

HOW DOES A GENRE GO GLOBAL?

Magical realism occupies a paradoxical space at the center of the relation between Latin America and the discourse of world literature. On the one hand, it has been portrayed (and still is today, after its aesthetic and cultural power has been manifestly exhausted) as the most local, most particular aesthetic form: that is, the aesthetic form that best expresses the cultural tensions and historical ethos of the region. On the other, as evidenced by its ubiquity in syllabi, anthologies, and *corpora*, it is the most established and stable world literary genre, the world literary genre par excellence, indeed, a global form, particularly since its rebranding as "the literary language of the postcolonial world" (Bhabha, "Introduction" 7). As analyzed in the previous chapter, the institutionalization of world literary reason solves this paradox by producing mappings of the discipline whereby the world's peripheries are represented by supposedly typical aesthetic forms, whose typicality needs to be naturalized in order to express the totality of the region or nation it is meant to represent. Here, then, is a first (albeit, immensely dissatisfactory) answer to the question that opens this section: magical realism goes global as a particularistic aesthetic that satisfies a demand for *local color* from marginal cultures in the global field of world literature.

But the triad of magical realism, postcolonialism, and world literature is a rather new development that dates back to the 1990s. Before that, in the 1970s and 1980s, magical realism was seen as a characteristically Latin American literary code. Critics like Josefina Ludmer, Enrique Anderson Imbert (*Realismo magico*), and Ángel Rama, among many others, read Alejo Carpentier's *lo real maravilloso* and Gabriel García Márquez's *realismo mágico* as overcoming the apparent contradiction between the region's desire for cultural modernity in sync with Europe and the United States, and the recuperation of its cultural particularity. Since the 1990s, however, several academics have denounced magical realism as the "reification of alterity" (Moreiras 145–46), consumed by metropolitan audiences that affirm their sense of superiority in their rejoicing in magical realist gimmicks because that "doesn't happen, couldn't happen, here" (Molloy, "Postcolonial Latin America" 375): magical realism as a form of critical domestication (Kadir, *Other Writing* 26).

These affirmations of, and this resistance to, the identification of magical realism with the putative cultural essence of the region coincide in their perception of magical realism as conspicuously Latin American. But since the 1990s, from quite different subject positions and with markedly distinct implications, a number of comparative literature scholars have characterized magical realism as the emblematic genre of a postcolonial world literature and, more generally, as a global literary currency (which would then include metropolitan texts like Angela Carter's *Nights at the Circus*, Peter Carey's *Illywhacker*, and Marie Darrieussecq's *Truismes*), now emancipated from the Latin American determinations that launched it onto the world scene. Besides Homi Bhabha's identification of magical realism with the postcolonial world that I quoted above, Gayatri Spivak describes it as a Latin American aesthetic form that "has been used to great effect by some expatriate or diasporic subcontinentals writing in English" ("Post-structuralism" 57); Fredric Jameson portrays it as an "alternative to the narrative logic of contemporary postmodernism" ("On Magic Realism" 129); Lois Parkinson Zamora and Wendy Faris, who edited the most ambitious critical compendium on the global scope of magical realism, consider it "an international commodity" (2); David Damrosch links it to the expansion of world literary markets from Latin America to India and the Balkans (*How to Read* 106–07); Franco Moretti calls it a liminal aesthetic of the modern world epic (*Modern Epic* 233); Michael Denning sees it as a part of a global tradition of proletarian, committed, and progressive literature (703); and Jean-Pierre Durix writes that it is "a new multicultural artistic reality" (162).

In spite of so many declarations certifying the perfect triple marriage between world literature, postcolonialism, and magical realism, this *ménage-à-trois* needs to be unpacked, denaturalized, and historicized. Indeed, the making of a new world literature—a new understanding of its critical discourse and the texts that interact in the most productive ways with it—calls for accounts of the global status of aesthetic forms that are invested in foregrounding the historical and hegemonic mediations that make up the global space where world literary discourses inscribe their cosmopolitan desires. We need to interrogate precisely the process through which an aesthetic formation becomes a world literary genre. How does a certain literary protocol, recognized beyond its singularity as a genre, become universally available as a productive and interpretative device? Only a historical narrative of the actual spread of a given genre across the globe, an account of material and concrete encounters, appropriations, resignifications, and transformations, can inform its world literary stature. Genres and texts belong to world literature not because of what they *are* but rather because of what they *do*: because they perform global desires, because they further transcultural goals, and because they resist the immediacy of meaning as a function of the local, whether national or regional. Or rather, they are made to behave like this, under the gaze of world literary critics. This is why I insist on the notion of world literary interventions, world literary disruptions that alter the epistemic geographies of literary history to produce new, contingent (ephemeral or not) large-scale spatial assemblages, redrawing the boundaries of the world with each utterance.[1]

Along the lines of *the globalization of the novel* that I proposed in the previous chapter, here I suggest that the world literary nature of magical realism should be sought, not in its formal generic traits, but in its concrete global trajectories from the 1920s to the 1990s and in the traces it leaves behind in the translations and rewritings that make up the literary materiality of its world: from the coining of the term *magical realism* by German art critic Franz Roh as a modality of post-expressionist art, to the essays and narratives of the Venezuelan Arturo Uslar Pietri, the Cuban Alejo Carpentier, and the Guatemalan Miguel Ángel Asturias, to the so-called Boom of Latin American literature and the worldwide cult developed around Gabriel García Márquez's *Cien años de soledad* (*One Hundred Years of Solitude*) and its rewritings between the 1970s and 1990s in Africa, South and East Asia, Eastern Europe, and the US South. Each of these global dislocations reconfigured magical realism according to the cultural politics of its appropriations: from avant-garde psychologism, to Latin Americanism as a redemptive discourse of cultural identity, to its global postcolonialization (or its postcolonial globalization), and finally to its commodification and the deactivation of its historico-political potential.

This global historical narrative is missing from the vast multilingual bibliography on magical realism that has grown exponentially since the 1980s and consists, for the most part, of formalistic and taxonomic analyses that try to define the genre through its difference from fantasy, science fiction, horror narratives, and other genres. Debates and divergence about the ways in which to characterize the term seem to be a central part of the aesthetic and critical tradition of magical realism. The proliferation of conflicting definitions does not have to do with the apparent oxymoron implied in the articulation of the realms of the marvelous and extraordinary within a conventionally conceived reality. Almost without exception, critics agree that magical realist narratives attempt to bridge the contradiction between its two terms—to depict magic and other phenomena that ordinary common sense cannot explain as naturally intervening in reality. The world of magical realist texts is one where the ordinary and extraordinary coexist without conflict, without even calling attention to each other's Otherness. In this sense, most critics would agree with Brazilian critic Irlemar Chiampi's working definition of magical realism as "a naturalização do irreal e a sobrenaturalização do real" (*Realismo maravilhoso* 26) ("the naturalisation of the marvelous and the denaturalisation of the real").

But the agreement on the definition of magical realism ends with this dialectic of estrangement and normalization. Specialists are divided as to whether magical realism is (1) an ability of artists (inherited from a romantic lineage that conceives the poet as seer) to unveil the spiritual determinations of the real in order to shed light on the marvelous that constitutes it, so that it cannot be explained through a rational logic of cause and effect; or (2) a code of representation that accounts for particular cultural formations where the historical experience of modernity coexists with a perception of the supernatural, understood in the broadest possible sense. To state it another way: Is magical realism a universal aesthetic that unveils the supernatural core of the real everywhere thanks to its universal antipositivistic (transhistorical, and often ahistorical) appeal? Or is it an aesthetic that belongs organically to marginal cultures marked by traumatic collective experiences of oppression (colonial or otherwise)? Most of the bibliography on magical realism and world literature tends to explain the genre's globality in terms of the first formulation, while those critics (like Bhabha and Spivak, among many others) that identify the coupling of magical realism and postcolonialism opt for the second argument. In this chapter, I attempt to historicize the gap that separates these two questions about the world literary nature of the genre.

TALES OF ORIGINS

If origins are historically determined, fictional, retrospective, and conventional constructions, it is not surprising that literary history assigns two different starting points to magical realism, each corresponding to one of the two ways of defining this narrative form described in the previous section: magical realism as the result of a universally available aesthetic perception of the intersections of the marvelous and the real, and magical realism as a narrative mode that contains the particular cultural experience of the underdeveloped world. Franz Roh, on the one hand, and Arturo Uslar Pietri and Alejo Carpentier, on the other, lay out the discursive matrices for each of these understandings of the cultural politics of magical realism.

In 1925, Franz Roh was the first to give critical substance to the concept of magical realism, albeit to interpret postexpressionist works of art, not narrative. Roh, an art historian, wrote a book/catalog on and for an exhibition of paintings that Gustav Hartlaub had organized in Mannheim, Germany, under the title *Neue Sachlichkeit* (alternately translated as "New Objectivity," "New Realism," or "Post-Expressionism"), with works by Otto Dix, George Grosz, and Max Beckmann among others. Roh saw *Neue Sachlichkeit* as a resolution of the historical opposition between impressionism and expressionism. In *Nach-Expressionismus, Magischer Realismus: Probleme der neusten eropäischen Malerei* (*Post-Expressionism, Magical Realism: Problems of the Most Recent European Painting*), Roh explains that whereas impressionist artists were concerned with objective representations, "giving maximal value and meaning to chromatic texture" ("Magic Realism" 19), "expressionism shows an exaggerated preference for fantastic, extraterrestrial, remote objects" (16). He saw this new school of *Neue Sachlichkeit* as an attempt to reconcile the referentiality of impressionism with the expressionist attempt to uncover the spiritual and mystical nucleus of reality: "Post-expressionism sought to reintegrate reality into the heart of visibility" while trying to "discover a more general and deeper basis [for it]. . . . This [art offers a] calm admiration of the magic of being, of the discovery that things already have their own faces" (18, 20). But this is as far as Roh went. He never gave a precise and cogent definition of magical realism, and because he limited himself to the reference in the title of his book, it could be said that it is only as a result of posterior elaborations on the concept that we recognize a foundational moment of the conceptual history of magical realism in his interpretation of postexpressionist art. In fact, Roh himself dropped the concept when he published *Geschichte der Deutschen Kunst von 1900 bis zur Gegenwart* (*German Art in the Twentieth Century*) in 1958 "in recognition that his terms *Magischer Realismus* and *Nach-Expressionismus* had been eclipsed by Hartlaub's *Neue Sachlichkeit*" (Guenther 35).

According to critics such as Irene Guenther and Chris Warnes, Roh inscribes his interpretation of postexpressionist painting in a Germanist philosophical tradition inaugurated by Novalis (Friedrich Freiherr von Hardenberg), who first delineated the concept of magical realism in 1798. Warnes explains that the German romantic Novalis envisioned in his notebooks the figure of a prophetic intellectual, whom he referred to as *magischer Idealist* and *magischer Realist* (*Schriften* 384): the prophet poet who lives outside the boundaries of enlightened discourse without losing touch with the real, grounding his poetic idealism in reality. "What Novalis and Roh have in common, then, is a concern with the limits of mimesis and a reliance on dialectics of inwardness and outwardness, subject and object, spirit and the world in their formulations of this concern. While each responded to the circumstances of his own times, and these dialectics are pronounced features of the post-Kantian tradition in general, the striking point of overlap lies in the two thinkers' attempts to synthesize such dialectical opposites through their uses of the term magical realism" (Warnes, *Magical Realism* 26).[2]

From the mid-1920s to the 1940s, Roh's concept of magical realism traveled through the marginal channels of Europe's avant-garde landscape. In 1927 Massimo Bontempelli, writer and director (with Curzio Malaparte) of *"900" Cahiers d'Italie et d'Europe*, published several articles (in French and Italian) calling for a magical realist aesthetic that would reinforce the role of imagination in literature and art:

"Unico strumento del nostro lavoro sarà l'immaginazione; ocorre rimparare l'arte di costruire, per inventare i miti freschi onde possa scaturire la nuova atmosfera di cui abbiamo bisogno per respirare" (750) ("The only instrument of our work will be the imagination. We have to relearn the art of creating; to invent fresh myths from which the new atmosphere we long to breathe in will emerge"). Erik Camayd-Freixas explains that Bontempelli's "magical realism sought to overcome futurism, but also a pastless primitivism, that zero degree of culture proposed by surrealist artists. From the very beginning, then, the literary concept of magical realism was contaminated with primitivism" (34). Bontempelli's proposal coincided with Roh's in the estimation that the roots of magical realism could be found in realism proper, but they differed in that Bontempelli wanted to broaden the scope of magical realism in order to include the representation of magical occurrences with realist techniques (Menton 213). The bilingual nature of Bontempelli's journal helped spread the concept throughout Europe.[3] When it reached Paris in the late 1920s, the history of magical realism merged with surrealism's attempt to reach deeper truths through nonrational, oneiric associations and the unexpected encounter of dissimilar objects and worlds.

This European elaboration of the concept of magical realism is construed in ahistorical terms. Neither Roh nor the romantic tradition he recuperated, nor Bontempelli and the avant-garde appropriations that followed suit, thought of a magical realist aesthetic defined and conditioned in its specificity by the cultural particularities of its differential spaces of emergence. Magical realism was born unbound by specific social relations; it was a discourse whose universality was determined by an epochal antipositivist exploration of the limits of rational approaches to the real. Only in its later displacement to the Caribbean does Carpentier conceptualize it as the aesthetic particularity of Latin America, opening the theoretical horizon to include its relation to marginality, subalternity, and postcolonialism.

THEORIES OF THE LATIN AMERICAN MARVELOUS

Magical realism came of age when a group of Caribbean and Central American writers—Arturo Uslar Pietri, Alejo Carpentier, and Miguel Ángel Asturias, who had befriended one another in Paris in the late 1920s and early 1930s—reformulated the concept into an aesthetic form derived from the hybrid nature of Latin American culture and society. In essays and novels from the late 1940s, they present magical realism as a way to achieve Latin America's aesthetic emancipation, when the region first gives itself a literary identity of its own, markedly differentiated from those translated from Europe. Carpentier made the most significant contribution to the redefinition of the concept, which he renamed "lo real maravilloso" ("the marvelous real") in the preface to his novel *El reino de este mundo* (*The Kingdom of This World*) (1949). However, when they met in Paris, the three writers were primarily concerned with conceiving a cogent aesthetic program capable of expressing their Latin American cultural particularity, and it was the Venezuelan novelist Uslar Pietri who first produced, albeit tentatively, a Latin American appropriation of the concept. In a 1986 essay, Uslar Pietri reminisces about those years:

> Desde 1929 y por algunos años tres jóvenes escritores hispanoamericanos se reunían, con cotidiana frecuencia, en alguna terraza de un café de Paris para hablar sin término de lo que más les importaba que era la literatura de la hora y la situación política de la América Latina que, en el fondo, era una misma y sola cosa. . . . En Asturias se manifestaba, de manera casi obsesiva, el mundo disuelto de la cultura maya, en una mezcla fabulosa en la que aparecían, como extrañas figuras de un drama de guiñol, los esbirros del Dictador, los contrastes inverosímiles de situaciones y concepciones y una visión casi sobrenatural de una realidad casi irreal. Carpentier sentía pasión por los elementos negros en la cultura cubana. Podía hablar por horas de los santeros, de los ñáñigos, de los ritos del vudú, de la mágica mentalidad del cubano medio en presencia de muchos pasados y herencias. Yo, por mi parte, venía de un país en el que no predominaban ni lo indígena, ni lo negro, sino la rica mezcla inclasificable de un mestizaje cultural contradictorio. La política venía a resultar un aspecto, acaso el más visible, de esas situaciones de peculiaridad que poco tenía que ver con los patrones europeos. ("Realismo mágico" 135)
>
> For a few years beginning in 1929, three young Hispanic American writers gathered frequently on the terrace of one Parisian café or another to talk endlessly of the things

> they cared most about, the literature of the moment, and the political situation in Latin America, which ultimately, were one and the same thing. . . . In Asturias there was an almost obsessive display of the destroyed world of Mayan culture: The dictator's henchmen, the improbable contrast of situations and conceptions, and an almost supernatural vision of an unreal reality, appeared in a fabulous mix as if they were strange figures in a Guignol drama. Carpentier felt passionate about the black elements of Cuban culture. He could talk for hours about santeros, voodoo rites, the magical mentality of the average Cuban faced with many pasts and heritages. I, on the other hand, was coming from a country where neither the indigenous nor the African predominated; a country marked by the unclassifiable mix of a contradictory cultural hybridity. . . . What came out of all those stories and evocations was the notion of the peculiar condition of the American world, which was irreducible to any European model.

These concerns (or obsessions, as Uslar Pietri calls them) about the cultural difference of Latin America, along with an exoticizing primitivist and ethnographic aesthetic, defined the early literary work of all three writers. In 1927, Asturias published (with the Mexican J. M. González de Mendoza) a Spanish translation of the Mayan sacred book, the *Popol Vuh* ("The Book of the Community" in Quiché—although their translation was from the French version their professor Georges Reynaud had published in 1925), followed in 1930 by *Leyendas de Guatemala* (*Legends of Guatemala*), a reinvention of the Mayan civilization, and of the mythical elements in its culture, written with an avant-gardist consciousness of the need to work with the inherited language (Yepes-Boscán 675).[4] During those same years, Carpentier published his first novel *Ecué-Yamba-ó* ("Praised be God" in Yoruba) (1933), which he had begun writing while imprisoned in Cuba in 1927. The novel depicts the reality of Afro-Cuban populations in Cuba, with special attention to the sorcery and mystical elements of the religious ceremonies of black ñáñigo groups, which the text presents in striking contrast to Havana's urban modernity. Uslar Pietri's novel *Las lanzas coloradas* (*The Red Lances*) (1931) does not attempt to give a voice to marginalized subjects; rather, it retells the history of the Venezuelan wars of independence interspersed with popular myths, in an attempt to code the Latin American particularity in national rather than ethnic terms. Shortly after, the Venezuelan wrote "La lluvia" ("The Rain") (1935), a short story that is often included in anthologies as an example of this incipient magical realist period and that deals with the everyday and apparently banal lives of two old rural peasants and their interaction with an environment that turns eerie during a drought.[5] Mario Roberto Morales explains that Asturias, Carpentier, and Uslar Pietri belonged to "todo un movimiento vanguardista latinoamericano de apropiación, inclusión, resignificación y fusión de las culturas subalternas al proyecto moderno de nación que comenzaba a prefigurarse sobre todo en las mentalidades de intelectuales liberals . . . la apropriación recreadora de la cultura popular tradicional, vista como insumo básico para crear versiones estéticas de identidades mestizas para diversos países de América Latina, yendo más allá, por supuesto, de toda suerte de negrismos e indigenismos asimilacionistas" (570–71) ("a whole Latin American avant-garde that appropriated, included, resignified, and fused subaltern cultures into the project of the modern nation-state that was beginning to take shape above all in the minds of liberal intellectuals . . . an appropriation that reinvented traditional popular cultures, seen as raw material to create aesthetic versions of hybrid identities for different Latin American countries, transcending, of course, any type of assimilationist *negrismos* and indigenisms"). If these three authors share the drive to redefine Latin America's historical specificity in terms of popular and subaltern subjectivities, they nonetheless appeal to different poetic strategies that, grouped together, establish the foundation of a certain Latin American narrative of marvels articulated around an incipient postcolonial consciousness of the need to remap and retell the history of a region whose narrative had been told from the perspective of the hegemonic *cultura criolla*.[6] Writing about mythical tales of talking animals that interact with archetypal human beings, Asturias recasts the place of Mayan culture in Guatemala. Depicting the Afro-Cuban world in his ethnographic account of *Ecué-Yamba-ó*'s main character, Menegildo Cué, and his religious and cultural practices (from music to rites of initiation), as well as his incursions into an urban world that marginalizes him, Carpentier begins the inquiry into what he sees as the magical dimension of Afro-Cuban reality, and the constitutive antagonism of hegemonic and subaltern subject positions as the entire region's trademark.[7] Defamiliarizing a received and unquestioned national culture and local mores by weaving together popular myths and a strikingly modernist style, Uslar Pietri explores the cultural potential of effecting the encounter of universally modern narrative techniques with local histories, narratives, and subjects. "Se trataba, evidentemente, de una reacción," wrote Uslar Pietri many years later, "reacción contra la literatura descriptiva e imitativa que se hacía en la América hispana, y también reacción contra la sumisión tradicional a modas y escuelas europeas" ("Realismo mágico" 136) ("It was a clearly a reaction. A reaction against the descriptive and imitative literature that was being written in Hispanic America, but also a reaction against the usual submission to European trends and schools"). In the same essay, Uslar Pietri defines the literature that he and his colleagues were writing in the 1930s and 1940s as an apprenticeship in learning to see Latin America with Latin American eyes, or, to put it differently, learning to naturalize a strangeness that was specific to Latin American because of its hybrid culture:

> Si uno lee, con ojos europeos, una novela de Asturias o de Carpentier, puede creer que se trata de una visión artificial o de una anomalía desconcertante y nada familiar. No se trataba de un añadido de personajes y sucesos fantásticos, de los que hay muchos y buenos ejemplos desde los inicios de la literatura, sino de la revelación de una situación diferente, no habitual, que chocaba con los patrones aceptados del realismo. Para los mismos hispanoamericanos era como un redescubrimiento de su situación cultural. Esta línea va desde *Las leyendas de Guatemala* hasta *Cien años de soledad*. Lo que García Márquez describe y que parece pura invención, no es otra cosa que el retrato de una situación peculiar, vista con los ojos de la gente que la viven y la crean, casi sin alteraciones. El mundo criollo está lleno de magia en el sentido de lo inhabitual y lo extraño. (139)

> Read with European eyes, a novel by Asturias or Carpentier might be seen as representing an artificial or a disconcerting and unfamiliar anomaly. It was not a mix of characters and fantastic events, of which there are many good examples since the beginning of literature, but the revelation of a different, unusual situation that clashed with accepted modes of realism. For Latin Americans themselves it was a rediscovery of their cultural position. This trajectory goes from

> *Legends of Guatemala* to *One Hundred Years of Solitude*. What García Márquez describes, which seems like pure invention, is none other than the portrayal of a peculiar situation, seen from the eyes of the people that live and create it, almost without alterations. The *criollo* world is full of magic in the sense of the strange and the unusual.

This 1986 essay has the retrospective benefit of posterior definitions and the general consolidation of magical realism as a clearly designated non-European aesthetic form. Uslar Pietri emphasizes that the Latin American writer's ability to perceive the magical core of the region's cultural reality was a rediscovery enabled by distance from that reality. Indeed, the two crucial factors that explain why these Latin American expatriates produced—out of anxiety around Latin America's historical specificity—proto-magical realist fiction, and would later fully develop the concept, must be found in the type of transcultural artistic interactions made possible by the coincidence of émigrés in Paris during the 1920s and '30s. Carpentier had arrived in Paris in 1928 thanks to the help of a friend, the poet Robert Desnos, who pushed the Cuban on board the ship *España* with Desnos's own passport to help him escape an asphyxiating and dangerous political situation in Havana. Carpentier arrived in Paris at the exact moment when Desnos and others were breaking away from André Breton's brand of surrealism. With Desnos's aid, Carpentier befriended the surrealist dissidents (while also frequently visiting Breton and Aragon), joined the chorus of reactions against Breton, and started collaborating on the journals *Documents* (1929–30) and *Bifur* (1929–31), which were edited by Georges Bataille and other former surrealists (Fass Emery 24–25). Breton's *Surrealist Manifesto* (1924) and its antirealist, antipositivistic aesthetic through which the artist would gain access to a superior reality had clearly made an impact on Carpentier, especially the investment of the marvel with aesthetic and even extra-aesthetic potential: "Tranchons-en: le merveilleux est toujours beau, n'importe quel merveilleux est beau, il n'y a même que le merveill eux qui soit beau" (*Manifestes* 22) ("Let us not mince words: the marvelous is always beautiful, anything marvelous is beautiful, in fact only the marvelous is beautiful"; *Manifestoes* 14). Within months of his arrival Carpentier had written an article on the surrealists for the Cuban magazine *Social*, and it is apparent that his relationship with the movement "marked a turning point in his literary development. . . . It brought him a greater sense of the role of faith in the magical, in the noncausal, the supernatural, as a factor in artistic creation" (Shaw 17). Together with the theorization of the marvel, the ethnographic and primitivist dimension present in the artistic practice of many surrealists (what James Clifford has termed "the ethnographic surrealism of the Parisian Avant-Garde," 118) resonated with Carpentier's sensibility and, evidently, coincided with the writing of *Ecué-Yamba-ó*. This cultural climate certainly favored the warm reception of his novel (as well as Asturias's *Leyendas*) in Paris.[8]

Neither Carpentier nor Uslar Pietri wrote about Latin American marvels or magical realism as a defining aesthetic of the region until 1948–49. The Venezuelan writer was the first to do so, in an otherwise forgettable book-length essay, *Letras y hombres de Venezuela* (*The Literature and Men of Venezuela*) (1948). Reflecting on narrative written in his country and throughout the continent since 1930, he tries to delineate a defining trait of this group of texts: "Lo que vino a predominar en el cuento y a marcar su huella de una manera perdurable fue la consideración del hombre como misterio en medio de los datos realistas. Una adivinación poética o una negación poética de la realidad. Lo que a falta de otra palabra podría llamarse un realismo mágico" (162) ("What became prominent in the short story and left an indelible mark was the consideration of man as a mystery surrounded by realistic facts. A poetic prediction or a poetic denial of reality. What for lack of another name could be called magical realism"). The definition is ambiguous and fails to provide a path for aesthetic innovations, underscoring the need to concentrate on the mysterious nature of the empirical world, and mandating a critical-aesthetical attitude toward the real. In Uslar Pietri, as in his European predecessors, magical realism is an individual, historically undetermined (and, in that sense, potentially universal, universally applicable) attitude toward a given reality. There are still no traces of a conceptualization of magical realism as an aesthetic dictated by the particular nature of Latin American culture and society. But even though his introduction of the concept into the Latin American literary field and imaginary did not contribute greatly to its critical definition (not nearly as much as Carpentier's later explanation of the marvelous real), Uslar Pietri was in fact the first to connect, more than two decades after Roh's initial conceptualization of magical realism, its European and Latin American incarnations. He later described how the concept came back to him, many years after he had taken part in discussions about magical realism in Paris. "De dónde vino aquel nombre que iba a correr con buena suerte? Del oscuro caldo del subconsciente. Por el final de los años 20 yo había leído un breve estudio del crítico del arte alemán Franz Roh sobre la pintura postexpresionista europea, que llevaba el título de 'Realismo mágico.' Ya no me acordaba del lejano libro pero algún oscuro mecanismo de la mente me lo hizo surgir espontáneamente" ("Realismo mágico" 140) ("Where did a name that would have such an impact come from? From the dark depths of the unconscious. In the late 1920s I had read a brief study by the German art critic Franz Roh about postexpressionist European painting titled 'Magical Realism.' I had long forgotten that book, some obscure mechanism in my mind brought it back spontaneously"). According to Roberto González Echevarría, the repressed concept might not have returned "spontaneously," given that the concept was present in the writings of many New York art critics at the time (*Alejo Carpentier: The Pilgrim* 109). In any event, what is important about Uslar Pietri's quotation is that it puts to rest the critical speculations about where he (and most likely, Carpentier and Asturias) got the notion of magical realism. The answer: in Paris, in 1927, in Fernando Vela's Spanish translation of Roh's piece that was published in the influential *Revista de Occidente* (*Western Journal*), edited by José Ortega y Gasset and widely circulated in European and Latin American circles.[9]

MARVELS AND NOVELS

The true breakthrough in this global history of magical realism's conceptualizations was Carpentier's article "Lo real maravilloso de América" ("The Marvelous Real in America") (1948), later published as the preface to *El reino de este mundo* (1949).[10] The novel, based on historical events that took place in Haiti between 1751 and 1822, spans the chronological arc of the rise and slow demise of the Haitian Revolution: from the scheming voodoo priest François Macandal and the uprising led by the Jamaican shaman Bouckman to the Napoleonic invasion of the island and the failed institutionalization of the revolution under King Henri Christophe. Carpentier weaves these different moments together, narrating the story from the point of view of a fictional character, Ti Noel, a slave that starts out as a witness to the rebellion and ends up the delusional hero of his own imaginary kingdom. Magical realism is intrinsically linked to the narration of historical events. Perhaps as a residue of the surrealist influence, Carpentier's marvelous real appears as an account of the *real* history of Latin

America, an interpellation of the Truth (to put it in Hegelian terms) of the region's history. The unearthing, manipulation, and rewriting of historical references is an omnipresent strategy in magical realism in Latin America and elsewhere.

During the eleven years he spent in Paris (returning to Cuba in 1939, as World War II loomed on the horizon), Carpentier worked as a correspondent for Latin American publications and also as a radio technician and editor. Yet intellectually, he was invested mainly in his quest to rediscover Latin American culture through *Ecué-Yamba-ó*, his journalistic practice, and his research and reading: "Sentí ardientemente el deseo de expresar el mundo americano. Aún no sabía cómo. Me alentaba lo difícil de la tarea por el desconocimiento de las esencias americanas. Me dediqué durante largos años a leer todo lo que podía sobre América desde las Cartas de Cristóbal Colón pasando por el Inca Gracilaso, hasta los autores del siglo dieciocho. Por espacio de ocho años creo que no hice otra cosa que leer textos americanos" (qtd. in Arias 63) ("I felt an ardent desire to express the [Latin] American world. I still did not know how. I was attracted by the difficulty of the task because of the lack of knowledge of American essences. I devoted myself for long years to read[ing] everything I could about [Latin] America, from the letters of Christopher Columbus through the Inca Garcilaso to the eighteenth-century authors. For the space of eight years I don't think I did anything except read [Latin] American texts"). Back in Latin America, he poured these energies into writing *El reino de este mundo*, and constructing the concept of the marvelous real. In the preface to *El reino de este mundo*, Carpentier explains that it was during a 1943 trip to Haiti from exile in Venezuela that he started to delineate the concept that, in his eyes, defined Latin American reality. He explains that in Haiti he encountered a kind of marvel he had never seen or thought of before, made of the ruins of Henri Christophe's kingdom with its shattered palace of Sans-Souci and the bulk of the Citadel of La Ferrière, and the colonial Cap Français, where black men lived like the rulers of Versailles for a short period in the nineteenth century. Carpentier saw the marvel that gave access to a "superior reality" (according to the surrealist mandate that he had absorbed in Paris) to be the result of the hybridization of cultures, religions, and polities.[11] The very modern desire for freedom was articulated in terms of magical emancipations: "una tierra donde millares de hombres ansiosos de libertad creyeron en los poderes licantrópicos de Mackandal, a punto de que esa fe colectiva produjera un milagro el día de su ejecución"

("Prólogo" 5) ("a land where thousands of men, anxious for freedom, believed in Macandal's lycanthropic power to the extent that their collective faith produced a miracle on the day of his execution"; "Marvelous Real" 87). These remnants of a kingdom of slaves were a miniature Latin America, a region where the marvelous arises "de una revelación privilegiada de la realidad, de una iluminación inhabitual o singularmente favorecedora de las inadvertidas riquezas de la realidad, de una ampliación de las escalas y categorías de la realidad, percibidas con particular intensidad en virtud de una exaltación del espíritu que lo conduce a un modo de 'estado límite'" (4–5) ("from a privileged revelation of reality, an unaccustomed insight that is singularly favored by the unexpected richness of reality or an amplification of the scale and categories of reality, perceived with particular intensity by virtue of an exaltation of the spirit that leads it to a kind of extreme state"; 86).

The key contribution of Carpentier's essay—one that would open up the possibility of conceptually linking magical realism and postcolonialism—lies in the notion of an "unexpected richness" of Latin American reality that favors "privileged revelation[s]." There was something about Haitian and Latin American culture that was different from the cultures of other regions of the world, particularly Europe. Other cultures may have experienced the marvelous (he cites Marco Polo's belief in birds that could carry elephants in their claws, Luther's vision of the devil and throwing an inkwell at it, and Victor Hugo's belief in ghosts and apparitions), but these were the fantastic imaginations of a hyper-rationalist culture that longed to compensate for a lack of magic, like people who "admiran el supermacho por impotencia" ("Prólogo" 5) ("admire the supermacho because of their own impotence"; "Marvelous Real" 86). In Latin America, according to Carpentier, the marvelous was a constitutive, organic element of reality. "A cada paso hallaba lo *real maravilloso*. Pero pensaba, además, que esa presencia y vigencia de lo real maravilloso no era privilegio único de Haití, sino patrimonio de la América entera, donde todavía no se ha terminado de establecer, por ejemplo, un recuento de cosmogonías. Lo real maravilloso se encuentra a cada paso en las vidas de hombres que inscribieron fechas en la historia del Continente" (5) ("I found the marvelous real at every turn. Furthermore, I thought, the presence and vitality of the marvelous real was not a privilege unique to Haiti but the heritage of all of America, where we have not yet begun to establish an inventory of our cosmogonies. The marvelous real is found at every stage in the lives of men who inscribed dates in the history of the continent"; 87).

Carpentier formulates a novel idea—indeed, foundational—that was not present in Roh, Bontempelli, or Uslar Pietri: the marvelous real is a cultural condition and not a universally available aesthetic perception of reality; it is the defining trait of Latin American reality. According to Carpentier, if Latin America had a literary and artistic tradition that, in the past, had dealt with the marvelous nature of the region (from the chronicles of conquest to his own *Ecué-Yamba-ó* and now *El reino de este mundo*), it was because these narratives stemmed directly, immediately, from a naturalized experience of the reconciliation of the real and the marvelous in the region.

This proposition of a marvelous Latin American cultural specificity allows Carpentier to criticize Breton's brand of surrealism and to burn the bridges that could have led critics to think of the marvelous real as a Third World offspring of surrealist aesthetics. If in Latin America the marvelous is an organic, omnipresent component of reality, in Europe and metropolitan cultures in general it is a mere artifice, an entertaining gimmick, a "agotante pretensión de suscitar lo maravilloso que caracterizó a ciertas literaturas europeas de estos últimos treinta años" ("Prólogo" 4) ("tiresome pretension of creating the marvelous that has characterized certain European literatures over the past thirty years"; "Marvelous Real" 84). Carpentier continues: "Lo maravilloso, pobremente sugerido por los oficios y deformidades de los personajes de feria — ¿no se cansarán los jóvenes poetas franceses de los fenómenos y payasos de la fête foraine, de los que ya Rimbaud se había despedido en su Alquimia del Verbo?—. Lo maravilloso, obtenido con trucos de prestidigitación, reuniéndose objetos que para riada suelen encontrarse: la vieja y embustera historia del encuentro fortuito del paraguas y de la máquina de coser sobre una mesa de disección, generador de las cucharas de armiño, los caracoles en el taxi pluvioso, la cabeza de león en la pelvis de una viuda, de las exposiciones surrealistas" (4) ("The marvelous, inadequately evoked by the roles and deformities of festival characters—won't young French poets ever get tired of the *fête foraine* with its wonders and clowns, which Rimbaud dismissed long ago in his *Alchemie du verbe*? The marvelous, manufactured by tricks of prestidigitation, by juxtaposing objects unlikely ever to be found together: that old deceitful story of the fortuitous encounter of the umbrella and the sewing machine on the dissecting table that led to ermine spoons, the snail in the rainy taxi, the lion's head on the pelvis of a widow, the Surrealist exhibitions"; 84–85). In Latin America, according to Carpentier, the marvelous does not have to be invented by poets because it can be found "at every turn" (87) and therefore its literary presentation results from an apparently simple mimetic operation. In Europe, in contrast, where a positivistic social structure lacking in magic is preeminent, the marvelous can only be artificially invoked through the mediation of aesthetic artifice determined by its own historical horizon.[12] Uslar Pietri also emphasized this difference between magical realism and surrealism. The European avant-garde, on the one hand, was merely "el juego otoñal de una literatura aparentemente agotada. . . . Era pintar relojes derretidos, jirafas incendiadas, ciudades sin hombres, o poner juntos las nociones y los objetos más ajenos y disparatados, como el revólver de cabellos blancos, o el paraguas sobre la mesa del quirófano . . . un juego que terminaba en una fórmula artificial y fácil" ("Realismo mágico" 137) ("an autumnal game of a literature that seemed exhausted. . . . It was painting melted watches, burning giraffes, cities without men, or putting together the most dissimilar and ludicrous notions and objects, like the white-haired gun, or the umbrella on the dissecting table . . . a game ending in an artificial and easy formula"); but the marvelous real and magical realism of Carpentier, Asturias, and Uslar Pietri himself aimed at "revelar, descubrir, expresar, en toda su plenitud inusitada esa realidad casi desconocida y casi alucinatoria que era la de la América Latina para penetrar el gran misterio creador del mestizaje cultural" (137) ("revealing, discovering, expressing in all of its rare splendor that almost unknown and almost delusional Latin American reality, to penetrate the great creative mystery of cultural hybridity").

But the importance of Carpentier's marvelous real to postcolonial determinations of the definition of magical realism may be said to reside in the contradiction between what the preface of *El reino de este mundo* says and what the novel does. While the preface stresses the lack of mediations in the way aesthetic formations—such as these new *marvelous* novels—express a Latin American social reality constituted by marvelous phenomena visible "at every turn," the novel itself performs the cultural presence of the marvelous as a result of mediation marked by the socially bound perspective of the spectator. Nowhere is this more evident than in the famous scene of Macandal's miracle, in the closing pages of the first chapter.

Macandal, mentor of Ti Noel and leader of a slave uprising, has gone into hiding. He has been coordinating a clandestine network that sought to terrorize whites by poisoning them and their animals, and has been recognized by slaves as a *houngán*, a voodoo priest in contact with *Radá* divinities. Slaves have attributed the success of Macandal's conspiracy to the fact that he operated under animal disguises that enabled him to be at different plantations simultaneously.[13] Following his capture, the French colonial authorities sentence the leader of the revolt to a spectacular exemplary punishment and set out to burn him on a pyre in the central square of the Cap Français. For Ti Noel, the sentence is meaningless, as Macandal is going to metamorphose into a mosquito and escape:

> Eso era lo que ignoraban los amos; por ello habían despilfarrado tanto dinero en organizar aquel espectáculo inútil, que revelaba su total impotencia para luchar contra el hombre ungido por los grandes Loas. Mackandal estaba ya adosado al poste de torturas. El verdugo había agarrado un rescoldo con las tenazas. Repitiendo un gesto estudiado la víspera frente al espejo, el gobernador desenvainó su espada de corte y dio orden de que se cumpliera la sentencia. El fuego comenzó a subir hacia el manco, sollamándole las piernas. En ese momento Mackandal agitó su muñón que no habían podido atar, en un gesto combinatorio que no por menguado era menos terrible, aullando conjuros desconocidos y echando violentamente el torso hacia adelante. Sus ataduras cayeron, y el cuerpo del negro se espigó en el aire, volando por sobre las cabezas, antes de hundirse en las ondas negras de la masa de esclavos. Un solo grito llenó la plaza.
>
> —Mackandal sauvé!
>
> Y fue la confusión y el estruendo. Los guardias se lanzaron, a culatazos, sobre la negrada aullante, que ya no parecía caber entre las casas y trepaba hacia los balcones. Y a tanto llegó el estrépito y la grita y la turbamulta, que muy pocos vieron que Mackandal, agarrado por diez soldados, era metido decabeza en el fuego, y que una llama crecida por el pelo encendido ahogaba su último grito. Cuando las dotaciones se aplacaron, la hoguera ardía normalmente, como cualquiera hoguera de buena leña. (El reino de este mundo 18)

> This was what their masters did not know; for that reason they had squandered so much money putting on this useless show, which would prove how completely helpless they were against a man chrismed by the great Loas. Macandal was

> now lashed to the post. The executioner had picked up an ember with the tongs. With a gesture rehearsed the evening before in front of a mirror, the Governor unsheathed his dress sword and gave the order for the sentence to be carried out. The fire began to rise towards the Mandigue, licking his legs. At that moment Macandal moved the stump of his arms, which they have been unable to tie up, in a threatening gesture which was none the less terrible for being partial, howling unknown spells and violently thrusting his torso forwards. The bonds fell off and the body of the Negro rose in the air, flying overhead, until it plunged into the black waves of the sea of slaves. A single cry filled the square:
>
> "Macandal saved!"
>
> Pandemonium followed. The guards fell with rifle butts on the howling blacks, who now seemed to overflow the streets, climbing toward the windows. And the noise and screaming and uproar were such that very few saw that Macandal, held by ten soldiers, had been thrust head first into the fire, and that a flame fed by his burning hair had drowned his last cry. When the slaves were restored to order, the fire was burning normally like any fire of good wood. (*Kingdom* 31–32)

This scene, the one most often cited as a perfect narrative performance of the marvelous real, is structured as an irreconcilable opposition of the rational, positivistic point of view of the white colonialists and the magical conception of the real of the slaves. González Echeverría first conceptualized the interpretative matrix that remains a constant in the criticism of magical realism; according to him, magical realist narratives conceived the marvel either as an ontological or as an epistemological construction. In these terms, then, Carpentier's foundational *El reino de este mundo* presents a clear tension between these two notions and inaugurates the Latin American genre that would later spread throughout the postcolonial world. If in the anthropological discourse of the preface the marvel is defined as an ontological condition of Latin American culture, in the novel magic is an effect of a particular and socially determined worldview. In the scene of Macandal's execution, the narrative voice is identified with the slaves' belief in his power to ridicule the French and escape; accordingly, the narrator describes with ostensible objectivity how he turns into smoke to escape the pyre. Were the chapter to end there, it would have been a literal demonstration of the preface's idea of *the marvelous found at every turn in Latin America*. But the production of a "naturalização do irreal" (Chiampi, *Realismo maravilhoso* 26) ("naturalization of the unreal") is interrupted when the narrator whispers that the crowd was so busy believing in Macandal's miracle "that very few saw that Macandal, held by ten soldiers, had been thrust head first into the fire, and that a flame fed by his burning hair had drowned his last cry" (Carpentier, *Kingdom* 32). The novel performs a marvelous real discourse very different from the one put forth in the preface/manifesto. The marvelous is no longer the constitutive core of Latin American reality, no longer its objective truth, but the predicate of the worldview of Latin American marginalized, subaltern populations. The narrator explains *what really happened* and thus reterritorializes the marvelous real as the delusion of an oppressed class that needs reassurance in order to survive hardship, needs to believe that "Macandal had kept his word, remaining in the Kingdom of This World" (32). The novel gives the reader a version of the marvelous real as a classical form of ideology, as a veil that deforms a perceived reality: the marvelous real as sociocultural pathology.

The chapter ends with Monsieur Lenormand de Mezy going to bed and thinking about the lack of sensibility of the black men, and with Ti Noel going back to work in the barn, suggesting a clear hierarchy between these opposing "fenomenologias da percepção" (Chiampi, *Realismo maravilhoso* 23) ("phenomenologies of perception"): actuality lies on the side of the French colonizers, while the marvelous is an epistemology of the oppressed, a willful projection of a subaltern who is motivated by the need to anchor hope in a better future. By discrediting the point of view of the slaves, Carpentier contradicts the proposal of his preface and reinscribes his conception of the marvelous within the frame of the primitivist mind-set of the French avant-garde. He also opens up the meaning of magical realism to future postcolonial self-conscious appropriations of the genre.

Within months of the appearance of *El reino de este mundo* in 1949, Asturias published *Hombres de maíz* (*Men of Maize*), a novel that explores the marvelous cultural practices of Mayan communities and their modern descendants.[14] In 1946, Asturias had published *El señor presidente* (*Mr. President*), a crucial text in the genealogy of the Latin American novel about the figure of the dictator, but *Hombres de maíz* returned to the exploration that Asturias had begun in *Leyendas de Guatemala:* the aesthetic and political potential of magical and ritualistic legends of wonders, which are also presented both as the constitutive ground of the community's cultural identity and self-representation and as an alternative to Western, bourgeois modernism.

The novel's plot deals with the impact of the process of colonial and neocolonial modernization between 1899 (the year of Asturias's birth) and the 1940s on the lives of Mayan Indian characters that are represented through archetypical elements of the culture's mythology. Gaspar Ilóm, for example, the hero of the first part of the novel, has supernatural powers that he uses to defend the hills and forests where his people live from the encroachment of capitalist planters backed by the state. Contrary to what Carpentier's narrator does with Macandal in *El reino de este mundo*, the narrator of *Hombres de maíz* does not seem to think that the psychological, mythological, or cultural source of these powers requires an explanation external to it; he adopts the characters' cultural point of view and never breaks with it. Asturias's novel contains no space of enunciation exterior to the universe of the indigenous characters; even the narrator's language reproduces a popular Guatemalan rural dialect. This is in stark contrast to the erudite, baroque tone of Carpentier's narrator. Asturias shows how the foundational narrative of the Mayas, the *Popol Vuh* sacred text, is at work in the lives of the twentieth-century descendants of the Mayas who once ruled Central America. For instance, the rural mailman Nicho Aquino's fall down a deep well after losing his wife is represented as an archetypical descent into the underworld, during which he witnesses the creation of the first man out of maize as it had been narrated in the *Popol Vuh* and the *Book of Chilam Balam*. But Asturias's is an eminently modern magical realism: he rewrites these classical Mayan texts with key modern theories in mind, from surrealism to Marxism and psychoanalysis (Martin, Introduction xxiv).[15] According to René Prieto, the pivotal elements of the story, such as corn, water, and fire, are linked with colors, animals, and numbers "in keeping with their ascribed spheres of action in Mayan cosmogony," and he affirms that these materials are in fact "the unifying principle of a novel which develops neither chronologically nor through its protagonists but, rather, through a character substitution principle that is based on clusters of elements interlinked amongst themselves" (155).[16] But the novel's specificity in comparison to Asturias's previous versions of the *Popol Vuh* in *Leyendas de Guatemala* reveals his intention to articulate the mythical and the cultural in the context of the dual challenges posed to them by the loss of the links to the earth that ensure their vitality and the social disruption of the colonialism of the nation-state.[17]

After Carpentier and Asturias set up theoretical and narrative practices of magical realism as the literary identity politics of Latin America, the Haitian novelist Jacques Stéphen Alexis gave a lecture at the first Congress of Black Writers in 1956 at the Sorbonne, "Du réalisme merveilleux des Haïtiens" ("On the Marvelous Realism of the Haitians"). He proposed an aesthetic capable of representing the social totality of a Caribbean culture that he saw deeply rooted in the living tradition of the mythic, the legendary, and the marvelous.[18] Amaryll Chanady points out that the crucial difference between Carpentier's and Alexis's approach is the latter's emphasis on the *merveilleux* as the language of non-Europeanized Haitians and Latin Americans. While Carpentier attempted to re-create the worldview of the Other from a position of exteriority, Alexis searches for an expressive form that springs from the local culture (Chanady, *Entre inclusion et exclusion* 109–21). Drawing from his formation in the context of the French Communist Party, Alexis proposed magical realism as the Caribbean's *réalisme social*, a narrative form capable of unveiling to the people their own political struggles (247). Alexis's specific contribution to the theorization of *lo real maravilloso americano* was to wed the aesthetic potential of this literary practice to an explicitly stated revolutionary goal. Magical realism was for Alexis a fully fleshed postcolonial, emancipatory aesthetic form, and not merely a self-affirming discourse that sought to create a new aesthetic identity.[19]

IN OR OUT? THE POSTCOLONIAL LIMITS OF MAGICAL REALISM

If the first formulations of magical realism in Europe were marked by its relation to the historical avant-garde of the 1920s, it was in Latin America, between 1949 and 1970, that the concept became identified as an emancipatory cultural discourse capable of expressing the region's historical particularity and desire to establish an aesthetic rhetoric independent of European modernism. In many cases these attempts were formulated in rather explicit postcolonial terms; in others, the postcolonial cultural politics were a retrospective theoretical attribution; and in yet a third group, magical realism was described in purely formal terms, without any allusion to its potential relation to the political and cultural projects of an imagined collectivity. It was a scholar, Ángel Flores, in a famous lecture given in 1954 and published a year later, "El realismo mágico en la narrativa hispanoamericana" ("Magical Realism in Spanish American Fiction"), who returned to a structuralist definition of magical realism that valued the concept for its "intrinsically aesthetic merits" (109) as a formal "amalgamation of realism and fantasy" (112). This tendency to define magical realism in strictly formal terms that overlook its historical, cultural, and political determinations has led many critics to include almost any text featuring a fantastic episode not explainable by the laws of physics, regardless of when or where it may have been produced, within the flexible boundaries of magical realism. Devoid of the specific historical context and cultural politics that differentiate it from mere fantasy and other forms of narrative that defy the "rational, linear worldview of Western realist fiction" (Ashcroft, Griffiths, and Tiffin, *Post-colonial Studies* 133), magical realism became an empty signifier that fit practically every text to critique the stability of the referential world and the possibility of accessing it in a transparent and direct manner.

This ahistorical definition of the concept led Flores to declare a misguided Latin American genealogy of magical realism composed of authors whose texts could not be further from Carpentier's proposal or Asturias's practice. Flores's genealogy begins with Jorge Luis Borges's *Historia universal de la infamia* (*A Universal History of Infamy*) (1935) and *El jardín de los senderos que se bifurcan* (*The Garden of Forking Paths*) (1941) and continues with María Luisa Bombal's *La última niebla* (*House of Mist*) (1935), Silvina Ocampo's *Viaje Olvidado* (*Forgotten Journey*) (1937), Adolfo Bioy Casares's *La invención de Morel* (*The Invention of Morel*) (1942), José Bianco's *Sombras suele vestir* (*Shadow Play*) (1944), and other texts that simply cannot be read under the rubric of magical realism.[20] Flores's missteps open up a critical question about the limits of a magical realist rhetoric that has been tested since the 1950s by liminal texts whose inclusion in the genre is undecidable at best. This is the case of Juan Rulfo's *Pedro Páramo* (1955), the story of Juan Preciado, a poor rural peasant whose mother sends him back to her home town of Comala in the Jalisco desert to claim what's owed to them, *lo nuestro* ("what's ours" [3]) from his father, the powerful landowner and local chieftain Pedro Páramo. Preciado eventually realizes that the people relating the stories of their suffering at the hands of Pedro Páramo are dead. Is a novel written about a character who talks to the dead without realizing it an unmistakable example of magical realism? It would be easy to see it this way, especially when magical realism is conceived as a discourse that emerges from the historical experience of a collective drama. On the other hand, a narrative so firmly grounded in the Mexican tradition of communing with the dead (the Day of the Dead, or All Saints' Day, occurs between November 1 and 2), whose backdrop is a tapestry of meticulous historical references to the social universe of postrevolutionary Mexico, can legitimately be read as allegorical.

In the 1980s, this same dehistoricizing move took hold of the notion of magical realism in the English-speaking world. After Gabriel García Márquez's 1982 Nobel Prize, David Young and Keith Holloman edited an anthology, *Magical Realist Fiction*, that defined the concept of magical realism in similarly vague terms and yet immediately became a textbook in classrooms worldwide:

> Whatever its limitations—and all such terms have them—we found the term and what it implied extremely useful in defining for ourselves a category of fiction that could be distinguished from traditional realistic and naturalistic fiction, on the one hand, and from recognized categories of the fantastic: ghost story, science fiction, gothic novel, and fairy tale. . . . The recent increase in popularity of the term has made us feel less defensive about our decision to stick with it, but there is also the fact that any other term, such as "fiction of the marvelous," or "fiction of conflicting realities," would be both more cumbersome and less expressive. (1)

This way of broadening the scope of magical realism, together with the lack of interest in its cultural, historical, and geopolitical determinations, permits the inclusion of texts by thirty-five writers (among them, Gogol, Tolstoy, Mann, Kafka, Mandelstam, Nabokov, Faulkner, Borges, Cheever, Reyes, Cortázar, Calvino, and Kundera), of which only Carpentier's and García Márquez's texts could productively be counted as marvelous and magical realist. The affirmation of the difference of magical realism from the merely fantastic that would determine a much more rigorous anthology is both formal and historical. Ato Quayson provides the most convincing definition of the formal specificity of the rhetoric of magical realism, distinguishing it from the fantastic by describing the differential relation it establishes between the real and the extraordinary in terms of a "principle of equivalence": "It is not that magical realism does not share elements of the fantastic with other genres, but that in confounding any simple or clear sense of spatial, ethical, or motivational hierarchies between the real and the fantastic, magical realism generates a scrupulous equivalence between the two domains" ("Fecundities" 728). This principle of equivalence, which recalls Chiampi's idea of the denaturalization of the real and the naturalization of the marvelous cited at the beginning of the chapter, is not at work in fantasy, where the abnormal and the marvelous are never normalized. On the contrary, in texts like Kafka's "Metamorphosis" and Robert Kroetsch's *What the Crow Said* (and most of the novels and stories in Young and Holloman's anthology), the pervasive "sense of the uncanny" permeates these narratives; the magical and fabulous remain strange, forever disrupting the real. However, the main hypothesis of this chapter is that a formal delimitation of magical realism is not enough to understand a genre that results from the complex interaction between aesthetic forms and their historicity because, as Zamora has argued, magical realism works by "erasing and redrawing the lines between fiction and history for particular political purposes" ("*One Hundred Years*" 31). In other words, magical realism should not be considered an aesthetic form that can be forged anywhere, under any sociocultural conditions, but rather as a discourse that emerges from cultural formations marked by the perception of a lack (in the Lacanian sense) and the registration of emancipatory desires that dislocate and reconfigure hegemonic mappings of world literature. Indeed, it could be said that the most important contribution of the Latin American writers who reinvented the category and practice of magical realism was to imprint in the genre's DNA an awareness of the indissoluble relation between aesthetic form and the specificity of the historical determinations that separate magical realism from other neighboring narrative discourses. As Christopher Warnes affirms in what may be the most rigorous study to date of the relation between magical realism and postcolonialism, it is in postcolonial conditions of enunciation "that magical realism fulfills its creative and critical potential to the fullest" (*Magical Realism* 28–29). Or to state it differently, between the 1940s and the first half of the 1980s, magical realism produced a critique (which in certain contexts might very well be called postcolonial) of the social and epistemological relations that give rise to hegemonic modes of symbolizing the real in the margins of global modernity.

The postcolonial potential that Warnes describes can be seen fleshed out in Michael Taussig's conception of the politics of magical realism, which he sees as an interrogation of the "persistence of earlier forms of production in the development of capitalism" in order to produce a discourse "that intermingle[s] the old and the new as ideals transfiguring the promise offered yet blocked by the present" (167). Taussig sees magical realism as the possibility of "rescuing the 'voice' of the Indian from the obscurity of pain and time. From the represented shall come that which overturns the representation" (135). Even though Taussig sees in magical realism a subversive potential to lay down the discursive basis for new political cultural and practices, he warns of the danger of becoming an aesthetic instrument of a hegemonic reappropriation, "a neo-colonial reworking of primitivism" (172). This does not annul, for Taussig, the latent potential of magical realism as a cultural and political project that might restore the voice of the popular, the subaltern, and the premodern. Taussig concurs with those who consider magical realism not only to emerge from societies structured through postcolonial imaginaries but in fact to produce them: "Magical realism creates a new and decolonized space for narrative, one not already occupied by the assumptions and techniques of European realism" (Faris, *Ordinary Enchantments* 135); or, as Faris has stated elsewhere, magical realism represents a "liberating poetics" whose effectiveness depends on adopting a form of representation antagonistic to a realist narrative seen as a "European import" (Faris, "Question of the Other" 103). Whether one agrees with the emphasis on the emancipatory potential that Taussig, Faris, and others ascribe to magical realism or is more inclined to focus on the rapid pace at which the promise of aesthetic emancipation is captured by a process of fetishization (and since the 1970s, of increasing commodification), one should not lose sight of the historical determinations that framed the efficacy of magical realism to forge a sense, shared by writers and readers across the world, of the genre's potential to create the necessary conditions to repair historical harms produced by different forms of oppression and exclusion.

GABRIEL GARCÍA MÁRQUEZ AND THE GLOBALIZATION OF MAGICAL REALISM

Neither the so-called Boom of Latin American literature and the novels that gained unprecedented visibility thanks to the synergy of its collective process—chief among them, Gabriel García Márquez's *Cien años de soledad* (1967)—nor the second Latin American life of magical realism can be understood outside the political and cultural space created by the 1959 Cuban Revolution. During the 1960s, and to a large extent in dialogue with the anti-imperialist content of the events taking place in Cuba, the literary field was dominated by discourses expressing the desire to achieve a self-determined Latin American identity, to engage in a process of modernization while remaining faithful to the cultural particularities of the region. The Boom in general, and García Márquez's novel in particular, were immediately received as the most perfect answer to these cultural and political dilemmas.[21] The attempt to negotiate the universality of modern narrative techniques and the particularity of Latin American history constitutes an invisible thread that strings together a literary genealogy from Carpentier, Asturias, and Rulfo to García Márquez, each deeply committed to one way or another of understanding the project of a socialist modernization of Latin America, before and after the rise of Fidel Castro in 1959.

Since 1948, García Márquez had been working on ideas, characters, and settings for what would become *Cien años de soledad* under the working title of *La casa* (*The House*). Until the mid-1960s, the project was little more than a handful of family stories and descriptions of the Colombian village where he had grown up with his grandparents, or a fictional version of the collective history of his elders. In addition to his journalistic work since 1948, he had published three brief novels, *La hojarasca* (*Leaf Storm*) (1955), *El coronel no tiene quien le escriba* (*No One Writes to the Colonel*) (1961), and *La mala hora* (*In the Evil Hour*) (1962), as well as a collection of stories, *Los funerales de Mamá Grande* (*Big Mama's Funeral*) (1962), and several short stories that would be collected after 1967, the most important of which is "Monólogo de Isabel viendo llover en Macondo" ("Monologue of Isabel Watching It Rain in Macondo") (1955). Many critics have read these pre–*Cien años* narratives as proto–magical realist laboratories where García Márquez played with forms of conveying the marvelous, which he would perfect and incorporate into his grand novel. This is clearly an exaggeration. *La hojarasca* and *El coronel no tiene quien le escriba* experiment with time, stretching the narrative duration of an instant in a clearly European modernist way (principally Joyce, but also Woolf and Faulkner), rather than a Latin Americanist magical conception of temporality. If these narratives are read as pre-texts, their most notable elements are the presentation of physical spaces, including Macondo and the house, and some of the Buendía family members, as well as references to traumatic episodes (the arrival of the banana company, an extended rainstorm) that would become part of the novel. Still missing, however, is the clear articulation of the rhetoric of magical realism—a naturalization of the magical aspects of both everyday occurrences and sociohistorical events.

"Mi problema más importante era destruir la línea de demarcación que separa lo que parece real de lo que parece fantástico. Porque en el mundo que trataba de evocar esa barrera no existía" (qtd. in Palencia-Roth 69) ("My problem was that I wanted to destroy the separation between what appeared to be real and what appeared to be fantastic because, in the world I was trying to evoke, that barrier did not exist"). García Márquez's challenge in *Cien años de soledad* was to find a rhetoric capable of presenting stories particular to a specific region of Colombia that he had heard from his grandmother in a narrative that represented what he understood to be the historical experience of Latin America as an undifferentiated whole: the productive ambiguity of that "world I was trying to evoke."[22] Macondo is the mediation between the idiosyncratic hyperlocalism of the Colombian tropical forest and the general situation of the continent. Macondo is the village-signifier that names the difference of Latin America and, perhaps later, of the entire Third World.

Cien años de soledad is the story of the mythical foundation of Macondo, and of the ways in which its traumatic social history—the roots of which are found in the formation of the Latin American nation-state—break up the Buendía family. The specificity of García Marquez's magical realism resides in the tension between myth and history, or rather, in the tense interrogation that myths, legends, beliefs, that is, culture at its most particularistic, pose to modern history and the wounds this history has inflicted on the world's peripheries. The difference between fantasy and magical realism becomes transparent in García Márquez's novel, and this newfound clarity becomes a critical tool to reexamine the limits of the genre throughout the world. Marvelous episodes occur throughout the novel: José Arcadio Buendía finds the skeleton of an old galleon in the middle of the jungle; the dead haunt the living in search of redemption; the whole town suffers, first, from an insomnia plague, and later, from a collective memory loss that only Melquíades can cure when he returns from the dead out of boredom; when the patriarch dies, it rains little yellow flowers; Remedios the Beauty ascends to heaven amid bedsheets; and Mauricio Babilonia, crazy in love with Meme, is followed wherever he goes by a cloud of yellow butterflies. These are not magical, marvelous, or strange episodes that take place under the eyes of delusional or prophetic individuals (as in the case of D. M. Thomas's *The White*

Hotel [1981]), or in unspecified and undetermined collectivities. On the contrary, their magical nature is a "categorical affirmation: there is no doubt that Remedios the beauty ascends to heaven; there's no doubt that butterflies always follow Meme and Mauricio Babilonia" (Rama, *Edificación* 125). In other words, magic is structurally determined: the community where these events occur is politically mediated by the traumatic experience of a clash between modernization and tradition, between oppression and a demand for justice typical of Latin American culture since the nineteenth century. The novel foregrounds the political nature of this contradiction through its attention to the civil war between factions of a failed state, and to the massacre of striking workers by a national army acting in defense of an American banana company. That is, because the magical occurrences in the novel end up being determined by the wind that wipes out Macondo, as well as the past, present, and future of the Buendías, the inexistence of "the separation between what appeared to be real and what appeared to be fantastic" is always colored by a tragic fate: Latin American history, the novel seems to say, inflicts wounds that hegemonic reason and realist forms of literary representation cannot suture.[23]

To a large extent, the importance of *Cien años de soledad* in the history of the postcolonial globalization of magical realism has to do precisely with the narrative and interpretative horizon that García Márquez opened up by making visible the relation between the universality of (colonial, postcolonial, capitalist) modern history and the particularity of local forms of oppression. It would be difficult to read the very productive uses of magical realism in Salman Rushdie's *Midnight's Children* (1980), Latife Tekin's *Dear Shameless Death* (1983), Toni Morrison's *Beloved* (1987), Ben Okri's *The Famished Road* (1991), Mia Couto's *Sleepwalking Land* (1992), and Mo Yan's *Big Breasts and Wide Hips* (1996) without accounting for the material history of the globalization of magical realism, and of García Márquez's novel in particular.[24] The debt of most of these novels to *Cien años de soledad*'s practice of "magical realism as a means of interrogating ideas about history, culture and identity" (Warnes, *Magical Realism* 96) is self-evident in two complementary, indeed, necessary, aspects: one formal, the other cultural-political. First, these novels follow García Márquez's postulation of a narrative whose objective (or rather, *objectivized*) point of view is identical to that of a culture that naturalizes the marvelous and denaturalizes social domination, massacres, wars, and other historical traumas. Second, they do so in the way they conceive and articulate the marvelous and the fantastic, not so much as a form of reflecting "multiple cultural influences" (Bowers 58) and belongings, but in relation to specific subaltern cultural experiences resulting from colonialism or other forms of local or global oppression.[25]

Post–García Márquez magical realist postcolonial novels—those that transformed what was by then a recognizable Latin American genre into a global aesthetic form—were deeply rooted in the postcolonial social reality that constitutes their context of enunciation. Thus in Rushdie's *Midnight's Children* the task at hand is to contest the colonial historical narrative of India through Saleem Sinai's *counter-realist* (because it is difficult to see it as straightforwardly magical realist) story of the twentieth-century process that goes from transition to partition. In this history of the genre, Rushdie's novels represent the intersection of postcolonial magical realism and postmodernism: for Saleem (as well as Rushdie, who returns to this aesthetic device in *The Satanic Verses*), history is nothing but an aggregate of stories told from particular, historically determined sociocultural locations. According to Warnes, the specificity of Rushdie's magical realism is that "the supernatural of this novel seems to arise from Rushdie's own eclectic imagination, nurtured as it has been by wide reading and a productive mixing of cultures. It does not arise ethnographically, from the world view of any specific culture, but linguistically, from the detail of language" ("Naturalising the Supernatural" 10). Even though this assessment may open a gap between Rushdie and Carpentier and García Márquez, because of their differential relation to a generalized cultural condition, *Midnight's Children*'s estranged history of India is still told from the perspective of a subject longing for self-determination, self-affirmation, and the overcoming of a social condition that he or she feels as a burden, in other words, the postcolonial determinations that define the particular strand of magical realism explored here.

In a similar vein, Mo Yan's *Big Breasts and Wide Hips* rewrites, with a keen eye for the strange, the eventful history of twentieth-century China—from the end of the Qing dynasty, the Republic, and the Japanese invasion, to Mao's Long March, to the Cultural Revolution, and all the way to the capitalist reforms of the 1980s—looking at their impact in a little fictional Chinese Macondo, Northeast Gaomi County. Through the use of folk stories, legends, and myths, Mo Yan effectively "deconstructs the grand historical narrative of China's revolutionary century" (Teng). In the case of Morrison's *Beloved*, the title character haunts her mother (and her family) for having killed her when she was two years old while she was attempting to get away from the men who would return her to the Kentucky plantation she had escaped from. Beloved's ghostly and marvelous harassment of Sethe and others enables the retelling of slavery's unspeakable stories. In this sense, she stands as the signifier of all enslaved women and all the suffering of slavery, and facilitates the possibility of healing. Both Latife Tekin's *Dear Shameless Death* and Mia Couto's *Sleepwalking Land* articulate a view of the magical dimensions of the worlds of Anatolia, Turkey, and Mozambique from children's perspective on traumatic historical experience. In the case of Tekin's novel, *Djinn* demons, a witch, and "the donkey boy" (myths drawn from Anatolian folklore) inhabit the rural world where Dirmit lives. These real threats punctuate the experience of a distressing modernization of the interior of Turkey and terrifying internal migrations to urban centers. Couto's story about Mozambique's fifteen-year-long civil war, from the second half of the 1970s until 1992, is told through Muidinga, an orphan boy who sets out on a quest to find his lost family with the help of an old man who guides him through a landscape of terror, hallucinatory memory, and magical events prompted by traumatized and desiring collective subjects. The zenith of these wanderings (at one point they realize they are traveling without moving, thanks to a manuscript that has introduced them to these marvels) is their search for a river that leads to the sea, where the boy hopes to find his mother. In Couto's novel, published shortly after the end of the civil war in Mozambique, magical realism functions as a political intervention in the discursive field of a present ravaged by war atrocities.[26]

And even in the case of novels whose relation to *Cien años de soledad*'s magical realism could only be described as negative, as in the case of Okri's *The Famished Road*, the *un*real is construed as the result of the internal and geopolitical effects of historically inflicted wounds. Ato Quayson, one of Okri's most lucid interpreters, describes his fiction with a concept borrowed from Harry Garuba, "animist realism" (*Strategic Transformations* 148). While the concept places Okri's novel closer to Carpentier, Asturias, and Rulfo than to García Márquez, it is still undoubtedly within the practice of magical realism as it has been outlined in this chapter. Azaro, the novel's protagonist, wanders in an indeterminate life-space suspended between the dead and the living (the space of ethico-political undecidability), which he experiences as "problematically equivalent" (Quayson, *Strategic Transformations* 136). This, along with the novel's representation of orality, inscribes it within both a local Nigerian literary tradition (exemplified by Amos Tutuola and Wole Soyinka) and the traditional Yoruba worldview, as it tries to re-create genetical Yoruba myths. Layering high-culture techniques and popular materials, Okri brings to the surface Africa's modern historical trauma as well as the marvelous dimensions of local traditional cultures that could not conform to a realistic representation of social existence.

The direct or allusive debt of these novels' historically inflected concept of the magical to *Cien años de soledad* is spelled out explicitly in the novel that has come to be seen as the ultimate embodiment of postcolonial fiction, Rushdie's *Midnight's Children*. A few pages into the novel, the reader encounters a meaningful rephrasing of the famous opening sentence of García Márquez's book. Aadam Aziz, the narrator's grandfather, has returned to Kashmir after studying medicine in Germany; seeing his home "through traveled eyes," he finds it a "hostile environment." And then, evoking the literary source of its magical realist constructive device ("Many years later, as he faced the firing squad, Colonel Aureliano Buendía was to remember that distant afternoon when his father took him to discover ice"; *Cien años de soledad* 1), the narrator inscribes his story, which overlaps with the history of India, in a tradition of magical realist representation: "Many years later, when the hole inside him had been clogged up with hate, and he came to sacrifice himself at the shrine of the black stone god in the temple of the hill, he would try to recall his childhood springs in Paradise, the way it was before travel and tussocks and army tanks messed everything up" (*Midnight's Children* 5). The publication dates of the texts analyzed above show that local re-elaborations of magical realism in diverse postcolonial sites outside Latin America began during the second half of the 1970s and acquired particular intensity after 1982. But the question persists. How did magical realism move from Latin America to the postcolonial peripheries of the rest of the world?

One of the most common explanations for the global ubiquity of magical realist rhetoric is to state its universality as an aesthetic form. Seymour Menton, one of the first critics to historicize and theorize the genre in American academia, has fleshed out the formalist premise that underlies most attempts to read the versions of magical realism that have emerged throughout the world: "I am of the opinion that magical realism is a universal tendency, which has not been engendered in American soil" (10). Much more persuasive than this affirmation of the universality of magical realism is Doris Sommer and George Yúdice's hypothesis about the reasons why these Latin American narratives were immediately understood and embraced across the world: "The appeal to foreign readers, no doubt, owed something to their degree of familiarity with or preparedness for the Latin American extensions of a European, sometimes called universal, literary tradition. That very familiarity allowed them to appreciate how supplements to that tradition were unpredictable and refreshing." But they explain that their appeal resided not only in the fact that "Spanish-Americans exploited the lessons of modernists to their own ends" but also perhaps in the very effective articulation in these novels of "a tenuous or paradoxical balance between aesthetic experimentation and ethico-political motivation" ("Latin American Literature" 860–61). Even though Sommer and Yúdice are thinking about García Márquez and others' success in world publishing markets, their hypothesis is particularly useful for exploring why Latin American magical realism was singled out as a productive aesthetic matrix to appropriate and reimagine from other peripheries of the world where writers felt the pressing need of "destabilising the binaries of imperial romance—coloniser and colonised, knowledge and inscrutability, western and other—upon which colonial fictions depend" (Warnes, *Magical Realism* 39). And yet this significant hypothesis about the *why* does not address the question of *how* it became a global narrative form, and in order to deal with this, one needs to explain the difference between the presumed universality of magical realism and its actual, concrete *universalization* through specific historical processes.

The question about the universality of magical realism has to be answered by reconstructing the material history of the globalization of *Cien años de soledad* that began with its explosive and unprecedented critical and commercial success upon its publication in 1967. The novel's publication had been carefully orchestrated by three people on both sides of the Atlantic: in Barcelona, García Márquez's literary agent, Carmen Balcells; and in Buenos Aires, Paco Porrúa, editor of Sudamericana, the press that released the book, and Tomás Eloy Martínez, director of the news magazine *Primera plana*, one of the most important "vectors of dissemination" (Sorensen, *Turbulent Decade Remembered* 109, 115) of a new Latin American cultural industry. In the 1960s, Latin America and Spain, like the rest of Europe and the United States, were experiencing an economic expansion that broadened middle classes and triggered the consumption of all sorts of material and cultural goods. This expansion had a very recognizable impact in the field of cultural production in Spain and Latin America: "refurbishing of the publishing industry; the mobilization across national lines of a reading public that had remained until then fragmented in local markets; the establishment of a sense of modernity . . . and finally, the relaxation of linguistic and poetic norms" (Santana 156). The Boom of publication, consumption, and demand for a literature that claimed to represent local experiences, imaginaries, and aspirations must be understood in terms of this transformation of the region's social structure. The magazine's promotion of *Cien años de soledad*, the investment in advertising, and the unprecedented coordination of efforts resulted in an immediate success: the first two printings of eight thousand copies sold out in two weeks. Second, third, and fourth editions sold out in two months, and the Argentine publishing house could not print the book fast enough to respond to demands of booksellers in Spain, Mexico, Colombia, and other regional markets that placed orders for tens of thousands of copies. Balcells took advantage of the novel's success to alter the balance of power between authors and editors and negotiated agreements that liberated the foreign rights of the book so that she could deal with European and American editors independently of Sudamericana. As a result, the novel was translated almost immediately, published in Italian in 1968 by Feltrinelli (translated by Enrico Cicogna as *Cent'anni di solitudine*), in French, also in 1968, by Editions du Seuil (translated by Claude and Carmen Durand as *Cent ans de solitude*), in German in 1970 by Kiepenheuer und Witsch Verlag (translated by Curt Meyer-Clason as *Hundert Jahre Einsamkeit*), and in English in 1970 by Harper and Row in the United States and Jonathan Cape in the United Kingdom (translated by Gregory Rabassa).

No Latin American writer before García Márquez had been translated into the languages of international success with such momentum, so soon after the first local edition. By the mid-1970s, and even more so after he won the Nobel Prize in 1982, readers in Europe and the United States (but also in countries from the Eastern bloc, the British Commonwealth and the Middle East) were devouring *Cien años de soledad*. For most of these audiences the book's appeal was linked to the interest in Latin America that the Cuban Revolution and the iconography of Che Guevara had triggered throughout the 1960s and '70s, and the work was received both as a technical prodigy and as an exotic commodity (Kennedy). But thanks to the unparalleled wide reach of the novel in translation, English-speaking postcolonial intellectuals were the ones first and most intensely interpellated by magical realism. They saw in the novel a mirror that reflected what they perceived as their own postcolonial reality, and the possibility of using García Márquez's rhetoric as a resource to express their specific aesthetic, cultural, and political anxieties. In a tribute to the Colombian writer organized by International PEN in New York, Salman Rushdie recalled that in 1975 a friend asked him if he had read *Cien años de soledad*. When he said he had never heard of the novel, his friend sent him a copy:

> And of course when I did read it, I had the experience that many people had described of being forever lost in that great novel. Unforgettable. I think all of us can remember the day when we first read Gabriel García Márquez; it was a colossal event. One thing that struck me, which was one of the things that first struck me when I went to Latin America, was the incredible similarity between the world he was describing and the world that I knew from South Asia, from India and Pakistan. It was a world in which religion and superstition dominated people's lives; also a world in which there was a powerful and complicated history of colonialism; also a world in which there were colossal differences between the very poor and the very rich, and not much in between; also a world bedeviled by dictators and corruption. And so to me, what was called "fantastic" seemed completely naturalistic. ("Inverted Realism")

At the same meeting of International PEN, the writer Edwidge Danticat expressed a similar sense of familiarity with the marvelous in her Haitian home, where Carpentier had imagined the most perfect example of the Latin American marvelous real: "Many of us who come from the Caribbean are astounded when people speak of the 'implausibility' of magical realism. For in our worldview, as in our much-loved Gabriel García Márquez's, a lot of what is considered magically realistic seems to us much more realistic than magical" ("Real Worlds"). In an excellent essay, "Streams Out of Control: The Latin American Plot," Carlos Rincón unveils the nearly unknown contemporary circulation of bootlegged editions of *Cien años de soledad* in Iran and the post-Soviet world. After the 1979 revolution, booksellers in front of Tehran's major universities promoted cheap copies of García Márquez as "*One Hundred Years of Solitude:* 100 pages for 100 Tuman!" (179), and in the Soviet landscape of Samarkand, Yerevan, Tbilisi, and Almaty, "Gabriel

García Márquez's novel circulated in *magnitisdat*, clandestine recorded cassettes that were the oral version of the *samizdat* [underground publications that circulated hand to hand between readers avid to get ahold of prohibited material]" (179). Rincón's analysis is akin to the one I have tried to articulate in this chapter: "The possibilities of appropriating these texts according to the specific codes of perception and deciphering of the postcolonial Muslim world and those of a multi-ethnic and multinational Soviet state" show that "these dissimilar recipients possessed cultural and symbolic resources that would be revalued and activated thanks to a great transfer of South-South cultural capital. . . . Because of this relationship, local cultures that depend on the historical condition of place and find themselves included in and marked by the process of cultural globalization have their own authority over that very process" (180). In other words, magical realism is a global form only because it has been appropriated and re-created in differential local contexts, where it was transformed by its interactions with the material historical conditions that have given the genre local and global cultural-political significance.

THE END OF MAGIC: COMMODITIES AND MODERNIST RUINS

If during the 1970s García Márquez was in Latin America and in Spain a writer for the masses, an enlightened best-selling author, and in world literary metropolitan centers a writer's writer, after his 1982 Nobel Prize his stature changed. He became the most visible global literary celebrity, and magical realism became the preeminent protocol for the representation of the underdeveloped world, an aesthetic form easily translatable to a wide range of cultural locations. The genre's rare stability beyond Latin America, achieved thanks to its postcolonial efficacy and global marketability, led to overstretched uses and abuses as pure aesthetic form disengaged from the traumatic historical displacement that had constituted its context of emergence at the height of its cultural-political power. This process transfigured the aesthetic value of magical realism into a commodity whose formulaic contours were shaped according to market niche expectations, as in the cases of Isabel Allende's *La casa de los espíritus* (*The House of the Spirits*) (1982), Angela Carter's *Nights at the Circus* (1984), Patrick Süskind's *Perfume* (1985), Laura Esquivel's *Como agua para chocolate* (*Like Water for

Chocolate) (1989), and Marie Darrieussecq's *Pig Tales* (1997), among many other cases.[27] These novels no longer operated within the terrain set up by Carpentier and Asturias (and later reinforced by García Márquez), a magical realism defined by an organic interaction with its cultural-historical situation, capable of codifying ethnic and racial tensions and hybridities in the context of the Caribbean, Central America and the Indian subcontinent, nor were they invested in political, emancipatory, messianic imaginaries, postcolonial or otherwise. These *post–magical realist* novels inscribed their poetics and circulated in a world literary field structured as a global market where magical realism had become a niche, a designated shelf in corporate bookstore chains.

From the late 1970s until the 1990s, many writers reacted against this *post–magical realist* commodification of the genre within and without Latin America. To be sure, their protest was not against historical magical realism and its *founding fathers* but against what had become of the genre after its globalization; against the naturalized identification, on the part of global reading audiences and publishing markets, of magical realism as the only aesthetic horizon of Latin American narrative literature; against the reduction of the antagonistic difference constitutive of the region's literary field to one essentialized and totalized aesthetic identity. Juan José Saer was one of the most notable writers who articulated a polemical discourse on the imposition of magical realist expectations for Latin American writers. At the end of the 1960s Saer had moved to Paris from Santa Fe, Argentina, thanks to a film scholarship. His experience as a Latin American writer in Europe, having to address magical realist demands in his dealings with editors, the press, and award-granting institutions, certainly informed the polemical position he articulated in the 1979 programmatic essay "La espesa selva de lo real" ("The Thick Forest of the Real"). There, he defended the project of a Latin American literature conceived, following the antinovelist Macedonio Fernández, as "una crítica de lo real" (268) ("a criticism of the real"), dispossessed of Latin American specificity: "La tendencia de la crítica europea a considerar la literatura latinoamericana por lo que tiene de específicamente latinoamericano me parece una confusión y un peligro, porque parte de ideas preconcebidas sobre América Latina y contribuye a confinar a los escritores en el gueto de la latinoamericanidad" (268–69) ("The tendency of European critics to consider what is specifically Latin American about Latin American literature seems confusing and dangerous to me, because it comes from preconceived ideas about Latin America and works to confine its writers to the ghetto of Latin Americanness"). He believed that magical realism set an identitarian trap for Latin American writers that put it back in a colonial relation with metropolitan reading publics, and therefore that it was an aesthetic that had to be avoided: "El vitalismo, verdadera ideología de colonizados, basada en un sofisma corriente que deduce de nuestro subdesarrollo económico una supuesta relación privilegiada con la naturaleza. La abundancia, la exageración, el clisé de la pasión excesiva, el culto de lo insólito, atributos globales de lo que habitualmente se llama realismo mágico y que, confundiendo, deliberadamente o no, la desmesura geográfica del continente con la multiplicación vertiginosa de la vida primitiva, atribuyen al hombre latinoamericano, en ese vasto paisaje natural químicamente puro, el rol del buen salvaje" (270) ("Vitalism, the true ideology of the colonized, based on an ordinary sophism that derives from our economic underdevelopment a supposedly privileged relationship with nature. Abundance, exaggeration, the cliché of excessive passion, the cult of the extraordinary, global attributes of what is usually called magical realism, which, confusing, whether deliberately or not, the continent's geographical excess with a dizzying multiplication of primitive life, attributed to the Latin American man, in his vast natural and chemically pure landscape, the role of the good savage"). Abundance, exaggeration, excessive passion, and the sovereignty of an unruly nature—what was the target of Saer's criticism? Was it the magical realist representation of Latin American cultural particularity, or the European demand of a vitalist literature from Latin America, even from writers like Saer, whose own aesthetic choices would go against performing an exoticizing relation to nature? Since 1979 (to use the arbitrary date of Saer's essay), the global travels of magical realism as avant-garde, postcolonial, and commodity forms make it impossible to distinguish the aesthetic program of magical realism from the European (and North American) expectations that constitute the historicity of the last moment of its globalization. In other words, Saer's criticism is directed to both, or rather, to the imaginary intersection and overlap between the two, which is the point where a hegemonic demand is met by the Latin American performance of a magical realist cultural identity.

The ideological opposition to magical realism took an interesting and polemical turn in Latin America in 1996 when the Chilean novelist Alberto Fuguet and Sergio Gómez gathered a group of young writers from Chile, Argentina, Peru, Bolivia, and Mexico to publish a collection of short stories under the title *McOndo*, identifying themselves as a generational break with García Márquez and the aesthetic of magical realism.[28] In "I Am Not a Magic Realist" (1997), Fuguet rewrites for the English-speaking reading public "Presentación del país McOndo" (1996), the introduction to the collective volume that he co-wrote with Gómez. There, he describes his experience at the prestigious International Writers' Program at the University of Iowa and the trauma of being told he was a bad Latin American writer because he "lacked magical realism." But beyond its anecdotic appearance, the purpose of the essay and the introduction to *McOndo* is to define the aesthetic horizon of his entire generation's literary enterprise in opposition to that of the writers of the Boom:

> Unlike the ethereal world of García Márquez's imaginary Macondo, my own world is something much closer to what I call McOndo—a world of McDonald's, Macintoshes and condos. In a continent that was ultra-politicized, young, apolitical writers like myself are now writing without an overt agenda, about their own experiences. Living in cities all over South America, hooked on cable TV (CNN en español), addicted to movies and connected to the Net. . . . I get suffocated by thick, sweet, humid air that smells like mangos, and I get the munchies when I begin to fly among thousands of colorful butterflies. I can't help it; I'm an urban dweller through and through. The closest I'll ever get to "Like Water for Chocolate" is cruising titles at my local Blockbuster. . . . Writers today who mold themselves after the Latin American "boom" writers of the 1960s (García Márquez, Carlos Fuentes, Mario Vargas Llosa, to name a few) have transformed fiction writing into the fairy-tale business, cranking out shamelessly folkloric novels that cater to the imaginations of politically correct readers—readers who, at present, aren't even aware of Latino cultural realism. . . . I feel the great literary theme of Latin American identity (who are we?) must now take a back seat to the theme of personal identity (who am I?). The McOndo writers—such as Rodrigo Fresán and Martín Rejtman of Argentina, Jaime Bayly of Peru, Sergio Gómez of Chile, Edmundo Paz Soldán of Bolivia and Naief Yeyha of Mexico, to name a few—base their stories on individual lives, instead of collective epics. This new genre may be one of the byproducts

> of a free-market economy and the privatization craze that has swept South America. . . . As a character from my second book said: "I want to write a saga, but without falling into the trap of magical realism. Pure virtual realism, pure McOndo literature. Kind of like 'The House of the Spirits,' only without the spirits."

Fuguet believes magical realism has already died, but world literature (which in his case is a restricted field of market forces and literary institutions encompassing Europe, the United States, and Latin America) has not acknowledged it yet. McOndo is the attempt to foreground the end of a Latin Americanist past (the Cuban Revolution, the Boom, and magical realism) and the birth of a Latin American literature fully inscribed in the global flows of neoliberal capital. In this sense, Fuguet's view of magical realism as a stigma, a plummet, a risible utopia, and a historical collective mistake should be read as an intervention in the field of world literature. On the one hand, he is addressing extra– and trans–Latin American reading publics: "politically correct" world readers who "aren't even aware" times have changed. World literature becomes a space where identities are redefined (from Macondo to McOndo) and their cultural particularity becomes visible in the context of transnational forms of legibility. On the other, McOndo signifies a new Latin American relation with world literature as a global market where the structural distance between high and popular culture has been collapsed. Fuguet has no problem with the circulation of literature as commodity; what concerns him is that Euro-American readers and literary institutions are buying antiquities, relics, without any current exchange value. Fuguet's rejection of magical realism is a Latin American symptom of a world-historical neoliberal break, a break that he sees as the condition of possibility of a new aesthetic ideology successfully determined by the social hegemony of postnational and deterritorialized economic forces and novel consumerist subjectivities.

At the same time, the articulation of literary concerns crystallized in the McOndo trademark, alluding to a fast-food chain, a line of globally popular computers, and residential units mass produced with ready-made materials, subverts the place of literature as a privileged site of cultural and political agency, the status it held for the Boom writers in general and García Márquez in particular. And again, as in the case of the desacralized circulation of commodities, this undoing of hierarchies and the elitism of the Latin American literary tradition directly relates (in Fuguet's eyes) to the extremely creative disruption of market forces in the cultural field and the way actors identify themselves in it.[29]

Beyond Latin America, opinions are divided regarding whether magical realism still preserves the potential to imagine emancipatory horizons for global peripheries where ethnic and racial tensions and hybrid forms of subalternity await aesthetic languages capable of articulating their cultural identity, or whether it is another ruin in a landscape of demolished modernist edifices. Regardless of our position in this regard, reconstructing the historicity of magical realism's global trajectories is crucial for understanding the material formation of transcultural literary fields and world literary mappings that contemporary writers in Latin America and other global peripheries are still trying to undo and redraw.

Part II

Marginal Cosmopolitanism, *Modernismo*, and the Desire for the World

CHAPTER 3

The Rise of Latin American World Literary Discourses (1882–1925)

How did Latin American writers represent their historical task at the turn of the century? Sylvia Molloy explains that it involved a rhetoric of foundations: "Darío, como otros contemporáneos, opera a partir de un vacío cultural. . . . Darío y sus pares [tienen] la sensación de un vacío que pide ser colmado. Este vacío y esta necesidad de colmar—y más aún: de colmatar—es la clave del modernismo" ("Voracidad" 7–8) ("Darío, like other contemporaries, operates out of a cultural void. . . . Darío and his peers [have] the sensation of a void that begs to be filled. This void and this need to fill up—and furthermore to cram and soak—is the key to modernism"). In filling this void, establishing a modern culture where, to them, there was none, *modernistas* took on the work of cultural and aesthetic modernization with confidence in the omnipotence of their modern sensibility. For *modernistas*, what was modern in a Latin America devoid of modernity was their own modern desire, in perfect synchronicity with what they imagined as the universality of European modernism; or, as Aníbal González has pointed out, "En vez de señalar la necesidad de ser modernos, los escritores modernistas hacen su literatura desde el supuesto de que *ya son modernos*" (*Crónica* 7) ("Instead of signaling the need to be modern, the *modernista* writers write their literature from the assumption that they *already are modern*").[1]

My contention in this chapter is that world literature, as a critical discourse on the literatures of the world, was for *modernistas* a significant way to address the question of the realization of their modern subjectivities in what they perceived as a desolate cultural field. If in Part One I argued that world literature was a form of critical engagement with the transcultural determinations of specific cultural phenomena, as well as with the historical and hegemonic formation of an enlarged field of symbolic exchanges, here I put forth that it also can be understood as the discursive articulation of a *deseo de mundo* or desire for the world that points to the modernization of Latin America in cosmopolitan terms. In this sense, world literature would be a constellation of discourses that invoke a world of literatures, imprecisely defined by a vague and abstract notion of universality, so welcoming to marginal cultures that Latin American writers see it as a blank screen for the projection of their modern hopes. It is a discursive attempt to posit a literature that is outside Latin American literature, one that they imagine as a universal repository of modernist aesthetics where marginal cosmopolitans find the bits and pieces they can put together to articulate a nonparticularistic cultural modernization. Aside from a handful of references beginning in the sixteenth century to foreign literatures, authors, and works that are individually identified as ostensibly foreign (and as an ontologically superior model), the systematic presence of these world literary desires in Latin American culture can be traced back to the beginning of the 1880s, to the cultural formation that has come to be known as *modernismo*.[2] This chapter reconstructs and analyzes this lost archive of world literary interventions, activating "the archontic power [of the archive], which also gathers the functions of unification, of identification, of classification . . . to coordinate a single corpus, in a system or a synchrony in which all elements articulate the unity of an ideal configuration" (Derrida, "Archive Fever" 10), while underscoring—in this very gesture of reinstitution and "consignation"—the historical tension introduced by constitutively "anarchivic" or "archiviolithic" forces seeking to destroy, erase, and veil archives, which Derrida conceives as figures of Freud's "death drive" (14).

The idea of a *modernista* discourse on world literature, with or without explicit reference to Goethe's concept of *Weltliteratur* (only the late modernist Baldomero Sanín Cano engages directly with the concept and its northern European genealogy), raises the question of its historical and theoretical specificity. Appeals to *other* literatures are frequent throughout the nineteenth century, but they always refer to one, two, or three privileged European traditions and always allude to them as national totalities. For instance, the romantic imagination (a paradigmatically particularistic tradition in terms of how it addresses Latin America's structural relation of inferiority to European culture) inscribes discrete cultural identities on an uneven transatlantic literary field mediated by the isolation of national/regional differences.[3] Conversely, *modernismo*'s world literary discourse does not invoke foreign literatures to signify "otherness" but rather views foreign works and authors, in classical cosmopolitan fashion, as distant relatives and kindred spirits whose names signify the presence of a world that includes Latin America—a community of modernizing aesthetics that determines the meaning of the *modernistas*' own practice. What defines their world literary discourse is not the accumulation of references to one or another foreign literature or text (even though they effectively accumulate those references) but the postulation of a world defined by an antagonistic relation with cultural forms of locality that connote, in the eyes of the *modernistas*, a backward sense of the past and the present. This world was radically exterior to their Latin American juncture, yet contiguous to their modern, cosmopolitan sensibility. In the context of the accelerated integration of a global economy that relied on Latin America as a crucial supplier of commodities, the *modernistas*' world literary discourse did not actually refer to the whole world.[4] Latin American intellectuals, unable to articulate their recourse to universalism as a discursive strategy to counter the provincialism they believed to be endemic to the region's culture, pointed to the term *world* as a label for their cosmopolitan demands on that culture. Thus I agree with Alejandro Mejías-López when he writes, in reference to Amado Nervo's defense of a Mexican *modernista* cosmopolitanism in "Nuestra insignificancia," that "the legitimacy of Spanish American literature to speak about anything and anyone, to define itself and define others, was an undeniable and remarkable accomplishment of *modernismo* that has not been sufficiently recognized" (76).

Modernismo is a complex cultural formation, made up of a variety of discourses that coexist harmoniously at times but more often in striking contradiction. World literature, understood as radical universalism and an antiparticularistic position, is admittedly a secondary road to the main avenues represented by the *modernistas* postulation of a vaguely unified Latin American identity as well as a Pan-Latin cultural identity that includes Hispanic America but also France, Italy, and Spain and was conceived in opposition to the United States as an emergent regional power, especially after the colonial war in Cuba and Puerto

Rico in 1898. But while the universalist discourse of world literature is less visible than the identitarian constructions that critical tradition has highlighted, its importance as a stepping-stone cannot be overstated.

The most radical and antiparticularistic world literary discourses within the *modernista* aesthetic formation can be found in essays, reviews, and chronicles by notable writers (albeit seldom read) like the Guatemalan Enrique Gómez Carrillo and the Colombian Baldomero Sanín Cano. Both were important actors in the transatlantic modernist theater, but were later marginalized by a critical field that was unwilling to open up the *modernista* canon. A world literary critical discourse (indeed, a world literary desire) is present in all their published work, and not just in passing, as in the case of many other *modernistas*.

The cosmopolitan orientation of their writing and professional itineraries determines Gómez Carrillo's and Sanín Cano's intellectual identity within the *modernista* cultural formation. However, when a cultural field emerges in the context of the globalization of modernity (as analyzed in Part One), as it was in turn-of-the-century Latin America, the affirmation of its own cultural difference is expected to be its most prevalent and visible dynamic. Thus the need to forge an oppositional identity during foundational or transitional moments (whether locally, in relation to the hegemony of cultural elites, or globally, challenging uneven cultural relations) leads most intellectual actors to produce particularistic rather than cosmopolitan discourses, to assert an independent cultural being rather than argue for formal equivalence with the literatures of the world in order to inscribe it as universal in that global space.[5]

World literature as a modernizing *modernista* desire, then, can be traced in the cracks of the particularistic *and* Francophile monuments of José Martí, Manuel Gutiérrez Nájera, Manuel González Prada, and Rubén Darío, as well as in the work of writers like Gómez Carrillo, who is frequently considered too insubstantial and derivative for his brand of cosmopolitanism to merit serious engagement. Even if their world literary demands were seldom articulated clearly, in seeking a radical universalism that defied the particularistic determination of the *modernista* project (and of late nineteenth-century literature in general), these writers opened a cosmopolitan horizon for Latin American culture, a condition that made it possible for others to challenge simplistic nationalist and regionalist imaginaries later in the twentieth century.

In this chapter, I reconstruct the presence of world literary discourses in the split body of modernism, where the desire to be part of the universality of cultural modernity (as *modernistas* conceived it) coexisted in a productive and unresolved tension with the particularistic goal of producing a differential identity. This split that prevents the possibility of a critical narrative of *modernismo* as a coherent project marked by its Latin Americanist, particularistic orientation and ideology (a characterization that is omnipresent in the critical tradition, from Pedro Henríquez Ureña to Ángel Rama and his heirs) must be registered in the divided bodies of some modernist writers themselves. If Martí, Gutiérrez Nájera, and González Prada, among others, are considered emblematic contributors to the foundation of a Latin Americanist identity for Latin America—that is, a differential identity defined by a particularistic determination—I argue that they also articulate a universalist discourse on the literatures of the world that is in blatant contradiction to their own particularistic goals. Recognition of this unresolved tension is essential to a complete and complex understanding of the discursive forces at stake for the *modernistas*, as well as in the Latin American cultural field through the first half of the twentieth century. To be clear, I propose that the cosmopolitan subject of world literary discourses does not coincide with the biological person of the writers but rather is a subject position that they assume at very specific historical junctions as a way of responding to specific modernizing demands that a particularistic, nationalist or regionalist discourse of cultural difference would not satisfy.

LATIN AMERICANISM'S THORN: MARTÍ AND WORLD LITERATURE

In January 1882, Oscar Wilde visited New York City as part of an extended North American lecture tour. Martí attended Wilde's talk at Chickering Hall, a 1,450-seat theater in Union Square. "Oscar Wilde," his chronicle of the event, was written for the Cuban newspaper *El Almendares* and reprinted in *La Nación* in Buenos Aires in December of the same year. In the opening paragraph, before describing the theatrics of the lecture and summarizing Wilde's arguments on the Pre-Raphaelite renaissance in English art, Martí called on Latin American intellectuals to turn to world literature as a force to break them out of the Hispanic tradition that prevented the modernization of their literary practices:

> Vivimos, los que hablamos lengua castellana, llenos todos de Horacio y de Virgilio, y parece que las fronteras de nuestro espíritu son las de nuestro lenguaje. ¿Por qué nos han de ser fruta casi vedada las literaturas extranjeras, tan sobradas hoy de ese ambiente natural, fuerza sincera y espíritu actual que falta en la moderna literatura española? Ni la huella que en Núñez de Arce ha dejado Byron, ni la que los poetas alemanes imprimieron en Campoamor y Bécquer, ni una que otra traducción pálida de alguna obra alemana o inglesa bastan a darnos idea de la literatura de los eslavos, germanos y sajones, cuyos poemas tienen a la vez del cisne níveo, de los castillos derruidos, de las robustas mozas que se asoman a su balcón lleno de flores, y de la luz plácida y mística de las auroras boreales. Conocer diversas literaturas es el medio mejor de libertarse de la tiranía de algunas de ellas; así como no hay manera de salvarse del riesgo de obedecer ciegamente a un sistema filosófico, sino nutrirse de todos, y ver cómo en todos palpita un mismo espíritu, sujeto a semejantes accidentes, cualesquiera que sean las formas de que la imaginación humana, vehemente o menguada, según los climas, haya revestido esa fe en lo inmenso y esa ansia de salir de sí, y esa noble inconformidad con ser lo que es, que generan todas las escuelas filosóficas. ("Oscar Wilde" 287)

We who speak the Spanish tongue live steeped in Horace and Virgil, and the frontiers of our spirit would seem to be those of our language. Why must foreign literatures be virtually forbidden fruit for us, rich as they are today in the natural setting, honest strength, and contemporary spirit so lacking in modern Spanish literature? Byron's reflection in Núñez de Arce, the influence of German poets on Campoamor and Bécquer, and the smattering of pallid translations from the German or English hardly convey an idea of literature of the Slavs, the Germans, or the English, whose poems contain at once the snowy swan, castle ruins, rosy-cheeked maidens in flower-filled balconies, and the serene and mystic light of the aurora borealis. The knowledge of different literatures frees one from the tyranny of a few, just as the danger of blind subjection to one philosophical system is best escaped by feeding on all. It is then one realizes

> that in all systems one spirit prevails, confronted by the same problems, whatever the form the human imagination, soaring or restrained, according to climate, takes to express its faith in the infinite, the desire to transcend itself and that noble non-conformity with one's own existence which is engendered by all philosophical schools. ("Oscar Wilde" 259–60)

Although often cited, this opening paragraph has never been recognized for what it is: the first Latin American world literary discourse, the first articulation of a concern, regarding not this or that individual *foreign* literature, text, or author (I will return to the foreign nature of the textual formation that Martí describes) but rather the universality of literature and the possible emancipatory effects of this inscription of universality in America's literary body. Martí condemns the state of the region's cultural field ("espíritu actual"): isolated, belated, and in need of modernity to help it transcend the limits of Hispanic sameness and cultural particularity ("las fronteras de nuestro espíritu son las de nuestro lenguaje").[6] Martí's call to world literature shows his impatience with the absence of *deseo de mundo*, a lack of interest on the part of Latin Americans about what lies beyond the limits of a monolingual existence, whether in the *metrópoli* or in its current and former colonies.

With his surprise and subtly expressed outrage, Martí names the anti-identitarian desire to negate oneself, to be another, to be one with the world that he sees as a universal cosmopolitan urge ("esa ansia de salir de sí, y esa noble inconformidad con ser lo que es"). To Martí, world literature can expand one's subjectivity to the point that the self dissolves into a world of universal, undifferentiated plenitude: world literature as a way of not-being Latin American, when Latin American identity feels culturally and aesthetically limiting, like a form of tyranny that calls for liberation. World literature, then ("conocer diversas literaturas"), is Martí's cultural-political prescription for modernizing a literary field defined by a lack ("lo que falta en la moderna literatura española").

The weight of the colonial situation in the Caribbean (the first but not the only context of Martí's poetic and essayistic writing) could lead us to interpret the denouncement of "la moderna literatura española" in relation to the symbolic constellation of "Nuestra América" ("Our America") (1891), as a declaration of cultural independence based on an affirmation of Latin American cultural difference. Instead, I believe (as I will demonstrate below through a close reading of the passage) that in choosing to direct his criticism at a universe formed by "los que hablamos lengua castellana," Martí in fact advocates against the narrowness of particularistic cultural politics to argue that an emancipated and modern Latin American culture must break free from Spain and overcome the inherited Hispanic tradition that isolates it from the modern world.

Although Martí was the first *modernista* to explicitly articulate the idea (and ideal) of world literature, others followed suit. In 1885, the Mexican Gutiérrez Nájera called for Latin American men of letters to adopt universal horizons: "No puede pedirse al literato que sólo describa los lugares de su patria y sólo cante las hazañas de sus héroes nacionales. El literato viaja, el literato está en comunicación íntima con las civilizaciones antiguas y con todo el mundo moderno" ("Literatura propia" 86) ("One cannot ask a man of letters to describe only the places of his homeland, to only sing of the feats of his national heroes. The man of letters travels, the man of letters keeps in intimate contact with ancient civilizations and with all the modern world"). In 1886, the Peruvian González Prada gave a lecture in Lima that echoed Kant's "An Answer to the Question: What Is Enlightenment?" in its call for Latin American intellectuals to mature into cosmopolitan adults; he recommended engagement with world literature as the most productive way to overcome Spain's backwardness and to synchronize Peruvian culture with the secular universality of modernity: "Dejemos las andaderas de la infancia y busquemos en otras literaturas nuevos elementos y nuevas impulsiones. Al espíritu de naciones ultramontanas y monárquicas prefiramos el espíritu libre y democrático del siglo. . . . Recordemos constantemente que la dependencia intelectual d'España significaría para nosotros la indefinida prolongación de la niñez" ("Conferencia" 26) ("Let's leave behind the habits of childhood and seek new elements and new impulses in other literatures. We prefer the free and democratic spirit of the present day to the spirit of Catholic monarchies. . . . Let us constantly remember that the intellectual dependency of Spain would signify for us an indefinite prolongation of childhood"; "Lecture" 24). Later, in 1901, the Nicaraguan Darío insists on the need for literary exchanges with a literary world as a way to finally shed the cultural particularity inherited from Spain (he calls it "españolismo") which "impide la influencia de todo soplo cosmopolita" (*España contemporánea* 311) ("prevents the inflowing of any cosmopolitan breeze";

Selected Writings 369). And to defend his cosmopolitan *modernismo* from its detractors in Spain, Darío explains that its rise in Latin America was triggered by a desire to connect with different cultures of the world, a modern desire articulated in relation to the world at large: "nuestro inmediato comercio material y espiritual con las distintas naciones del mundo, y principalmente porque existe en la nueva generación americana un inmenso deseo de progreso y un vivo entusiasmo, que constituye su pontencialidad mayor" (*España contemporánea* 314) ("our immediate material and spiritual commerce with the many nations of the world, and also because there is, in the new Latin American generation, an immense desire for progress and an intense enthusiasm, which is that generation's greatest potential" (*Selected Writings* 371–72). Between the 1890s and 1920s, the Guatemalan Gómez Carrillo revised the emblematically modernist category of "literatura extranjera" ("foreign literature") into "literatura universal" ("universal literature"), in the same way that he turned the imperialistic nucleus of Orientalist representations of Japanese culture into a cosmopolitan discourse with emancipatory overtones. Between 1893 and 1894, the Colombian Baldomero Sanín Cano (a transitional figure in Latin American literature who bridged *modernismo* and the liberal humanism of Alfonso Reyes and Victoria Ocampo) wrote "De lo exótico," a lecture first and an essay later, that invited Latin American writers to expand the region's restricted set of intellectual interests: "No hay a falta de patriotismo, ni apostasía de raza en tratar de comprender lo ruso, verbigracia, y de asimilarse uno lo escandinavo. . . . 'Ensanchemos nuestros gustos' dijo Lemaitre. . . . Ensachémoslos en el tiempo y en el espacio; no nos limitemos a una raza, aunque sea la nuestra, ni a una época histórica, ni a una tradición literaria" (92–93) ("There is no lack of patriotism, nor racial apostasy in trying to understand Russian, for example, and trying to absorb Scandinavian. . . . 'Let us broaden our tastes', Lemaitre said. . . . Let us broaden them in time and in space; let us not limit them to any race, not even our own, nor to any historic period, nor to any literary tradition").

Once the archive of *modernista* discourses on the literatures of the world reveals itself in its vast complexity, its structural presence within the *modernista* cultural formation can no longer be minimized. In this archive made up of fragmentary, dispersed, yet exceptionally revealing discourses, one can read the *modernistas*' consistent postulation of a universal literary space where they will try to inscribe their aesthetic practice and trace the constitution of their cosmopolitan subjectivity in a dynamic tension with their concern with Latin America's differential cultural particularity.

It is not surprising that Ángel Rama was the only critic to pay attention, albeit in passing, to Martí's universalist declaration and to note its significance as a symptom of a larger, epochal phenomenon in an essay published right before his tragic death in 1983. In this utterly overlooked essay, Rama recognized that in Martí's "conocer diversas literaturas es el medio mejor de libertarse" throbs a universal desire that cannot be achieved: "encerrándose en las estrechas y arcaicas fronteras nacionales, como reclamaban rezagados románticos o los conservadores, y mucho menos prolongando la dependencia de la cultura española, sino avanzando aún más en el internacionalismo de la hora mediante una audaz ampliación del horizonte universal de la cultura. . . . La internacionalización, como vía adecuada para alcanzar la libertad y un más alto grado de soberanía intelectual, se constituiría en adelante en el principio rector de la cultura latinoamericana" ("José Martí" 97) ("shutting himself off within the narrow and archaic national borders, as the romantic stragglers or the conservatives demanded, and much less prolonging the dependence on Spanish culture, rather advancing furthermore in the internationalism of the hour through an audacious amplification of the universal cultural horizon. . . . The internationalization, as an adequate path toward liberty and a higher degree of intellectual sovereignty, would establish itself from then on as the guiding principle of Latin American culture").[7]

Rama exaggerates when he argues that the cultural norm in the region after the 1880s would be regulated by the internationalist orientation of its intellectual field. That was not the case even for Martí himself, who would go on to write "Nuestra América" and several speeches and journalistic pieces (among them "Nuestras tierras latinas" ["Our Latin Lands"] in 1885, and "Madre América" ["Mother America"] in 1891) that would contribute to the definition of a Latin American identity in particularistic, differential terms. Rama's generalization may owe to the context of the early 1980s, when his thinking was turning away from the construction of national/regional cultural identities to focus on the international dynamics of cultural capital and the ways in which the lettered class had shaped the culture of the region in its own image: in other words, from *Rubén Darío y el modernismo* (1970) to *La ciudad letrada* (1984) and *Las mascaras democráticas del modernismo* (left unfinished when he died in 1983, and published as he had left it a year later).[8] Rama also downplays the centrality of the particularistic politics of modernism, which he had highlighted in previous writing on Darío and Martí. While internationalization may have been a "vía adecuada," it was by no means the "principio rector" according to which the *modernistas* (except for Gómez Carrillo and Sanín Cano) imagined the path to modernity.

Indeed, in Latin America, the critical imaginaries that might have given visibility to the structural presence of a discourse on the literatures of the world and the *deseo de mundo* that sustained it have always traveled secondary roads. Whether articulated by writers in the margins of the modernist canon (Gómez Carrillo, Sanín Cano) or canonical figures (Martí, Darío, Gutiérrez Nájera), their world literary discourse has always been overwhelmed by their self-defining, particularistic drives and the critical tradition that constructed *modernismo*'s pantheon of heroic, male Latin Americanist intellectuals. González Prada, for example, whose "Conferencia en el Ateneo de Lima" clearly calls on Latin American writers to imagine themselves as part of a world literary network, is generally read only as the author of "Nuestros Indios" ("Our Indians") and as a crucial figure in the history of *indigenista* discourses in Peru. My point is that radical discourses of cosmopolitan universalism and the positing of a Latin American differential identity suppose contingent subject positions that Martí, Darío, Gutiérrez Nájera, and González Prada embodied at different points in time, as a strategic means to anxiously pursue the goal of cultural modernization. And in the context of this constitutive tension, world literary discourses represented the noncoincidence of *modernismo* with itself, or at least, with its established critical characterization as a rather homogeneous formation.

In the case of Martí, the tendency has been to monumentalize him as the heroic founding father of a modern Latin American identity, or to turn him into what Michel Foucault has called an author-function, "the ideological figure by which one marks the manner in which we fear the proliferation of meaning" (Foucault 119). When the figure of Martí is recognizable only as the transparent, unified author of "Nuestra América" and the programmatically reconciling poem "Dos patrias" ("Two Homelands"), it is difficult if not impossible to also read him as the author-function of a world literary discourse and to make sense of the universalist moment of proliferation of meanings that he triggers, in order to account for the structural emergence of a radical cosmopolitan imagination that disrupts the production of a differential Latin American cultural identity.

The emphasis on the cultural politics of identity is a combination of the historically determined need for cultural self-affirmation constitutive of *modernista* aesthetics, and the critical gaze that conceptualized and stabilized its canon. If *modernistas* produced the Latin American cultural particularism that retrospectively authorized the emergence of both their aesthetic intervention and the Eurocentric universal archive they affiliated themselves with, the most visible critical narratives have tended to interpret this double maneuver from the perspective of a self-asserting *Latin Americanist* identity politics, a number of particularistic demands meant to interpellate the totality of a field made up of a multiplicity of aesthetic and intellectual relational positions. Thus this diverse discursive production becomes a system oriented by the desire to articulate the region's differential cultural character. But the discursive construction of a Latin American cultural identity preceded the critical interventions that foregrounded that aspect of *modernismo*. In this sense, no text was more important to a tradition of affirming differential, identity-forming signifiers than Martí's "Nuestra América"—a text that established the centrality of cultural particularity in Latin American culture: "Se ponen de pie los pueblos y se saludan '¿Cómo somos?' se preguntan, y unos a otros se van diciendo cómo son. Cuando aparece en Cojímar un problema, no van a buscar la solución a Dantzig. Las levitas son todavía de Francia, pero el pensamiento empieza a ser de América" (36–37) ("The nations stand up and salute each other. 'What are we like?' they ask; and they begin to tell one another what they are like. When a problem arises in Cojimar, they do not send to Danzig for the answer. The frock coat is still French, but thoughts begin to be American" ("Our America" 147). "Nuestra América" laid down, for the following century and beyond, the account of the antagonistic genesis of Latin America's singularity and, perhaps more importantly, gave to the figure of the intellectual and its lettered practices the political task of emancipating and managing the symbolic weight of the region's overdetermining cultural particularism:

> Conocer el país, y gobernarlo conforme al conocimiento, es el único modo de librarlo de tiranías. La universidad europea ha de ceder a la universidad americana. La historia de América, de los incas acá, ha de enseñarse al dedillo, aunque no se enseñe la de los arcontes de Grecia. Nuestra Grecia es preferible a la Grecia que no es nuestra. Nos es más necesaria. Los políticos nacionales han de reemplazar

> a los políticos exóticos. Injértese en nuestras repúblicas el mundo; pero el tronco ha de ser el de nuestras repúblicas. Y calle el pedante vencido; que no hay patria en que pueda tener el hombre más orgullo que en nuestras dolorosas repúblicas americanas. ("Nuestra América" 35)

> To know one's country, and govern it with that knowledge, is the only alternative to tyranny. The European university must give way to the American university. The history of America, from the Incas to the present, must be taught until it is known by heart, even if the Archons of the Greeks go by the board. Our Greece must take priority over the Greece that is not ours: we need it more. Nationalist statesmen must replace cosmopolitan statesmen. Let the world be grafted on our republics; but the trunk must be our own. And let the vanquished pedant hold his tongue: for there are no lands in which a man can take greater pride than in our long-suffering American republics. ("Our America" 143)

The contrast—indeed, the contradiction—between "Nuestra América" and the beginning of "Oscar Wilde" is remarkable, and Martí poses two different normative mandates—one particularistic, one universalist—for Latin American intellectuals, with the explicit common objective, in both essays, of cultural and political liberation. In "Nuestra América" he prescribes the examination of the region's cultural particularity ("Conocer el país, y gobernarlo conforme al conocimiento, es el único modo de librarlo de tiranías") and codifies the relation between *nuestra América* and Europe in terms of an irreconcilable and insurmountable contradiction (Cojímar versus Dantzig, Latin America versus France). In "Oscar Wilde," the same goal requires leaving the Latin American particularity behind (at least to arrive at a more open and cosmopolitan definition of Latin American culture later) in order to examine the wide universe of the literatures of the world: "Conocer diversas literaturas es el medio mejor de libertarse de la tiranía de algunas de ellas." *Know thyself* versus *Forget about your belated, limited self momentarily and know the World*: a particularistic production of the self, versus the universalist reflection on the conditions that make possible that self's inscription in the world. These two parallel formulations of a single emancipatory desire call on intellectuals to perform radically opposed critical tasks in order to modernize Latin America.[9] I

argue that this contradiction between the particularistic and universalist drives in Martí's work is, in fact, constitutive of the whole *modernista* aesthetic and cultural formation.

UNIVERSALISM, PARTICULARISM, AND THE QUESTION OF LATIN AMERICAN IDENTITY

Both Martí and the critical tradition that has made him the epitome of the modern Latin American intellectual emphasized on the region's differential identity as the most effective discursive path to a modernity understood as self-determination and progress. The presence of these particularistic readings began to be felt in Latin America in the late 1960s, with the politicization of the literary and academic fields following the Cuban Revolution and the Boom.[10] Many critical narratives took a militant Latin Americanist turn that stressed Latin America's differential identity and strived for a postcapitalistic, postimperialistic political and economic emancipation. During the first half of the twentieth century, the most important critical accounts of *modernismo* focused on the aesthetic nature of its singularity as a mere break—within a linear literary history—with romantic forms that could no longer express the modernizing processes of new social, economic, and cultural forces.

Pedro Henríquez Ureña, perhaps the most important Latin American literary and cultural critic of his time, alternated in his writings on *modernismo* between a substantive and a formalist characterization of its specificity (although even he remained focused on the aesthetic nature of the modernist dislocation as a quest for an expression of their true identity) (*Seis ensayos* 35), and a description of the aesthetic break with a number of variations of neoclassicist and romantic poetics, with an emphasis on the use of new syntaxes, terminologies, versifications, prose features, and imageries ("Literatura contemporánea" 286). And Max Henríquez Ureña, author of the period's definitive work on *modernismo*, *Breve historia del modernismo* (*A Brief History of Modernism*) (1954), crystallized the formalist critical approach: "El modernismo rompió con los cánones del retoricismo seudo-clásico que mantenía anquilosado el verso dentro de un reducido número de metros y combinaciones. . . . El impulso inicial del modernismo se tradujo, por lo tanto, en un ansia de novedad y de superación en cuanto a la forma" (16) ("Modernism broke with the canons of pseudoclassical

rhetoricism, which limited verse to a reduced number of meters and combinations. . . . The initial impulse of modernism was translated, therefore, into an anxiety for novelty and for overcoming, in terms of form").

After the Cuban Revolution, however, formalist and literary-historical approaches were dropped in favor of a reading that tracked down the historical determinations of the modernist construction of Latin America's cultural particularity (an interpretation that was already present, albeit incipiently, in Pedro Henríquez Ureña's work). Critics looked mostly at Martí, but also at a vague, totalized idea of *modernismo*, in order to construct the genealogical origins (with various degrees of deconstructive self-consciousness, depending on the particular critical ideologies) of a modern, autonomous Latin American identity, emancipated from sociocultural and epistemological colonial and neocolonial determinations. In one of the most radical and extreme cases, Roberto Fernández Retamar's "Calibán" (1971) characterized this genealogy as a Castrist teleology with Martí at the beginning and the Cuban Revolution at the end, of the history of the aesthetic and cultural self-determination of the region:

> Así se conforma su visión calibanesca de la cultura de lo que llamó "nuestra América." Martí es, como luego Fidel, conciente de la dificultad incluso de encontrar un nombre que, al nombrarnos, nos defina conceptualmente; por eso, después de varios tanteos se inclina por esa modesta fórmula descriptiva, con lo que, más allá de las razas, de lenguas, de circunstancias accesorias, abarca a las comunidades que con problemas comunes viven, "del [Río] Bravo a la Patagonia, y que se distinguen de 'la América Europea." Ya dije que, aunque dispersa en sus numerosísimas páginas, tal concepción de nuestra cultura se resume felizmente en el artículo-manifiesto "Nuestra América." (*Todo Calibán* 43)
>
> This is the way in which Martí forms his Calibanesque vision of the culture of what he called "our America." Martí is, as Fidel was later to be, aware of how difficult it is even to find a name that in designating us defines us conceptually. For this reason, after several attempts, he favored that modest descriptive formula that above and beyond race, language, and secondary circumstances embraces the

> communities that live with their common problems "from the [Rio] Bravo to Patagonia," and that are distinct from "European America." I have already said that although it is found scattered throughout his very numerous writings, this conception of our culture is aptly summarized in the article-manifesto "Our America." ("Caliban")

Fernández Retamar's critical discourse might be an extreme example, but it nevertheless articulates the most prominent elements present in the political-particularistic approach to *modernismo*: the identification of a Latin American identity at the center of Martí's work; the construction of his heroism as the founder of an intellectual genealogy extending forward all the way to the 1970s (as evidenced by the use of the first person); and a militant Latin Americanist view of Latin American culture as a discursive function of the Cuban Revolution.[11]

Ángel Rama's *Los poetas modernistas en el mercado económico* (*The Modernist Poets in the Economic Market*) (1967), later included as a chapter in the groundbreaking *Rubén Darío y el modernismo* (*Rubén Darío and Modernism*) (1970), together with the long essay "La dialéctica de la modernidad en José Martí" ("The Dialectic of Modernity in José Martí") (1971), inaugurated a sociological approach to *modernismo*. This approach accentuated the production of the region's historical and cultural difference vis-à-vis former colonial powers and present global hegemons, which entered the critical narrative as a relational other in regards to the identity formation process. In these texts, Rama works through two notions of autonomy. The first is the paradoxical autonomy of the literary sphere produced by a process of specialization of writers that is not supported by a full-blown market in symbolic goods: "Producida la division del trabajo y la instauración del mercado, el poeta hispanoamericano se vio condenado a desaparecer. . . . La actividad específica del escritor, y especialmente del poeta, no tenía un sitio previsto en la estructura económica que estaba siendo transplantada de Europa a tierras americanas" (*Rubén Darío* 50, 55) ("Given the division of labor and the establishment of the market, the Spanish American poet found himself condemned to disappear. . . . The specific activity of writer, and especially of poet, did not have a planned place in the economic structure that was being transplanted from Europe to the American lands"). Second, autonomy as a process of differentiation from Spain produces a particularly Latin American aesthetic identity: "la primera independencia poética de América que por él y los modernistas alcanza mayoría de edad respecto a la península madre, invirtiendo el signo colonial que regía la poesía hispanoamericana" (*Rubén Darío* 10–11) ("the first poetic independence of America that because of him [Darío] and the modernistas reached its age of maturity, with respect to the mother peninsula, inverting the colonial sign that had ruled Spanish American poetry").[12] Both notions of autonomy are crucial to an understanding of the prevalent critical narratives about *modernismo* since the 1970s.[13]

Rama represents the highest and most sophisticated point in the Latin American critical tradition of a dialectical approach to the problem posed by the contradiction between cosmopolitanism and *criollismo*, universalism and particularism, world literature and national literature, and so on. For this tradition, the contradiction between the self-enclosing tones of the vindication of *our* cultural, social, and political particularity (as in "Nuestra América") and the striking openness to the world (as articulated at the beginning of "Oscar Wilde") is only apparent and in fact stands for a moment of dialectical negation that produces a modern cultural formation at once particular in its Latin American nature and universal in its inscription in the globality of modernity. This is quite evident in Rama's concept of "transculturación narrativa" ("narrative transculturation"), which he devised during the early 1970s with the intention of mediating the binaries that, he believed, had structured Latin American culture since colonial times, chiefly the popular and lettered in all its different manifestations—country and city, traditional and modern, and particular and universal, among others. Rama argues that the modernization of the novel that took place between the 1940s and '60s (through a heterogeneous group of texts usually labeled as the Boom) represents the moment of *transculturación* par excellence.[14] In "Los procesos de transculturación en la narrativa latinoamericana" ("Processes of Transculturation in Latin American Narrative"), originally published in *Revista de Literatura Hispanoamericana* in 1974, Rama explains that the novels of Alejo Carpentier, Mario de Andrade, Juan Rulfo, Gabriel García Márquez, José María Arguedas, and João Guimaraes Rosa construct an identity for Latin American literature that reconciles the universality of modern aesthetic techniques with the popular particularity of the region (207–08). Rama describes this dialectical movement as a three-part process that involves, first, "una parcial desculturación" ("Procesos" 211) ("partial deculturation"; "Processes" 159) that results from a modernizing impulse that has little regard for local specificity; second, a "reculturación" (211) ("reculturation"; 159) that reintroduces the elements that were initially negated; and finally, the moment of the Hegelian *Aufhebung*, when the new cultural formation is produced in an "esfuerzo de neoculturación por absorción de elementos externos de una cultura modernizada. . . . una figura donde las dos fuerzas enfrentadas generan tres focos de acción que se conjugan diversamente: habría pues destrucciones, reafirmaciones y absorciones" (211) ("the process of 'neoculturation'—through the absorption of elements external to a modernizing culture. . . . A pattern whereby two conflicting forces generate three types of action that combine in different ways is thus formed. The process reveals destructions, reaffirmations and absorptions"; 159–60).[15] Key to this process of transculturation is the ideological orientation of these formal mechanisms; what defines the dialectical formation of the transculturating novels (as opposed to cosmopolitan narratives) is precisely its contribution to the realization of national-popular imaginaries that cultural-political leadership can help translate into actual social transformations. With the concept of transculturation, as Jean Franco explains, "popular culture succeeded in breaching the walls of 'the lettered city'; through this breach, indigenous languages and cultures entered into productive contact with lettered culture" (10).

If many notable critics have seen *modernismo*, the avant-garde, and the Boom as moments when the antagonism between universalism and particularism is resolved in favor of an identity that overcomes the contradiction between them, I propose that this seeming resolution is the function of a willful Latin Americanist ideology that has been the consistent identitarian trademark of this critical tradition since the 1960s.[16] Instead of celebrating Latin America as an alternative form of aesthetic modernity (as in Rama's teleological narrative of the evolution of the region's literature, in which the Boom is an aesthetic *end of history* that corresponds to the political *end of history* represented by the Cuban Revolution and other epochal anti-imperialistic struggles across the region), I suggest that the tension between universalism and particularism is never resolved. On the contrary, the incommensurability between the cosmopolitan desire for a universal belonging and the self-representation of the marginal particularity of Latin American culture reinforces and reproduces its tension throughout the twentieth century and even defines the split at the center of Latin American cultural and aesthetic debates today.[17]

I am not arguing for a return to old binarisms that might uphold the universal against the particular, or vice versa. Instead, I am highlighting the overbearing presence in the most consecrated provinces of

Latin American criticism of a teleology within which the *modernista* moment represents closure in the nineteenth century's quest for identity.[18] I do not deny the need to interrogate the moments when modernist intellectuals posit a differential identity, for example, Martí's "Nuestra América," Rodó's *Ariel*, and Darío's "El triunfo de Calibán" ("The Triumph of Caliban"), among many others, but I argue that it is important to address contradictory evidence (as in Martí's "Oscar Wilde" and "Nuestra América"), resisting the temptation to subsume the traces of a minoritarian cosmopolitan push within *modernismo* into the particularistic determination of a fetishized identity that results from the totalizing and particularistic political project of Latin Americanism. Because, and that is the point of this chapter, in the midst of multiform and chaotic relations to the European archive that has been a staple of Latin American literature since the fifteenth century, there is a drive I am trying to isolate and study that is irreducible to notions of influence, translation, or even appropriation and creolization at stake in Federico de Onís's classical 1932 definition of *modernismo* as "la forma hispánica de la crisis universal de las letras y del espíritu que inicia hacia 1885 la disolución del siglo XIX" (xv) ("the Hispanic form of the universal crisis of letters and of the spirit that in 1885 begins the dissolution of the nineteenth century"), or in Pedro Henríquez Ureña's characterization of it as a movement that "toma sus ejemplos de Europa pero piensa en América" (*Seis ensayos* 34) ("draws its examples from Europe but thinks in America"). The desire articulated in "Oscar Wilde" and in the *modernista* world literary tradition Martí inaugurates is not an inward local actualization of universal experience. World literature is an outward move, a reaching out to the world instead of a translation of it into our terms. It is reading the world in order to inscribe ourselves in it. Indeed, the *modernistas* put together their poetic edifice appropriating tropes and topics from European literature, but it matters whether critics emphasize Latin America or the world outside its cultural particularity. When Martí, Darío, Gutiérrez Nájera, Gómez Carrillo and Sanín Cano channeled this desire to perform a world literary task, they were actually trying to produce a world *from* Latin America in order to inscribe themselves in it, rather than crafting a Latin American identity using odds and ends from the world. The latent liberal humanism at work in the *modernistas'* notion of Literature would transform the European archive and its others into the universal patrimony that authorized the *modernistas'* self-representation as universal aesthetic subjects with "a keen desire for participation in a cosmopolitan world of modernity as much as for timeless universals" (Kirkpatrick 31).

WORLD LITERATURE AND *MODERNISMO*'S OUTWARD DRIVE

Martí's "Oscar Wilde" provides what I believe to be the key to *modernista* world literary discourse: the reconceptualization of the idea of the foreign, not as an exterior Other, but as the antiparticularistic (non-Hispanic) potential of being with the world. This critical operation can be traced in the conceptual trajectory of the opening paragraph: "Parece que las fronteras de nuestro espíritu son las de nuestro lenguaje. ¿Por qué nos han de ser fruta casi vedada las literaturas extranjeras, tan sobradas hoy de ese ambiente natural, fuerza sincera y espíritu actual que falta en la moderna literatura española?" (287). Those critics who have paid attention to this *crónica* have insisted that this paragraph, crucial to the intellectual history of *modernismo*, shows that Martí is interested, not *only* in local aesthetic, social, and political affairs, but *also* in that which is not Latin American, in the Others of Latin American literature understood as foreign. At the core of these analyses the notion of the foreign is always present, as a radical Other to the Latin American self, an antagonist against which a particularly Latin American identity can emerge (see Pérus 102; Portuondo 22; Fernández Retamar, "*Nuestra América*"; Marinello 303).

These readings, always already determined by the particularistic orientation analyzed above, rely on a hasty interpretation of Martí's mention of "las literaturas extranjeras," but Martí's understanding of the foreign is completely different—as are Darío's, Julián del Casal's, and José Asunción Silva's. The point is that, when the *modernistas* gave a voice to the world literary subject (even when it coexisted in them with particularistic voices), there was nothing foreign to them. They never saw the cultures of distant regions as alien Others; rather, they saw them as triggers of their desire to escape belatedness and exclusion. "Esa ansia de salir de sí, y esa noble inconformidad con ser lo que es" ("Oscar Wilde" 287) is Martí's version of Rimbaud's "Je est un autre" ("Lettres" 202) ("I is someone else"; *Complete Works* 371) that precedes Martí's world literary call by eleven years. The foreign Other that is not strange but is the signifier of my own cosmopolitan desire does not appear to Martí and the *modernistas* as either a Hegelian dialectical Other that must be conquered and colonized to achieve a form of knowledge and subjectivity that transcends the merely individual or a Lacanian Other that determines the subject's inscription in the symbolic/social order. It is rather an Other whose foreignness stands for the outside exterior of particularistic identity, at a moment when that identity bears the marks of isolation and exclusion from the order of modernity. That is, it is an Other that represents the opposite of a present lack and therefore represents the desired modernist plenitude of Latin American culture. The Other, the foreign, as the potentiality of the *modernista*'s self, already actualized in the modern condition of a privileged (European or, in some cases and with different overtones, US) Other. The supposedly foreign, then, was a horizon of futurity for a modernizing aesthetic agency, which is exactly how Octavio Paz conceptualized the modernist peregrination to Paris or London because, for the *modernistas*, "ir a París o Londres no era visitar otro continente sino saltar a otro siglo" (*Cuadrivio* 19) ("a trip to Paris or London was not a visit to another continent but a leap to another century"; *Siren* 23).

This may not be apparent to a reader who stops after Martí's reference to foreign literatures in "Oscar Wilde." It could be argued that once the literatures of the world are deemed "foreign," a cosmopolitan discourse on world literature that stresses circulation, commonalities, hegemonic relations, connections, and interpellations in a transcultural field of exchanges becomes impossible. However, as I show below, Martí is not instituting "fronteras" ("borders") that separate the Latin American literary imagination from the literatures of the world but rather breaking them down and bridging that gap. Why then would he refer to "literaturas extranjeras" when naming that which seems to be forbidden to those working within "la moderna literatura española"? I believe the answer is to be found in the substitution of "the diverse" for "the foreign" when he calls on Latin American writers to engage "diversas literaturas." Moreover, "literaturas extranjeras" could be read as a reference to the way in which "la moderna literatura española" perceives that which lies beyond "las fronteras de nuestro espíritu" and "nuestro Lenguaje." My hypothesis is that Martí establishes the pillars of a cosmopolitan discourse on world literature in his complex articulation of the notions of "diversas literaturas," "la tiranía de algunas de ellas," and "esa ansia de salirse de sí" that I unpack below.

After complaining about the cloistering of Latin American literary practices in a Hispanic cell, Martí continues: "Ni la huella que en

Núñez de Arce ha dejado Byron, ni la que los poetas alemanes imprimieron en Campoamor y Bécquer, ni una que otra traducción pálida de alguna obra alemana o inglesa bastan a darnos idea de la literatura de los eslavos, germanos y sajones" ("Oscar Wilde" 287). This can be read as a harsh judgment of the peninsular mediation in Latin America's relation to the literatures of the world, and it is yet another instance of Martí's desire for the kind of cultural autonomy and self-determination that Rama and Ramos highlighted in his discourse. *Modernistas* want to read the world for themselves, and even translations—perhaps because of their peninsular origin—are an obstacle to overcome. And the assertion that "conocer diversas literaturas es el medio mejor de libertarse de la tiranía de algunas de ellas" can be interpreted along these same lines of breaking free of a Hispanic tradition with a monopolistic and tyrannical presence in the Latin American intellectual field. These are certainly sensible interpretations, but I do not think the critical meaning of these passages is exhausted in the description of an antipeninsular feeling that exudes an antagonistic affirmation of Latin American autonomy. I would like to propose that they bring up something that exceeds the specificity of the colonial and postcolonial presence of Spain in Latin America. These passages articulate the normative demand according to which Latin America defines itself within a universal geography of Literature instead of in relation to itself and to any single, individualized *foreign* literatures ("la tiranía de algunas de ellas"), such as Spanish, French, or any *one* literature in particular.[19]

Or to put it differently, is there *a world* in the opening paragraph of "Oscar Wilde," or just *foreign literatures*? And what is the difference between foreign literatures and world literature? Where would one find the notion of world literature here? First of all, in the seemingly random enumeration that includes Slavic, German, and Saxon literatures and deliberately avoids the more predictable non-Hispanic literatures: English, French, and Italian. This is the first meaning of Martí's normative call to investigate "diversas literaturas," in order to modernize Latin American letters. It is not about an affirmative desire to become French, or American, or English (never Spanish); rather, it points to the cosmopolitan dynamics of a world literary desire, "esa ansia de salir de sí, y esa noble inconformidad con ser lo que es, que generan todas las escuelas filosóficas" ("Oscar Wilde" 287). It is the need to escape one's fixed place of belonging and the desire to be universal, to make the totality of the world one's place of cultural residence. *The world* is a rhetorical artifice that, as I stated in the Introduction, does not coincide with the referential world but is instead the spatial imagination of a cosmopolitan modernity to come. And that is the meaning of Martí's enumeration of literatures that lie outside Latin American, and even Pan-Latin, culture—because, I insist, the call to look at "diversas literaturas" to escape Hispanic particularity posits this world, a world where a marginal aesthetic subject can hope to inscribe him- or herself, to become one with the assumed universality of a world system of literary exchanges.

A necessary precondition for *modernismo*'s desire for universality is a highly ideological and voluntaristic discursive cancellation of difference, that is, the conceptualization of the relation between singularities, within an imagined global cultural field, in terms not of difference but of diversity. Because, while the concept of "difference" accentuates the break and the antagonism between one and its Other (an Other that is necessarily foreign in the way it triggers the process of antagonistic self-affirmation), the concept of "diversity" presupposes a field of equal singularities whose difference can be overcome because of their structural equivalence.[20] Diversity is a willful fiction built upon actually existing material difference. Or to explain it differently, the concepts of difference and diversity are markedly opposed ways of answering the question of how separate, singular sociocultural elements relate to one another. Diversity answers: they coexist harmoniously, one next to the other. This is the meaning of both *modernismo*'s marginal cosmopolitanism and, a century later, multiculturalism. Difference, however, offers, not a single answer, but several. I have stressed the particularistic vindication of Latin American identity that has characterized the Latin Americanist ideological discourse on Latin American culture since the 1960s, but I have also insisted (especially in chapter 1) that the concept of hegemony is a way to address the uneven power relations that constitute sociocultural bonds. But the Latin American discourse of world literature that Martí inaugurates inscribes itself conceptually in the *diversity camp*, since it attempts to posit a world of undifferentiated symmetric relations among equivalent literary cultures. Only in such a world, internally structured as an aggregate of diverse singularities, can the Latin American modernist intellectual hope to stand on the same ground as any other particular aesthetic tradition and therefore to be as modern as the best of them. This is how *the world*, summoned up by "diversas literaturas" toward the end of the paragraph, resignifies the reference to "literaturas extranjeras" in the opening lines.

But *the world* is also implied in the idea of "la tiranía de algunas de ellas," which invokes the conflictive relation between metropolitan and marginal literatures. On the one hand, we have the tyranny of a particular literature over another; on the other, Literature (with a capital L to underline its idealistic nature) as an emancipatory universal horizon for cosmopolitan aesthetic, cultural, and political agency.[21] If the link between the foreign and nonforeign in the idea of *foreign literature* is always hierarchical and ethnocentric, and the identities of one and its *otherized* Other are fixed in a hegemonic relation, the notion of world literature that Martí articulates in "Oscar Wilde" dehierarchizes the relation between Latin America and the plurality of literatures of the world through his recommendation to read "diversas literaturas" and "nutrirse de todos," because "en todos palpita un mismo espíritu, sujeto a semejantes accidentes."

Another world literary articulation of the critique of the Hispanic tradition in Latin America and the cosmopolitan desire to transcend a local identity defined in particularistic terms can be found in the crucial lecture that González Prada delivered at the inauguration of the Arts and Letters section of El Ateneo de Lima on January 30, 1886 (drastically rewritten and published in 1894), which reads like a panoramic master class on world literature, prescribing new, non-nationalistic paths for Peruvian culture:

> Dejemos las andaderas de la infancia y busquemos en otras literaturas nuevos elementos y nuevas impulsiones. Al espíritu de naciones ultramontanas y monárquicas prefiramos el espíritu libre y democrático del siglo. . . . Recordemos constantemente que la dependencia intelectual d'España significaría para nosotros la indefinida prolongación de la niñez. . . . La inmigración de los extranjeros, no viene al Perú como ráfaga momentánea, sino como atmósfera estable que desaloja a la atmósfera española i penetra en nuestros pulmones modificándonos física i moralmente. Vamos perdiendo ya el desapego a la vida, desapega tan marcado en los antiguos españoles, i nos contagiamos con la tristeza jemebunda que distingue al indíjena peruano. . . . Seamos americanos y del siglo xix. I no tomemos por americanismo la prolija enumeración de nuestra fauna i de nuestra flora o la minuciosa pintura de nuestros fenómenos meteorolójicos,

> en lenguaje saturado de provincialismos ociosos i rebuscados. ("Conferencia" 26–27)

> Let's leave behind the habits of childhood and seek new elements and new impulses in other literatures. We prefer the free and democratic spirit of the present day to the spirit of Catholic monarchies. . . . Let us constantly remember that the intellectual dependency of Spain would signify for us an indefinite prolongation of childhood. . . . The immigration of foreigners doesn't reach Peru like a sudden gust, but like a stable atmosphere gradually displacing the air from Spain and penetrating into our lungs and changing us physically and morally. We are gradually losing our alienation from life, an alienation so marked in Spaniards of old, and we are becoming infected with the keening melancholy that characterizes the native Peru. . . . [We] should be nineteenth century Americans. And let's not accept as an Americanism the lengthy enumeration of our flora and our fauna, or the meticulous description of our meteorological phenomena, in a language saturated with gratuitous and recherché provincialisms. ("Lecture" 24–25)[22]

The fact that González Prada conveys a developmental conception of cultural change, inherent in the call on Peruvian intellectuals to leave their infancy behind (a developmental metaphor with a long tradition in Western thought, from classical Greek philosophy to Kant's "An Answer to the Question: What is Enlightenment?" where he characterizes the pre- or un-modern as a state of *Unmündigkeit* or immaturity), is less interesting than the identification of immaturity with the perpetuation of the colonial bond to Spain, and the world literary prescription to break it. As in "Oscar Wilde," the insistence on the need for Peruvian elites to move on from their constitutive dependence from Spain could suggest an interpretation that is limited to the break with Spain. However, as in the case of Martí, I read the presence of an antiparticularistic world literary desire (and not a mere postcolonial break) in González Prada that points in two different directions.

On the one hand, the lecture introduces the créole audience to a world literary maneuver in which writers are presented as cosmopolitan originals inscribed in a universal literary field, rather than specific national cultures that should serve future Peruvian artists as mirrors.

González Prada draws attention to Heinrich Heine, for instance, because of his "inspiración nómade y cosmopolita" ("Conferencia" 12) (he is "gifted with a nomadic and cosmopolitan spirit"; "Lecture" 15), and because of the global circulation of his texts: "el hombre que forma escuela en Alemania, se populariza en Francia, penetra en Inglaterra, invade Rusia, se hace traducir en el Japón i viene a ejercer irresistible propaganda en América i España" (8–9) ("this man who founds his school in Germany, becomes popularized in France, penetrates England, invades Russia, gets translated in Japan, and ends up having an irresistible influence in America and Spain"; 12–13), and presents his work as a textual site where Latin American writers should look for "nuevos elementos e impulsiones" (26) ("new elements and new impulses"; 24). In other words, the essay performs its own world literary demand.

In attempting to widen the boundaries of Peruvian literature, González Prada does not only point to a world beyond Latin America and Spain; he also looks at ways of reconfiguring the national from within, by considering the cultural effects of the massive Chinese immigration promoted in Peru from the 1850s (immigrants were employed as semi-slave labor on sugarcane plantations) and the cultural production of indigenous peoples of the Andes. If in the 1890s, as a result of the War of the Pacific against Chile, González Prada would adopt a discourse of *indigenismo* and flirt with nationalistic rhetorics (Suárez Cortina 70), at the time of this lecture in 1886 he was still a fervent cosmopolitan who, rather than favor the assimilation of *Coolies* and Indians into an already constituted Creole and Hispanophile nation-state, points out their potential as socially concrete forms of cultural alterity. Hence, a familiarity with other literatures, the transformative power of immigration, and the refreshing cultural difference of the Indians' sadness are specific strategies to both de-Hispanize Peruvian culture and overcome the definition of a given cultural formation in particularistic terms (whether Hispanic or Latin Americanist) in favor of a modern cultural identity ("Seamos americanos y del siglo xix") posited in a language that avoids "provincialismos ociosos i rebuscados."

A reading of Martí's "conocer diversas literaturas" and González Prada's "busquemos en otras literaturas nuevos elementos" in a series with Gutiérrez Nájera's "no puede pedirse al literato que sólo describa los lugares de su patria," Darío's description of *modernismo* as a "comercio material y espiritual con las distintas naciones del mundo" (*España contemporánea* 314), and Sanín Cano's "ensanchemos nuestros gustos . . . no nos limitemos a una raza, aunque sea la nuestra" ("De lo exótico" 92–93), among other remarks, makes evident a discursive formation that cannot be explained away as a function of the *modernistas*' cultivation of *foreign* literatures, a will to remove themselves from the orbit of Madrid's cultural influence, an Occidentalist ideology, or different aesthetic forms of Euro- or Francophilia.[23] Instead, I propose the structural presence of a world literary discourse that posits a world understood as a universal totality of modernist culture where the *modernistas* could inscribe their aesthetic practice and become cosmopolitan subjects and conduct a cosmopolitan modernization of Latin American culture. The *modernistas*' cosmopolitan drive must be understood as the reparatory demand for universal equality of those who feel excluded from the banquet of aesthetic modernity. That is why Martí underscores the universality of the spirit of modernity ("en todos palpita un mismo espíritu") that determines the global literary system and each of its singular elements and participants.[24]

Whether Martí, Gutiérrez Nájera, González Prada, Darío, Gómez Carrillo, and Sanín Cano called this discourse "world literature" or not is beside the point; they were the first intellectuals to establish a rigorous and conceptually specific discourse on the relation of necessity between their own literature and the literatures of the world—a world they felt they inhabited and deserved. Turn-of-the-century modernists (in Latin America and elsewhere) represented the space of literary culture as a world community of modern aesthetic subjects. This construction effectively broke down the symbolic borders between local modernisms at the same time that it produced, especially in artists from the periphery, a sense of belonging to a modernist brotherhood, even if metropolitan writers were largely unaware of those in the periphery and were not at all invested in reinforcing meaningful transatlantic bonds. This global unevenness was crucial to the politics of Latin American world literary discourses vis-à-vis the critical imaginaries of their European and American counterparts. As I state in the Introduction, while hegemonic world literary discourses are based on a notion of universality that is identical to its imaginary self-representation, the politics of Latin American world literary discourses is always determined by a strategic goal: to transform a cultural field obsessed with its difference and particularity (often coded as a symptom of backwardness) into a formation whose identity is determined by its openness to the world and its representation of local processes of cultural modernization as part of overarching global phenomena.

That is precisely what the *modernista* world literary discourse does: it dilutes the emphasis on Latin American singularity to redefine Latin American literature and culture in relation to a world conceived as the backdrop for the actualization of the universality of modern literature.

Recognition of the unevenness of socioeconomic and cultural positions of enunciation within a geopolitically determined global system of literary exchanges is crucial to an understanding of the specificity of the marginal cosmopolitanism at work in the *modernistas*' world literary discourse. For instance, in describing Wilde's performance, Martí stresses Wilde's confidence in the place he occupies in this global network; this aesthetic plenitude is in striking contrast with the Cuban's complaint about the isolation of Latin American letters. Martí is self-conscious about his marginal position of enunciation, and the presence of Wilde on stage allows him to articulate that difference. The asymmetry between lecturer and spectators is echoed in the unevenness between Wilde and Martí's cultural locations. Even if conservative North Atlantic readers marginalize and censor Wilde ("Es un elegante apóstol, lleno de fe en su propaganda y de desdén por quienes se la censuran" ("Oscar Wilde" 287) ("He is an elegant apostle, filled with faith in his message and scornful of those who criticize it"; 261), to Martí, on that evening at Chickering Hall, he stands for the universality of a renewed modern culture—"predica lo Nuevo" (288) ("the new is proclaimed"; 261); Wilde is "el innovador" (288) ("the innovator"; 261)—and becomes both the signifier of Latin America's exclusion and the figure of a sense of belonging to come.[25]

If the opening of the *crónica* signals the need to refound a stale Latin American literature, Wilde's lecture accounts for an aesthetic sumptuousness (manifest in the very title of the talk, "English Renaissance of Art") achieved by symbolist, decadent, and Pre-Raphaelite aesthetic enterprises. For Wilde, it is not English art that has been reformed but Art in general; it is the universal practice and institution that has been renewed thanks to the discourses of British but also French and Italian artists: "I call it our English Renaissance because it is indeed a sort of new birth of the spirit of man, like the great Italian Renaissance of the fifteenth century, in its desire for a more gracious and comely way of life" (58). The *English* renaissance signals to Wilde a new birth of *the spirit of man*, which means either that English literature (and, in more general terms, metropolitan literatures within the mappings of modernity) welcomes a new stage of spirit, modernity for the whole of humanity, or that the particularity of English literature is identical with the universality of human kind.

Martí, the cleverest of observers, takes note of Wilde's performance of queer difference: "aderezado con un traje extravagante que no añade nobleza ni esbeltez a la forma humana, ni es más que una tímida muestra de odio a los vulgares hábitos corrientes" (292) ("attired in a garb whose extravagance adds neither dignity nor grace to the human form and is nothing more than a timid demonstration of hate for ordinary dress"; 268–69). Sylvia Molloy was the first to point out that Martí "is clearly disturbed by the extravagance he has before his eyes" ("Too Wilde" 188). Indeed, Martí goes back and forth between awe at the aesthetic performance and the need to re-stabilize his threatened moral center: "Embellecer la vida es darle objeto. Salir de sí es indomable anhelo humano, y hace bien a los hombres quien procura hermosear su existencia" (289) ("Beautify life and you give it meaning. The desire to rise above oneself is an unrelenting human longing, and he who beautifies man's existence serves him well"; 260), but "Hiere los ojos ver a un galán gastar chupilla de esta época, y pantalones de la pasada, y cabello a lo Cromwell" (289) ("It is distressing to see this young man dressed up in the latest waistcoat, outmoded breeches, an antiquated hairdress"; 262).[26] Martí translates this anxiety into the geopolitical terms of his world literary discourse; he sees self-assuredness—"Sonríe seguro de sí" (289) ("He smiles confidently"; 263)—in Wilde's display of symbolic difference and fullness, and an abundance of material and symbolic resources that he interprets in opposition to his situation, which is marked by poverty, lack, and uncertainty: "Oscar Wilde pertenece a excelente familia irlandesa, y ha comprado con su independencia pecuniaria el derecho a la independencia de su pensamiento. Este es uno de los males de los que mueren los hombres de genio: acontece a menudo que su pobreza no les permite defender la verdad que los devora e ilumina, demasiado nueva y rebelde para que puedan vivir de ella. Y no viven sino en cuanto consienten en ahogar la verdad reveladora de que son mensajeros, de cuya pena mueren" (288) ("Oscar Wilde comes from an excellent Irish family, and he has purchased intellectual independence with his personal wealth. For here is one of the evils that beset men of genius: it often happens that the consuming and illuminating truth they bear is too new and revolutionary for the public, and their poverty does not permit them to be its champion. So they must bury within themselves the revelation of which they are the messengers in order to survive, and from the pain caused by this, they die"; 261–62). Martí, the exile in New York, the dislocated subject who identifies with Wilde's literary queerness but is uneasy about his sexualized manner—"No viste como todos vestimos, sino de singular manera" (289) ("He is dressed in singular fashion, not at all like the rest of us"; 262)—underscores that ambiguity: *We agree on our desire for aesthetic modernization* ("Esos son nuestros pensamientos comunes: con esa piedad vemos nosotros las maravillas de las artes" [291] ["These are our daily thoughts; this the reverence with which we regard the miracles of art"; 268]), *but we clearly speak from different places.*

The juxtaposition of the world literary call at the beginning of the *crónica* with Martí's formulation of the difference between his and Wilde's situations constitutes the grounds for a *modernista* world literary marginal imagination. Its specificity is the imaginary attempt to bridge the gap that separates Latin America and the margins of the universal from the fully achieved modern aesthetic formation that Martí portrays as Wilde's site of enunciation. This *modernista* world literary discourse produces cosmopolitan subjectivities and cosmopolitan cultural formations that operate, one could argue, in the same way as Lacan's *imaginary* (*Ego in Freud's Theory* 166): narrowing the split between the hegemonic and the marginal, constituting a unified, undifferentiated universal aesthetic field—"la iglesia del arte hermoso universal" (287) ("the church of beautiful universal art"; 260)—that incorporates every singular aesthetic manifestation on equal terms. This implicit demand for equality, for equal access to the ontologically privileged realm of modernity, marks the marginal nature of the desire that triggered it. Every world literary discourse (and the very act of positing the idea of *the world*) presupposes a certain geopolitical position. However, cosmopolitan discourses enunciated from metropolitan cultural locations tend to pronounce universalist signifiers to mask their hegemonic making, while marginal cosmopolitanisms that represent themselves as defined by a lack negate their overbearing local and particular determinations to overcome the social and aesthetic particularities that they see as symptoms of their exclusion. In a strategic and highly ideological fashion, *modernismo* called on Latin American writers to open up to a world where hegemonic social relations and substantive difference have been undone; a self-reconciled world of literature in and for itself, without marginal or metropolitan predicates.

GUTIÉRREZ NÁJERA: INDIVIDUAL WORLDS AND IMPORT/ EXPORT CULTURES

As I have noted, after Martí's "Oscar Wilde," other intellectuals in the region followed suit, prescribing a path to aesthetic modernity that went through *the world* rather than the Latin Americanness of Latin America. A few years after Martí's inaugural world literary discourse, the Mexican poet, novelist, and chronicler Manuel Gutiérrez Nájera, "fundador de lo moderno" (Pacheco 20) ("founder of the modern"), director of *Revista Azul* (Mexico, 1894–96), went even further than the Cuban in his universalist redefinition of the scope of the local and national.[27] In 1885, he wrote one of the most important and prescient *modernista* essays, "Literatura propia y literatura nacional" ("One's Own Literature and National Literature"), in which he affirms the secondary importance of the national question in literary matters. "¿Hay una literatura mexicana?" (86) ("Is there a Mexican literature?"), Gutiérrez Nájera asks. His answer prefigures Borges's, sixty-five years before "El escritor argentino y la tradición": yes, there is, but national belonging is irrelevant.[28] What matters to Gutiérrez Nájera is achieving a place in the universal sphere of Literature:

> Las literaturas no se forman al antojo de nadie. Aparecen en los pueblos cuando éstos llegan a cierto grado de desarrollo. . . . Ahora bien, para que esta literatura tenga un carácter propio, se necesita que los literatos cuyas obras la compongan, estén dotados de poderosa individualidad. . . . Una literatura propia, no es, en resumen, más que la suma de muchas poderosas individualidades.
>
> Poco importa que éstas hayan contribuido al fondo común de la literatura con obras en que se pinten otros países o se canten proezas de héroes extraños. Si en esas obras han estampado el sello de su genio propio, como lo estampó Schiller en *María Estuardo* y en *Guillermo Tell*, Racine en *Fedra* y *Atalía*, Byron en *Sardanápalo*, Víctor Hugo en *Cromwell* y *Lucrecia Borgia*, esas obras pertenecen respectivamente al círculo de las grandes creaciones alemanas, inglesas y francesas. Hoy no puede pedirse al literato que sólo describa los lugares de su patria y sólo cante las hazañas de sus héroes nacionales. El literato viaja, el literato está en comunicación íntima con las civilizaciones antiguas

> y con todo el mundo moderno. Las literaturas de los pueblos primitivos no eran así, porque el poeta sólo podía cantar los espectáculos de la naturaleza que su tierra le ofrecía y los grandes hechos de sus mayores o coetáneos. Hoy las circunstancias son diversas. Lo que se exige a un poeta, por ejemplo, para considerarlo como un gran poeta en la literatura propia, es lisa y llanamente que sea un gran poeta, que la luz que despida sea suya y no refleja. (85–86)
>
> Literatures are not formed at the fancy of anyone. They appear among peoples when they arrive at a certain degree of development. . . . That is to say, in order for this literature to have its own character, it is necessary that the writers whose works would constitute said literature be endowed with powerful individuality. . . . One's own literature is not, after all, more than the sum of many powerful individualities.
>
> It is not important that these individualities contribute to the common fund of literature with works in which other countries are painted or feats of foreign heroes are sung. If in these works they have stamped the seal of their own genius, as Schiller stamped his in *Mary Stuart* and *William Tell*, Racine in *Phaedra* and *Athalie*, Byron in *Sardanapalus*, Victor Hugo in *Cromwell* and *Lucrezia Borgia*, these works belong respectively to the circle of the great German, English, and French creations. Today one cannot ask a man of letters to describe only the places of his homeland, to sing only of the feats of his national heroes. The man of letters travels, the man of letters keeps in intimate contact with ancient civilizations and with all the modern world. The literatures of primitive peoples were not like this, because the poet could sing only about the spectacles of nature that his own land offered him and the great acts of his elders and contemporaries. Today, the circumstances are diverse. That which is expected of a poet, for example, in order to consider him a great poet in native literature, is plainly and straightforwardly that he be a great poet, that the light that he gives off be his and not reflexive.

Within the context of the Porfiriato (General Porfirio Díaz's de facto presidency from 1876 and 1911), a period of modernization of infrastructure through foreign investment and a positivistic conception of governance as bureaucratic administration, Gutiérrez Nájera's call to produce universal rather than Mexican literature combines well with the forms of cultural cosmopolitanism that were popular among Mexico City elites.[29]

The pervasiveness of a liberal individualistic ideology during the rise of the Mexican bourgeoisie can be read in Gutiérrez Nájera's conception of world literature as the sum of irreducibly personal literatures: a sphere whose universality depends on its indetermination and uprootedness, composed of individual works that cannot (or should not) be inscribed within the national particularity of a given culture but rather are the products of their authors' unique genius. Thus the genius of Schiller, Racine, Byron, and Hugo does not express the cultural essence of the German, French, or English peoples; to the contrary, it is the manifestation of their individual artistic subjectivity ("el sello de su genio propio"). Gutiérrez Nájera explains that the value of their texts is measured according to their contribution to the universal patrimony of Literature ([el] "fondo común de la literatura"), while their national meaning is deferred. National literary formations have a place in his consideration, but they are secondary to the preeminent value of the individual writer and his (authorship is a male social relation to Gutiérrez Nájera) masterwork, and his talent is the mediation that articulates the national and world literary realms.[30]

If in "Oscar Wilde" Martí sends Latin Americans to *read* world literature, in "Literatura propia y literatura nacional" Gutiérrez Nájera is concerned with what Mexican and Latin American intellectuals should *write* in order to be part of the world of modern literature. That is why he describes the modern world literary practices of writers "hoy," as opposed to those of "las literaturas de los pueblos primitivos." Writers today should not limit themselves to represent "hazañas de sus héroes nacionales" and "espectáculos de la naturaleza que su tierra le[s] ofrecía"; they travel and "está[n] en comunicación íntima con las civilizaciones antiguas y con todo el mundo moderno." In other words, Latin American writers should be world literary writers, and Gutiérrez Nájera equates modern Literature with world literature.

But a few years later, in 1890, he sees that it is impossible to separate the reading and writing of world literature, that writers from marginal literary cultures have to engage world literature as readers. In "El cruzamiento en literatura," published in *Revista Azul* on September 9, 1894 (although most of the ideas appeared in an article with the same title in the newspaper *El Partido Liberal* in 1890), he considers the question of literary importation in marginal contexts through the case of Spanish novelists:

> Mientras más prosa y poesía alemana, francesa, inglesa, italiana, rusa, norte y sudamericana, etc., importe la literatura española, más producirá, y de más ricos y más cuantiosos productos será su exportación. Parece que reniega la literatura de que yo le aplique estos plebeyos términos de comercio; pero no hallo otros que traduzcan tan bien mi pensamiento. No puede negarse que en España hay mejores novelistas que poetas líricos. ¿Y a qué se debe esta disparidad? Pues, a que esos novelistas han leído a Balzac, a Flaubert, a Stendhal, a George Eliot, a Thackeray, a Tolstoi, a muchos otros, y este roce con otros temperamentos literarios, ha sido provechoso para ellos. . . . El renacimiento de la novela en España ha coincidido y debía coincidir con la abundancia de traducciones publicadas. Leen hoy los españoles mucho Zola, mucho Daudet, mucho Bourget, mucho Goncourt, mucho Feuillet. . . . En otras palabras: la novela española ha viajado y ha aprendido bastante en sus viajes. (102)
>
> The more important the prose and poetry from Germany, France, England, Italy, Russia, South and North America are for Spanish literature, the more Spanish literature will produce, and its exportation will feature richer and more bountiful products. It seems as though applying such commercial terms to literature is improper; but I do not find other terms that translate my thought as well. It cannot be denied that in Spain there are better novelists than lyric poets. And to what is such disparity due? Well, it is because such novelists have read Balzac, Flaubert, Stendhal, George Eliot, Thackeray, Tolstoy, and many others, and this contact with other literary temperaments has been beneficial to them. . . . The rebirth of the novel in Spain has coincided and should coincide with the abundance of published translations. Spaniards today read a lot of Zola, a lot of Daudet, a lot of Bourget, a lot of Goncourt, a lot of Feuillet. . . . In other words: the Spanish novel has traveled and has learned quite a bit from its travels.

While avoiding a mechanistic relation of reflection between the socioeconomic and the aesthetic, Gutiérrez Nájera's consequential and subversive translation of global literary exchanges into the language of commerce (at the height of Latin America's integration into world capitalism as a provider of commodities) can be understood in terms of what Ericka Beckman has called "capital fictions," a term she proposes to account for the ways in which "Latin American elites thought about and responded to the world(s) emerging from early economic liberalization and modernization . . . [since] the dawn of the Export Age in the 1870s and 1880s, when it seemed as though the realization of America's vast stores of natural wealth was not only possible but imminent" (x, 5). For my argument, however, the crucial aspect of Gutiérrez Nájera's rhetoric is that it makes visible the fragmented networks of symbolic borrowings, appropriations, readings, translations, overwritings, and geological diggings that make up a global literary field. The journeys of the Spanish novel through the works of Balzac, Flaubert, Thackeray, Tolstoy, and others are less meaningful as affirmations of a *modernista* canon of nineteenth-century novels—the usual interpretation of this list of writers—than they are in highlighting the internal dislocations of the uneven field of world literature. Spanish novelists and the Spanish novel are signifiers of a marginal cultural location (available to *also* signify the place of Latin America) within these global mappings, which becomes a point of departure for travels through "otros temperamentos literarios."

World literary travels and translations can bring about the modernization of marginal cultures, understood as renaissance and abundance; as emancipation from exclusion and an isolated, poor, preuniversal aesthetic existence characterized by the lack of the "productos ricos y cuantiosos" that it will eventually gain through world literary importations. But Gutiérrez Nájera does not limit himself to identifying the global scope of marginal cultures, or to recognizing their poor and backward particularity. "Mientras más prosa y poesía alemana, francesa, inglesa, italiana, rusa, norte y sudamericana, etc., importe la literatura española, más producirá, y de más ricos y más cuantiosos será su exportación": the very form of the first sentence of the cited passage, with its anaphoric flair (more, more, and more), expresses his optimistic outlook on world literary approaches to cultural production as a way out of a sense of lack, want, and need.

Gutiérrez Nájera, like Martí before him, proposes cultural transactions that go beyond French and English literatures. That *beyond* is the world, a world posited in the vague language of a desire to transcend the limitations not only of the local but also of neocolonial relations, whether with Spain or new powers like France or Britain. The world as the promise of an indeterminate multiplicity of engagements ("más . . . más . . . más") signifies the plenitude and riches to come. The list in the opening sentence of the paragraph ("alemana, francesa, inglesa, italiana, rusa, norte y sudamericana, etc."), especially the "etc." that closes the enumeration, echoes Martí's "diversas literaturas" and points to a world of numerous cultural locations for entering into dealings. Gutiérrez Nájera imagines, rather willfully, a world literary field with loosened hierarchies, where Spanish writers borrow from North and South Americans, from Russians or Italians, and, yes, from French and English authors. But this is not a flat, horizontal world of even exchanges; Zola did not read José Mármol, and Huysmans did not read Darío (much to his chagrin).[31] Gutiérrez Nájera articulates a *modernista* cosmopolitan discourse, and rather than focusing on the differential places of strong and weak global traditions, stresses the unevenness between those who have inscribed their practice in the world of literary exchanges (Spanish novelists) and those who have not (Spanish poets). For marginal writers, the illusion of horizontal equality and flatness, and the dismantling of hierarchies, begins *after* the triumph of world literature over the impoverished condition that results from a lack of exposure ("roce") to the universality of capital-L Literature.

Even before Spain or Mexico or other Latin American countries engage the world, their marginal situation determines their role as cultural importers. But through importation, they modify the sign of their marginality and become importing/exporting cultures ("Mientras más prosa y poesía . . . importe la literatura española . . . de más ricos y más cuantiosos productos será su exportación"). This notion is extraordinary in the context of *modernismo*: the idea that Latin America's destiny is not only to import aesthetic forms and strategies but also, once it reaches the stage of modernity where it is itself a world literary culture, to export. This is a point Oswald de Andrade will make three decades later with respect to Brazilian culture in "Manifesto Pau Brasil" (*Pau Brasil* or Brazil wood was one of this country's most import export commodities and in "Manifesto antropófago," where he declares that Brazilian culture not only devours European culture but also provides the French with the necessary Other against which they define their universality during the revolution: "Sem nós a Europa não teria siquer a sua pobre declaração dos direitos do homem" (3) ("Without us, Europe would not even have its meager Declaration of the Rights of Man" ("Anthropophagite Manifesto" 97). But the idea of a Latin American literary culture fully integrated into the world as exporter is actualized as a global reality (as opposed to its discursive articulations) only with, on the one hand, the magical realist genealogy that begins in the 1930s with Alejo Carpentier, Miguel Ángel Asturias, Arturo Uslar Pietri, and later, Gabriel García Márquez; and, on the other, Borges's philosophical appropriations in France between 1955 and 1964, when Sartre's *Les Temps Modernes* published a significant number of his texts in translation, and *Cahiers de L'Herne* canonized him with a special issue of almost five hundred pages with essays on the Argentine writer by the most renowned French intellectuals at the time—together with the Formentor Prix that Borges shared with Samuel Beckett in 1961.

Gutiérrez Nájera's contribution to a tradition of world literature in Latin America, although overlooked, is highly significant. Within the internal tensions of *modernismo*, he breaks down Darío's law of French culture's ontological privilege (which I analyze in the next chapter) vis-à-vis Latin America's minoritarian and secondary place. Instead, he designs a model of world literary intervention for the Latin American writer that privileges the individual over the national and conceptualizes that relation in the language of commerce, thus grounding his critical prescriptions in the materiality of concrete literary exchanges.

NEGOTIATING COSMOPOLITANISM AND REGIONALISM IN *COSMÓPOLIS*

Gutiérrez Nájera's rhetoric of novels and writers that travel across a global network of literary exchanges ("La novela española ha viajado y ha aprendido bastante en sus viajes," and "El literato viaja, el literato está en comunicación íntima con las civilizaciones antiguas y con todo el mundo moderno") can be traced in several *modernista* world literary discourses, always with a constant semantic structure in the conceptualization of literary universality. While Gutiérrez Nájera emphasizes world literature as a way of naming the field in which aesthetic forms (and ideas, more generally) travel, the Venezuelan poet and essayist Pedro Emilio Coll focuses in many texts on the tracks that literary texts leave behind as they transform readers and cultures. In 1901, he writes in "Decadentismo y Americanismo" that "las literaturas extranjeras [son] algo como un viaje ideal, que nos enseña a distinguir lo que hay de peculiar en las cosas que nos rodean" ("Foreign literatures

[are] somewhat like an ideal voyage, which teaches us to distinguish the peculiar among the things that surround us") and explains that, thanks to these travels, "nuestros ojos han aprendido a ver mejor, y nuestro intelecto a recoger las sensaciones fugaces" (68) ("our eyes have learned to see better, and our intellect to capture fleeting sensations"). World literature is not only an unpredictable network of connections but also a perspective or point of view that radically affects the perception of the local and particular, now seen as part of the universal system of Literature.

Coll was the founder and director of the magazine *Cosmópolis* (Caracas, 1894–95), the most dynamic cultural site in turn-of-the-century Venezuela, but he shared editorial duties with Pedro César Dominici and Luis Manuel Urbaneja Achelpohl, both of whom were more interested in the formation of Venezuelan national culture. As a result, *Cosmópolis* (which published only twelve issues over a fifteen-month period) displayed the constitutive tension between a universalist and a particularistic understanding of the discourse of cosmopolitanism in Latin America—indeed, opposing interpretations of its polysemous title. While Coll proposed, albeit not very consistently, a universal horizon for the magazine (and for Latin American aesthetic practices), Urbaneja Achelpohl emphasized the differential traits of the Venezuelan polis within a world of particular nations. In its first nine issues, published between May of 1894 and May of 1895, *Cosmópolis* displayed three conflicting positions: "El *criollista* proponía la dotación de la literatura de originalidad y sentir nacional, el *conservador* luchaba por la preservación de la lengua, la demarcación identitaria de la nación y exigía la congruencia de la producción literaria con los rasgos caracterizadores de lo histórico cultural, y el *modelo cosmopolita* otorgaba un papel secundario a los anteriores y perfilaba el hecho literario hacia la liberación del marco identitario que la encasillaba" (Moré 130) ("The *creole-ist* proposed the endowment of literature of originality and national feeling; *the conservative* fought for the preservation of the language, the demarcation of the national identity, and demanded the congruence of literary production with the characterizing historical and cultural traits of the nation; and the *cosmopolitan model* granted a secondary role to the previous notions and directed the literary toward its liberation from the identity framework in which it had been pigeonholed").

These three lines are roughly identified with the positions articulated by Urbaneja Achelpohl and Coll (Moré excludes Dominici's broad decadentism as nonantagonistic).[32] Some of these tensions were reflected in the first issue's editorial statement, presented as a conversation titled "Charloteo" ("Chatter") in which each editor outlined his expectations for the magazine. Urbaneja Achelpohl "enfrenta a los contenidos nacionales con los cosmopolitas del modernismo" (Infante 408) ("contrasts national subject matters with modernism's cosmopolitan subject matters") and defends a literature of Latin American particularities: "Desaparece el nombre de patria y queda humanidad: el arte universal; la santa y última expresión de la confrternidad artística. ¡Pero diablos! Admito el programa siempre que vibra en él la nota criolla. ¡Regionalismo! ¡Patria! Literatura nacional que brote fecunda del vientre virgen de la patria" (qtd. in Santaella 16) ("The country's name disappears and what is left is humanity; universal art; the holy, greatest expression of artistic fellowship. But hell! I allow such a program as long as the creole note still vibrates in it. Regionalism! Homeland! National literature that fertilely sprouts from the virgin womb of the homeland").[33] Conversely, for Coll, *Cosmópolis* was a space for Venezuelan writers to learn about the major trends of a world literature with a conspicuous Francophile bent. For him, as Graciela Montaldo has explained, "El patrimonio cultural de Occidente le pertenece por derecho a los intelectuales, a la aristocracia del espíritu, que es universal y está por encima de las contingencias" (*Ficciones culturales* 95) ("The cultural patrimony of the West belongs by right to the intellectuals, to the aristocracy of the spirit, which is universal and is above any contingency"). In that first "Charloteo" of May 1894, he defines *his Cosmópolis*, listing all the topics of the *modernista* world literary discourse:

> En este periódico como lo indica su nombre tendrán acogida todas las escuelas literarias, de todos los países. El cosmopolitismo es una de las formas más hermosas de la civilización pues que ella reconoce que el hombre rompiendo con preocupaciones y prejuicios, remplaza la idea de patria por la de Humanidad. La literatura ha hecho en favor de la confraternidad humana más que todas las intrigas diplomáticas; los países más lejanos se conocen, se acercan y simpatizan por el libro y el periódico; las ideas viajan de una nación a otra sin hacer caso de los empleados de aduana, ni de los ejércitos fronterizos, las razas se estrechan, y la Paz se impone. (*Pedro-Emilio Coll* 103)

> In this journal, as its name indicates, all the literary schools of all countries will be welcomed. Cosmopolitanism is one of the most beautiful forms of civilization because it recognizes that man, breaking from preoccupations and prejudice, replaces the idea of homeland with that of Humanity. Literature has served human fellowship more than any diplomatic intrigue; the furthest countries become acquainted, draw near and sympathize with each other through the book and the newspaper; ideas travel from one nation to another without obeying the customs agents, the border patrols; the races become close and Peace is imposed.

Coll's is one of the most explicit articulations of a cosmopolitan literary project in the context of *modernismo*: ideas that travel and thereby reconfigure a world without borders, customs, prejudices, or armies. This global circulation of ideas and literary forms undoes the interpretative power of national cultures in favor of the universality of literature as the indivisible capital of humanity. Or rather, it is *in* literature that humanity, a "confraternidad humana," is produced. If in Kant's essay "Perpetual Peace" peace was the result of both commercial convenience and a vigorous ethical demand, in Coll "las razas se estrechan, y la Paz se impone" thanks to the aesthetic labor of a literary discourse capable of interpellating the universal grounds that he calls humanity.

In 1897, in a preface to *Confidencias de psiquis*, a collection of short stories by the Venezuelan modernist Manuel Díaz Rodríguez, Coll goes one step further: "Paréceme que en la esfera de la ideología hay una tendencia superior a la ley de nacionalidad y aun a los postulados del método científico y del momento histórico, y es aquella tendencia de algunos espíritus cultivados por la lectura y la meditación a crearse un ambiente fuera del tiempo y del lugar en que han nacido o viven" (*Pedro-Emilio Coll* 79) ("It seems to me that in the sphere of ideology, there is a tendency that is superior to the law of nationality and even above the postulations of the scientific method and of the historical moment, and it is the tendency of the spirits cultivated by reading and thought that creates an environment beyond the time and place in which they have been born or live"). Reading provides a cosmopolitan space outside the historical time of nations and national belonging; furthermore, cosmopolitanism is a form of aesthetic existence exterior to social being. But this cannot be achieved through the kind of literary cult of national particularity put forth by his friendly antagonist, Urbaneja Achelpohl. It is the literature that Coll personally selects for translation and publication in *Cosmópolis* (Hugo, Daudet, Tolstoy, Turgenev, Taine, Renan, Schopenhauer, Maupassant, Heine, and Baudelaire, among others) that creates a literary world that might be experienced as an "ambiente fuera del tiempo y del lugar en que han nacido o viven." Even if, following Darío, Coll's world literature has a French inclination, or experiences *the world* through a French symbolist sensibility (he explicitly linked his idea for the magazine with the *Revista de América* [*American Review*] that Darío published in Buenos Aires at the same time), it is still conceptualized as a cosmopolitan enterprise. The French and decadent texts, as well as the French favorites from the Russian canon that he includes in *Cosmópolis*, are there not as expressions of a particular French culture but as works representative of a French culture whose particularity is identical to the universality of modernity and that expresses a cosmopolitan desire to abandon a local, historical time and place, whether French, Venezuelan, or Latin American.[34]

If Martí's world literary discourse consisted of prescribing engagement with the literatures of the world, and Gutiérrez Nájera's paid attention to the global displacements of literary forms and the ways they affect the individual's literary practice, Coll articulated a cosmopolitical discourse about the formation of a universal community of aesthetic sensibilities through literature. While Martí and Gutiérrez Nájera attempted to address concrete cultural and aesthetic agents how to go about their intellectual practices (*you should stop worrying about your Hispanic tradition and be concerned with the modern world out there*), the terms Coll chose for the cosmopolitan fabric of his world literary discourse (*humanity*, *homeland*, *ideology*, *peace*, etc.) empty the meaning of the universal. World literature as it is normatively demanded by Martí and Gutiérrez Nájera had the concrete content of the actually existing literatures of the world, but Coll's invocation of a world community whose content is as abstract as the notion of humanity exposed itself to challenges about the effectiveness of its cultural politics. Coll later addressed these criticisms, downplaying his initially abstract radical universalism.

The abstract universality of the classical discourse of cosmopolitanism that Kant inaugurates (see chapter 1) and that Coll reinscribes in the Latin American context depends largely on an essentialist affirmation of the given, naturalized, and self-reconciled identity of a hegemonic particular with the universality of mankind. This ideological fantasy, in which the particularity of every culture disappears in favor of their shared actualized universality, would be translated, not into "diversas literaturas," but into one single, homogeneous global literature. This literature could perhaps be exemplified by the formal universality of genres such as the nineteenth-century novel considered synchronically (as in the comparison between Jules Verne and Eduardo Holmberg in chapter 1).

In October 1894 the rift between Coll and Urbaneja Achelpohl caused the group that had founded *Cosmópolis* to disband. Coll resigned his position with a letter they agreed to publish in the ninth issue of the magazine, in October 1894. In his "Farewell," Coll outlines his differences with his coeditors' aesthetic project: "Urbaneja Achelpohl, con entusiasmo admirable en esta época de desalientos trabaja incansablemente por aclimatar el criollismo, la pintura exacta de nuestra vida nacional" (qtd. in *Pedro-Emilio Coll* 105) ("Urbaneja Achelpohl, with admirable enthusiasm in this era of discouragement, works tirelessly to acclimate *criollismo*, the precise portrait of our national life"), while in his case, "mi diletantismo era una nota discordante en el periódico y bastante dañino para el progreso de nuestra patria" (105) ("my dilettantism was a discordant note in the journal and quite hurtful for the progress of our homeland"). All three editors decided to end the magazine and travel to Europe. When they returned to Caracas in early 1895, they relaunched *Cosmópolis*, but the new journal lasted only three months.[35]

In this last stint, Coll's discourse was significantly different from the uncompromised universalism he had proclaimed a year before. As if conceding a point to Urbaneja Achelpohl, or as a way of unifying the magazine, Coll tried to reconcile *Cosmópolis*'s universalist and particularistic dimensions in the last three issues. In "A propósito de *Cosmópolis*" ("About Cosmopolis"), the text that opens this second and last phase in May 1895, he explains that "hay que considerar a Cosmópolis desde dos puntos de vista: como órgano vulgarizador de la producción artística y científica extranjera y como paladín de la literatura patria" (107) ("One must consider *Cosmopolis* from two points of view: as a popularizing organ of foreign artistic and scientific production and as a champion of national literature"). And he goes on to develop what he sees as the magazine's dual cultural-political goals: a space to gain Venezuelan adherents to his old conviction about the cosmopolitan social function of literature in building universal communities of solidarity and empathy, but also a place to articulate the cultural specificity of the nation:

> Si esta revista tiene una marcada tendencia cosmopolita, no debe verse en ello un fatuo esnobismo, una garrulería presuntuosa de rastaqouere, muy a la moda de hoy, sino algo más serio: una necesidad de nuestras almas inquietas, solicitan en las literaturas extranjeras no sensaciones sino ideas, solución a los problemas que apenas salidos a la vida empiezan a torturarnos, horizontes, aires para nuestras inteligencias, que por una ley de equilibrio buscan el nivel del progreso universal. Es una labor más bien ética que estética la que acometemos. Abogamos por la solidaridad humana y la literatura es uno de los medios por la que ella se establece. . . .
>
> La otra faz de *Cosmópolis* me parece por muchos respectos digna de atención. Siendo como es esta revista una antología mensual de los escritores jóvenes venezolanos. . . . Es por consiguiente un excelente campo de inducción para el que anhele, si no prever, á lo menos, presentir cuál será el porvenir de la nación. (108–09)
>
> If this magazine has a marked cosmopolitan tendency, one should find in it, not a fatuous snobbism, a presumptuous garrulity of the *nouveau riche*, quite in style today, but rather something more serious: a necessity of our restless souls, they seek in foreign literatures not sensations but ideas, solution to the problems that quickly begin to torture us, horizons, airs for our intelligences, which, because of a law of equilibrium, seek the level of universal progress. It is a labor more ethical than aesthetic that we undertake. We plead for human solidarity, and literature is one of the mediums through which it can be established. . . .
>
> The other face of *Cosmópolis* seems to me in many ways worthy of attention. Given that this magazine is a monthly anthology of the young Venezuelan writers. . . . It is therefore an excellent field of induction for he who desires, if not to foresee, at least to presage what the future of the nation will be.

To incorporate Urbaneja Achelpohl's nationalistic position, Coll characterizes the magazine as a vehicle for expression by young Venezuelan writers, something which only partially describes *Cosmópolis* and deliberately leaves out its world literary element. Coll clearly seeks to show that the cosmopolitan and national horizons that signify the possibility of modernizing intellectual and aesthetic practices are not in opposition and can be articulated as compatible means toward the same goal of modernization. What appears to be a mere rhetorical gesture in these last three issues of the magazine will resurface as Coll's new creed. In the 1901 essay "Decadentismo y Americanismo" ("Decadentism and Americanism"), he forcefully formulates the necessary relation between the local and the worldly, the particular and the universal: "Una moda extranjera que se acepta y se aclimata es porque encuentra terreno propio, porque corresponde a un estado individual o social y porque satisface un gusto que ya existía virtualmente" (57) ("A foreign fashion is accepted and acclimated because it finds its own grounding, because it corresponds to an individual or social state and because it satisfies a taste that already existed virtually"). He continues: "Pues hasta en los que suponemos que rinden un culto a las hegemonías extranjeras, obra la energía que brota de las entrañas de las razas y del medio" (67) ("Because even in those whom we suppose to worship foreign hegemonies, the energy that breaks forth from the innards of the races and the environment is at work").

Coll's shift is open to different interpretations. Gerard Aching sees it as the recognition of a Latin American need to overcome the apparent contradiction between universalist and particularistic discourses that "suggests the possibility of belonging to national and transnational spaces simultaneously and, moreover, without contradiction. . . . The 'nota criolla,' in other words, must remain a vital force if the cosmopolitan program is to succeed" (*Politics* 142). Aching's analysis is part of a tradition of Latin Americanist criticism of Latin American literature (analyzed in the previous section) that considers radical universalism an elitist stance, one that should be circumvented by looking at the instances of its reconciliation with popular forms of cultural particularism. This approach produces a dialectical Latin American identity presented as a mode of cultural existence higher than the naive universalism of *modernismo* and higher than nationalistic or ethnical forms of particularism. Preserved *and* negated, the universalism of *modernismo* would then give birth to cultural forms grounded in the historical specificity of the institutions and practices that represent the region's cultural particularity, while articulating the cosmopolitan aspiration of translating the universality of modernity in their own terms: in other words, a Latin American culture at once particular and universal.

Coll's last contributions to *Cosmópolis*, those dated May 1895 or later, highlight this particularistic determination of the universal, now plainly identified with the foreign. The idea that world literary practices "satisface[n] un gusto que ya existía virtualmente" supposes that the universal always already exists as some aspect of the particular and that cosmopolitan practice simply activates it. The determining end, the *telos*, would be the particular culture within whose boundaries the agent of "cosmopolitan" appropriation acts. Cultural particularity is the *telos* (finality) and *archē* (origin) that conditions cosmopolitan discourses and subjectivities, because, according to this late Coll, "la energía que brota de las entrañas de las razas y del medio" will always be at work in the universalism of world literature. This could not be further from the desire to replace "la idea de patria por la de Humanidad" and from the declaration of a "tendencia superior a la ley de nacionalidad" in the first issues of *Cosmópolis*. While it is entirely legitimate to interpret Coll's conversion, as Aching does, as the realization of the need for a concrete ground for the Latin American enunciation of a universalist discourse of world literature, I prefer to see it as a reactionary defensive reflex in regard to the symbolic dispossession that is part of the negation of a given particular identity and the embrace of humanity in all its abstract, groundless universality.

GÓMEZ CARRILLO AND THE MEDIATING LABORS OF THE WORLD LITERARY CRITIC

The place of the Guatemalan Enrique Gómez Carrillo in the modernist canon has always been dubious. Since the first totalizing critical accounts of *modernismo* in the 1920s, Gómez Carrillo's writing has been considered banal and superficial. The most prolific and commercially successful author of his generation, he has been relegated to the corners where texts are never read and names are mentioned only in footnotes. As I will discuss in chapter 5, he has been recognized as a traveler, a dandy, a journalist, and a socialite, but he has rarely been credited with any significant contribution to the collective production of modernist aesthetics. Gómez Carrillo would have never imagined an afterlife of marginality for his work; to the contrary, he was convinced of his own importance and saw himself as the glue that held together the community of Hispanic American modernist émigrés in Paris at the beginning of the twentieth century. He arrived in Paris in 1891, at eighteen years of age, with a letter of recommendation from Rubén Darío, and he resided there, aside from brief forays to Madrid, until his death in 1927.[36] He repaid Darío's favor when Darío visited France for the first time in 1893, hosting him and introducing him to the French literary world, even fulfilling Darío's dream of meeting Verlaine, with whom Gómez Carrillo had become well acquainted in the wee hours of his bohemian nights.

Gómez Carrillo's texts are hardly ever part of the academic curriculum in the United States and Latin America (with the exception of some of his travel writing), but the reason why he is the ultimate marginal is the general consensus that his is the most perfect and irredeemable embodiment of the lightest and most trivial side of *modernismo*. This accusation has been articulated by Manuel Ugarte, who spoke of "la zona frívola en la que él mismo quiso encasillarse" (*Escritores iberoamericanos* 133) ("the frivolous zone in which he himself wanted to be pigeonholed"), and by Darío himself, who wrote in a letter to Miguel de Unamuno that "las tonterías de Gómez Carrillo—pues las tiene grandes—no harán sino que se distinga entre lo que París tiene de sólido y verdaderamente luminoso, y el *article de Paris* que fascina a nuestros *snobs* y bobos de la moda" (*Epistolario I* 28–29) ("Gómez Carrillo's silliness—and his is complete silliness—will do nothing that distinguishes between the truly solid and luminous aspects of Paris and the *article de Paris* that fascinates our snobs and idiots of fashion"). Sylvia Molloy echoes Darío's sentiment about Gómez Carrillo's banality: "Si le dépaysement *modernista* de Rubén Darío, de Gutiérrez Nájera, de Julián del Casal eut pour bout la mise à jour de la littérature hispano-américaine, le dépaysement de Gómez Carrillo semble avoir eu l'effet contraire. Gómez Carrillo assimila l'aspect le plus superficial de cet effort non moins naïf que sérieux du *modernismo* pour enrichir la littérature d'Amérique hispanique" (*Diffusion* 28) ("If the *modernista* displacements of Rubén Darío, Gutiérrez Nájera, Julián de Casal, culminated the process of bringing Spanish American literature up to date, the displacement of Gómez Carrillo seems to have had the opposite effect. Gómez Carrillo assimilated the most superficial aspects of the *modernista* effort, in no way less naive than serious, to enrich Spanish American literature").[37] Even María Luisa Bastos, in an essay that constitutes the most significant contribution to the criticism of Gómez Carrillo's work in its conceptualization and historicization of the structural function of frivolity understood as a very modern anxiety about the new, explains that "si hubiera que caracterizar sintéticamente su obra, antología sería la denominación más acertada" (56–57) ("if one had to characterize synthetically his work, anthology would be the most accurate description").[38] And even when some critics, like Max Henríquez Ureña, have acknowledged his cultural function as a collector and disseminator of modernist aesthetics for Spanish and Latin American reading audiences, he has been seen as a propagandist interested only in reproducing the global hegemony of French literature.

The problem with this oversimplifying characterization of Gómez Carrillo is not its unfairness but rather its failure to account for the Guatemalan writer's centrality in the reconstruction of a world literary moment within the *modernista* formation. This moment, in turn, could then serve as the origin for a Latin American cosmopolitan aesthetic tradition—albeit a retrospectively constructed origin that aims to confer redeeming, teleological meaning to that tradition (what Walter Benjamin terms *Ursprung* in *The Origin of German Tragic Drama*). Indeed, Gómez Carrillo's role in the rise of a *modernista* world literature was not only crucial but also complex, sophisticated, and at times even self-contradictory. I propose that he could be considered the most relevant subject of a world literary discourse at the turn of the century in two distinct ways. First, he took it upon himself to disseminate modernist literatures from all over the world to Latin American and Spanish reading publics (admittedly, with an emphasis on French authors but by no means restricting himself to them; I return below to the question of whether Gómez Carrillo's was—as in the case of Darío, which I will discuss in chapter 4—a *French* world literature). Second, in contrast to some of the other *modernistas*, he did not concentrate on the discursive articulation of a call for Latin American writers to look for sources of a new aesthetic modernity out in the world. Instead, he made a deliberate effort to become a world literary critic and shape his intellectual identity as a practitioner of world literature, making sense of novels, poems, and plays by establishing world literary connections and placing Latin American, Spanish, and French literatures in global, comparative contexts. In this respect, and in the scope of the world he captured in his reviews and essays, Gómez Carrillo went further than most of his contemporaries.

The first of these two contributions—and the only one he has been given credit for—was acting as a mediating figure, an intellectual capable of translating French, northern and eastern European, Balkan, Japanese, Chinese, and Middle Eastern modernisms for Spanish reading audiences. If most *modernistas* wrote chronicles and reviews about the wide array of new aesthetic practices they experienced in their travels and residencies throughout Europe, only Gómez Carrillo was systematically dedicated to the dissemination and introduction of new literatures utterly strange to Spanish-speaking reading publics (M. Henríquez Ureña 384; Picón vi).[39] Not only was he the most curious and knowledgeable reader of modernist literatures from cultures beyond the usual (French) suspects, but from 1900 on he was entirely dedicated to writing expository and nonfictional texts. If Martí reinvented the *crónica* by introducing the language of poetry in his diasporic narratives, and Darío tapped into new rhythms, metrics, and arsenals of images that radically transformed the lyrical mind of the region, Gómez Carrillo's great contribution to the modernization of Latin American literature (besides the most substantial corpus of books on eastward travels in the Spanish language) was his guidance of reading audiences through a forest of unknown world literary texts. Unlike his cohorts (most notably Darío), who saw almost nothing of interest beyond the dazzling lights of Paris, Gómez Carrillo was fascinated by the aesthetic world he could access *through* France.

Of the eighty-seven books Gómez Carrillo published during his lifetime (including the dozen that rehashed and rearranged old pieces under new titles), seventy consist of world travel writing and essays on world cultures and literatures. Five of these in particular—*Esquisses* (*Sketches*) (1892); *Sensaciones de arte* (*Sensations of Art*) (1893); *Literatura extranjera* (*Foreign Literature*) (1895); *Almas y cerebros* (*Souls and Brains*) (1898); and *Literaturas exóticas* (*Exotic Literatures*) (1920)—gathered essays and reviews published in Spanish, Latin American, and French periodicals and show Gómez Carrillo's deep-rooted commitment to the cosmopolitan task of introducing world literature to a transatlantic Hispanic field. These essays did not limit themselves to the stars of the *modernista* firmament (Coppée, Verlaine, Huysmans, Wilde, Verlaine, Zola, *la* Bashkirtseff, Villiers de l'Isle-Adam, and Nordau, among others); in an unprecedented stretch, they also included August Strindberg, Marquis de Sade, Leopold von Sacher-Masoch, Gerhardt Hauptmann, Paul Heyse, Alexander Pushkin, Demetrios I. Polemis, Spyridōn Basileiadēs, Kostis Palamas, Alexandros Papadiamantēs, Abu Naddara, Shin Jaehyo, Kikuchi Yūhō, and Li Tai Pe, as well as hardly known authors and anonymous texts from China, Japan, Korea, Albania, Montenegro, Russia, Norway, and England.[40]

Gómez Carrillo wore his unparalleled familiarity with world novels, poems, and plays as a mark of distinction. He was virtually the only writer who could bring news from a wide world (wider than the one that Ibero-Americans were accustomed to acknowledging) to a Spanish-speaking province that seemed all the more isolated in light of Gómez Carrillo's discourse. In this sense, it is interesting to pay attention to the meaning of "literaturas extranjeras," the title of the most organic of these four volumes of criticism. The mention of "las literaturas extranjeras" in Martí's "Oscar Wilde" described the new Latin American culture he envisioned in terms of an emancipatory embrace of a foreign world whose noncoincidence with the backward particularity of "nuestra América" would liberate it from the dangers of nationalism and Hispanism. In contrast, Gómez Carrillo's familiarity with "las literaturas extranjeras" speaks of a cultural capital whose possession he flaunts as a badge of distinction (in Bourdieu's sense of the concept), one that sets him apart and shapes his own individual intellectual identity.

Literatura extranjera refers to a global modernism that may contain the keys to a transatlantic Hispanic aesthetic cosmopolitan modernity of the kind Gómez Carrillo aspires to, and his repeated claims of authority over it in these books reduplicates the distinction already present in merely invoking the *foreign* signifier. He presents his critical reviews as a pedagogic mission to enlighten the public *and* the members of the literary intelligentsia about new aesthetic trends in the world: "Entre las muchas obras literarias que han aparecido en estos últimos tiempos ninguna me parece tan interesante como *Sept Sages et la Jeunesse contemporaine* de Julien Leclercq. . . . Los ignorantes pueden aprender en él muchas cosas amenas, y los letrados encontrarán pretexto, recorriendo sus breves capítulos, para meditar de nuevo sobre algunos de los más grandes escritores modernos" ("Siete maestros" 309) ("Among the many literary works that have appeared in recent times, none seemed to me as interesting as *Sept sages et la jeunesse contemporaine* by Julien Leclercq. . . . Ignorant people can learn quite a few pleasant things through it, and the men of letters will find pretext, wandering through its brief chapters, to meditate again on several of the greatest modern writers"). He sees his digressive and subjective critical prose as a model that could be imitated in Spain and Latin America: "'El buen crítico es el que sabe contarnos las aventuras de su alma en medio de las obras maestras.' Yo, por lo menos, encuentro tanta verdad en estas dos líneas [de Anatole France], que durante mucho tiempo he tratado de popularizarlas en España y América con objeto de que mis amigos busquen en ellas una regla de conducta literaria" ("Notas dispersas"

330) ("'The good critic is he who knows how to tell us the adventures of his soul through the masterpieces.' I at least, find so much truth in those two lines [by Anatole France] that for ages I've tried to popularize them in Spain and in America, with the objective that my friends look to them for a rule of literary conduct"). In other words, readers from marginal, backward cultures have to be taught world literature as a modernizing strategy.

But world literary criticism as a didactic enterprise is not without its challenges. First among them is the resistance and dislocation that Latin readers in America and Spain experience when they encounter texts from remote cultures. In his long essay on Henrik Ibsen, Gómez Carrillo typifies this potential opposition in the person of a poet friend, Marcelo, who accompanies him in the fictional setting of going to see three plays: *Peer Gynt*, *Nora*, and *Rosmersholm*. Gómez Carrillo depicts himself as the cosmopolitan spectator whose universal, all-encompassing aesthetic sensibility allows him to appreciate the plays, whereas his companion is baffled by their foreignness: "Y bien—le dije a Marcelo cuando salimos del teatro—¿Qué piensas de *Rosmersholm*? El poeta no quiso responderme y se contentó con sonreír. Su espíritu latino se sublevaba contra la bruma del Norte que envuelve todas las frases de Ibsen, y su cerebro harmónico sentíase desconcertado ante la rudeza del carácter bárbaro; pero su alma de hombre se encontraba dominada por el genio del poeta enemigo y se estremecía ante el recuerdo de Rebeca y Rosmer" ("Henrik Ibsen" 251) ("And so—I said to Marcelo when we left the theater—What do you think about *Rosmersholm*? The poet did not want to respond, satisfying himself with just a smile. His Latin spirit rose up against the fog of the North that envelops all of Ibsen's phrases, and his harmonic brain felt disconcerted before the rudeness of the barbarous character; but his soul of man found itself dominated by the genius of the enemy poet and shivered before the memory of Rebecca and Rosmer"). Gómez Carrillo's cosmopolitan subject position differentiates him from Marcelo and, through him, the transatlantic Hispanic cultural field. Not only is he at home with Ibsen, but Gómez Carrillo is also able to see "su alma de hombre," the universal commonality underneath Marcelo's differential and particularized Latin character. His pedagogic task is to *cosmopolitanize* Marcelo and Spanish and Latin American reading audiences to be able to *estremecerse*, to shudder and harmonize with Ibsen and other world literary texts that feel foreign to them at first. Gómez Carrillo repeats this gesture over and over again in his essays. When writing about

Gerhardt Hauptmann's *Einsame Menschen* (*Lonely Lives*), for example, he writes that "su forma literaria desconcierta a todos los que, más o menos, conservan la huella de la educación latina y el amor de los ritos tradicionales" ("Gerhardt Hauptmann" 21–22) ("its literary form disconcerts all those who, more or less, conserve the trace of Latin education and love of traditional rituals"). In "Alejandro Pouchkine," he insists on the Latin American obstacles to non-French or Italian world literature with the example of nineteenth-century Russian narrative:

> Naturalmente, Gogol, Turgueniev y Tolstoi no entraron en nuestra patria sin trabajo. Los académicos les hicieron la guerra en nombre de cierta tradición castiza, y los profesores de las universidades nos hablaron, al verlos venir, de herencia grecolatina. . . . Nuestro abolengo latino y meridional nos preocupaba. Pero luego fueron cayendo entre nuestras manos las obras maestras del genio eslavo: leímos *Taras Bulba*, *Las almas muertas*, *Ana Karenine*, *Krotkaia*, *Los Poseídos*, etc., y la lectura de esas novelas nos hizo comprender que los hombres del Norte que las habían escrito eran más compatriotas nuestros por el sentimiento. ("Alejandro Pouchkine" 72–73)

> Naturally, Gogol, Turgenev and Tolstoy didn't enter our country without trouble. The academics battled against them in the name of pure tradition, and the professors of the universities spoke to us, upon seeing them, of Greco-Latin legacies. . . . Our Southern and Latin lineage worried us. But then, the masterpieces of Slavic genius were falling in our hands: we read *Taras Bulba*, *Dead Souls*, *Anna Karenina*, *A Gentle Creature*, *Demons*, etc. and the reading of those novels made us understand that the men of the North that had written them were more our compatriots because of their sentiment.

Gómez Carrillo identifies the resistance to world literature not only as a question of cultural predisposition and character, as in the case of his friend's reaction to Ibsen's plays, but also as the result of institutional design that prevents a cosmopolitan discourse on Latin American aesthetic modernity from taking root. He sees his role as an antidote to an academia dominated by a particularistic Hispanophilic or Latinist cultural ideology, as a mediating agent who can bring the literatures of the world to Latin American and Spanish readers, breaking down the cultural and institutional resistances to aesthetic difference and helping them realize that by reading novels such as the Russian realist classics they can be one ("compatriotas . . . por el sentimiento") with a world unified by the aesthetic experience of modernity.

However, the mediating subject position that Gómez Carrillo assumed—and, to a large extent, actually occupied—would not be as effective, or even possible, if it were not grounded on French culture as a privileged instance of universal mediation. The fact that French authors and texts were highly visible in his world literary disseminating agency and, more importantly, that Gómez Carrillo read German, Nordic, Japanese, Chinese, Korean, Serbo-Croatian, and Russian texts in French translations casts a shadow on the cosmopolitan nature of my argument regarding Gómez Carrillo's world literary discourse. If his was a French discourse on the literatures of the world, if his aspiration to apprehend the universality and globality of modernist aesthetics was produced through the prism of a worldview structured around a belief in the ontological privilege of French culture (French *civilization* in the language of the time), then it could not fall within the tradition I am tracing in this chapter; it would be, not a form of cosmopolitan universalism, but rather a Latin American strain of French particularism.

To some degree, this was the case. Gómez Carrillo, like many of the *modernistas* and Darío in particular, thought of French culture as a master-signifier in the order of modernity and considered Paris the capital of global modernism (I dedicate the next chapter to this issue). But this is only part of the story. Like every other *modernista*, Gómez Carrillo was not a systematic thinker; he was unconcerned with contradicting himself or articulating critical discourses with strikingly different cultural implications. And if, on the one hand, he configured his world around a French culture that represented its particularity as always already universal, on the other he also displayed in his readings of global modernisms a wide and decentered world literary network of aesthetic relations (as I discuss below). The question, I believe, is not whether Gómez Carrillo's French inclination canceled out his cosmopolitanism but rather how to interpret and conceptualize it in a way that takes into consideration the ways in which French culture weighed in the mind of a Latin American writer living in Paris at the turn of the twentieth century. Besides his efforts to promote the writers that, he believed, were spearheading the new aesthetic trends of the Parisian literary scene (many of whom were his friends and acquaintances), the French determinations of Gómez Carrillo's world literature assumed two different forms.[41]

First, Gómez Carrillo presented French literature as the universal norm of modernism, a parameter that measured the capacity of an author or a given marginal literature to be modern *like* France, their ability *to be French.* He met Yakub Sanu (aka Abu Naddara), the Jewish writer from Cairo, in Paris and wrote about him in 1906: "En todos los pueblos árabes o musulmanes se le conoce con el nombre de 'El Molière egipcio'" (*Literaturas exóticas* 89) ("In all parts of the Arab and Muslim worlds they knew him by the name 'the Egyptian Molière'"). Molière becomes an aesthetic identity for a marginal writer (a Jew, an Egyptian) who might agree with Gómez Carrillo in his representation of the particularity of French culture as universally modern. Being Molière, for an intellectual writing within a culture he or she diagnoses as backward, supposes a rejection of a particular cultural tradition and the embrace of a ready-made universalism provided by a French culture that is believed to represent Men rather than Frenchmen: "Lo primero que llama la atención es el sentimiento nacionalista de los helenos. En un universo cosmopolita, ellos siguen siendo soberbiamente exclusivos. Mientras lo turcos imitan a George Ohnet y los egipcios copian a Moliere; mientras los japoneses mismos parecen dispuestos a olvidar las historias trágicas de sus 'ronines' para tratar de europeizarse, los griegos, siempre griegos, no piden inspiración sino a sus tradiciones" ("Teatro griego moderno" 7) ("The first thing that stands out is the nationalist sentiment of the Hellenic people. In a cosmopolitan universe, they remain proudly exclusive. While the Turkish imitate George Ohnet and the Egyptians copy Molière; while even the Japanese seem ready to forget the tragic stories of their 'rōnin' and try to Europeanize themselves, the Greeks, always Greeks, do not seek inspiration in any tradition but their own"). Here Gómez Carrillo constructs two antagonistic axes, modernity/tradition, future/past, and French-inflected cosmopolitanism/marginal nationalism. French culture as a universal norm is commensurable with the cosmopolitan, future-oriented pole and therefore becomes a preferred form of aesthetic identification vis-à-vis the particularism of a "soberbiamente exclusiv[a]" Greek culture.

The second determination has to do with the status of French as a language that worked as a universal platform for cosmopolitan literary relations, with translation as the operation that mediated and thus constituted the material transcultural nature and the desired universality of that literary field. For Gómez Carrillo, as for much of the Latin American cultural and intellectual elite, French was the universal lingua franca of marginal global modernisms—not because the Egyptian Molières, Turkish Ohnets, or Latin American Verlaines wrote in French (although, as I analyze in the next chapter, Darío made it a point to problematize this notion), but because French was the language of exchange between local modernisms, the universal currency that made it possible for a Latin American writer to be acquainted with texts originally written in German, Norwegian, Russian, Chinese, Japanese, Albanian, and Serbo-Croatian, among other languages. Besides Spanish, Gómez Carrillo spoke English and French and read Italian, Portuguese, and, to a lesser extent, German. Living in Paris gave him mediated access to a wide world of literature that was not accessible to Latin American and Spanish readers without the linguistic means or wealth of literary resources at hand: "Lo único que todavía nos hace falta para acabar de comprender el gran secreto del alma eslava, es familiarizarnos con los poetas de Rusia. Hasta ahora el público español sólo sabe los nombres de algunos de ellos; pero estoy seguro de que no pasarán muchos años sin que un escoliasta piadoso que ya ha vertido a nuestra lengua algunos poemas de Pouchkine ponga en castellano las obras esenciales de Kozlor, Lermontof, Baratinski, Delvig, Polonski, Tziganov, Vizige y Nadson. Entre tanto, aprovechamos las traducciones francesas. Algunas de ellas son excelentes" ("Alejandro Pouchkine" 74) ("What we still need in order to finally comprehend the great secret of the Slavic soul is a familiarity with the Russian poets. Up until now, the Spanish public knows the names of only a few of them; but I am sure that many years will not pass before a pious scholastic, who has already translated some of Pushkin's poems into our tongue, renders the essential works of Kozlov, Lermontov, Bartynsky, Delvig, Polonsky, Tsyganov, Vizige and Nadson. In the meantime, we take advantage of the French translations. Some of them are excellent"). Because of the lack of translations of world literary texts in languages other than French, Italian, and English, French translations became the precondition for the introduction of texts utterly unknown in Spain and Latin America: from the Russian romantic poets listed in this passage, to anonymous Chinese narratives and poems from the Tang dynasty (translated by the Marquis d'Hervey de Saint-Denys and Théodore Marie Pavie), to *La Tsarine des Balkans*, a Serbo-Croatian drama written by Nikola Petrović-Njegoš—king of Montenegro at the turn of the century—and translated by Il'ja Halpérine-Kaminsky, the

renowned translator of Dostoyevsky, Turgenev, Gogol, Tolstoy, and Gorki.[42] Gómez Carrillo's unwavering world literary militancy would have been impossible without the French translations that articulated the world as an imagined totality of modernist meaning.

But the uniqueness of Gómez Carrillo's contribution to the rise of a world literary discourse in Latin American letters lies in its casual and self-contradicting nature. Even if the world literary formation that emerges from his essays and reviews is grounded in the unavoidable centrality of French culture, it is possible to trace in his writings other, significantly less centered ways of mapping the literatures of the world. With or without France in the equation, Gómez Carrillo had a comparative critical eye, and his interpretative readings place texts (particularly those coming from marginal cultures) in wider, transcultural networks of aesthetic relations. His world literary interventions attempted (and, to some extent, failed) to resignify in explicitly cosmopolitan terms the meaning of the process of aesthetic modernization that was taking place in Latin American and peninsular modernist literature and to engage with institutions that held different forms of power in that discursive debate. Two of these institutions were Walt Whitman—a paramount "place" of global modernism—and Rubén Darío. In the essay "Walt Whitman," Gómez Carrillo questions Darío's reading of the US poet and, implicitly, the relation that *modernismo* has to establish with this forefather. The essay opens with a dedication to Darío that is at once an homage and a challenge, followed by a footnote explaining that the text is a response to Darío's poem "Walt Whitman" (published in *Azul*): "Este artículo fue escrito, cuando W. Whitman vivía aún, en respuesta al siguiente soneto de Rubén Darío" (51) ("This article was written while W. Whitman was still living, in response to the following sonnet by Rubén Darío"). The footnote then quotes Darío's poem in its entirety before concluding: "Para el poeta de *Azul*, en efecto, Whitman es un cantor del porvenir, mientras que para mí es el cantor de un pasado fabuloso" (51–52) ("For the poet of *Azul*, in effect, Whitman is a voice of the future, while for me he is the voice of a fabulous past"). The opening lines of the essay itself reiterate the challenge to Darío: "El viejo cantor yankee de *Leaves of Grass* y de *Drum Taps* vive aún. Su voz, empero, ya no suena en nuestros oídos como una voz contemporánea, ni siquiera como una voz moderna, sino como el eco lejano y vibrante de una raza antiquísima. Más que un poeta de este siglo, parece un bardo anterior a la era de Jesús" (51) ("The old Yankee singer of *Leaves of Grass* and *Drum* still lives. His voice, however, no

longer sounds in our ears like a contemporary voice, not even like a modern voice, but rather like a distant, trembling echo of an antique race. More than a poet of this century, he is like a bard from before the age of Jesus"). He compares Whitman to Poe: "Entre Walt Whitman y Edgar Poe hay tres mil años de distancia" (52) ("Between Walt Whitman and Edgar Poe there are three thousand years of distance"). For Gómez Carrillo, then, Whitman's poetics of nature identify him with a primeval temporality, whereas the future is spatialized in the city: "Él no escribe para nosotros los habitantes de las grandes ciudades . . . sino para los hombres fuertes y para los hermanos de la Naturaleza. Sus versos son salmos de una religión primitiva cuya base es el Amor general. . . . En este respecto, el hombre civilizado le parece inferior a los animales silvestres" (55–56) ("He does not write for us, the dwellers of great cities . . . rather for strong men and for the brothers of Nature. His verses are psalms of a primitive religion whose foundation is general Love. . . . In this respect, the civilized man seems to him inferior to wild animals"). As he did in the footnote, Gómez Carrillo contrasts this view to Darío's vision of Whitman as a "profeta nuevo" ("modern seer"), or a voice from the future, focusing on these verses in Darío's poem:

> Y con un harpa labrada de un roble añejo,
> Como un *profeta nuevo* canta su canto.
> Sacerdote que alienta soplo divino,
> Anuncia en el futuro, tiempo mejor.
> Dice al águila: '¡Vuela!', '¡Boga!' al marino,
> Y '¡Trabaja!' al robusto trabajador.
>
> (Darío, "Walt Whitman" 184)

> He sings his song like a modern seer,
> strumming on a lyre cut from ancient oak.
> He is a priest of that first breath's holy
> omen of better times for the future.
> He tells the sailor, "Row!" and says, "Fly free!"
> to eagles; "Work!" to the strong who labor.
>
> (Darío, *Selected Writings* 136)

In the same way that Gómez Carrillo was willing to engage with *modernismo*'s most revered institutions, he played with different comparative scales and contexts in conducting the paradigmatic operation of *modernista* criticism, that is, placing Latin American literature in a wider *Latin* or Romance context (*our* textual production vis-à-vis French, Italian, and peninsular literatures). He was able to think beyond given binaries and relations, for example analyzing the shortcomings of what he saw as the consolidated block of Latin narrative in relation to German short stories:

> Monsieur Edouard de Morsier tiene razón. Los escritores de raza latina ya no saben "contar." La historieta sencilla, fresca y amable, la buena historieta que nació en Roma y que entretuvo a nuestros abuelos, ha emigrado desde hace muchos lustros de los países meridionales, para refugiarse entre la bruma fría del Norte. Los cuentos italianos, franceses o españoles de esta época, son epigramas rápidos que provocan sonrisas maliciosas, o novelas abreviadas que conmueven de un modo intenso, pero ya no son cuentos en el verdadero sentido de la palabra. Los cuentos alemanes, en cambio, son relatos seguidos que comienzan diciendo: "éste era un rey" y que terminan por una consideración filosófica o moral. Pablo Heyse es una prueba de lo que digo. Leed una de sus *geschichtes* después de haber leído una *nouvelle* de Maupassant, y notaréis sin dificultad la diferencia literaria que hoy existe entre la narración bárbara y el relato romántico. ("Cuentista aléman" 31–32)

> Monsieur Edouard de Morsier is right. Writers of the Latin race no longer know how "to tell stories." The simple, fresh and friendly short story, the good short story that was born in Rome and entertained our grandfathers and grandmothers, has emigrated from the southern countries many lustra ago, taking refuge in the foggy cold of the North. The Italian, French, or Spanish stories of today are quick epigrams that evoke malicious smiles, or abbreviated novels that are intensely touching but no longer stories in the true sense of the word. The German stories, on the other hand, are straight relations that start by saying: "This man was a king" and conclude with a philosophical or moral consideration. Paul Heyse is a proof of what I say. Read one of his *geschichtes* after having read a *nouvelle* by Maupassant, and without difficulty you will note the difference that there is today between barbarous narration and the romantic story.

Besides Gómez Carrillo's preference for morally bound German narrative over sentimental or witty Latin literature, his apparently superficial value judgment is highly original. He considers Latin American literature, not as an irreducible cultural identity determined by geopolitical oppositions to the United States and Spain, but rather as the province of a larger Latin formation (as imaginary as any other national or regional aesthetic community). But he also goes one step further to affirm that when compared with their northern European peers, writers working within the aesthetic boundaries of Spanish, French, and Italian lack an essential literary asset ("ya no saben contar") and can be defined by their crippling difference ("la diferencia literaria que hoy existe") from a German mode of narration that is attuned to the present instead of entertaining "a nuestros abuelos."

The radicalism of Gómez Carrillo's commentary resides in his ability, not shared by any other *modernista*, to disregard Latin America altogether. That is, he takes an interest in the world itself (or what he takes to be *the world*), rather than paying attention *only* to the cosmopolitanizing and modernizing impact the world might have on Latin America. This view of the world as a mere set of local effects in the transformation of the region's cultural particularity had limited the cosmopolitanism of *modernistas* from Martí and Gutiérrez Nájera, to Coll and Darío. Gómez Carrillo does not feel tied in any meaningful way to Latin America or Spain (other than considering the reception of his texts there), and thus he is the only one able to think about the potential universality of the plot of an Albanian short story in relation to *King Lear:* "Hay, por lo menos uno, entre sus cuentos de tendencias éticas, que, lejos de chocar por su acento primitivo, podría brillar en la literatura europea cual una de las más preciosas joyas del *folk-lore* universal. ¿Queréis que, en pocas palabras os cuente esta historia de un rey Lear que encuentra en su nieto una Cordelia más eficaz que la del drama shakespeariano?" ("Cuentos albaneses" 116) ("There is, at least one, among their stories of ethical tendencies, that, without shocking because of a primitive accent, could shine in European literature as one of the most precious jewels of universal folklore. Do you want me to tell you, in a few words, this story of a King Lear that finds in his grandson a more efficacious Cordelia than the one in the Shakespearian drama?").

When Gómez Carrillo engages in this type of relational criticism, placing a text from a marginal literature within a world literary network of aesthetic relations, he does not tend toward equalizing outcomes.

That is, in his reading, the Albanian short story does not transcend its marginality to stand on equal footing with Shakespeare's classicality. Instead, it remains marginal, a marginal Shakespeare at best, because its primitive features ("acento primitivo") confine it to the realm of (particularistic, lowercase-c culture) folklore, the exact opposite of the literary realm where Shakespeare belonged. For Gómez Carrillo, world literature was not a means to an emancipatory modernization, as it was to Martí, who believed that "conocer diversas literaturas es el medio mejor de libertarse de la tiranía de algunas de ellas." World literature was a transcultural field of aesthetic exchanges in which power relations of canonicity were rarely altered.

Yet Gómez Carrillo was a firm believer in the ubiquity of modernism at the turn of the century. Whether Albanian, Korean, Japanese, German, Norwegian, French, or Latin American, the world texts he read formed the map of a global modernism that, even if still organized around cores and peripheries, made visible the universalizing potential of literature. In the essay "Dos obras japonesas" ("Two Japanese Works"), his comparative perspective works to dislocate the rhetoric of modernism in a novel and a play whose plots take place in Japan: *L'amour de Kesa* (1911), a comedy of Japonaiseries by the French playwright (and famous Rudyard Kipling translator) Robert d'Humières, set "en plena atmósfera legendaria del Japón caballeresco" (168) ("in the middle of the legendary atmosphere of knightly Japan"), and *Ono ga tsumi* (1899), by the modernist Japanese writer Kikuchi Yūhō: "una historia psicológica sin grandes aventuras, sin samurayes, sin paisajes románticos y sin musmés amorosas hasta el sacrificio" (171) ("a psychological story without great adventures, without samurais, without romantic landscapes and without the *musumes* so in love they would sacrifice everything") that Carrillo read in the English translation *One's Own Room*. After analyzing each text, he comes to a subversive conclusion that dislocates the presumed marginality of Kikuchi's novel and the modernist Orientalism of the French play:

> Comparando la novela y la comedia es seguro que cualquiera tomaría la primera por una obra de un europeo y la segunda por obra de un japonés. Toda la psicología de Yuho Kitutchi [*sic*], en efecto, es occidental. Las situaciones de su libro las hemos visto en Alejandro Dumas (hijo), en Paul Bourget, en Gabriel D'Annunzio. Su manera misma de escribir, sobria y precisa, es lo que en Francia se llama un estilo

> narrativo clásico. En cambio, de Humières, tan abundante, tan lleno de imágenes, tan enamorado de lo estupendo, tan esclavo del honor caballeresco y del sacrificio romántico, aparece, en su *Amor de Kesa*, como un continuador de aquellos maravillosos cuentistas nipones que escribieron las aventuras extraordinarias. (173–74)

> Comparing the novel and the comedy, it is certain that anyone would take the former for the work of a European and the latter as the work of a Japanese person. All the psychology of Yuho Kitutchi [*sic*], in effect, is Western. The situations of his book we have found in Alexandre Dumas (II), in Paul Bourget, in Gabriel D'Annunzio. His way of writing, sober and precise, is what in France is called classical narrative style. On the other hand, de Humières, so abundant, so full of images, so in love with the stupendous, so enslaved by knightly honor and romantic sacrifice, appears, in his *Amor de Kesa*, as one who continues those marvelous storytellers of Japan who wrote the extraordinary adventures.

While Kikuchi is a contemporary of modern European aesthetics, Gómez Carrillo inscribes d'Humières in a millenary Japanese narrative tradition. If he is thoughtful about the possibility of an emergence of modernism anywhere in the world (because he and his fellow *modernistas* are themselves Latin American Kikuchis), he also fails to acknowledge the deeply French and western European roots of the Orientalist aesthetic displayed in d'Humières's play. Gómez Carrillo's map of global modernism is articulated by this kind of dislocation whereby *King Lear* can be rewritten in Albania and *Genji Monogatari* re-created in a French theater. Gómez Carrillo sees d'Humières's *L'amour de Kesa* as an Oriental, not an Orientalist, play.

In mistaking nineteenth-century French Japonaiseries for a Japanese aesthetic tradition, Gómez Carrillo's world literary practice could be seen as a form of elitist exoticism, the fetishism of cultural difference that has nothing to do with the cosmopolitan desire to attack the imagined self-sufficiency of any given cultural location. In other words, is his world literary discourse caught in a contradiction between the hegemonic stereotyping of all forms and themes that come from the East, and his conviction that literature is a universal network of aesthetic exchanges, appropriations, and reinscriptions within new comparative contexts, and that meaning emerges from the interactions, contrasts, and relations that give shape to the global literary system?

Even though, as I discuss in chapter 5, Gómez Carrillo has been known to assume exoticist and Orientalist discourses, a cosmopolitan perspective on the circulation of aesthetic meaning prevails in his writings. Exoticism is a protocol of representation that asserts the radical, unbridgeable difference between the writer's own identity and the (distant or close) cultural situation he or she narrates. Gómez Carrillo, however, constantly plays with, and attempts to bridge whatever distance separates him from literary and cultural Otherness. His willingness to undo both the Orientalist tradition and the Orientalist in himself can be read in the account of his arrival to Tokyo extracted from his *De Marsella a Tokio: Sensaciones de Egipto, la India, la China y el Japón* (1906):

> ¡Tokio, Tokio! . . . Ya sus primeras casa empiezan a aparecer entre árboles floridos. Es la realización de un ensueño muy antiguo y que todos hemos hecho leyendo descripciones pintorescas. He allí las paredes de madera, los techos en forma de tortugas, las ventanas que, en vez de vidrios, tienen papeles. He allí las tiendecillas sin mostrador, en las cuales todo está en el suelo en cajitas misteriosas. He allí a los japoneses sentados sobre sus esteras, como en las estampas, con posturas singulares, en equilibrios inverosímiles. Sin duda, todo es tal cual yo me lo había figurado; pero con algo menos de vida, o mejor dicho, con algo menos de poesía, de color, de capricho, de rareza. ¡Singular y lamentable alma del viajero! En vez de alimentarse de realidades lógicas, vive de fantasmagóricas esperanzas y sufre de inevitables desilusiones. (147–48)

> Tokyo! Tokyo! . . . Already its first houses begin to appear among the flowery trees. It is the realization of an ancient fantasy and one that all of us have read in picturesque descriptions. I have here the wooden walls, the turtle-shaped roofs, the windows that, instead of glass, are paper. I have here the little stores with no counters, in which everything lies on the floor in mysterious little boxes. I have here the Japanese people sitting on their mats, as in the prints, with singular postures, improbable equilibriums. Without a

> doubt, everything is exactly how I had figured it would be; but with somewhat less life, or rather, with somewhat less poetry, less color, less caprice, less strangeness. The singular and sorrowful soul of the traveler! Instead of feeding off the logical realities, he lives off of phantasmagoric hopes and suffers from inevitable disappointments.

Upon seeing Tokyo for the first time, Gómez Carrillo confesses his disappointment when he does not find the picturesque images that his manipulation of the Orientalist archive has led him to expect: two-dimensional, traditional Japanese houses and stores, locals acting their ethnically determined role, everything "como en las estampas." He recognizes some of these features, but what he sees is devoid of the exotic qualities (less poetic, colorful, capricious, and strange) that define the Orientalist imagery he studied before his voyage. There is a gap between Orientalist phantasmagorias and the rather disappointing, mundane landscape in front of his eyes. Whenever he finds himself voicing an exoticist point of view, Gómez Carrillo wriggles free and assumes a different subject position. In fact, his cosmopolitanism could be defined precisely in terms of his mobility, his refusal to stand still in a fixed cultural place of enunciation, whether hegemonic or subaltern. This cosmopolitanism is not a positive universal belonging to culture but rather an ability to switch points of view (albeit arbitrarily) to *otherize* oneself upon entering into the literatures of the world.

Indeed, he demands that Latin American and Spanish reading publics do just this. For instance, when reviewing Gerhardt Hauptmann's 1891 play *Einsame Menschen*, he tells Spanish readers that they should find it strange, because "su forma literaria desconcierta. . . . No tiene esa encantadora frivolidad que nuestro público admira generalmente" ("His form of literature is disconcerting. . . . It doesn't have that enchanting frivolity that our audience generally admires"). Gómez Carrillo prescribes a radical, self-transformative cosmopolitanism for the backward, provincial collective he identifies as "nuestro público" as a way of engaging with the literatures of the world: "Para saborearlo, es preciso 'hacerse un alma alemana'; para comprenderlo es necesario tener una idea neta de los grandes problemas ideológicos que agitan hoy a los hombres del Norte; para sentirlo es indispensable haber vivido algún tiempo entre la bruma penetrante de los países septentrionales" ("Gerhardt Hauptmann" 21–22) ("In order to savor it, it is necessary to 'become a German soul'; in order to understand it, one must have a clear idea of the great ideological problems that today agitate the men of the North; in order to feel it, it is indispensable to have lived some time amidst the penetrating fog of the northern countries"). To be part of the world of modern literature, a reader must be willing to inhabit other bodies, other cultures, or, as he puts it, other souls; it is necessary to interrupt one's sense of selfness, to be able to wander out of oneself and one's own cultural determinations.

"Bueno es, una vez que otra, salir de nuestro mundo europeo" ("It is good, once in a while, to leave our European world"), he writes in the 1892 essay "Del exotismo" ("On Exoticism") that was his most ambitious accomplishment in world literary criticism. "Los viajes intelectuales a través de países lejanos abren nuevos horizontes a la imaginación y proporcionan a la inteligencia puntos de vista originales. . . . El exotismo bien entendido es cosa excelente" (87) ("The intellectual voyages through faraway countries open new horizons for the imagination and provide, for one's intelligence, original points of view. . . . Exoticism, well understood, is an excellent thing"). This essay displays (1) Gómez Carrillo's chameleonic identity switching; the point of view changes from one identified with French culture—as he tends to do when faced with the imaginary and vast formation of the Orient—to a playful, marginal position that gives him (toward the end of the essay) complete freedom to produce comparative, cosmopolitan aesthetic constellations; and (2) the tension between exoticism as an ethnocentric European mode of representation that focuses on the picturesque, sensuous, and artificial nature of a cultural Other that turns out to be irreconcilable in its premodern difference, and exoticism as the characterization of an excellent curiosity about cultural difference that constitutes the foundation of any cosmopolitan aesthetic discourse aimed at overcoming the isolation of the national or the regional.

In this piece, Gómez Carrillo tackles "lo exótico" through two French editions of classical Chinese literature: *Poésies de l'époque des Thang* (seventh to ninth centuries) translated by the Sinologist Marquis D'Hervey de Saint-Denys in 1862, and *Choix de contes et nouvelles traduits du Chinois* (eighth to twelfth centuries), edited by the traveler and Orientalist Théodore Pavie in 1839 (Gómez Carrillo discovers these books through media coverage of D'Hervey de Saint-Denys's death in 1892). Although the essay is titled "Del exotismo," his cosmopolitan reading emphasizes the familiar aesthetic flavor of these medieval pieces: "Las sorpresas abundan, como lo saben por experiencia monsieur Pavie y monsieur Saint-Denys. Ambos hicieron un viaje literario a China, en busca de monstruos espantosos, y lo único que lograron encontrar fue hombres civilizados. . . . Yo también esperaba ver salir de las obras de los anónimos *tshaïtsen* de la China, una gran caravan de monstruos dobles. . . . La decepción fue tan completa como dulce" (88–89) ("Surprises abound, as Monsieur Pavie and Monsieur Saint-Denys know through experience. Both men underwent a literary voyage to China, in search of terrifying monsters, and the only thing that they were able to discover were civilized men. . . . I also hoped to see huge caravans of two-headed monsters trail forth from the works of the anonymous Chinese *tshaïtsen*. . . . The disappointment was as complete as it was sweet").

Gómez Carrillo's essay is written against the omnipresent Orientalist construction of Asian cultures in France and Europe, for it instead foregrounds a transhistorical and transcultural world literary commonality between these texts and his own aesthetic sensibility: "Lo que más admiración me causó, cuando leí por primera vez el libro de Pavie, fue la multitud de semejanzas que existen entre los poetas chinos del siglo VII y nuestros poetas contemporáneos" (98) ("What inspired in me the most admiration when I read Pavie's book for the first time was the multitude of similarities that there are between the Chinese poets of the seventh century and our contemporary poets"). Most of the essay is dedicated to summarizing the plot of "Les pivoines" ("The Peonies") (an anonymous nouvelle in which Tsieu-sien, a gardener attacked by a nobleman, is consoled by a child who descends from heaven and helps him plot his revenge), as well as historicizing seventh-century Chinese literature. However, this predictable and didactic review takes a surprising cosmopolitan turn at the end: "Li-tai-pe—me dije al leerlo—es un precursor de Baudelaire, un abuelo de Wisewa, un maestro de Rubén Darío" (Esta es una paradoja, que pongo desde luego a la disposición de mi querido maestro Valera). . . . Lo único malo, para quien se propusiera hablar seriamente de estas coincidencias es que todos estamos seguros de que ni Baudelaire, ni Rubén Darío, ni Wisewa conocen los poemas del viejo cantor amarillo. Y éste es un detalle, sin duda, pero hay detalles que echan a perder cualquier argumento" (98–100) ("Li-tai-pe—I said to myself as I read it—Baudelaire's precursor, Wisewa's grandfather, Rubén Darío's teacher [This is a paradox, that I make available to my beloved teacher Valera]. . . . The only bad thing about it, for he who sets out to seriously speak about these coincidences, is that all of us are sure that neither Baudelaire nor Rubén Darío, nor

Wisewa knows of the work of the old yellow poet. And this is a detail, without a doubt, but there are details that throw off any argument"). In Gómez Carrillo's account, the famous and often-anthologized eighth-century Tang poet Li Bai (known in the West by various transliterations: Li Po, Li Tai-po, and, yes, Li Tai-pe), included in Saint-Denys's and Pavie's books, is not a marvelous and rarely sculpted jade stone but a fatherly figure in the best modernist tradition. The idea of Li Tai-pe as a precursor of Baudelaire and Darío (who quotes the Chinese poet in his "Divagación," which I analyze in chapter 4) bears a striking resemblance to Borges's hypothesis in "Kafka y sus precursores" ("Kafka and His Predecessors") (1951): literary genealogies are formed retrospectively, determining the endpoint's aesthetic traits and inventing a tradition for it. For Borges, the past does not influence the present but the other way around: the true meaning and beauty of Zeno of Elea, Han Yu, and Kierkegaard emerge only in light of Kafka's literature.

Gómez Carrillo anticipates Borges by almost sixty years. He cannot help but read Li Tai-pe *from* Baudelaire, Darío, and the modernist prescriptions of the French-Polish critic and translator Téodore Wyzewa, who was famous in Paris at the turn of the century for his forceful defense of symbolist aesthetics. But Gómez Carrillo is not Borges and, understandably, is attached to a nineteenth-century conception of literary historiography that is based on chronological formations and influence as the link that binds past and present in a rationalist and linear manner (in the same way as Juan Valera, whom both Darío and Gómez Carrillo identify as the embodiment of the literary institution in Spain). And even if he plays with a notion that he cannot uphold, his world literary imagination inscribes Darío in a global network of transhistorical modernist meaning that cancels out aesthetic forms of cultural particularity, universalizing his poetics through proximity to Li Tai-pe and Baudelaire while obviating any affiliation with Hispanic letters.

Ten years earlier Martí had asked Latin American writers to get acquainted with "diversas literaturas" to emancipate themselves from the tyranny of provincialism. No other *modernista* took Martí's mandate as far as Gómez Carrillo; instead of merely postulating the need for literary cosmopolitanism, he practiced it.

SANÍN CANO, FROM WORLD LITERATURE TO INTERNATIONAL COMPARATIVE CRITICISM

The historical task of bringing *modernismo*'s world literary discourse to a close fell to the Colombian critic Baldomero Sanín Cano. This was not only due to his intellectual longevity—his writings span 1888 to 1957. Also, and more importantly, he negotiated the transition between a *modernista* sensibility and a humanist discursive frame with regard to the universality of Latin American culture. Like most other modernists, he was dissatisfied with the narrow Hispanist definition of Latin America and the need to transcend the particularistic determinations of the local, and he produced a textual corpus that proposed paying less attention to the local and the particular and concentrating more on the universality of literature as it was expressed in northern European culture. He criticized the *modernistas*' ontological privileging of French culture and shifted the center of the world to Shakespeare's Britain, Goethe's Germany, and Georg Brandes's Denmark. He argued against reading literature as a function of national traditions (for him, literature was and had always been produced in the interstices between cultures) and moved toward a redefinition of the humanist cultural and aesthetic criticism practiced by his renowned contemporaries Alfonso Reyes and Pedro Henríquez Ureña.

Sanín Cano is hardly ever recognized outside Colombia for what he was: the author of the most systematic cosmopolitan discourse on the literatures of the world and the relation that Latin American and Spanish writers should establish with them—at least until Borges's 1951 "El escritor argentino y la tradición." His preeminent place in the tradition of nineteenth- and early twentieth-century Latin American world literature does not rest only on his ability to read European languages (he knew English, Italian, French, German, and Danish); or on his writings on Brandes, Maeterlinck, or Altenberg, whom he presented to Latin American and Spanish readers for the first time; or on his essays on Taine, Nietzsche, Fitzmaurice-Kelly, Ibsen, Wordsworth, Carducci, Marinetti, Max Nordau, T. S. Eliot, Shakespeare, W. H. Hudson, Eugene O'Neill, and George Bernard Shaw, among others. The configuration of his world literary project is different from Gómez Carrillo's because he did not rely on linguistic or cultural translation as the necessary mediation for imagining the universal grounds of Literature out of a world of literary differences. The disciplinary rigor inherent in his premise that world literary critics should read works in their original language set him apart from the *modernista* paradigm and made him a precursor of the school of humanist philologists that would flourish at the Centro de Estudios Históricos in Madrid under the direction of Ramón Menéndez Pidal at the turn of the century.[43] In any case, his linguistic skills and extensive European library were just the instruments of his systematic engagement with a world where "las ideas y los ideales se propagan con grande prisa. Es insensato el pueblo que quiera hacer de los suyos patrimonio exclusivo. Es insensato si pretende que los extranjeros no vengan a mezclarse con los propios" ("De lo exótico" 344) ("Ideas and ideals spread with great haste. Insensible is the country that insists that its own [ideas and ideals] are exclusive patrimony. It is insensible if it expects that foreign ideas and ideals will not come and mix with its own").[44]

Sanín Cano's world literary discourse can be traced through sixty years of critical texts produced in Bogotá, London, Paris, and Buenos Aires, where he was, at different times, a literary critic, a foreign correspondent for Colombian and Argentine newspapers, a diplomat, and a university scholar. But his most important contribution to a cosmopolitan understanding of the place of Latin American literature in relation to the globalization of modernity was "De lo exótico." This world literary manifesto, given as a lecture in Bogotá in 1893 and published in *Revista Gris* (*Gray Review*) one year later (when Sanín Cano was only twenty-three years old), is explicitly affiliated with Goethe's project of *Weltliteratur:* "El arte es universal. Que lo fuese quería Goethe cuando dijo en su epigrama sobre la literatura universal: 'Que bajo un mismo cielo todos los pueblos se regocijen buenamente de tener una misma hacienda'" (344) ("Art is universal. Goethe wanted it so when he said, in his epigram on universal literature: 'Under the same sky, all the peoples cheerfully enjoy the same estate'").[45]

Sanín Cano's declaration of cosmopolitan principles in "De lo exótico" was particularly controversial in Colombia in the early 1890s. The 1886 constitution had consolidated the Catholic Church's power over cultural and social affairs, in striking contrast to the regional process of secularization that was occurring from Mexico to Brazil and Argentina, encouraged by liberal elites in positions of power in positivist state institutions. Colombia's conservative turn, led by Rafael Núñez, was translated into a cultural climate of isolation and raging nationalism (often articulated as a return to the Spanish tradition), against which Colombian *modernistas* like José Asunción Silva, Guillermo Valencia, and Sanín Cano rose up to promote "lo artificial y lo exótico" (the artificial and the exotic) as "la *diritta via* para liberar el espíritu de la asfixia que les imponía un mundo provinciano y legalista, tanto en las artes como en la vida social" (Ruiz xii) ("the *diritta via* to liberate the spirit from the asphyxiation imposed on it by a provincial and legalist world, in terms both of the arts and of social life").[46]

In contrast to Silva's and Valencia's postromantic poetics of symbolist exoticism (which are rather straightforward examples of *modernismo*'s quest for aesthetic estrangement), the specificity of Sanín Cano's radical cosmopolitanism lies in its critical and programmatic nature and his articulation of it around two dislocations of Colombian and Latin American tradition. First, he strongly criticizes both Bogotá's fascination with all things peninsular and the reactionary nature of Menéndez Pelayo's philological modernization in Spain, which carried a lot of weight in Colombia and other parts of the region: "En una época en que escribieron Renán, Ruskin, Turgueniev, los Goncourt, Flaubert y Walter Pater, el autor de *Heterodoxos españoles* continuaba ofreciendo a las Españas el entusiasmo verbal de César Cantú como *desiderátum* de estilo, por el vigor de la expresión y la claridad del pensamiento . . . cuál es la idea predominante en la obra de Menéndez Pelayo. . . . Tal idea era la necesidad de conservar en España ciertas formas tradicionales, y ciertos sentimientos, sin los cuales se descomponía seguramente la levadura nacional" ("Menéndez Pelayo" 160) ("In an era in which Renán, Ruskin, Turgenev, the Goncourt brothers, Flaubert, and Walter Pater wrote, the author of *Heterodoxos españoles* continued to offer the Spanish world the verbal enthusiasm of César Cantú as a *desideratum* of style, because of the vigor of expression and the clarity of thought . . . which is the predominant idea in Menéndez Pelayo's work. . . . The idea was the need to preserve in Spain certain traditional forms, and certain sentiments, without which the national leavening would break down"). Had Sanín Cano stopped at the rejection of Madrid as the organizing vector of Latin America's cultural life, his ideas could simply be understood as yet another *modernista* assertion of autonomy. Instead, unlike Silva and Darío and Nervo and Gómez Carrillo, for whom the French signifier had served as the means to break with Spain, Sanín Cano snubs their Francophilia as pitiful ("lastimoso") and relocates the center of his world literary map further north, to England, Germany, Scandinavia, and Russia:

> Es miseria intelectual esta a que nos condenan los que suponen que los suramericanos tenemos de vivir exclusivamente

> de España en materia de filosofía y letras. Las gentes nuevas del Nuevo Mundo tienen derecho a toda la vida del pensamiento. No hay a falta de patriotismo, ni apostasía de raza en tratar de comprender lo ruso, verbigracia, y de asimilarse uno lo escandinavo. Lo que resulta no precisamente reprensible, sino lastimoso con plenitud, es llegar a Francia y no pasar de ahí. El colmo de estas desdichas es que talentos como el de Rubén Darío, y capacidades artísticas como la suya se contente de lo francés. . . . Es doloroso quedarse en el borde las formas. ("De lo exótico" 345)

> Intellectual poverty is the situation to which those who suppose that we South Americans depend exclusively on Spanish arts and sciences condemn us. The new people of the New World have a right to all the life of thought. There is no lack of patriotism or racial apostasy in trying to understand Russian, for example, and trying to absorb Scandinavian. What would not be precisely reprehensible, rather fully pitiful, would be to arrive at France and never go beyond there. The height of misfortune is that talents like Rubén Darío's, and artistic strengths like his, are satisfied with the French. . . . It is painful to remain within the limits of forms.

His criticism of Darío for mistaking France for the world opens a crack in the facade of *modernismo*'s cosmopolitan front, often seen by critics as solidly homogeneous in its opposition to all forms of cultural particularism. Sanín Cano is disappointed in Darío's modernism because, although Darío is willing to reject the self-absorption of nationalism and Latin Americanism, he is not inclined to take his cosmopolitan subjectivity beyond the borders of a French imaginary of aesthetic modernity.

Naturally, turning his back on Spain and expressing his lack of enthusiasm for a Pan-Latin cultural identity with Paris as its modernist capital cost Sanín Cano dearly and ensured his marginality in Latin American letters. Luis María Mora, a poet and contemporary of Sanín Cano, summarized the general view of Sanín Cano's dislocated space within the Colombian literary field at the turn of the century: "No ama la literatura sencilla, clara, transparente de los pueblos que se bañan en las ondas azules del Mediterráneo, sino que se embelesa en las lucubraciones oscuras de pensadores del Norte y en las figuras abstractas de los dramas escandinavos" (136) ("He does not love the simple, clear, transparent literature of the peoples who bathe themselves in the blue waves of the Mediterranean; rather he embellishes himself in the obscure lucubrations of the northern thinkers and in the abstract figures of the Scandinavian dramas").

Mora's harsh criticism reveals, on the one hand, the radical horizon of Sanín Cano's literary cosmopolitanism when compared to the narrowness of the *modernista*'s universalist *doxa*. On the other, it shows the threat that cosmopolitan subject positions posed to an intellectual field that tolerated only rather predictable forms of aesthetic cosmopolitanism, understood as the appropriation of a well-known European archive of names, tropes, and poetic genres. But when writers like Sanín Cano (and, at times, Gómez Carrillo) went beyond the limits of the familiar into markedly foreign and unexplored corners of world literature, they were condemned and deemed suspicious; cosmopolitanism was seen as symbolic treason, a perversion and a threat to the national foundation of the state in the European and Latin American *fin-de-siècle*.[47] In this sense, Martí's discomfort with Oscar Wilde's queerness is not all that different from Mora's view of Sanín Cano's trafficking in obscure and radically foreign cultural discourses (not Hispanic, French, or Italian) whose lack of transparency threatened the harmonic and transparent *Latin* constitution of Colombia.

The second dislocation of the Colombian and Latin American tradition that constitutes Sanín Cano's world literary critical discourse is the call to overcome local imaginaries (whether national or regional) when reading and writing literature, expressed most cogently in "De lo exótico." This polemical essay's cosmopolitan proposal has two nuclei: the rejection of national literature as an unproductive ideological matrix that writers and critics should discard, and the proposal to modernize "regiones estériles o aletargadas de su cerebro" (345) ("the sterile or lethargic regions of its mind"), like Latin America and other margins of the world, by expanding their literary subjectivities: "Ensachémoslos [nuestros gustos] en el tiempo y en el espacio" (345) ("Let us broaden [our tastes] in time and in space").

As I have explained above, "De lo exótico" can be considered a crucial if utterly overlooked precursor to Borges's seminal cosmopolitan essay, "El escritor argentino y la tradición," at least in the way it characterizes "the national" as an ineffective and artificial cultural epistemology: "El sentimiento de las nacionalidades . . . divide a las gentes en literaturas, lo mismo que si se tratara de hacer una clasificación de razas. Así han pasado al mercado de valores literarios las denominaciones, sin duda muy artificiales, de literatura francesa, alemana, rusa, escandinava, con que están llenas hoy las obras de crítica y hasta los periódicos" (335) ("The sentiment of the nationalities . . . divides the people in literatures, in the same way as if one were trying to classify them by races. Thus the denominations, surely artificial, that fill the critical works and even the magazines, denominations of French literature, German, Russian, Scandinavian, have passed to the market of literary values"). Although he avoids a polemic on the usefulness of the category of "race" (notwithstanding that everything in the essay points in the direction of a criticism of positivism's racial epistemologies), Sanín Cano censures the racial overtones of forms of European and Latin American literary criticism that adopted taxonomies oriented by the belief in the nation as an irreducible analytical unit. He explains that literature has always been produced in between cultures, through borrowings, imitations, and acts of pillage, that "los poetas de Roma crearon la literatura imitando a los griegos" ("the poets of Rome wrote literature imitating the Greeks"), and that even "Cervantes enriqueció su lengua agregándole todos de decir italianos que hoy son rematadamente castizos" (337) ("Cervantes enriched his language by adding Italian idioms that are considered utterly authentic"). Literature is an inherently transcultural institution, a window into the human soul: "Los modernos que dejan su tradición para asimilarse otras literaturas se proponen entender toda el alma humana" (343) ("The modern people that leave their tradition in order to absorb other literatures seek to understand all of the human soul"). In contrast, the insistence on viewing literary texts as part of an "obra nacional, genuina, libre de mácula extranjera" (338) ("national work, genuine, free of foreign blemishes") is a nationalist illusion, "un ofuscado amor patrio" (341) ("obfuscated patriotism").

His final coup in the systematic abasement of national literature as the master concept that structured the field of critical signification is the simple question: What does it mean "hacer obra nacional" ("to make a national work of art")? What does it take to be author of a text unequivocally identified with the national culture it is seen to emerge from? And he demands an answer: "que se nos diga si ello consiste en el asunto tratado, en la manera de tratarlo, en los autores más o menos servilmente imitados. Es justo que se nos diga, de una vez, si para ser uno autor nacional ha de tener ciertas cualidades del espíritu, aquellas, en efecto, que la gente reconoce como virtudes y atributos fundamentales del alma nacional, y que están como vinculadas en la raza" (338) ("that it be told to us if it consists of a subject matter, of the mode of representation, of the authors more or less slavishly imitated. It is crucial that we are told once and for all, if in order to be a national author one has to have certain qualities of the spirit, those that, in effect, the people recognize as fundamental virtues and attributes of the national soul, and that are somewhat linked to race"). By interrogating nation-bound aesthetics and listing the formulaic answers that often authorize them (the display of essentialized national themes or authorial virtues), Sanín Cano denaturalizes their hegemony in the Latin American literary field. Not only does he reject the nation's role as the organizing principle of cultural production, but in the essay's closing maneuver he radicalizes his antagonism with a conception of literary phenomena restricted to national imaginaries and articulates the cosmopolitan stance he is calling for as an approach to the indeterminate universality of literature.

If, in his first move, he defined the cosmopolitan horizon of a new Latin American attitude toward the literatures of the world as the mere negation of national determinations, he now argues that the only path for Latin American and Spanish writers to achieve the aesthetic modernity they crave is by attempting to "renovar sus sensaciones estudiando las que engendra una civilización distinta" (343) ("renew their sensations studying those that a distinct civilization has engendered"). He sees nationalism as a pathology that writers and critics need to overcome in order to escape the stagnation and sterility of their intellectual practices: "Ni las naciones, ni los individuos pierden nada con que un habitante de Australia y un raizal de Costa Rica, enfermos del mal de pensar, sientan vivamente las letras extranjeras y se asimilen parte del alma de otras razas. Vivificar regiones estériles o aletargadas de su cerebro debe ser . . . la preocupación trascendental del hombre de letras" (345) ("Neither nations nor individuals lose anything because an Australian resident and a Raizal person from Costa Rica, infected by the illness of thought, vividly sense foreign literatures and absorb part of the soul of other races. To vivify sterile or cerebrally lethargic regions should be the transcendental concern of the man of letters"). Sickly thoughts and sluggish brain functions: Sanín Cano prescribes an intense, sympathetic proximity with "las literaturas distintas de la literatura patria" (345) ("literatures different from the national literature"), or, better yet, an assimilation of their "soul" ("se asimilen parte del alma de otras razas") as a cure for this transatlantic intellectual *condition*. Latin American and Spanish writers should learn to become Other, to alienate themselves in order to identify with the nonidentical nature of a world literature defined by its difference from any given particular national identity.

What I find provocative and original in Sanín Cano's world literary demand is the articulation of literary cosmopolitanism as a question of, again, healing the self-inflicted maladies of isolation and backwardness but also as a matter of justice, humanity, and elegance, in other words, a question of politics, ethics, and aesthetics:

> Los ambientes diversos, los heredamientos acumulados en razas vigorosas les van dando a las letras savia rica, que algunos no se atreven a llamar sana. Sería injusticia no explorar una forma de arte nuevo solamente porque salió de una alma eslava. 'Ensanchemos nuestros gustos' dijo Lemaitre. . . . Ensachémoslos en el tiempo y en el espacio; no nos limitemos a una raza, aunque sea la nuestra, ni a una época histórica, ni a una tradición literaria. . . . Esta actitud de la inteligencia es más humana que la que proscriben lo extranjero. . . . Es más humana, y sin comparación, más elegante. (345–46)

> The diverse environments, the accumulated legacies of the vigorous races, are giving literature rich vitality that some do not dare to call healthy. It would be an injustice not to explore a new form of art only because it was product of a Slavic soul. "Let us broaden our tastes," Lemaitre said. . . . Let us broaden them in time and in space; let us not limit them to any race, not even our own, or to any historic period, or to any literary tradition. . . . This attitude of the intelligence is more human than that which outlaws the foreign. . . . It is more humane and incomparably more elegant.

Sanín Cano challenges Latin American and Spanish intellectuals and artists to expand their subjectivities, to be one with the world in all of its historical and global diversity. This larger, wider, and curious critical and aesthetic identity will open the region to vigorous and vital, indeed, modern literatures of the world, and this close contact will have the potential to reinvigorate and inject "savia rica . . . sana" into the cultural blood vessels of Colombia, Latin America, Spain, and any marginal formation that may suffer from a pathological attachment to their aesthetic particularities.

Sanín Cano attenuated his cosmopolitan universalism after 1893 as the national-Catholic feeling that prevailed after the constitutional reforms in Colombia began to wane, showing that the radical dismissal of national literature he articulated in "De lo exótico" should be understood in the context of that asphyxiating cultural climate. In the following years, especially during Rafael Reyes's moderate conservative administration from 1904 to 1909, Sanín Cano held several positions in the national government. In 1909, he went to London as the Colombian representative on the board of a British company that operated an emerald mine in the province of Boyacá; he stayed until 1927, long after his governmental appointment had expired. During this period, Sanín Cano gradually abandoned his universalist stance. The experiences of historical change in Bogotá and diasporic subjectivity in London were surely important to the development of this new critical agenda, but the crucial factor in Sanín Cano's world literary discourse was his acquaintance with the writings of Georg Brandes, the Danish literary critic and creator, between 1871 and 1917, of one of the most consistent comparative approaches to nineteenth-century European literatures as well as a rearticulation of the concept of world literature that revived a critical discourse that had been practically forgotten after Goethe's death.

If in 1893 the notion that organizes Sanín Cano's prescribed relation with the literatures of the world is Goethe's *Weltliteratur*, explicitly referred to in "De lo exótico" ("El arte es universal. Que lo fuese quería Goethe" (344) ("Art is universal. That was Goethe's wish"), by the early twentieth century he no longer affirmed that the path to aesthetic modernization depended on a new generation of writers and readers with a cosmopolitan perspective on the production of literature both at home and in the world. This new position is much closer to Brandes, who wrote in 1899: "I do not believe that nationality and cosmopolitanism are incompatible. The world literature of the future will be all the more interesting, the more strongly its national stamp is pronounced and the more distinctive it is, even if, as art, it also has its international side" ("World Literature" 147). Sanín Cano's shift from Goethe to Brandes, as the shorthand reference that structures a coherent world literary discourse, illuminates a change of heart regarding the status of national culture in artistic and critical practices: from the need to overcome overbearing national determinations (in 1827, Goethe told Eckermann that "national literature has not much meaning nowadays: the epoch of world literature is at hand"; Strich 349), to seeing them as a necessary dimension of a literary work's meaning and circulation.

Sanín Cano first encountered Brandes's essays when he moved to Bogotá from the province of Antioquía. In his autobiography he explains:

> Por los años 1888 y 1889 estaba yo suscrito a la *Deutsche Rundschau* de Berlín, y en uno de sus números tropecé con un originalísimo estudio sobre Emilio Zola, notable por la novedad del pensamiento y por su desusada libertad y simpatía. . . . Nunca había leído nada de Brandes. Ignoraba su nombre y los títulos de sus obras. Le escribí. . . . Mi carta le impresionó. Decía en la suya que había sido "rührt" (conmovido) por el hecho de que un español le escribiese desde Bogotá acerca de sus trabajos literarios. En el segundo tomo de sus memorias menciona el caso. (*De mi vida* 117–18)
>
> In the years 1888 and 1889 I subscribed to *Deutsche Rundschau* from Berlin, and in one of its numbers I stumbled across a quite original study about Emile Zola, notable for the novelty of its thought and for its unusual liberty and sympathy. . . . I had never read anything by Brandes. I did not know his name or the titles of his works. I wrote him. . . . My letter impressed him. He said in his response that he had been "rührt" (moved) by the fact that a Spanish person would write him from Bogotà about his literary works. In the second tome of his memoirs he mentioned the case.

In 1915, while living in London, Sanín Cano traveled to Sweden and Denmark on a special mission to recover a sizable sum of money for the Colombian government. He made a personal detour to visit Brandes in his house in Copenhagen. Their conversation lasted less than an hour, and even though Brandes agreed to see him merely out of courtesy—"Contestó una esquela de cita para las dos de la tarde, no sin advertir que la entrevista había de ser corta, porque estaba en esos días muy ocupado" ("He answered with an appointment card for two in the afternoon, not without warning that the interview had to be short, because he was very busy in those days")—their conversation (about British and German literature, the Great War, and French politics) was one of the most meaningful episodes of Sanín Cano's intellectual life, and he dedicates an entire chapter to it in his autobiography (*De mi vida* 117, 119). After that fateful afternoon in Copenhagen, Sanín Cano learned Danish, following Brandes's recommendation that he read his books in the original—"Volvió a decirme que si me interesaba su obra desde el punto de vista de la forma debía leerla en danés" (121) ("He replied that if I was interested in his work from the point of view of the form that I should read it in Danish")—and wrote three significant and thorough essays on the writing and intellectual environment of his hero: "Nietzsche y Brandes" (published in *La civilización manual y otros ensayos*, 1925), "Jorge Brandes" (*Indagaciones e imágenes*, 1926), and "Jorge Brandes, o el reinado de la inteligencia" ("Georg Brandes, or the Rule of Intelligence") (*Ensayos*, 1942).

Sanín Cano's profound interest in Brandes as a standard-bearer for modern literary criticism is in large part a result of the way in which the limits and potentialities of the Danish writer's cultural context reflected Sanín Cano's own conditions of discursive production: "El habría podido trasladarse a Berlín y ganarse allí la vida escribiendo en alemán. . . . Prefirió escribir en una bella lengua hablada solamente por tres millones y medio de seres pensantes" (*De mi vida* 121) ("He could have moved to Berlin and earned a living there writing in German. . . . He preferred to write in a beautiful language spoken by only three and a half million thinking beings"). The question of minor linguistic and literary traditions is central to the articulation of both of their critical discourses. Each insists in a meaningful way on the uneven relation that constitutes the marginality of certain literary languages, an insistence that serves the dual purpose of affirming the possibility of a cultural identity for marginal literatures and "the world" in which those identities are supposed to be formed. For Brandes and for the post–"De lo exótico" Sanín Cano at the turn of the century, cultural identity was shaped in a world structured by the opposition between hegemonic and subaltern national traditions. In this (inter)national field of differential relations, marginal conditions can be translated as political complaints articulated in the form of a minor identity defined by the lack of symbolic resources, and not necessarily by any counterhegemonic potential. Brandes, for instance, raises the question of minor literatures in relation to a world literary field conceived as a marketplace characterized by the unequal distribution of success and recognition:

> It is incontestable that writers of different countries and languages occupy enormously different positions where their chances of obtaining worldwide fame, or even a moderate degree of recognition, are concerned. The most favourably situated are the French writers. . . . When a writer has succeeded in France, he is known throughout the world. English and Germans, who can count on an immense public if they are successful, take second place. . . But whoever writes in Finnish, Hungarian, Swedish, Danish, Dutch, Greek or the like is obviously poorly placed in the universal struggle for fame. In this competition he lacks the major weapon, a language, which, for a writer, is almost everything. ("World Literature" 144)

Along similar lines, Sanín Cano reflects in a 1937 essay on the subaltern status of Spanish as a language for aesthetic pursuits, a situation that placed it in danger of losing its autonomy: "El mozo que formaba su estilo en la América española de 1830 a 1880 no armonizaba los encantos de la lengua española de que se servía diariamente para la expresión de sus necesidades y afectos con las formas excelentes y la retórica discreta de los escritores franceses en los cuales formaba su pensamiento. . . . En momento de nuestra evolución literaria corrió peligro nuestra lengua materna" ("Influencias" 271) ("The young man that formed his style in Spanish America from 1830 to 1880 did not harmonize the charms of the Spanish language that he used daily in service of the expression of his needs and affections with the excellent forms and discreet rhetoric of the French writers through whom he formed his thought. . . . In this moment of our literary evolution our mother tongue was in danger"). These comparative assessments of particular literatures based on uneven power relations must be understood in relation to the conviction that literature is, above all else, a window into the cultural history of a given nation. In his master oeuvre, *Main Currents in Nineteenth-Century Literature* (six volumes published between 1872 and 1890), Brandes explains—in the markedly historicist terms he acquired through his systematic study of Hegel's philosophy of history—that the task of the literary critic is to make literature speak to the historical context it emerges from:[48] "Literary history is, in its profoundest significance, psychology, the study, the history of the soul. A book which belongs to the literature of a nation, be it romance, drama, or historical work, is a gallery of character portraits, a storehouse of feelings and thoughts. . . . The more remarkable and at the same time representative the characters, so much the greater is the historical value of the book, so much the more clearly does it reveal to us what was really happening in men's minds in a given country at a given period" (*Emigrant Literature* viii). Sanín Cano, having abandoned the stance he had assumed in "De lo exótico," adopted Brandes's nation-bound critical discourse. In 1944, he wrote a book entirely dedicated to Colombian literature—something that would have been inconceivable for him in 1893—where he echoes the Danish intellectual: "Las obras literarias de un pueblo o de una nación son uno de los testimonios más dignos de crédito sobre el significado histórico de la nación o la raza productora de estas obras" (*Letras colombianas* 13) ("The literary works of a people or of a nation are one of the testimonies most worthy of credit about the historical significance of the nation or race that produced these works"). Similarly, he wrote elsewhere that "es verdad adquirida en el estudio comparativo de las literaturas que toda obra de mérito debe tener hondas raíces en el ambiente físico, en la patria espiritual del autor" ("¿Existe la literatura hispanoamericana?" 284) ("it is a truth acquired in the comparative study of the literatures that every work of worth should have deep roots in the physical environment, in the spiritual homeland of the author").

Sanín Cano's world literature now had an entirely different configuration. Instead of the *world* as a globe of aesthetic difference whose unity and universality was defined in opposition to Latin America's banal provincial particularism, it had the form of an aggregate of national literatures that contributed their cultural and aesthetic difference to the totality of the system. If minor literatures could not compete on the uneven global playing field where established traditions reproduce their privileged positions on the backs of consolidated institutions and extended hegemonic consent, Brandes suggested a different account of the place of minor literatures in world literature to Sanín Cano. If the contours of this atlas were drawn from critical values oriented by the global readership and circulation of a given text, then the hegemonic relation between the powerful and the marginal remained untouched. But if the map was designed in accordance with a cosmopolitan (or rather, *cosmonational*) appreciation of the sociocultural singularity expressed in works emerging from the different nations of the world, minor and major literatures now stood on equal grounds, since their value was measured by the potential to make unique but formally equal contributions to the global whole.

Brandes's formalist conception of world literature (as a senate in which each state is represented by a member expressing its differential cultural and ethical life—what Hegel called *Sittlichkeit*) serves minor literatures well. Danish literature will be a meaningful member of this world parliament of letters, not by experimenting with aesthetic forms, literary strategies, and tropes believed to be universal, but by forging a literature of plots, tones, and forms that deliberately and intensely express its own cultural particularity. In this sense, Denmark (or Colombia, or Ibero-America in general) will not be hostage to feelings of inferiority vis-à-vis France or England. The task of the critic, then, will be to discover and sort structural "currents" (as the title of Brandes's multivolume master oeuvre indicates) underlying "the chaos of hundreds of thousands of books in many languages" (*Young Germany* 411), in order to recognize moments of perfect identity between specific aesthetic forms and the singular historical experience of one nation or another. Brandes (and, to a lesser extent, Sanín Cano) organizes the literatures of the world, not so much as a world literature, but as an (inter)national literary system with special emphasis on cultural/national diversity, rather than common sensibilities, estrangements, and symbolic transactions that articulate its contingent unity: "The comparative view possesses the double advantage of bringing foreign literature so near to us that we can assimilate it, and of removing our own until we are enabled to see it in its true perspective. . . . The different nations have hitherto stood so remote from each other, as far as literature is concerned, that they have only to a very limited extent been able to benefit by each other's production" (*Emigrant Literature* vii–viii). But what remains of Sanín Cano's cosmopolitanism after the 1890s? Does he find any hints of a cosmopolitan outlook in Brandes's literary history, where the particularity of the national context of production determines the meaning of a text and the possibility of entering into a relation of a comparative nature? Sanín Cano turns his attention to the critic's intellectual practice, to highlight the fact that there, rather than in his discourse, resides the cosmopolitan task of promoting understanding, communication, and justice across global difference; the cosmopolitan potential of criticism resides in the act of reading Literature, and not necessarily in what the critic reads in each literary work. In a lecture he gave in Buenos Aires in 1925, Sanín Cano introduces Brandes as an intellectual model to be imitated:

> Es menos conocido en América de lo que debiera ser. . . . Representa un anhelo general de la especie humana, un anhelo desvirtuado por la incomprensión, por el juego sombrío de tahúres fulleros en el destino de los pueblos. . . . Jorge Brandes ha usado de toda su inteligencia, de su inexorable voluntad y de su excepcional perspicacia para promover el entendimiento de unos pueblos con otros. Es internacional en el sentido generoso de la palabra, porque presume que hay ciertas nociones generales de justicia, de humanidad, de cortesía, comunes a todos los pueblos cultos. ("Jorge Brandes" 193–94)

> He's less well known in America than he should be. . . . He represents a general desire of the human species, a desire distorted by incomprehension, by the shady play of cheating gamblers in the destiny of peoples. . . . Jorge Brandes has used all his intelligence, his inexorable will, and his exceptional insight to promote the understanding of some peoples through others. He is international in the generous sense of the word, because he presumes that there are certain general notions of justice, of humanity, of courtesy, notions common to all the cultivated peoples.

Sanín Cano seems to be addressing the cosmopolitan intentions behind Brandes's critical enterprise, but how can he judge intentions? What does it mean to be "international in the generous meaning of the word"? If Brandes was concerned with the national mediation in the comparative analysis of literary works, and if this illuminates the gap between the international and the cosmopolitan, Sanín Cano tries to illuminate the cosmopolitan purpose behind Brandes's international comparative criticism: its cosmopolitan value will be found, not in its enunciated statements, but rather in the function that it fulfills. This explanation helps Sanín Cano to legitimize the distance from his position in "De lo exótico"—the call on Latin American intellectuals to read the wide world of aesthetic elective affinities that was unknown to conservative writers too focused on their Hispanic heritage and to modernizing poets too obsessed with French determinations of nineteenth-century modernity. It will also authorize his adoption of a comparative methodology after 1900—with Brandes as its perfect European model—meant to establish relations and differences between, *inter*, national literatures, never undermining the postulated homogeneity of the nation as the indivisible unit of a conception of comparative literature that had been established in 1797, when Herder published his "Results of the Comparison of Different People's Poetry in Ancient and Modern Times."

From world literature to comparative (inter)national literature: the trajectory of Sanín Cano's cosmopolitan comparative literature runs from Goethe to Brandes, not necessarily as a function of political changes in the Colombian state, or the centrality of national categories in the European imagination before and after the Great War, but perhaps as a result of the circumstances of his biographical dislocations. Rafael Gutiérrez Girardot wrote that "la crítica de Sanín Cano propuso a Colombia las condiciones para que echara una mirada al mundo, adaptara los instrumentos para hacerlo y saliera, al fin, de su pacato aislamiento" (502) ("Sanín Cano's critique proposed to Colombia the conditions through which it could look out at the world, adapt instruments to do so, and, finally, leave its timid isolation"). This is certainly the underlying idea that bridges the gap between cosmopolitan and international comparativism: the desire to escape the smothering isolation of the Latin American ideology of Latin Americanism.

CHAPTER 4

Darío's French Universal and the World Mappings of *Modernismo*

Following the 1888 publication of *Azul* (*Azure*) in Santiago de Chile—where he had been living and publishing since 1885—many *modernistas* considered Rubén Darío their guide to navigating the waters of aesthetic modernization. For most critics his name has become the signifier of *modernismo*. Because of their metonymic function for Latin American modernism, his poetry and chronicles as well as his diasporic persona are central to critical discussions of the cosmopolitan nature of *modernismo*.[1] A universalist drive coexists in Darío's writing with particularistic reterritorializations—appropriations, translations, and local reinscriptions of Latin America's cultural difference, as well as the postulation of a Pan-Hispanic tradition, as in the significative "Salutación del optimista" ("Salutation of the Optimist"), "Inclitas razas ubérrimas, sangre de Hispania fecunda" (233) ("Illustrious, prolific races, blood of fecund Hispania"; Aching, *Politics* 75).[2] In the previous chapter I proposed that, notwithstanding their importance, universalist and world literary drives were second to a predominant particularistic-regionalist discourse within the *modernista* imaginary. In Darío's writing, however, these proportions are somewhat altered in favor of the universal, especially in the period between 1893 and 1905. This period begins with Darío's arrival in Buenos Aires and the writing of the poems and essays that will comprise *Prosas profanas* (*Profane Hymns*) (1896) and *Los raros* (1896), and it ends with the publication in Madrid of *Cantos de vida y esperanza* (*Songs of Life and Hope*) in

1905, in which he effectively repositions himself in relation to his past ("Yo soy aquel que ayer nomás decía" [231] ["I am the one who just yesterday spoke"; *Selected Poems* 161]), assesses the opening verse of the book's first poem) and closes the first chapter of his cyclothymic relation with Paris and French culture. During this period Darío invented an expansive poetic subjectivity that can be described as cosmopolitan, even if that cosmopolitanism needs to be qualified.

Darío's poetic subject is open to the world and its strangeness: "He expresado lo expresable de mi alma y he querido penetrar en el alma de los demás, y hundirme en la vasta alma universal. He apartado asimismo, como quiere Schopenhauer, mi individualidad del resto del mundo, y he visto con desinterés lo que a mí yo parece extraño, para convencerme de que nada es extraño a mi yo" ("Dilucidaciones" 274) ("I have expressed what is expressible in my soul and I have wanted to penetrate the souls of others, and sink in the great universal soul. I have also, as Schopenhauer would have it, distanced my individuality from the rest of the world, and have impartially seen what to my 'I' seems strange, in order to convince myself that nothing is strange to my 'I'"), he writes in "Dilucidaciones" ("Elucidations"), the preface to *El canto errante* (*The Wandering Song*) (1907).[3] Sylvia Molloy has characterized this poetic subject as "un yo voraz que, al proyectarse en lugares y personas, los despoja de sus características propias para transformarlos en aspectos de ese yo" ("Conciencia" 449) ("A voracious 'I' that, as it projects itself into places and people, strips them of their own characteristics to turn them into aspects of that 'I'"). Molloy does not link the voracious eagerness of this poetic "I" to local or global objects and places, but her conceptualization opens up the possibility of metaphorizing cosmopolitan desire in the figure of hunger for the world. This subject becomes universal when he makes the world his, when he—to use Molloy's image—devours it. If strangeness is the signifier of Otherness, this subject familiarizes the world to the point of eradicating the experience of difference; only a cosmopolitan subject can affirm that "nada es extraño a mi yo." But, as we shall see below, these notions of the world and the strangeness in it need to be interrogated. For Darío, the world is not a plural universe of multiplied difference but rather a uniformly French formation, or a world seen through a French looking glass, divided into modern and premodern camps. Darío's passion is for a controlled strangeness that does not destabilize the modernist subject in formation. Instead of exploring the cosmopolitan questions and problems behind Darío's enthusiasm for all things French, critics have tended to view it as a form of neocolonial subjection, to the point that, from that perspective, cosmopolitanism becomes a mask for colonial mimicry. This misunderstanding has its origins in discussions of *modernismo* contemporary to Darío's literary production and is crystallized in a polemical exchange between him and José Rodó.

Rodó criticized "la poesía enteramente antiamericanista de Darío" ("Darío's entirely anti-American poetry"), complaining that the poet "evoca siempre, como por una obsesión tirana de su numen, el *genius loci* de la escenografía de París" (*Obras completas* 2: 74) ("always evokes, as if by a tyrannical obsession of his muse, the *genius loci* of Parisian scenery"). Because of its excessive recurrence to European marquises, Greek mythological figures, and Japonaiseries, Rodó believed that Darío's strain of *modernismo* suffered from "trivialidad y frivolidad literarias: una tendencia que debe repugnar a todo espíritu que busque ante todo, en literatura, motivos para sentir y pensar" (qtd. in Aching, *Politics* 8) ("literary triviality and frivolity: a tendency that has to repudiate every spirit that seeks above all, in literature, motives for feeling and thinking"). Two years later, Rodó wrote *Rubén Darío, su personalidad literaria*, a book that reviews Darío's poetic innovations, particularly those of *Prosas profanas*, published in Buenos Aires in 1896. Although the book is full of praise, Rodó cannot hide his uneasiness with Darío's lack of attachment to Latin America: "Indudablemente, Darío no es el poeta de América. ¿Necesitaré decir que no es para señalar en ello una condición de inferioridad literaria?" (5). ("Certainly, Darío is not the poet of America. Must I say that this is not a condition of literary inferiority?"). Rodó characterizes Darío's aesthetics as an "americanismo en los accesorios; pero aun en los accesorios, dudo que nos pertenezca colectivamente el sutil y delicado artista de que hablo. Ignoro si un espíritu zahorí podría descubrir, en tal o cual composición de Rubén Darío, una nota fugaz, un instantáneo reflejo, un sordo rumor, por los que se reconociera en él al poeta americano de las cálidas latitudes y aun al sucesor de los misteriosos artistas de Utatlán y Palenke" (7) ("Americanism in the accessories; but even in the accessories, I doubt that this subtle and delicate artist belongs to us collectively. I do not know if a clairvoyant spirit could discover, in one or another of Rubén Darío's compositions, a fleeting note, an instantaneous reflection, a low murmur, by which we could recognize the American poet of the warm regions and even the successor to the mysterious artists of Utatlan and Palenque"). Rodó claims that he is not making a value judgment but merely describing Darío's aesthetics.

His portrayal of Darío as an uprooted poet, detached from a Latin American cultural particularity that can be linked directly to an indigenous past (with which Rodó's work also had no connection), however, is hardly neutral. It is Darío who writes about "Palenke y Utatlán" in "Palabras liminares" ("Preliminary Words"), the preface to *Prosas profanas*, where he situates his own poetry in both pre-Hispanic and modern genealogies: "(Si hay poesía en nuestra América, ella está en las cosas viejas: en Palenke y Utatlán, en el indio legendario, y en el inca sensual y fino, y en el gran Moctezuma de la silla de oro. Lo demás es tuyo, demócrata Walt Whitman)" (187) ("([If there is poetry in our America, it is in the old things, in Palenque and Utatlan, in the legendary Indian, and in the courtly and sensual Inca, and in the great Moctezuma on the golden seat. The rest is yours, democratic Walt Whitman]"; *Selected Poems* 113). These parentheses follow a question: "¿Hay en mi sangre alguna gota de sangre de África, o de indio chorotega o nagrandano?" (187) ("Is there in my blood a drop of blood from Africa or of Chorotega or Nagrandan Indian?"; *Selected Poems* 113). And an answer: "Pudiera ser, a despecho de mis manos de marqués; mas he aquí que veréis en mis versos princesas, reyes, cosas imperiales, visiones de países lejanos o imposibles: ¡qué queréis!, yo detesto la vida y el tiempo en que me tocó nacer" (187) ("It may well be, despite my hands of a Marquis; yet note here that you will not see in my verses princesses, kings, imperial matters, visions of lands remote or impossible: what do you expect? I detest the life and times into which I had to be born"; *Selected Poems* 113).

Rodó reads Darío's acknowledgment that, while his veins may contain African and indigenous blood, he still hates his life and times as an admission of his exteriority to a *Latin Americanist* Latin American tradition. Darío does not reject the idea of continuity from the precolonial past to the cultural present (in fact, in the poem "Caupolicán" from *Azul*, he constructed the heroic figure of a warrior whose body was part Greek, part biblical, and part Mapuche), but he does express uneasiness in relation to it. In "Palabras liminares," for instance, the figure of Walt Whitman breaks the linear, smooth continuity that Rodó demands from the poet who is the supposed "sucesor de los misteriosos artistas de Utatlán y Palenke." Darío does not repudiate a potential Latin American affiliation, but he decidedly places himself outside "la vida y el tiempo en que me tocó nacer."[4] "The life and times into which I had to be born" should be interpreted, not simply as "Latin America," but rather as a certain notion of Latin American culture, conceived as a formation determined by a cultural particularity defined a priori, outside a concrete historical situation. To Rodó, that particularity is marked by an indigenous presence, which is difficult for Darío in 1896 to reconcile with the modernizing impulse of his cosmopolitan subjectivity and his desire to be free of the cultural particularity that he detests. When Darío declares, "Detesto la vida y el tiempo en que me tocó nacer," he sets up the discursive conditions for a cosmopolitan subject position; this subject sees the possibility of an emancipating modernization in the horizon of universality.[5] But, as I have already advanced, Darío's universal, however, is a limited, particularized universal, a French universal. One of my goals in this chapter is to interrogate this intersection between Darío's Francophilia and his cosmopolitan desire (as Rodó and others accuse him) to de–Latin Americanize his literature. In other words, what is the (universalist, particularistic) meaning of Darío's Francophilia? My second goal is to trace a specific discourse on world literature in Darío's critical writing, within or without the French determination.

WHAT WORLD, WHOSE FRANCE?

Before Rodó, and perhaps more insightful in his comments, the Spaniard Juan Valera was the first to put a finger on what many saw as the lack of a Latin American flavor in Darío's poetry, indicting his Francophilia as a synonym for cosmopolitanism. After reading *Azul*, Valera wrote a few letters to Darío—later compiled in his *Cartas americanas*—that summed up his views on Darío's *modernista* poetic practice: "Si el libro, impreso en Valparaíso, en este año de 1888, no estuviese en muy buen castellano, lo mismo pudiera ser de un autor francés, que de un italiano, que de un turco o un griego. El libro está impregnado de espíritu cosmopolita. Hasta el nombre y apellido del autor, verdaderos o contrahechos y fingidos, hacen que el cosmopolitismo resalte más. Rubén es judáico, y persa es Darío: de suerte que, por los nombres, no parece sino que Ud. quiere ser o es todos los pueblos, castas y tribus" (215–16) ("If the book, published in Valparaíso in this year of 1888, were not written in very good Castilian, it might as well be by a French author, or an Italian, or a Turkish or Greek one. The book is impregnated with cosmopolitan spirit. The author's first and last names, real or invented and fake, make its cosmopolitanism stand out even more. Rubén is Jewish, and Darío, Persian: so that, from your names, it seems as though you want to be or are all people, castes and tribes"). According to Valera, Darío "no tiene carácter nacional" (218) ("has no national character"), and he manifests his cosmopolitanism "no diré exclusivamente, pero sí principalmente a través de libros franceses" (251) ("I will not say exclusively, but I will say principally through French books"). Valera says, "Aplaudiría muchísimo más, si con esa ilustración francesa que en usted hay se combinase la inglesa, la alemana, la italiana y ¿por qué no la española también?" (236) ("I would applaud far louder if, together with your French Enlightenment, you mixed in English, German, Italian and—why not?—Spanish, too"). Perhaps because of his patronizing attitude toward Latin American writers, he perceives that Darío's cosmopolitanism sees the universe from a French standpoint, or, rather, from a Latin American conception of the French ontological privilege within the order of modernity. In spite of Valera's general condescension toward Darío in diagnosing the Latin American's "galicismo de la mente" (216) ("mental Gallicism") (as we will see, in a debate with Paul Groussac, Darío will take up the challenge and turn it on its head), Valera is a trenchant observer of the cultural politics of Darío's aesthetics. He demands a wider span of international materials (international and not universal, because Valera sees world literature as nationally organized), including those from the peninsula. He is bothered by the place of the French, not as another particular world culture, but as a mentality, a cultural subjectivity, a lens through which the world is perceived and captured—a role that he believes Spain should fulfill for the new generation of Latin American writers. In "Palabras liminares," Darío responds to Valera:

> El abuelo español de barba blanca me señala una serie de retratos ilustres: "Éste—me dice—es el gran don Miguel de Cervantes Saavedra, genio y manco; éste es Lope de Vega, éste Garcilaso, éste Quintana." Yo le pregunto por el noble Gracián, por Teresa la Santa, por el bravo Góngora y el más fuerte de todos, don Francisco de Quevedo y Villegas. Después exclamo: "¡Shakespeare! ¡Dante! ¡Hugo . . . ! (Y en mi interior: ¡Verlaine . . . !)"
>
> Luego, al despedirme: "—Abuelo, preciso es decíroslo: mi esposa es de mi tierra; mi querida, de París." (187)

> My white-whiskered Spanish grandfather points out to me a series of illustrious portraits: "This one," he tells me, "is

> the great Don Miguel de Cervantes Saavedra, a one-armed genius; this one is Lope de Vega, this one Garcilaso, this one Quintana." I ask him about the noble Gracián, about Theresa the Saint, about the courageous Góngora and the strongest of all, Don Francisco de Quevedo y Villegas. Then I exclaim: Shakespeare! Dante! Hugo . . . ! (And in my heart: Verlaine . . . !)
>
> Later, when saying good-bye: "Grandfather, I have to tell you: the woman I married is from my native land; the woman I love, from Paris." (*Selected Poems* 113)

With these "Palabras liminares," written in 1896, eight years after he included Valera's condescending letter as a preface to *Azul*, Darío answers Valera, his venerable but ill-tempered Spanish grandfather whose expectations correspond to an era that predates Darío's modernist literary universe, which credits Western classics (including Hispanic milestones) but privileges a French-symbolist sensibility.

Gracián, Teresa de Ávila, Góngora, Quevedo, Shakespeare, Dante, Hugo, and above them all, Verlaine. If the presence of the Spanish writers represents, for Darío, a linguistic tradition that needs to be reconfigured from the Latin American, *modernista* perspective; if Shakespeare and Dante do not have a substantive place in his aesthetic imaginary; and if Verlaine, the name he yells out with true (interior) desire, constitutes the center of his aesthetic militancy, the question jumps from the page: Is it possible to speak of a strict concept of world literature in Darío? Is he interested, as Martí demands and as I discussed in chapter 3, in the exploration of "diversas literaturas"? In other words, is there a world literary discourse, or a world literary practice, in a critical view so inclined toward a particular, decadentist, symbolist, *maudit* (cursed) canon?

When it comes to Darío and his vast, heterogeneous, changing textuality, it is unwise to generalize. On the one hand, Darío conceptualizes and performs Latin American literature's uneven relation with the universality he assigns to western European culture in *Prosas profanas* and *Los raros* and many of the *crónicas* he wrote from Spain, Paris, Tangier, Italy, Germany, Vienna, and Budapest between 1899 and 1901, later collected in *España contemporánea* (*Contemporary Spain*) (1901), *Peregrinaciones* (*Pilgrimages*) (1901), and *Tierras solares* (*Solar Lands*) (1904). On the other, *Cantos de vida y esperanza* (1905) and *El canto errante* (1907) present a conspicuous particularism that features

Pan-Hispanic articulations, racial vindications, and the exaltation of national states, their iconographies, and many of their political and intellectual leaders. The problem with much of the critical tradition focused on *modernismo* is its characterization of all of Darío's poetry as the coherent center of post-Martí *modernismo*, dehistoricizing both the *modernista* formation and Darío's heterogeneous and ever-changing writing. To avoid these empty generalizations, I want to explore the question of world literary discourse in Darío by historicizing both the writer and the aesthetic formation.

I will argue that from 1893 to 1905 (I have already addressed *Azul*'s initial transatlantic reception in 1888), Darío posits the universal potential of his own literature to inscribe itself—alongside *modernismo*—as a structural function of the universality of French culture that should be understood in relation to the (French-mediated) global spread of modernist aesthetics in the last quarter of the nineteenth century. Darío's restricted and narrow world literature, then, points not to the world but rather to an extra–Latin American promise. Instead of an infinite set of aesthetic possibilities, in his discursive practice *world* is a *Weltanschauung*, a worldview, an image whose putative universality results from a creative act determined by the particularity of the cultural location from which it is produced and perceived. This world is a *captured world*, a particular aesthetic space from which various literatures are apprehended. The fact that Darío occupies a French symbolist site—that is, the fact that he inhabits the signifier of aesthetic modernity—introduces a temporal dimension to the notion of world literature: modern and modernist predication upon world literature, because, for Darío, literature—the universal form at the core of world literary practices and discourses—is modern literature.[6] Literature is not all of the literature in the world but literature worth reading, the kind of literature that disrupts tradition to introduce a new sensibility that enables the experience of the (modern) world. He finds these potentialities in French symbolist texts, as well as certain other aesthetic discourses seen through a French symbolist style.[7]

Again: If Darío's is a French world, is it possible to speak with some rigor of a world literary discourse in his literature? And is there a world in Darío or just the hegemony of a French culture that views the globe as the site of its *mission civilisatrice*? Even if Darío's world does not extend far beyond Spain, France, and western Europe (because his Japonaiseries and Chinoiseries are not attempts to reach Japan or China but rather exoticist representations at the heart of nineteenth-century

French culture), he sees that narrow map as the extent of a world that is universal because it is devoid of marks of cultural particularity or Latin American local color.[8] What Darío cannot see—what his modernist subjectivity prevents him from seeing—is that his world is imprinted with some of the most salient markers of French culture.

The aesthetic and critical practice of a world literary discourse in Darío is determined by the French inflection of his notion of universality. His universal Francophilia, I believe, must be read as the horizon of *modernismo*'s worldly imagination. The fact that "France" was the signifier of choice is already a commonplace in Latin American cultural history, and it suffices to say that the semantic privilege that "France" enjoyed from the Hispanic colonies' independence until the end of World War II should be understood as a double transatlantic operation. On the one hand, France—as a cultural formation that spoke the language of modernity in the most compelling terms—represented its particularity as identical to the universality of modernity (for example, Victor Hugo wrote that "[Paris] falls drop by drop upon humanity and everywhere leaves its impression"; qtd. in Casanova 89). On the other, Latin American intellectuals affirmed and reproduced this cultural truism without questioning its essentialist premises. For Darío (and most *modernistas*), French poetry was always already modern and universal, and its modern-universal nature did not need to be questioned . His examples of modern universality are Hugo and Verlaine. Darío wrote in "El Dios Hugo y la América Latina" ("Hugo the God and Latin America") that Hugo had conquered the globe: "No ha vuelto a verse después de Hugo, un espíritu de poder tan universal. El conquistó el globo. Su nombre llegó luminoso a todas partes, casi como entre un soplo legendario. . . . En China, en la India, en países lejanos de extrañas civilizaciones y razas distintas, la gloria del poeta hizo vibrar algunos rayos" (116–17) ("Since Hugo there has not been a spirit of such universal power. He conquered the globe. His name arrived shining to all parts, as if on a legendary breeze. . . . In China, in India, in faraway countries of strange civilizations and different races, the poet's glory made rays vibrate"). And he speaks of Verlaine as being "el más grande de todos los poetas de este siglo" (*Raros* 55) ("among the greatest poets of this century"; *Selected Writings* 414), someone whose "obra está esparcida sobre la faz del mundo" (*Raros* 55) ("work is scattered over the face of the earth"; *Selected Writings* 414). Darío does not hesitate to identify Verlaine with the universality of *humanity:* "Verlaine fue un hijo desdichado de Adán, en el que la herencia paterna apareció con mayor fuerza que en los demás" (*Raros* 53) ("Verlaine was a wretched son of Adam in whom the paternal bequest was stronger than in other men"; *Selected Writings* 412). Only a French poet (like Verlaine, and with him, sometimes above him, Hugo), could naturally, organically, overcome his aesthetic and cultural particularity to become identical to the all-encompassing world-modernism within which Darío would like to inscribe his own writing.[9]

This is the challenge Darío set for himself: How can I be modern? How can I acquire the universal attributes of modernity when I am not French, and therefore, not essentially, naturally, always already modern? "France" (and "Paris" even more so) was key to a Latin American discourse on the experience of modernity, a discourse of fullness opposed to his perception of a Latin America marked by a lack of modernity; "France" and "Paris" were the paradisiacal places of plenitude where a modern/modernist subjectivity could be realized:

> Yo soñaba con París desde niño, a punto de que cuando hacía mis oraciones rogaba a Dios que no me dejase morir sin conocer París. París era para mí como un paraíso en donde se respirase la esencia de la felicidad sobre la tierra. Era la Ciudad del Arte, de la Belleza y de la Gloria; y, sobre todo, era la capital del Amor, el reino del Ensueño. E iba yo a conocer París, a realizar la mayor ansia de mi vida. Y cuando en la estación de Saint Lazare, pisé tierra parisiense, creí hallar suelo sagrado. (*Autobiografía* 69)

> I had dreamed of Paris since I was a boy, so much that when I said my prayers I begged God not to let me die without seeing Paris. Paris was for me like a paradise where you could breathe the essence of happiness on Earth. It was the City of Art, of Beauty and of Glory; and above all, it was the capital of Love, the kingdom of Dreams. And I was going to go to Paris, to fulfill my life's greatest desire. And when I walked on Parisian ground in Saint Lazare Station, I believed I had found sacred ground.

Even if "peu d'Hispano-Américains ont chanté, comme Rubén Darío—sur tous les tons, de toutes les manières—leur amour de la France" (Molloy, *Diffusion* 33) ("few Hispanic-Americans have sung, like Rubén Darío—in every tone and all manners—their love for France"), he was not alone in feeling the allure of Paris. Paris and French culture were at the center of the world imaginary mappings of some of the most important Latin American writers through the 1950s (Schwartz, *Writing Paris*). Sarmiento expressed his excitation and anxieties as he approached the shores of France for the first time in 1846: "Las costas de Francia se diseñaron por fin en el lejano horizonte. . . . Saltábame el corazón al acercarnos a tierra, y mis manos recorrían sin meditación los botones del vestido, estirando el frac, palpando el nudo de la corbata, enderezando los cuellos de la camisa, como cuando el enamorado novel va a presentarse ante las damas" (*Viajes* 94) ("The French coast could finally be seen on the distant horizon. . . . My heart pounded as we approached land, and my hands moved unthinkingly across the buttons of my clothes, stretching my jacket, touching the knot of my tie, straightening the collar of my shirt, as when an inexperienced lover introduces himself to a woman"). When faced with the modern plenitude that Paris and French culture represented, Darío becomes the adoring child who worships the city of all modern saints, and Sarmiento becomes the lover lost in his desire to surrender to the will of his loved one. Their self-figurations are portraits of *subjects subjected* to the modern sovereignty of Paris.

The postulation of France's universality can be read in Darío's poetry beginning with *Azul* in that he appropriates French poetry, French symbolist tropes and topics, and the French language as the signifying horizon for *any* attempt at aesthetic modernization. For Darío, French culture is universally modern (its particularity is identical to the universality of modernity), and the universal can be named only in French, or at least through a French imaginary. This is true in *Azul*, but between 1893 and 1900, between his first trip to Paris (immediately before he moved from Santiago to Buenos Aires) and his return to stay, Darío articulated and reproduced the universality of France as the necessary signifying condition of a new Latin American literary and cultural practice. The essay on Verlaine from *Los raros* (published in *La Nación* in 1896, a few months before its inclusion in the book) cited above is very telling in this regard. While many other texts could also be cited, one of the most interesting is a rare chronicle, "La fiesta de Francia" ("French Holiday") (published on July 14, 1898, in *La Nación*), that has never been critically analyzed, perhaps because it was reprinted only once, in the 1917 Mundo Latino edition of Darío's *Obras completas* (*Complete Works*).

Darío's *crónicas* have an unmistakable style that is part reportage, part poetic essay, and part programmatic declaration of aesthetic principles, and this one, commemorating the 109th anniversary of the storming of the Bastille, is no different. Darío writes as if he were reporting from France; only in the last two paragraphs does he reveal that *la fiesta de Francia* took place in Buenos Aires, at the French Embassy and in the street outside. He artfully avoids adverbs of place, the deictics that would indicate whether he wrote from *here* or *there*. It is only at the end that he admits to being *here* ("fueron anoche los franceses de Buenos Aires, a saludar a su ministro, a sus diarios, a su club. Pues *aquí* en la República Argentina hay también un pedazo de Francia" (129, emphasis mine) ("last night the French residents of Buenos Aires went to see their minister, their newspapers, their clubs. Because *here* in the Argentine Republic there is also a piece of France"), rather than *there* ("*allá* en París, *allá* en Francia entera, hierve el inmenso entusiasmo" [131, emphasis mine] ["*there* in Paris, *there* in all of France, there is immense enthusiasm"]). In this overlooked *crónica*, Darío playfully articulates his interstitial cultural location—the ambiguous and unstable gap between a Latin American *here* and a Parisian *there*. His aesthetic cosmopolitanism emerges from his overconfident conviction that, as he wrote in "Los colores del estandarte" ("The Colors of the Standard"), he can bridge the gap between these discursive spaces, "pensando en francés y escribiendo en castellano . . . publiqué el pequeño libro que iniciaría el actual movimiento literario Americano" (162) ("thinking in French and writing in Castillian . . . I published the little book that was to begin the current Latin American literary movement"; *Selected Writings* 485).

France is not another particular culture, or even a cultural *primus inter pares*; it is the linguistic and cultural body of the universal itself, the condition of possibility of culture as humanity's shared patrimony. In "La fiesta de Francia," Darío asks the question of France's universality—"¿Cuál es el secreto de que Francia sea amada de todos los corazones, saludada por todas las almas?" (123) ("What is the secret that makes France loved by all hearts, saluted by all souls?")—and finds the answer in its filiation with a genealogy of modern culture that dates back to the classical world: "El áureo París derrama sobre el orbe el antiguo reflejo que brotaba de la Atenas marmoreal. . . . El idioma de Francia es el nuevo latín de los sacerdocios ideales y selectos, y en él resuenan armoniosamente las salutaciones a la inmortal Esperanza y al Ideal eterno" (123) ("Golden Paris scatters the ancient reflection that sprung from marble Athens across the globe. . . . The French language is the new Latin of the ideal and select priests, and in it the greetings to immortal Hope and the eternal Ideal resound harmoniously"). At the same time, he identifies the French Revolution—the event his *crónica* celebrates—as the epicenter of a universally desired modernity:

> A Europa toda, a Oriente, al continente nuestro, el fuego de la vasta hoguera de la Revolución ha llevado una parte de su resplandor. Parece que algo del alma de todas las naciones hubiese salido libre de la bastilla en el día siguiente de su asalto. . . . El mongol, el abisinio, el persa, el descendiente del inca, el cacique, no hay quien, por bárbaro o ignorado, no alimente el gran deseo de contemplar la ciudad soñada. París es el paraíso de la vida, Francia es el país de la Primavera y del Gozo para todos los humanos. (124–26)
>
> The flames of the Revolution's vast bonfire have brought a piece of its brilliance to all of Europe, to the Orient, to our continent. It seems that something of the soul of all nations was freed from the Bastille on the day after its assault. . . . The Mongolian, the Abyssinian, the Persian, the descendant of the Inca, the Indian chief, there is no one, however barbarian or ignorant, who does not cultivate the great desire to contemplate the imagined city. Paris is the paradise of life, France is the country of Spring and Joy for all humans.

Beyond its global political echoes, Darío sees the French Revolution as the event that triggers aesthetic desire for Paris, "el gran deseo de contemplar" the spectacle of modernity. It was Hugo who identified the Revolution as "the city's major form of 'symbolic capital'—what set it apart from all other cities. Without 1789, he wrote, the supremacy of Paris is an enigma" (Casanova 24). Darío goes one step further and, following Hugo's line of thought (as he prided himself on doing), thinks about the Revolution's specific effects on marginal (he deems them "barbarian" and "ignorant") aesthetic configurations and subjectivities: the desire for Paris is what allows them, *bárbaras* or *ignoradas* as they might be, to imagine themselves part of "el gozo de todos los humanos."

Darío's notion of universality here refers to the abstract conceptualization of a generalized need for transcendence (to be part of a "paraíso de la vida"), a shared desire for plenitude as the end of lack that is again signified by the idea of paradise (an idea that he repeats in his *Autobiografía:* "París era para mí como un paraíso en donde se respirase la esencia de la felicidad sobre la tierra"), and the rebirth and reinvention expressed in "el país de la primavera." However, I want to add a Lacanian interpretative layer regarding the notion of *gozo* (enjoyment), which Darío could not have intended but which can further illuminate the meaning of Paris for the Latin American *modernistas.* What happens if we read *gozo* as *jouissance*? *Jouissance*, explains Lacan, is the experience of pain that results from an attempt to satisfy a drive in the form of a demand that can never be met, and thus *jouissance* points to the transgression of the prohibition established by the emergence of the Law in Freud's pleasure principle (*Ethics of Psychoanalysis* 177, 194, 209). *Jouissance*, then, is the painful, damned pleasure of violating the prohibition to enjoy oneself and get close to the Thing, the forbidden and unattainable object of desire (which Lacan will call *objet petit a* after 1963), which is so loaded with the promise of enjoyment that it becomes unbearable for the subject (*Other Side* 17). Darío isolates the constitutive desire of subjects from marginal cultures—whether Latin American or Mongolian, Abyssinian, or Persian: to access the Parisian experience of modern plenitude and become joyous members of a universal human collective. Octavio Paz sees the *modernistas*' love for Paris as a "voluntad de participación en una plenitud histórica hasta entonces vedada a los latinoamericanos" (*Cuadrivio* 21) ("the will to participate in a historical plenitude that Latin Americans had been forbidden until then"). By foregrounding the marginal subject's cosmopolitan desire, Darío underscores its exclusion from the realm of self-realization and reconciliation that he calls Paris. The "gozo de todos los humanos" is akin to Lacan's *jouissance* in that the pain at the core of a desire for Paris is the pain of a desire that can never be fulfilled.

Darío's French religion ("rogaba a Dios que no me dejase morir sin conocer París") and the construction of Paris as an altar have been read as a form of displaced Eurocentrism, or symptoms of the *modernistas*' need to flee Spain's shadow in order to enter into a new relation of cultural tutelage; Darío and Latin American modernist intellectuals (with the exception of Martí and Rodó, who supposedly escaped this neocolonial trap) would remain subjects of European culture's global hegemony. This interpretation is common within the critical genealogy described at the beginning of this chapter, a tradition that celebrates, rather normatively, the particularistic discourse and identity politics of *modernismo* (and all Latin American literature and culture), to the point that it engages in flawed readings of its cosmopolitan and universalist impulses.

TRANSLATING FRANCE, BECOMING FRENCH

Between October and December of 1896, while living in Buenos Aires as a diplomatic representative of Colombia and working as a staff writer at *La Nación*, Darío published two books considered to be foundations of the *modernista* cultural formation (M. Henríquez Ureña 94), *Los raros* and *Prosas profanas*. They were the most significant aesthetic world literary interventions within the limits of Darío's French universalism.

Los raros was a book of literary portraits of Parnassian, naturalist, positivist, symbolist, and decadent writers that Darío had published in *La Nación* over the previous two years. He presents this eclectic pantheon as a transgressive and alternative *canon de fin-de-siècle* (turn-of-the-century canon) made up of fourteen French writers, plus Poe, Nordau, Ibsen, Martí, and Eugenio de Castro. His own emerging poetics could become legible and relevant in the context of this canon and within the literary universe dominated by French signifiers that was Darío's conception of the world beyond Latin America. The key to the world literary nature of *Los raros* must be sought in Verlaine's *Les poètes maudits* (*The Cursed Poets*) (1884), the source of the self-affirming operation of *Los raros*. *Les poètes maudits* codified a tradition that began with the romantics and crystallized in Baudelaire: new, modernizing poetics, incarnated in marginal forms of aesthetic subjectivity that challenged established canons and attempted to invert the hierarchical relation between them. Verlaine's profiles of the *maudits* Corbière, Rimbaud, Mallarmé, Desbordes-Valmore, Villiers de L'isle de Adam, and himself disguised under the anagram of his own name "Le pauvre Lelian" defy the artistic status quo by claiming that *we, the unknown, the accursed, the marginalized are the real artists, the true poets*. Darío appropriates Verlaine's intervention for the Spanish-speaking literary world. Indeed, the narrowly French conception of world literature at work in *Los raros* ostensibly does not attempt to import and translate the Western canon in order to introduce it in Argentine and Latin American literature as Paul Groussac was doing at the same time (Siskind); to the contrary, its maneuver consists in universalizing a particular, discrete, and marginal French aesthetic formation Darío wanted to use to define the identity of his own modernist project.[10]

It is interesting that *Los raros* and *Prosas profanas* do not posit world literature as a critical discourse but instead are aesthetic performances of Darío's French-inflected world literature from Latin America. Rather than a conceptualization and predication on the literary world beyond the Latin American cultural particularity, these books display the desire for a literature configured around a French archive of poetic figures, syntaxes, and topics, whose perceived universality would allow it to be inscribed in the imagined synchronicity of a global modernism that, to Darío in 1896, marginalized Latin America. The world literary nature of *Los raros* and *Prosas profanas* can be read in the desire—at play in the writing and aesthetic choices—to access the world of modernity through its French gateway.

The asynchronous dislocated marginality that triggered Darío's world literary writing can be read in the first stanza of "Divagación" ("Digression"), one of the poems that define the aesthetic identity of *Prosas profanas*:

> ¿Vienes? Me llega aquí, pues que suspires,
> un soplo de las mágicas fragancias
> que hicieran los delirios de las liras
> en las Grecias, las Romas y las Francias. (189)

> Are you coming? I feel here, now that you are sighing,
> a breath of the magical fragrance
> that would have delighted the lyres
> of Greece, Rome, and France.
>
> (*Stories and Poems* 93)

Two very significant elements of this stanza point to the world beyond the imaginary horizon of the Latin American premodernist poet: the adverb of place *aquí* and the invitation that opens the poem. In the case of *aquí*, its deictic function maps the geo-aesthetic distance between the poet's location and "las Grecias, las Romas y las Francias" that are plentiful places of poetry ("las mágicas fragancias que hicieran los delirios de las liras"). His lover's breath transmits the classical and French inspiration that enables the poem and poetic voyage. The poem is preoccupied with the asymmetry of a *here* that receives lyres whose natural residence is *there*.

Darío himself thought of "Divagación" as a "curso de geografía erótica" ("course in erotic geography") and an "invitación al amor bajo todos los soles, la pasión de todos los colores y de todos los tiempos" (*Vida* 145) ("invitation to love under all suns, the passion of all colors and all times"). Critics have followed his lead, reading the opening "¿Vienes?" as a sexual invitation but disregarding his suggestion that the poem could be read as a world-mapping device.[11] Indeed, in this poem of irregular hendecasyllabic verses, the "I" invites the feminine muse that stands for Poetry on a journey ("¿Vienes?") of love through a world of manneristic cultural references: in other words, an invitation to loving/writing a world literary poetry.[12]

> ¿Te gusta amar en griego? Yo las
> fiestas galantes busco . . .
> . . . .
> Amo más que la Grecia de los griegos
> la Grecia de Francia, porque en Francia
> el eco de las risas y los juegos,
> su más dulce licor Venus escancia. (190)
>
> Do you enjoy love in a Greek mode? As for me, I seek
> The fêtes galantes . . .
> . . . .
> More than the Greece of the Greeks I love
> the Greece of France, because in France
> Venus serves her sweetest beverage,
> the echo of laughter and jollity.
> (*Stories and Poems* 93–95)

As is always the case, modern France is the mediation that constitutes Darío's world—in this case, Verlaine is the measure of a world literature hierarchically differentiated: "Verlaine es más que Sócrates" (190) ("Verlaine is more than Socrates"; *Stories and Poems* 95). The Spanish station is Merimée's Andalucía from *Carmen* (1845):

> O amor lleno de sol, amor de España,
> amor lleno de púrpuras y oros;
> amor que da el clavel, la flor extraña

regada con la sangre de los toros. (191)

O love full of sunshine, love in Spain,
Love full of purple and gold;
Love given by the carnation, the strange flower
Watered with blood of the bulls.

(*Stories and Poems* 97)

China is, plainly, a bazaar of Chinoiseries:

¿Los amores exóticos acaso . . . ?
Como rosa de oriente me fascinas:
me deleitan la seda, el oro, el raso.
Gautier adoraba a las princesas chinas.
. . . .
Ámame en chino, en el sonoro chino
de Li-Tai-Pe. Yo igualaré a los sabios
poetas que interpretan el destino. (191)

Exotic loves, perhaps . . . ?
You fascinate me like an Oriental rose:
I am delighted by silk, gold, satin.
Gautier adored Chinese princesses.
. . . .
Love me in Chinese, in the sonorous Chinese
of Li Bai. I shall be a match for the sage
poets who interpret destiny.

(*Stories and Poems* 97)

Japan is utterly exotic, pure and untouched by turn-of-the-century modernization:

Ámame, japonesa, japonesa
antigua, que no sepa de naciones
occidentales: tal una princesa
con las pupilas llenas de visiones. (191)

Love me Japanese woman, Japanese woman
of olden days, you that know nothing about Occidental
nations: like a princess

whose eyes are filled with visions.
(*Stories and Poems* 99)

Darío's global tour makes stops in other loci of a French-conceived genealogy of world poetry, summoning his muse to materialize wrapped in guises borrowed from Germany, India, and biblical Jerusalem. To conclude, the poem makes a cosmopolitan demand of Latin America to embrace universality in the name of Poetry:

Ámame así, fatal, cosmopolita,
universal, inmensa, única, sola
y todas. (192)

Love me in that way, my predestined, cosmopolitan
woman,
universal, immense, unique, a single person
comprising all women.
(*Stories and Poems* 99)

Darío's call for a cosmopolitan Latin American literature capable of loving and embracing universality echoes Martí's 1882 injunction in "Oscar Wilde" to realize "esa ansia de salir de sí" (287) ("the desire to transcend oneself").

In November of 1896, only a few weeks after the publication of *Los raros*, Paul Groussac reviewed the book harshly in *La Biblioteca* (*The Library*), the journal he edited as director of Argentina's National Public Library—a position he held from 1885 until his death in 1929. A few days later, on November 27, 1896, Darío responded to Groussac's criticisms in "Los colores del estandarte," which was published in *La Nación* and summarized Darío's poetics in the most forceful fashion. Two months later, in January 1897, Groussac published a slightly less critical review of *Prosas profanas*, toning down the polemical tone of an exchange that had already addressed some of the most important challenges of Latin American modernity. Even though Darío's "Los colores del estandarte" has been widely read and quoted, Groussac's reviews have been overlooked. Looking at all three pieces of this exchange provides an opportunity to focus on a crucial and emblematic disagreement over the different imaginary mappings that intellectual elites conceived in order to establish the place of Latin American literature within the (French) world of modern aesthetics.

Groussac and Darío disagreed about specific cultural forms: What was the nature of the Latin American particularity that would enable the region to inscribe itself in the universal modern world without losing that same cultural particularity? Through their asking and developing these questions, *modernismo* became a foundational moment, and Darío the most important cultural figure of the turn of the century.

The very few critics to pay attention to the three tiers of this polemic have analyzed them reductively as a clash of individual sensibilities rather than the expression of structural antagonism between intellectuals regarding the strategies of Latin American modern culture, in the context of a global modernity organized around the hegemony of French signifiers. Ángel Rama, for example, describes Groussac as a rigorous academic intellectual guided by "el deseo de investigar sistemáticamente" ("the desire to investigate systematically"), while Darío and the *modernistas* "leen mayoritariamente lo que se produce en su tiempo, en especial las novedades" (*Máscaras democráticas* 40) ("read mainly what was produced in their time, especially the new and different"). The relation of the *modernistas* to French culture is seen as a symptom of an epidemic trend: "Son hijos del tiempo, de sus urgencias, de sus modas, por lo cual extraordinariamente receptivos a las influencias del momento. Su autodidactismo les concede una libertad atrevida, propicia alevosos robos literarios, les hace caer fácilmente en las epidemias artísticas" (40–41) ("They are the sons of their time, of its urgencies, of its fashions, which makes them extraordinarily receptive to the influences of the moment. Their autodidactism gives them an audacious freedom, causes premeditated literary thefts, makes them the easy victims of artistic epidemics"). The origin of their disagreement lies in the incompatibility of these approaches to the aesthetic phenomenon. Rama explains that Groussac could never have liked *Los raros*: "La serie era de un exitismo periodístico algo ramplón que tenía que disgustar a Paul Groussac, pues estaba concebida oportunísticamente para el paladar de los lectores" (93) ("The series was a kind of vulgar journalism that Paul Groussac could not possibly have liked, as it was opportunistically conceived to appeal to readers' tastes").

Although it is difficult to agree with Rama's characterization of *Los raros*, and a clash of individual sensibilities is a partial explanation of this polemic at best, it is true that Groussac and Darío could not have been more opposed as readers and writers. The tone and concerns of Groussac's lectures and essays in *La Biblioteca* were strikingly different from those of Darío's pieces in *La Nación*. So were the intellectual sensibilities and social trajectories of the two men (including their success or failure to establish stable institutional relations within the sphere of the state).[13] For Beatriz Colombi, *Los raros* "desordena el campo, invierte las jerarquías [y] por eso Groussac le asigna operaciones de lo seudo, de lo falso" ("En torno" 79) ("disturbs the field, inverts the hierarchies, and for that reason Groussac attributes pseudo- or false operations to it"). The fact that *Los raros* undermines an order and a set of parameters that were a part of Groussac's own intellectual practice makes it difficult to read his reaction as mere personal dislike for Darío's *maudit* aesthetic.

For all their disagreements, Groussac and Darío coincided in their understanding of France (and at times, western European culture more broadly) as the epicenter of a global map of modernity marked by radical unevenness. They differed, however, in the way that they believed Latin America had to conceive the necessary relation to that culture which organized the grammar of modernity for the rest of the world. But to understand Groussac's position in the debate, it is necessary to know something of his position in the Argentine cultural field of the turn of the century, as well as his migratory experience and the discursive production of his French ontological and epistemic privilege.

Groussac's place in the Argentine intellectual field must be considered in relation to his experience of the global dislocation of French culture and his ability to place himself simultaneously inside and outside Argentine culture. Born in Toulouse in 1848, he arrived at the port of Buenos Aires in 1866 without any form of symbolic capital and yet managed to become the highest cultural authority in the country.[14] For Groussac, his French identity far exceeded his French nationality; his Frenchness was a social relation, a deliberate, especially meaningful device that he laboriously produced in all of his writings, including essays of literary and art criticism, academic historiography, novels, drama, travel writing, and journalism, but also in his social and cultural interactions and practices as a cultural agent of the state.

Groussac's intellectual trajectory is unique in nineteenth-century Latin American letters.[15] His notable rise to power has to be attributed to determination, talent, and good fortune. Coming to Argentina at the age of eighteen without a degree, credentials, or any knowledge of the Spanish language, he worked on a cattle ranch and as a tutor for patrician families. In 1871, solely on the basis of an essay on José de Espronceda that Groussac had published in *Revista Argentina* that same year, Nicolás Avellaneda, minister of education and future president, appointed him school inspector for the province of Tucumán.

The Argentine cultural field, like Groussac himself, perceived his French origin in terms of Derrida's "metaphysics of presence": origin as the a priori essence that determines an ontological privilege that, in a circular movement, authorizes the very hierarchies that give rise to an imagination of origins and originality.[16] Groussac was never dismissed as a foreigner when he lectured on national culture.[17] Quite the opposite, he was listened to even more carefully because he was French.[18]

It is not irrelevant that Groussac, an intellectual who represented his life in Latin America in terms of the *mission civilisatrice* that legitimized the late nineteenth-century French colonial enterprise, entered public life through the educational system. Groussac saw himself as the subject of this world-historical task, in a continent without a tradition that could ground a truly modern culture. He imparted these civilizational lessons through interventions in the cultural field, always assuming the asymmetrical nature of pedagogic relations. In an article published just after Groussac's death in 1929, Borges wrote that the Frenchman thought of himself as "un misionero de Voltaire en medio del mulataje" ("Paul Groussac" 233) ("a missionary of Voltaire among mongrels").[19]

The debate between Darío and Groussac revolves around one of the main concerns of the *modernista* project, the symbolic and imaginary relationship that Latin America should establish with the French signifiers of global modernity: imitation, rejection, translation, appropriation, and resignification. What poetic configurations would allow Latin America to synchronize itself with the Greenwich meridian of modernity that Paris represented (Casanova 87)?

Groussac writes about Darío and *modernismo* with utter contempt. He describes *Los raros* as a "reunión intérlope" ("Raros" 475) ("fraudulent gathering") brought about by "un joven poeta centroamericano que llegó a Buenos Aires hace tres años *riches de ses seuls yeux tranquilles*" (474) ("a young Central American poet who came to Buenos Aires three years ago and whose only wealth was his quiet eyes") and then characterizes Darío as an "heraldo de pseudo-talentos decadentes, simbólicos, estetas" (475) ("herald of decadent, symbolist, aesthete pseudotalents"). From the very beginning of the review of *Los raros*, Groussac establishes an asymmetric relation between the reviewer as aesthetic arbiter and the poet and his *raros*. Groussac describes Darío, condescendingly, as a newcomer, lacking in symbolic capital and judgment—sins that he attributes to Darío's youth. He despises the notion of *rareza*, the pretentious falsity of artists who pose as *maudits* to differentiate themselves from their contemporaries and predecessors: "Para sobresalir entre la muchedumbre, al gigante le basta erguirse: los enanos han menester abigarrarse y prodigar los gestos estrepitosos" (475) ("To stand out from the crowd, the giant has only to stand up straight: the dwarf must paint himself multicolored and make noisy gestures"). Groussac is not only impatient with their gestures, body language, and clothes but also with the imposture displayed by the materiality of their books, which allows Groussac to equate Darío with the objects of his veneration:

> Por eso ostentan la originalidad, ausente de la idea, en las tapas de sus delgados libritos, procurando efectos de iluminación y tipografía. . . . A este propósito, séame lícito reprochar al señor Darío las pequeñas "rarezas" tipográficas de su volumen. Aquel rebuscamiento en el tipo y la carátula es tanto más displicente, cuanto que contrasta con el abandono real de la impresión: abundan las incorrecciones, las citas cojas . . . las erratas chocantes sobre todo en francés. Créame el distinguido escritor: lo *raro* de un libro americano no es estar impreso en bastardilla, sino traer un texto irreprochable. (475–76)
>
> For this reason they show off their originality, free of ideas, on the covers of their skinny little books, using lighting and typographical effects. . . . In this regard, it would be fair to reproach Mister Darío for his volume's little typographical "oddities." Such affectedness in the type and cover is even more disagreeable when it contrasts with neglected printing: abundant mistakes, defective cites . . . shocking typos, especially in French. Believe me, the distinguished writer: what is *strange* in an American book is not its printing in italics but rather its being an impeccable text.

Groussac mocks the rare core of the book and in doing so makes his principal aim in the review evident: to construct himself as an authoritative figure in relation to at least three different problems. The first is criticism as the power to distinguish reputable and virtuous art from pseudopoetry on the extended global modernist scene, from France and western Europe to North and Latin America, where turn-of-the-century desires to express new aesthetic sensibilities and social discontents are leading symbolist and decadent writers into inadvisable aesthetic terrain. Second, related to his most immediate space of intervention, is the organization of the Argentine (and to a certain extent, Latin American) poetic field by establishing aesthetic parameters and foregrounding the French source of authority that determines what is included in and excluded from it—among other things, Groussac ridicules Darío for the book's "shocking typos, especially in French." And the third problem is Latin American poetry's relation to France as the particular cultural formation that incarnates the universality of the global system of modernity. Should it aspire to be original, that is, faithful to its own cultural particularity, and disregard the example set by the hegemony of France? Or should it acknowledge its marginal condition and produce an adequate imitation, an accurate reflection of French poetic modernity? Originality and imitation: Groussac sets these as the core concepts of the polemic, a binary Darío does not accept and furthermore subverts and deconstructs.

In a subtle but sure manner, Groussac intertwines his criticism of Darío's *modernismo* with a structural critique of Latin American culture—or rather, American culture, because he conflates the Americas in their identical immaturity and unoriginality, at least when contrasted with Europe.[20] This maneuver begins with an imaginary primal scene of Darío's misguided infatuation with French decadent aesthetics:

> Vagaba, pues, el señor Darío por esas libres veredas del arte, cuando por mala fortuna, vínole a las manos un tomo de Verlaine, probablemente el más peligroso, el más exquisito: *Sagesse*. Mordió esa fruta prohibida que, por cierto, tiene en su parte buena el sabor delicioso y único de esos pocos granos de uva que se conservan sanos, en medio de un racimo podrido. El filtro operó plenamente en quien no tenía la inmunidad relativa de la raza ni la vacuna de la crítica; y sucedió que, perdiendo a su influjo el claro discernimiento artístico, el 'sugestionado' llegase a absorber con igual fruición las mejores y las peores elaboraciones del barrio Latino. ("Raros" 475)

> Mister Darío wandered along those unbounded paths of art, when by bad luck, a volume by Verlaine fell into his hands,

> probably the most dangerous, most exquisite one: *Sagesse.* He ate that forbidden fruit, whose good part, of course, has the delicious and unique flavor of the few grapes to remain edible on a rotten vine. The love potion worked easily on him, as he had neither the relative immunity of race nor the vaccine of criticism; and, losing clear artistic discernment to its power, the "influenced man" came to absorb with equal delight the Latin Quarter's best and worst productions.

Beyond his sarcasm and condescension, Groussac's imputation contains a double hypothesis about the constitutive shortcomings in Darío and Latin American *modernismo* that lead to a foolish attraction to these "pseudo-talentos decadentes, simbólicos, estetas" (475). On the one hand, there is a lack of critical judgment: Groussac admonishes that those who are ill-prepared to discern the worthy and the worthless should not attempt aesthetic criticism, a trade that only *some of us* can exercise judiciously. On the other, and here Groussac reads Darío as a mere symptom of Latin America's marginality, there is a lack of natural ability to resist the most superficial aesthetic temptations, a power that is innate to some superior races, especially when it comes to aesthetic and cultural criteria in the world order of modernity. By "race," Groussac refers to the shared cultural traits—primarily, language—and experiences of the members of a national community (in the vein of Ernest Renan's "What Is a Nation?") rather than an imagined biological unity, and points to the ontological privilege of a monolithic French identity in the nineteenth century. Darío and the *modernistas* are not French and therefore cannot recognize aesthetic falsity, whereas Groussac, like any intellectual from a superior European culture, is naturally immune to such vulgarity.

Groussac does not waste time, moving swiftly on to what he sees as the most important conceptual issue at stake in Darío's relation to the French *maudits*, the question of imitation: "Lo peor del caso presente, lo repito, es que el autor de *Los raros* celebra la grandeza de sus mirmidones con una sinceridad afligente, y ha llegado a imitarlos en castellano con desesperante perfección. Es lo que me mueve a dirigirle estas observaciones, cuyo acento afectuoso no se le escapará" (475) ("The worst part of the present case, I repeat, is that the author of *Los raros* celebrates the magnificence of his Myrmidons with distressing sincerity, and imitates them in Castilian with infuriating perfection. This is what moves me to make these observations, whose affectionate accent will not be lost on him"). The emphasis on imitation is not an indictment of Darío's personal inability to produce an original aesthetic project autonomous from an immature French infatuation but rather and once again a cultural symptom of the degraded conditions that inhibit art making in Latin America. To Groussac, imitation is the only productive device in a region condemned to a Platonic, parasitic, mimetic existence on the margins of the universal whose culture can only aspire to reflect truly original modern cultural formations. In reviewing *Prosas profanas*, Groussac writes about himself, Darío, and their marginal cultural location:

> Me resigno sin esfuerzo a envejecer lejos del foco de toda civilización, en estas tierras nuevas, por ahora condenadas a reflejarla con más o menos fidelidad. Es, pues, necesario partir del postulado que, así en el norte como en el sud, durante un período todavía indefinido, cuanto se intente en el dominio del arte es y será imitación. Por lo demás, hay muy poca originalidad en el mundo: el genio es una cristalización del espíritu tan misteriosa y rara como la del carbono puro. . . . El genio es la fuerza en la originalidad, toda hibridación es negativa del genio, puesto que importa una mezcla, o sea un desalojo parcial de las energías atávicas por la intrusión de elementos extraños—es decir, un debilitamiento; ahora bien, la presente civilización americana, por inoculación e injerto de la europea, es una verdadera hibridación: luego, etc. *Et voilá pourquoi votre fille est muette.* ("Prosas Profanas" 157–58)

> I resign myself without a struggle to growing old far from the center of all civilization, in these new lands that are condemned for the time being to reflect civilization with more or less fidelity. It is, therefore, necessary to depart from the premise that, in the North as well as the South, for a still-indefinite period, whatever attempts are made in the realm of art are and will be imitation. Otherwise, there is very little originality in the world: genius is the crystallization of a spirit as mysterious and rare as pure carbon. . . . Genius is the force of originality, hybridization is the negative of genius, amounting to a mixture or a partial removal of atavistic energies through the intrusion of

> foreign elements—that is, a weakening; further, present American civilization, inoculated by and grafted from the European, is truly hybrid: then, etc. *And this is why your daughter is mute.*[21]

Groussac's global map of modernity and its Others is organized around the concepts of originality and imitation, and the binary cultural identities that find their place within this uneven distribution of genius. This map is an exercise in essentialism: relations of power cannot be subverted, and the agents that constitute them remain unaltered by the historical change that Groussac resists. For him, Latin American culture was inherently hybrid and thus could never host the genius of an original modern culture at once particularly Latin American and universally modern because that cultural particularity would always already be "inoculated" and corrupted by the presence of "elementos extraños"—indeed, *raros*—"and this is why your daughter is mute."[22] If imitation is the only aesthetic operation open to marginal modernities devoid of genius (for Groussac, the manifestation of originality), Latin American modernist poets would do well to choose *really* valuable aesthetic formations to emulate, such as "el prerrafaelismo o espiritualismo inglés . . . que se ha[n] preocupado mucho menos de los detalles exteriores que de la esencia artística" ("Raros" 477) ("Pre-Raphaelism or English spiritism . . . which are far less concerned with outward details than with artistic essence").[23]

Though "la América colonizada no debe pretender por ahora la originalidad intelectual" ("Prosas profanas" 158) ("colonized America cannot yet attempt intellectual originality"), one exceptional American poet manages to escape the structural determination of *modernity-by-way-of-imitation* to be original, a poet of the future who stands on the other side of the "por ahora" that marks literature's limitations at that time and on that side of the Atlantic: Walt Whitman, whose poetry is the "expresión viva y potente de un mundo virgen" ("Raros" 480) ("true and powerful expression of a virgin world").[24] Groussac sees in Whitman an invitation to the Americas, and Latin America in particular, to join the world of aesthetic modernity on their own terms: *Express your genius*! In other words, American artists in general, and Latin American writers in particular, should not concern themselves with producing their own universality through the shortcut of French culture; instead, like Whitman, they should write an original literature that expresses the continent's cultural particularity: "El arte americano será original—o no será. ¿Piensa el señor Darío que su literatura alcanzará dicha virtud con ser el eco servil de rapsodias parisienses, y tomar por divisa la pregunta ingenua de Coppée? *Qui pourrais-je imiter pour être original*?" ("Raros" 480) ("American art will be original—or it will not be at all. Does Mister Darío think that his literature will attain this virtue as the servile echo of Parisian rhapsodies, taking as its motto Coppée's ingenuous question? *Who can I imitate in order to be original*?"). Describing Darío's *Los raros* and *Prosas profanas* as servile echoes of French symbolism, Groussac believes that he has settled the question of the aesthetic and cultural value of *modernismo*, a debate that, in fact, was taking place throughout Latin America in 1896. The path for young Latin American poets is the one that Whitman has cleared: a Latin American poetry original in its Latin Americanness; original in the *particular* way that it can be original. It can be original in its display of the unique cultural particularity of the Americas, not in the manner of the innovative originality of a French culture that defines the content of aesthetic universality at a given historical time. Groussac ends the review by citing a character from *Le trésor* (*The Treasure*) (1879), a piece that François Coppée wrote for La Comédie Française: "To imitate in order to be original." Groussac reads the crux of the quotation as a naive faux pas that he equates with the immature self-deception at the core of Darío's aesthetics.[25] But it could also be seen as a paradox ingrained in the relation between originality and imitation, and thus the possibility of undoing the naturalized hierarchy between the two.

In "Los colores del estandarte," Darío uses this mocking slap in the face as the starting point for his response to Groussac. Turning the quotation from Coppée into a banner for his *modernista* aesthetic, he reformulates the meaning of "originality" to encompass inventive, proactive forms of imitation and in turn reconceives creative imitation as the subversive and necessary means of modern cultural production for cultures relegated to the margins of French universality. Darío brushes aside Groussac's concern with the absolute binary opposition between originality and imitation and sets his eyes on the prize of modernity. The point is to be modern, and for him, this means being French: adopting a French aesthetic identity, thinking in French, feeling French, and writing in Spanish. And creative imitation drives this process of becoming French:

> Mi éxito—sería ridículo no confesarlo—se ha debido a la novedad: la novedad ¿cuál ha sido? El sonado galicismo

> mental. Cuando leía a Groussac no sabía que fuera un francés que escribiese en castellano, pero él me eseñó a pensar en francés: después, mi alma gozosa y joven conquistó la ciudadanía de Galia. . . Al penetrar en ciertos secretos de armonía, de matiz, de sugestión que hay en la lengua de Francia, fue mi pensamiento descubrirlos en el español, o aplicarlos. . . . Y he aquí como, pensando en francés y escribiendo en castellano que alabaran por castizo académicos de la Española, publiqué el pequeño libro que iniciaría el actual movimiento literario Americano. . . . El *Azul* es un libro parnasiano, y por lo tanto, francés. En él aparecen por primera vez en nuestra lengua, el "cuento" parisiense, la adjetivación francesa, el giro galo injertado en el párrafo castellano. . . . *Qui pourrais-je imiter pour être original*? me decía yo. Pues a todos. A cada cual le aprendía lo que me agradaba, lo que cuadraba a mi sed de novedad y a mi delirio de manifestación individual. Y el caso es que resulté original. ("Colores" 162–63)

> My success—it would be absurd not to confess it—has been due to novelty. And this novelty, what has it consisted of? A mental Gallicism. When I read Groussac I did not know he was a Frenchman writing in Spanish. But he taught me to *think in French;* after that, my young, happy heart claimed Gallic citizenship. . . . As I penetrated into certain secrets of harmony, of nuance, of suggestion that one finds in the language of France, I believed I might discover those same secrets in Spanish, or apply them. . . . *Azure* is a Parnassian book, and therefore French. For the first time in our language the Parisian "tale" appears, French adjectivization, the Gallic turn injected into a paragraph of classic Castillian. . . . *Qui pourrais-je imiter pour être original*? I asked myself. Why, everyone. From each I took what I liked, what suited my thirst for novelty and my delirium for art: the elements that would go on to constitute a medium of personal expression. And it turned out to be original. (*Selected Writings* 483–85)

Admitting boastfully that he imitates and borrows indiscriminately, obeying only the dictates of his desire, Darío renders Groussac's mandate of originality irrelevant. The goal is to be, not original, but modern, and by any means necessary, and this means acknowledging the productive role that creative imitations, translations, appropriations, and resignifications have for marginal cultures.[26] "Los colores del estandarte" reduces Groussac's essentialist vindication of the power of origins not to a mere ideological position but rather to a blatant anachronism that is out of step with new cultural relations and aesthetic sensibilities. In the context of global modernism—a world structured as a discursive network of texts and aspirations that use colonial, neocolonial, commercial and diplomatic routes to travel quickly throughout the world, to and from Europe—Darío discovers that being modern means modulating the universality of modernity (effectively crystallized in French culture) in one's own language and then articulating the aesthetic syntax of that language according to the premises of the universal grammar of modern art. In other words, it is particularizing the universal and universalizing the particular in a dizzying maneuver that renders any preexisting hierarchical relation between them useless and inoperative.

Darío's reference to his own "galicismo mental" must be interpreted in relation to this reversibility. As with Coppée's passage, Darío takes the subtly derogative phrase that the Spaniard Juan Valera had used to describe the poet's inclination in *Azul* and uses it to define France's ambiguous role in the formation of his modernist aesthetic subjectivity. The adoption of "galicismo mental" as a self-describing motto presupposes the interiorization of a French disposition that is supposed to be foreign to a Latin American artist. Darío turns the demeaning accusation of Francophilia into an innovative predisposition to the modern, a sensibility that is no longer exterior to the modernist poet but the constitutive core of an aesthetic subjectivity that Darío called "el reino interior" ("the inner kingdom") in the famous poem of the same name from *Prosas profanas*.

Gerard Aching explains that "this internal realm or space has been characterized as the site of the *modernista* interiority, the ivory tower of the movement's members, the place of their hermetic literary production" (*Politics* 22). However, he proposes thinking of the trope "beyond its representation of internal spaces," as a symbol of "the social circumstances that gave rise to its literary creation and refinement in modernist texts" (23). Beginning with its epigraph by Poe ("with Psychis [*sic*], my soul"), Darío's poem laboriously constructs the differential interiority of the artist as a "selva suntuosa" with "extrañas flores de la flora gloriosa de los cuentos azules" and rare birds like "papemores" and "bulbules" that sing their "canto extasiado" ("Reino interior" 219) ("a sumptuous forest" with "strange flowers, from the glorious flora of fairy tales" and rare birds like "'papemors' whose song would enrapture the bulbuls with love"; *Stories and Poems* 127). Rather than condemn the poem for the sin of aestheticism, Aching insightfully highlights its social determinations and the subjectivity associated with it.[27] Far from retreating from the historicity of Latin American power relations at the turn of the century, the production of a *modernista* subjective interiority that uses the signifiers provided by the aesthetic universe of French symbolism presupposes a forceful discursive intervention in a social field where antagonistic agents struggle to shape social subjectivities (the professional writer, the symbolist esthete, and yes, the *modernista afrancesado*) that do not exist in the absence of the cultural practices and discourses that name them into existence.

"*Azul* es un libro parnasiano, y por lo tanto, francés," but in what sense is *Azul* French? For Darío, to be modern is to be French. He empties France of its particular French content and makes it the signifier of the universally modern: France as the name and exterior guise of a modernity that Darío wants Latin America to try out. If Groussac's essentialist epistemology concedes an ontological privilege to French culture, for Darío its favorable position is a structural function of the universal order of modernity; it is the master signifier (a *point de capiton* in Lacan's terms) around which the system of modernist signification is organized. *Azul* is a French book because it is modern, because it introduces, "por primera vez en nuestra lengua," new textual formations, a new sense of poetic musicality ("ciertos secretos de armonía"), and new rhetorics and vocabularies. Of course, Darío is not a French poet, and *Azul* and *Prosas profanas* are not, literally, French books. Their Frenchness results from an operation of translation. If France is immediately modern, in and for itself, in Darío's books of the 1890s (written "pensando en francés y escribiendo en castellano"), Latin America is modern *through* France—France as mediation, as the instance that enables a Latin American translation of modern forms, images, and desires. Darío's literature is *Latin Americanly French.*

Darío returned to this idea of French translation as the condition that makes aesthetic modernity possible in Latin America toward the end of his life, after he had made Paris his adopted home, in a poem he wrote in French, "France-Amérique" ("France-America"). Published in 1914 in *Mundial Magazine* (which he had edited from Paris since

1911), the poem was included in *Canto a la Argentina y otros poemas* (*Song to Argentina and Other Poems*), published later that same year. Surprisingly, the poem, which is a perfect window into the status of French culture in Darío's aesthetic imagination, has been utterly ignored by critics of *modernismo*. Darío wrote it directly in French under the original title "Ode à La France," to be read in his absence by Madeleine Roche—an actress of La Comédie Française—at a gathering organized by the Comité France-Amérique on June 25, 1914, to celebrate the Comité's fifth anniversary (Saavedra Molina 106).

The poem portrays France as the last ray of hope—"Car la France sera toujours notre espérance" ("France-Amérique" 337) ("Because France will always be our hope")—for a cosmopolitan peace based on the French concept of universal *fraternité* on the eve of World War I: "Crions Paix! sous les feux des combattants en marche . . . / Crions: Fraternité!" (337) ("We cry Peace! Under the fire of marching fighters . . . / We cry: Brotherhood!"). By writing it directly in French, Darío performs—rather than just enunciates—his faithful attachment to France as the horizon of modern cosmopolitan cultural practices, "le foyer béni de tout le genre humain" (337) ("the blessed home of all mankind"). But these are the usual topics in Darío's discourse of French universality. The truly original dimension of this poem is its translation of modern universality in order to link it to a Latin American condition that is expressed by a *nous* constantly invoked as the liminal place of enunciation, a textual mark of the tense relation between the desire for inclusion and universal belonging *with* France, and the experience of exclusion from the "blessed (modern) domain":[28]

> Marsellaises de bronze et d'or qui vont dans l'air
> sont pour nos coeurs ardents le chant de l'espérance.
> En entendent du coq gaulois le clairon clair
> on clame: Liberté! Et nous traduisons: France! (337)
>
> Bronze and golden Marsellaises coming in the air
> Are for our ardent hearts a song of hope.
> Listening to the Gallic rooster's clear bugle
> they proclaim: Liberty! And we translate: France!

The introduction of this notion of a Latin American translation of French modernity closes the circle around Groussac's summary judgment of imitation (good or bad, fortunate or misguided) as the sole aesthetic instrument of Latin American literature. Darío dismisses the idea that Latin America is condemned to a mimetic modernity and with "France-Amérique" suggests a far more complex relation between Latin America's marginality and the global modernist hegemony of French culture.

If France is the emblem of liberal modernity ("On clame: Liberté!"), inhabiting that modern imaginary requires a complex double operation of translation. On the one hand, French universality must be translated into the terms of Latin America's own specificity—or, rather, the universal modernity that France incarnates must be actualized in the Latin American particularity. On the other hand is the interesting admission that freedom and France don't *naturally* belong together. It is Darío and the *modernistas* who produce this identification, translating one term into the other. "On clame: Liberté! Et nous traduisons: France!": we translate France, *for* and *in* Latin America, and we translate liberty as France, and France as liberty. Darío's translational intervention makes France and freedom interchangeable, where freedom is understood as the pillar of the discourse of modernity and, in the case of Latin American *modernismo*, points to the idea of freedom from want and from aesthetic and cultural marginality. This, in turn, makes possible the nontransparent, nonmimetic translation that constitutes the *modernista* aesthetic formation.

Writing at the moment of the rise of the modern, Darío cannot be aware of the disappointment that Latin American intellectuals would come to feel about his optimistic universalization of French modernity as a world aesthetic that could include Latin America. The image of France as full and self-reconciled was, of course, a fantasy that said little about the breaks, voids, and unbridgeable gaps within French culture and everything about the specificity of the gap in Darío's modernist imaginary. And even Darío's Parisian faith was not without moments of crisis; it is a mistake to assume that his relation to France was unchanging or stable.

PARIS AS TRAUMA: THE DRAMA OF MISRECOGNITION

"Paris, die Hauptstadt des XIX Jahrhunderts" ("Paris, Capital of the Nineteenth Century"), wrote Walter Benjamin in 1939, and until the death of the historical avant-garde in the late 1920s the notion had universal applicability. Paris was the capital of the nineteenth century, the capital of the modernist literary world, and the capital of desire. Pascal

Casanova has argued that the map of global literary modernity was organized around Paris ("a standard that is universally recognized as legitimate") (17), whose centrality depended on the structural function of attributing aesthetic value to singular texts and the world system as a whole. Naturally then, those writers in search of recognition beyond the particular idiosyncrasies of local (national or regional) fame, that is, cosmopolitan desiring writers who imagined themselves in sync with a modern world beyond the particularity of their home cultures, saw Paris as the place that could make them universal writers in their own right. The *modernistas* expected Paris to be the mirror that would reflect the image of their universality.

Casanova explains that all marginal cultures can be defined by the ascension to Paris from the lowly peripheries of global modernity, and she stresses the codification of this movement to the center in terms of gain, capitalization, and plenitude—in other words, recognition and authorization are actively demanded, or even taken, rather than begged for. The articulation of the desire for Paris is a form of agency and a change in the valuation of the artist's subjectivity: "Those who, like Darío, Paz, Kiš, and Benet, go to the centre to seek—to understand, assimilate, conquer, rob . . .—literary wealth and possibilities that hitherto had been denied them help accelerate the process of building up literary assets in the small nations of the world" (326). Casanova's narrative is accurate as a description (it is far more problematic in its prescriptive modalities), but it accounts for only half of the experience of Parisian desire, the half that corresponds to the quest for recognition. Missing is the modernist writer's traumatic discursive articulation of his exclusion and misrecognition (once again, Parisian desire among *modernistas* is a male affair), in the face of his inability to represent himself as a fully constituted universal (that is, French) artist. Or, to say it differently, Casanova writes about the instances when Paris is gained but not about those when Paris is lost.

I want to conclude the examination of Darío's construction of Paris as the signifier of the world beyond Latin America by exploring those moments when he articulates his sense of exclusion from the Parisian modernist plenitude. At those times, he mourns the loss of a French universality that is evidently out of reach for his particularly Latin American self, resorting to a rhetoric of lamentation to explicitly articulate an aesthetic subjectivity disrupted by the irredeemably particular cause of his exclusion.

In 1899, *La Nación* sent Darío to Spain to report on both the peninsular repercussions of the American invasion of Cuba, Puerto Rico, and the Philippines and the effects of war in Spanish society and culture. A few months later, he went to Paris to cover the Universal Exhibition for the newspaper. Although he had briefly visited Paris before, in June 1893, moving there provided him the opportunity to test the idealized construction of French culture seen in *crónicas* like "La fiesta de Francia" against the real, concrete experience of the city. If Darío had seen Paris as the ideal horizon of all modern aesthetic practices, after a few months there the cracks in his faith in that "suelo sagrado" (*Autobiografía* 69) started to become apparent.

Darío spent his first months in Paris covering the Universal Exhibition, getting acquainted with the city's artistic and bohemian ambience, and sending weekly dispatches about both to *La Nación* in Buenos Aires.[29] His chronicles from those first months in Paris reveal his excitement that he was finally able to experience life in the cosmopolitan capital of world modernism. In the first chronicle, "En París" ("In Paris"), dated April 20, 1900 (he had arrived from Spain only two weeks earlier), Darío can hardly hide his fascination with the Universal Exposition's display of cosmopolitan sociability and the spatialization of modernity. The fair had opened on April 14 and occupied the square mile between the Trocadéro and the Pont des Invalides, and the Champ de Mars and L'Esplanade des Invalides: "La obra está realizada y París ve que es buena. Quedará, por la vida, en la memoria de los innumerables visitantes que afluyen de todos los lugares del globo, este conjunto de cosas grandiosas y bellas que cristaliza su potencia y su avance en la actual civilización humana. . . . Y el mundo vierte sobre París su vasta corriente como en la concavidad maravillosa de una gigantesca copa de oro. Vierte su energía, su entusiasmo, su aspiración, su ensueño, y París todo lo recibe y todo lo embellece" ("En París" 11–13) ("The work is done and Paris sees that it is good. Countless visitors from all over the globe will forever remember this collection of grandiose and beautiful things that crystallize the power and progress of current human civilization. . . . And the world pours its vast current over Paris, as if into a gigantic and marvelously concave golden cup. It pours its energy, its enthusiasm, its aspirations, its dreams, and Paris takes it all and makes it all beautiful").

The exhibition, however, is full of tourists. Darío despises them, in part because he is afraid of being confused with them. They cannot appreciate what he, as a poet, sees in the modern plethora of Paris.

Darío strolls through streets, gardens, and buildings that belong to him because he has thought, read, written, and dreamed about them. In contrast, the tourists, who are strange and foreign to the universal modernity of Paris, cannot blend in: "Allí va la familia provinciana que viene a la capital como a cumplir un deber, van los parisienses desdeñosos de todo lo que no sea de su circunscripción; van el ruso gigantesco y el japonés pequeño . . . y el chino que no sabe qué hacer con el sombrero de copa y el sobretodo que se ha encasquetado en nombre de la civilización occidental; y los hombres de Marruecos y de la India con sus trajes nacionales" (18–19) ("There goes the provincial family that comes to the capital as if to fulfill a duty, there go the Parisians disdainful of everything not from their district; there go the gigantic Russian and the small Japanese man . . . and the Chinese man who does not know what to do with the top hat and overcoat he pulled on in the name of Western civilization; and the men from Morocco and India in their national costumes"). Tourists, and even ordinary Parisians, are too implicated in their own cultural particularities to participate organically in the universalist meaning of Paris and the exhibition it was hosting. Darío asserts his privileged subject position by differentiating himself and his aesthetic community from them: "En cuanto a los poetas, a los artistas, estoy seguro de que hallarán allí campo libre para más de una dulce *rêverie*" (33) ("Regarding the poets, the artists, I am sure that they will find room there for more than one sweet dream").[30] Parisians can see nothing beyond their narrow Frenchness, and Russian, Japanese, Moroccan, Indian, and Chinese tourists are unable to transcend their peripheral difference. Only poets—modernist poets like Darío—are armed with the sensibility to see Paris and the exhibition's scenery as the ultimate space to enact cosmopolitan dreams and desires.[31]

Darío's initial impressions of Paris confirm his monumental expectations regarding his potential to become Parisian and understand Paris but also to be understood and recognized by Paris. He soured on the city only a few months later. From that point on, his relation to the city is a schizophrenic back and forth between modernist ideological faith and the quotidian experience of cultural rejection and economic need. On June 27, 1900, less than four months after his arrival in France, Darío complains, "Se nos conoce apenas . . . como nadie sabe castellano, salvo rarísimas excepciones, nos ignoran de la manera más absoluta. . . . No se hace diferencia entre el poeta de Finlandia y el de Argentina, el de Japón o el de México" ("Hispano-Americanos" 68)

("They hardly even know us. . . since, with extremely rare exceptions, no one speaks Castilian, they are completely unaware of us. . . . They do not distinguish between the poet from Finland and the one from Argentina, the one from Japan or the one from Mexico"). Darío resents the ignorance and condescension of the Parisian cultural field and inscribes his complaint in a world literary map of aesthetic exchanges whose center fails to perceive the larger structure. Over the next fifteen years, he will not miss an opportunity to lament the miserable conditions of a Latin American writer living in Paris:

> El artista hispano-americano que viene a Paris, viene siempre con una lamentable pensión de su Gobierno. . . Y acontece que, cuando menos piensa un joven de esos, con su porvenir casi asegurado, con su labor de estudio al terminar, se ve abandonado por la luminosa ocurrencia de un Gobierno que no cree de gran importancia el progreso artistico de su pais. De esos hay quienes se quedan aquí, en una triste "struggle-for-life," dándose a labores industriales, vendiendo su producción a la diabla, cuando logran que se la compren, y destrozados de desesperanza ante la imposibilidad de domar la suerte. ("Impresiones de Salón" 193–94)

> The Hispanic-American artist who comes to Paris always comes with a pitiful stipend from his government. . . . And then, when one of these young men least expects it, with his future almost assured, with his studies almost finished, he finds himself abandoned by a Government with the bright idea that the artistic progress of its country is not of great importance. Some of these young men stay here, in a sad "struggle-for-life," working as industrial laborers, selling their work carelessly when they can find anyone to buy it, and destroyed by hopelessness at the impossibility of overcoming their luck.[32]

Darío emphasizes the difference between the pains of true struggling artists, who should be recognized and embraced by the Parisian arbiters of aesthetic value, and the *rastaquoère*, the South American *parvenu*, the tasteless new-rich type to whom he had already dedicated an entire essay, "La evolución del rastacuerismo" ("The Evolution of *Rastacuerismo*," *La Nación*, December 11, 1902).[33] The *rastacuero* appeared in French theater and novels beginning in the 1860s, first in Henri Meilhac and Ludovic Halévy's play *Le Brésilien* (*The Brazilian*), which opened May 13, 1863, at the Palais-Royal, and later in several novels by Aurelien Scholl, the most famous of which was *Paris aux cent coups* (*Panicking in Paris*) (1888), featuring a character named Don Iñigo Rastacuero, "marquis de los saladéros" ("marquis of salted-meat factories") who lives at the Hôtel du Louvre, "d'oú il rayonne sur la societé parisienne. . . . Peu d'étrangers ont osé se presenter aux Café de la Paix sans s'être affublés d'un titre quelconque" (qtd. in Aubrun 430–31) ("from which he covers Parisian society. . . . Few foreigners have dared to present themselves at the Café de la Paix without a title of some sort").[34] This sardonic novel popularized the term and serves as a platform for Darío's tirade against this character with "dedos cargados de sortijas; una cadena de reloj que hubiera podido servir para atar el ancla de una fragata; tres perlas, gruesas como huevos de garza, le servían de botones de camisa. . . . El personaje . . . se puede aún encontrar" ("Evolución" 135) ("fingers loaded with rings; a watch chain that could anchor a frigate; three pearls, thick as herons' eggs, served as buttons on his shirt. . . . The character . . . can still be found"). Gonzalo Aguilar points out that "el rastacuero no puede dejar de delatar su origen, siempre arrastrando consigo, como una condena, el lugar polvoriento del cual salió" (*Episodios* 18) ("the *rastacuero* cannot help but reveal his origin, always dragging with him, like a punishment, the dusty place that he came from"); this understanding of the stigma of the *rastacuero* might explain why Darío resents being associated with these figures that, according to him, give all Latin American émigrés a bad name. The *rastacuero*'s irredeemable particularism stands out in Paris as foreignness and lack of familiarity with the universalism of a *modernista* aesthetic conceived in French and written in Spanish. Identification with a *rastacuero* therefore represents the peril of a Latin American particularity that Darío perceives as an obstacle to the inscription of his cultural practice in the universality of French modernity.

Darío never entirely got over from the disappointment of not being embraced by Paris. Midway through his fifteen years in the city, he wrote "París y los escritores extranjeros" ("Paris and Foreign Writers," *La Nación*, August 21, 1907), a rant about the bleak life of foreign artists in Paris. Darío quotes a character from *El Torrente* (*The Torrent*), a play by the Dominican and fellow émigré Tulio Cestero, who expresses the frustrations of misrecognition that dominated the private conversations of Latin American *modernista* artists in the French capital: "París es inconquistable, indomable. . . . Los que llegan fuertes, jóvenes, sanos, con la primavera en el alma, París los devuelve enfermos, viejos, rotos" (467–68) ("Paris is unconquerable, untamable. . . . Those who arrive strong, young, healthy, with springtime in their souls, return from Paris sick, old, broken").[35] At the same time, Darío again articulates the paradox of this capital of world modernism that is uninterested in the aesthetic world beyond its narrow cultural self: "Para el parisiense no existe otro lugar habitable más que París, y nada tiene razón de ser fuera de París. Se explica así la tradicional ignorancia de todo lo extranjero y el asombro curioso ante cualquier manifestación de superioridad extranjera. Ante un artista, ante un sabio, ante un talento extranjero, parecen preguntar: ¿Cómo este hombre extranjero y sin embargo tiene talento?" (463) ("To the Parisian, there is no habitable place but Paris, and no reason for anything to be outside of Paris. This explains the traditional ignorance of all foreign things and the curious surprise at any manifestation of foreign superiority. Faced with an artist, a wise man, a foreign talent, they seem to ask: How is this man foreign and nonetheless he has talent?").

The traumatic side of Darío's Parisian experience points to the constitutive unevenness of the global map of modernism, specifically in relation to the question of recognition. What happens to the modernist writer who confers on Paris the authority to draw the boundaries of that map? What happens to his aesthetic subjectivity when Paris ignores him as an artist? Darío's perception of his failure to be recognized and have his aesthetic subjectivity acknowledged by the only meaningful counterpart that could have mediated his place in the social space of global modernism reveals the limits of his *modernista* ideological fantasy about France's benevolent and welcoming universality. In Darío's bitterness is the evidence that the notion of universality that structures his extra–Latin American world literature in fact results from the hegemony of French modernism. The traumatic kernel of his experience of exclusion lies in the unbridgeable gap between his cosmopolitan desire to be recognized by the French Big Other as a French (that is, modern) poet who wrote in Spanish, and the actuality of a Parisian cultural field incapable of embracing him as an instantiation of global modernism. Although Darío never lost hope, he was disappointed time and time again: he would always be cast as the *poète rastaquoère* who could never overcome the cultural stigma of his marginal particularism.

CHAPTER 5

Gómez Carrillo Eastbound: Travel, Orientalism, and the Jewish Question

Enrique Gómez Carrillo asked his friend and mentor Rubén Darío to write the prologue to his first travel narrative, *De Marsella a Tokio: Sensaciones de Egipto, la India, la China y el Japón* (*From Marseille to Tokyo: Sensations of Egypt, India, China, and Japan*) (1906), which gathered the crónicas published the previous year in *La Nación* and *El Liberal,* the Buenos Aires and Madrid newspapers that funded most of Gómez Carrillo's journeys. In this prologue, Darío wrote: "Para mí un hombre que vuelve del Japón es siempre interesante; y si, como en este caso, ese hombre es un poeta, el hecho me resulta encantador. Este poeta, me digo, viene del país de los dragones, de las cosas raras, de los paisajes milagrosos y de las gentes que parecen caídos de la luna" ("Prólogo" vii) ("To me, a man who returns from Japan is always interesting; and when, as in this case, that man is a poet, I am delighted. This poet, I tell myself, comes from the country of dragons, of strange things, of miraculous landscapes and people who seem to have fallen from the moon"). Darío confesses—and this is also true of the broader cultural field and reading public—that for him Asia remains the exotic Orient, and narrative accounts of the continent should be modeled on the exoticist poetic protocols of the *voyage en orient* that François de Chateaubriand, Gérard de Nerval, Alphonse de Lamartine, and Gustave Flaubert had codified for the Middle East, and Pierre Loti for Japan, among other Oriental destinations. Travel writing, for Darío, belongs to the realm of poetry, not journalism or proto-ethnography; he therefore admonishes Gómez Carrillo to be suspicious of "los que dicen: 'Señor Gómez Carrillo, usted ha contado muy bien los sacos de trigo que produce Rusia y los sacos de arroz que produce Japón.' Crea al que le diga: 'Esta página brilla hermosamente'" (xii) ("those who say: 'Mister Gómez Carrillo, you have counted very well the sacks of wheat that Russia produces and the sacks of rice that Japan produces. Believe the one who says: 'This page shines beautifully'"). For this reason, Darío believes that his superficial familiarity with Parisian Japonaiseries authorizes him to pontificate on representations of Japanese culture, even though he has never ventured east of Vienna.

It would be a mistake, however, to interpret Darío's Orientalist sensibility as yet another way in which modernist cultural elites reinforce their subaltern place in the context of global modernism by imitating French culture. On the contrary, the motivation behind Darío's call to Latin American writers traveling eastwards to see Japan through the eyes of the French Orientalists that preceded them (*ignore the process of modernization, pay attention to dragons and enchanting rarities*) is the desire, which I explored in chapter 4, to inscribe the new Latin American culture that he saw himself founding within the solid and stable grounds of French modernity's universality.

In *De Marsella a Tokio*, Gómez Carrillo only partially follows Darío's injunction. On the one hand, he shares his mentor's view of the place of French culture in the world and therefore is inclined to see Japan as "un país de muñecas y de sonrisas" (viii) ("a country of dolls and smiles") and to mourn the fact that "el modernismo ha suprimido los sables" (viii) ("modernism has eliminated the cutlass"). On the other, Gómez Carrillo grounds his Orientalist representations in his far superior knowledge of the nineteenth-century French Orientalist archive. For example, he dedicates an entire chapter to his fascination with the sensuous *bayaderes* who perform for him in Ceylon (Sri Lanka) "una danza de seducción. . . . Los brazos se alzan ondulando, parecen subir, subir sin cesar. ¡Es la serpiente sagrada de la India! La música, que encuentra al fin su verdadero empleo, redobla su penetrante, su angustiante, su exasperante melancolía. Y alucinados por el ritmo, acabamos por no ver . . . sino una bella serpiente de voluptuosidad" (76, 78–79) ("a seductive dance. . . . The arms are raised in a ripple, they seem to rise, rise without stopping. It is the holy serpent of India! The music, which at last finds its true purpose, redoubles its penetrating, distressing, exasperating melancholy. And hallucinating from the rhythm, we end by seeing none other . . . than a beautiful voluptuous snake").

This exoticizing gaze reproduces all the features of romantic and *modernista* forms of European Orientalist eroticist representations of women, including "the stylization of the harem, the scopic pleasure, the overabundance of *jouissance*, the desire for domination, the objectification of women, their lascivious sexuality" (Behdad 69). Passages such as this one may have led Darío to see Gómez Carrillo's work as a Latin American subspecies of French Orientalism, the same way that he would have viewed his own writing if he had ever made the journey. But at the same time, in Gómez Carrillo's narrative, the Orientalist posture is constantly interrupted—indeed, disrupted—by his ability to analyze the material underpinnings of the experience of colonialism, denaturalize his exoticizing expectations, and insert counterpoints and dissenting voices that make for a complex portrayal of the process of colonial modernization. He begins the chapter "La India regenerada" ("India Regenerated") by praising the British presence on the subcontinent ("Es, en efecto, dentro de los gobiernos coloniales, el que más se acerca a la perfección" (62) ("Indeed, among colonial governments, it comes closest to perfection") but then interviews a local anticolonial intellectual, who analyzes the effectiveness and dangers of British colonialism:

> Los verdaderos enemigos de la política colonial debemos odiar más la liberalidad inglesa actual que la antigua ferocidad española. Vea usted, si no, los resultados. España ha perdido su imperio mientras Inglaterra, después de la independencia americana, lo ensancha. . . . Un yugo de flores, todos lo aceptan. Así, mientras los cubanos, los portorriqueños y los filipinos levantábanse en armas, los coloniales ingleses proclamaban su libertad, llenos de agradecimiento hacia la metrópoli que, lejos de tiranizarlos, los protege. Esto es una lástima, creálo V., pues tal sistema acostumbra a los pueblos a soportar las cadenas, y arraiga en Europa la idea de que es necesario colonizar todo el resto del mundo. (64–65)

> The true enemies of colonial politics must hate English liberality more than the old Spanish ferocity. If not, you see the results. Spain has lost its empire, while England, after

> American independence, has expanded its empire. . . . A yoke of flowers, everyone accepts it. Therefore, while the Cubans, Puerto Ricans, and Filipinos rise up in arms, the English colonies proclaim their freedom, full of gratitude to a metropolis that, far from tyrannizing, protects them. This is a shame, believe me, because this system gets people used to living in chains, and establishes in Europe the idea that it is necessary to colonize the whole rest of the world.

This voice, opposed to the British imperial regime, analyzes the relation of colonial domination through hegemonic consent and contrasts with Gómez Carrillo's own view of the process as one of mere bureaucratic, infrastructural, and cultural modernization: "Él [inglés] es quien ha cruzado de líneas férreas las selvas vírgenes; él quien ha hecho revivir las antiguas culturas muertas; él quien ha implantado el dominio de la justicia" (61) ("The Englishman is the person who has crossed the virgin forests with railroad tracks; the person who has revived the ancient dead cultures; the person who has established the realm of justice"). But it is Gómez Carrillo who introduces the militant anticolonial voice and juxtaposes it with the exotic dancer. In the same way, in Tokyo, he second-guesses his exoticizing perception and denounces it as an ideological apparition: "¡Singular y lamentable alma del viajero! En vez de alimentarse de realidades lógicas, vive de fantasmagóricas esperanzas" (147–48) ("Strange and pitiful soul of the traveler! Instead of nourishing itself with logical realities, it lives on illusory hopes"). Gómez Carrillo's eastbound travel is far more complex than Darío's Orientalist lens gives him credit for.

To make sense of Gómez Carrillo's ambivalent, oscillating attitude toward the otherness of his Eastern destinations and the social worlds he encounters there, it is useful to think about it in relation to the writings of Victor Segalen, a contemporary French poet, essayist, linguist, critic, and eastbound traveler whom Gómez Carrillo greatly admired (Colombi, *Viaje* 234). In *Essai sur l'exotisme, une aesthétique du divers* (*Essay on Exoticism: An Aesthetic of Diversity*) (which he began in 1904 and left unfinished after his death in 1919), Segalen developed a notion of exoticism capable of producing an aesthetic critique of the colonialist rhetoric that had characterized French and British Orientalism since the eighteenth century: "For Segalen, writing in a time when financial capital already occupied the political economic horizon and imperialist powers competed madly to seize and colonize much of the globe outside of Euro-America, the appeal to exoticism promised to trade the vast unevenness of this moment for the poetic dream of aesthetic diversity and the fantasy of irreparable loss of what never was" (Harootunian vii–viii). Segalen proposed a notion of exoticism that was emptied out of the clichés produced by the imaginaries of imperialism and tourism—"le palmier et le chameau; casque de colonial; peaux noires et soleil jaune" (*Essai* 35) ("palm tree and camel; pith helmet; black skins and yellow suns"; *Essay* 19)—and that in turn opened the epistemological space to consider "la sensation d'exotisme qui n'est autre que la notion du different; la perception du Divers; la connaisance de quelque chose qui n'est pas soi-même; et le pouvoir d'exotisme, qui n'est que le pouvoir de *Concevoir autre*" (35) ("the sensation of Exoticism, which is nothing other than the notion of difference, the perception of Diversity, the knowledge that something is other than one's self; and Exoticism's power is nothing other than the ability to conceive otherwise"; 19). If the rhetoric of Orientalism reifies alterity and transforms it into a transparent commodity ready to be imported, consumed, and reinscribed within the epistemological parameters that reproduce the hierarchies between global cultural singularities, Segalen proposes an exoticism that "n'est donc pas une adaptation; n'est donc pas la compréhension parfaite d'un hors soi-même qu'on étreindrait en soi, mais la perception aiguë et immédiate d'une incompréhensibilité éternelle. Partons donc de cet aveu d'impénétrabilité. Ne nous flattons pas d'assimiler les moeurs, les races, les nations, les autres; mais au contraire éjouissons-nous de ne le pouvoir jamais; nous réservant ainsi la perdurabilité du plaisir de sentir le Divers" (38) ("is therefore not an adaptation to something; it is not therefore not the perfect comprehension of something outside oneself which one would contain in oneself, but the keen and immediate perception of an eternal incomprehensibility. Let us proceed from this admission of impenetrability. Let us not flatter ourselves for assimilating mores, races, nations and others who differ from us. On the contrary, let us rejoice in our inability to do so"; 21). Against the prevalent understanding of exoticism as it had been practiced by eastbound and southbound French travel writers since the eighteenth century (from Bernardin de Saint-Pierre and Chateaubriand to Loti and Saint-Pol-Roux), Segalen's desire to preserve difference undoes the assumption of the superiority of the West at the core of the accounts of alterity in those writers. But, as Christopher Bush explains, it also expands the scope of the concept and transforms into a democratic epistemology for global modernism: "The true exotic for Segalen might be said to be the foreignness of the object to the subject, but only if object is taken in the broadest sense of any object of consciousness, including the self" (Bush, introduction 12).

In this chapter I propose a reading of Gómez Carrillo's eastbound travel writings that places them in the gap between these two notions of alterity. Against what many critics have put forth, Gómez Carrillo did not simply mimic the tradition of French Orientalism from the dislocated position of enunciation he occupied between Paris, Spain, and Latin America but regularly contradicted it by opening up a counterpunctual space of cosmopolitan contestation.[1] Indeed, Segalen's critique of the colonial underpinnings of a commonplace conception of exoticism is a very productive point of departure to render visible the cosmopolitan tension (which I call cosmopolitan interruption) in Gómez Carrillo's eastbound travels—not only in *De Marsella a Tokio* but also in accounts of journeys to other Orients such as Russia (*Sensaciones de Rusia: Paisaje de Alemania* [*Sensations of Russia: Passage from Germany*] [1905] and *La Rusia actual* [*Russia Today*] [1906]) and the Middle East (*Romerías* [*Pilgrimages*] [1912] and *Jerusalén y la Tierra Santa* [*Jerusalem and the Holy Land*] [1912]). My point is that, even when his itineraries and perceptions are guided and conditioned by the Orientalist library he has internalized, his writing opens a space for the articulation of a point of view that contradicts and interrupts hegemonic mimicry, producing a discourse of marginal cosmopolitanism that posits a world beyond Paris and London—like that of Captain James Cook, which I looked at briefly in chapter 1, but with an awareness of the Latin American cultural field's overcontentment with its provincial world mappings. At the same time, in this process of world making that redefines the region's representations of the scope of the world, I highlight a number of instances where the hegemonic perspective breaks down as the Orientalist traveler recognizes the oppression and sorrow of an eastern European Jewry that interpellates a cosmopolitan subjectivity in Gómez Carrillo.

WORLD MAKING AND THE DISLOCATION OF PARIS

In the global maps of *modernismo*'s travels, the most traversed routes connect the cultural capitals of Spanish America (Buenos Aires, Mexico City, Lima, Bogota, Caracas, Havana, and Santiago), and each of them with New York, Paris, Madrid, and, to a lesser extent, London.

Imagined as curved red lines drawn on a map, these itineraries of *modernismo* show its limited geographical scope: a striated space with an inter-American, transatlantic, and Franco-Hispanic core.[2] Although the Oriental journey is clearly marginal, the fact that it was taken at all forces us to revise established certainties about a *modernismo* conceived exclusively in relation to its inter- and transatlantic horizons.

Before and after Gómez Carrillo's excursions to Russia (1905), to India, Thailand, China, Korea, and Japan (1905), and to the Levant and Jerusalem (1910), and especially after the 1868 Meiji-era reforms opened Japan to the West and sent shock waves throughout Asia, a handful of Latin American intellectuals traveled east, writing books and *crónicas* that underscored the exceptional nature of their experiences east of Paris.[3] But those *modernistas* who traveled to China and Japan during the same period as Gómez Carrillo codified the subjective experience of an "Orientalized" Orient (Said 5) in the narrative protocols of eastbound travel writing. These writers included the Mexican José Juan Tablada, sent by the *Revista Moderna* to spend the year 1900 in Japan and report on a country that fascinated the local cultural elite; Efrén Rebolledo, who lived in Tokyo between 1908 and 1918 and represented Mexico in different diplomatic functions; and the Salvadorean Arturo Ambrogi, who reproduced Gómez Carrillo's trajectory in a *viaje de juventud* from the Indian Ocean to East Asia in 1915.[4]

Beatriz Colombi argues convincingly that the construction of the Orient in the *modernistas*' travel writing should be understood as an attempt to estrange Latin American culture, "el modo de imaginar otro escenario, no tan sólo de evasión, sino de estímulo a la imaginación y superación de los temas adocenados en las literaturas nacionales. Una función, podríamos pensar, liberadora del gravamen de lo nacional" (*Viaje* 225) ("a way of imagining another scenario, not just by evasion but rather stimulation of the imagination and improvement upon the mediocre subjects of national literatures. We could think of it as a liberation from the burden of the national"). I want to contextualize my analysis of Gómez Carrillo's travel writing not in terms of the estrangement that Colombi registers but rather in terms of a historical function specific to those world-making writers, that is, those whose travels veered from the most frequented Euro-American routes and destinations.

Gómez Carrillo's *crónicas* and travel books reached readers from Paris to Madrid, Mexico to Buenos Aires, and everywhere in between—thanks to a well-oiled network of newspapers and magazines that reprinted every installment of his overseas adventures—and shaped the perception of the world as a larger frame within which Latin America had a place. Indeed, eastbound travel narratives produced a *Latin American* world that now stretched well beyond Paris (although that city remained its structural center); the world did not preexist the global circulation of *modernistas* like Gómez Carrillo, whose itineraries, both physical and discursive, materialized a wider world before their readers' eyes.

In Europe since the 1880s, the reading audience's experience of a world that "was now genuinely global" (Hobsbawm 13) was overdetermined by a variety of cultural discourses but also by the intense and uneven flow of people, goods, and information between metropolis and colonies, formal or informal. In Latin America, however, those members of the elite interested in the local impact of the aesthetic, cultural, and economic reshuffling of global relations depended almost entirely on narratives of travel to East Asia to represent a world larger and more diverse than their transatlantic confines. But even when texts like Gómez Carrillo's display the global spread of modernist practices and rhetorics beyond familiar Franco-American itineraries, Paris remains the center that determines the particular nature of the universality that mediates this Latin American world. If for Darío the world was an abstract idea made up of names mediated by the universality of French culture, in Gómez Carrillo there is an actual, material world that displays that universality as a true process of cultural globalization articulated by colonial and cosmopolitan epistemologies, dislocated trajectories, and very effective imaginaries.

And yet, I would like to avoid presenting the difference between these figurations of the world in Darío and Gómez Carrillo as an irreducible contradiction between the world as idea and imaginary modernist horizon and the world as a concrete planetary field of transcultural historical interactions. In *Ideographic Modernism*, Christopher Bush explains that texts' citational uses of China (those reciting conventional topoi "in ways that would [supposedly] render referential accuracy essentially moot"; xxvi) and referential uses (those relying on some representation and account of a real place) are closely interrelated and depend on one another. According to Bush, we should not deny referential value to purely imaginary relations to the signifier "China," or overlook the fictional construction of its referentiality. Instead he proposes to weaken the distinction between these two uses in order to shed light on the fact that "citation constitutes a mode of reference"

and that "reference involves an irreducible element of citation" (xxvi). I think these are very productive terms to think about the uses of the world in cosmopolitan literary traditions, and in the case of Gómez Carrillo's eastward travels they illuminate his writing's complex, contradictory, and markedly modernist discursive constructions of Paris and, as I shall demonstrate, the Oriental.

First, Paris. In Gómez Carrillo's writing, the capital of French culture makes it possible to pose the world as an internally undifferentiated totality of modernist culture; the city is the ontologically privileged point of departure and arrival that grounds both a Latin American discourse on universality and the meaning of his travels. In his classic text "La psicología del viajero" ("The Psychology of the Traveler") (1910), Gómez Carrillo explains that "no sentimos ni la fatiga del viaje, ni las molestias de los hoteles, ni los mareos de los barcos, ni las tristezas de las interminables tardes solitarias, porque, gracias a todo eso, podemos ahora sentir la dulce belleza parisina mejor que hace tres meses. . . . De todo el viaje y de todos los viajes, tú constituyes en verdad nuestro único placer infinito" (139) ("We do not feel the fatigue of the journey, or the nuisances of the hotels, or the queasiness of the ships, or the sadness of endless lonely afternoons, because, thanks to all that, we can feel the sweet Parisian beauty better now than three months ago. . . . Of all the journey, and of all journeys, you are truly our only infinite pleasure"). One travels in order to return to Paris; the meaning of travel is found, not in the experience of the culture encountered at the destination, but rather in the distance and absence from Paris. Paris is *oikos*: the home that fixes the meaning of travel as an economy of gains and losses (Van den Abbeele xviii).[5] Travel here is merely a function of the relation between Paris and its global others, an interval away from home.[6]

In spite of its lucid analysis of the pervasiveness of travel and dislocation in Latin America at the turn of the century, which situates Gómez Carrillo close to Segalen's sensibility ("La afición por los viajes va convirtiéndose, según las estadísticas de las agencias ferroviarias y marítimas, en una pasión inquietante" ("La psicologia del viajero" 125) ("The affinity for travel is becoming, according to railway and maritime statistics, a worrying passion"), it is surprising that the same essay that puts forth this compelling "travel theory" also complains about the historical forces that take us away from home, declaring that global modernity has erased the markers of cultural difference that made travel worthwhile centuries and decades earlier: "Lo exterior, la

cultura, el barniz es, por lo menos en tiempos normales, casi uniforme en el mundo entero. Las levitas y los sombreros han nivelado el tipo europeo y americano. En Londres como en Berlín, y en Nueva York como en Buenos Aires, el hombre vive del mismo modo, se viste del mismo modo, habla del mismo modo y, en las cuestiones generales, piensa poco más o menos del mismo modo, recortando sus ideas según los mismos figurines intelectuales" (127) ("The outside, the culture, the varnish is, at least at normal times, almost uniform throughout the whole world. Frock coats and hats have equalized the European and American man. In London as in Berlin, in New York as in Buenos Aires, men live the same way, dress the same way, speak the same way, and, on general issues, think more or less the same way, refining their ideas according to the same intellectual fashions"). Traveling is pointless in a world where the globalization of modernity prevents the experience of difference in terms of everyday life, embodied culture, and intellectual discourse. But a year later, in June 1912, upon returning from Istanbul, Smyrna, and Rhodes (a trip he writes about in *Romerías*; he had been to Lebanon and Palestine the year before), he writes an essay that refutes the central argument of "La psicología del viajero." Now the markedly Orientalist poetic experience of his Middle Eastern voyage stands in striking contrast to the modernist *ennui* of a gray and ordinary Paris that Charles Baudelaire depicted in *Les fleurs du mal* (*The Flowers of Evil*):

> ¿Quién ha dicho que el mayor placer de un viaje, para los que vivimos en París, es el retorno? Yo, probablemente, entre otros. Pero, de seguro, fue al volver de alguna ciudad de aguas bulliciosas y tristes, en los días luminosos en que el sol, "ese dorador," convierte en áureas madejas las cabelleras de las obreritas. . . . Ahora, en verdad, rectifico. Este París pálido bajo el inmenso cristal ahumado de su cielo que tiene entre sus muros estrechos más gente que toda la Siria, con Jerusalem y Damasco y Beirut, me causa, al regresar de Oriente, una sensación infinita de congoja. . . . Estas lástimas yo mismo la experimento ahora, comparando la existencia que acabo de dejar con la que voy a adoptar de nuevo. . . . Hoy, por lo menos, que aún no he recibido el contagio de la existencia vibrante, estoy seguro de que cualquier beduino de Damasco, cualquier árabe de Jafa, cualquier *felá* de Luxor, es más feliz que mis amigos del Bulevar,

> los triunfadores de las artes, los que se sienten superiores porque tienen un automóvil trepidante, una querida trepidante y un alma trepidante. (*Romerías* 107–09)
>
> Who said that the greatest pleasure of a journey, for those of us who live in Paris, is to come home? I, probably, among others. But, to be sure, it was upon coming back from some city with noisy and sad waters, on the luminous days when the sun, "that gilder," turns the young workers' hair into golden mops. . . . Now, in truth, I correct myself. This pale Paris under the immense smoked crystal of its sky that contains more people within its narrow walls than all of Syria, with Jerusalem and Damask and Beirut, gives me, upon returning from the Orient, a sensation of infinite anguish. . . . These woes that I now experience, comparing the existence that I just left behind to the one that I will once again adopt. . . . Today, at least, when the vibrant existence has not yet infected me, I am sure that any Bedouin from Damask, any Arab from Jafa, any *felá* from Luxor, is happier than my friends on the *Bulevar*, triumphant in the arts, who feel superior because they have an exciting car, an exciting girlfriend, and an exciting soul.[7]

There is no doubt that Gómez Carrillo's discourse reinforces the colonial episteme of Orientalism, which, according to Edward Said, produces the Orient as the silent Other of a supposedly stable West, making "more rigid the sense of difference between the European and Asiatic parts of the world" (204), as well as promoting "the difference between the familiar (Europe, the West, 'us') and the strange (the Orient, the East, 'them')" (43). Orientalism creates a global field of cultural unevenness that restores the experience of travel, understood as leaving one's home to enter into a world of (backward and exoticist or hypermodern) difference. The differential surplus of orientalist exoticism is the signifier of a discontinuity between a world divided against itself that the discourse of Orientalism attempts to reconcile with a language that invokes the violent symbolic practices embedded in the long tradition of colonial relations.

Gómez Carrillo reinscribes Baudelaire's *ennui* in a global map structured around the binary opposition between sameness and otherness, but I propose that when he travels eastwards he oscillates between drawing on a ready-made Orientalist toolkit and attempting to undo and destabilize the exoticist fascination with the landscape of Asian cultural difference. If one essay panders to the Orientalist expectations of elite peninsular and Latin American readers, the other underscores the continuity or lack of difference between these supposedly irreconcilable cultural spaces. In a remarkable scene in *De Marsella a Tokio*, he recalls his dumbfounded reaction upon arriving in Saigon, Indochina (Vietnam), which leads him to reflect on the entirety of his eastern voyage:

> Media hora más tarde, cuando el cochero anamita os abre la portezuela de su "malabar," os figuráis despertar de un ensueño de exotismo. Vuestro viaje de más de un mes, vuestros paseos por las callejuelas de Adén, pobladas de árabes que agonizan de sed bajo el sol implacable; vuestros entusiasmos entre las palmeras de Colombo; vuestra estupefacción infantil en las calles chinas de Singapur, olorosas á ajo, á miel, a vainilla y a grasa . . . todo fue un ensueño.
>
> La realidad, héla ahí: estáis en París, no habéis salido de París. . . . Esa gran iglesia cuyas campanas cantan sus himnos crepusculares, es un San Agustín ó una Trinidad cualquiera. La arquitectura es la misma. . . . Del otro lado de la plaza, el Palacio de Correo. Es bello y amplio. Un tumulto inmenso lo llena. Debe de ser la hora del correo para Marsella, para Lyon, para Burdeos. En las ventanillas, los empleados, antentos y nerviosos, os sirven precipitadamente, hablando el francés de *faubourg*. Al salir del correo . . . a uno y otro lado, casas elegantes con jardines y verjas de hierro. Es una avenida de Neuilly, no hay duda. . . . En una esquina el café de la Música; en la otra, el café Continental; en la de más allá, el café de la Terraza; en la cuarta, el café de Francia. . . . Sí, no hay duda, esto es París. En provincia no hay ni tantos cafés, ni tantos bebedores, ni tanto lujo, ni tantas músicas. Es París una tarde de Agosto. (108–09)

> Half an hour later, when the Annamese driver opens the door to your "*malabar*," you imagine that you are waking from an exotic dream. Your journey of more than a month, your strolls through Aden's little streets, populated by thirsty Arabs under an implacable sun; your excitement

> among the palm trees that smelled like garlic, honey, vanilla, and lard . . . it was all a dream.
>
> Reality, there it is: you are in Paris, you have not left Paris. . . . That large church whose bells sing twilight hymns is any Saint Augustine or Trinity. The architecture is the same. . . . On the other side of the Plaza, the Post Office. It is beautiful and large. An immense uproar fills it. It must be time for the mail to Marseille, to Lyon, to Bordeaux. At the counter, the employees, attentive and nervous, serve you hastily, speaking the French of the *faubourg*. Upon leaving the Post Office . . . on one side and the other, elegant houses with gardens and iron gates. It is clearly an avenue in Neuilly. . . . On a corner, the Music Café; on the other corner, the Continental Café; on one far corner, the Terrace Café; on the fourth corner, the France Café. . . . Yes, there is no doubt, this is Paris. The provinces do not have so many cafés, or so many people drinking, or so much luxury, or so much music. It is Paris on an August afternoon.

Gómez Carrillo is stunned and disappointed not to find the exotic landscape he was expecting in Saigon, and it is this disconcerting moment when he instead finds himself right at home that interests me. I want to explore this antiexoticist approach and Gómez Carrillo's use of Paris as a measure of home.

The cultural politics of orientalist exoticism has a prominent place in imaginaries of *modernismo*; almost every major Latin American modernist writer has constructed poems or fictions around Orientalist tropes, a collection that includes Del Casal's poems "Kakemono," "Sourinomo," and "Japonerías" ("Japonaiseries"), Darío's short stories "La muerte de la emperatriz de China" ("The Death of the Empress of China") and "El rey burgués" ("The Bourgeois King"), Asunción Silva's *De sobremesa* (*After-Dinner Conversation*), and Nervo's poems in *El estanque de los lotos* (*The Lotus Pond*) and essays "Las crisantemas" ("The Chrysanthemums") and "El dragón chino" ("The Chinese Dragon"), among others.[8] As I have already pointed out, Gómez Carrillo actively participates in this discursive formation even to a larger extent than most other *modernistas*. For this reason, it is particularly interesting that his first reaction upon descending to the streets of Saigon is a sense of familiarity. He conveys the same impression about Shanghai, his next stop after Saigon: "Algo que no tiene nada de exótico, ni de lejano, ni de raro. Ningún follaje extraño aparece en las riberas, y en el horizonte ningún color luce violento. Es un panorama de paz laboriosa, como los que, todos los días, vemos en Europa" (119) ("Something that is not at all exotic, or distant, or strange. No strange foliage appears along the banks, and no color shines intensely on the horizon. It is a panorama of industrious peace, like those that we see every day in Europe"). The exotic destinations that preceded Saigon and Shanghai in his voyage (Egypt, Ceylon) were a dream, a hallucination; they belong to a fictional cartography of imagined Oriental contiguities.[9]

The absence of an exoticizing gaze in Gómez Carrillo's first impressions of Saigon and Shanghai, in contradiction to the Orientalist vein of his traveling subjectivity, can be understood in relation to the development of a cosmopolitan point of view that is able to produce an unlikely even, smooth, and homogeneous global territory, a cosmopolitan continuity between Paris, Saigon, and Shanghai. Gómez Carrillo's cosmopolitanism places him as far away from Loti as from Segalen: he avoids colonial commodifications of these cities for metropolitan consumption, but his universalizing outlook bridges the differential gap that separates Paris from its modernist margins in ways that exclude him from the multicultural world embraced by Segalen. Gómez Carrillo's cosmopolitan traveler feels at home in the world, or rather feels at home in a world that results from the modernist universalization of Paris's hegemonic particularity: *Paris is wherever I feel at home,* or *I feel at home wherever in the world I find Paris.* Eight years later, during his first trip to Argentina, he feels the same familiarity in his hotel room in Buenos Aires:

> Al abrir mi balcón esta primera mañana, singulares sensaciones me perturban el alma. Todo lo que hecho desde el día en que abandoné París se desvanece de pronto cual un sueño. Cádiz, un sueño . . . El barco, un sueño . . . Montevideo, un sueño . . . Y la realidad aparece ante mis ojos, obligándome a notar que no me he movido, que no he salido de mi casa, que no he abandonado mi rinconcillo habitual. Lo que veo, en efecto, es lo de siempre: cielo, calle, gente, coches. Ya antes de salir de la cama, el ruido que desde la calle sube hasta mi estancia habíame sorprendido con sus notas familiares. Porque, así como los ciegos de El Cairo reconocen cada barrio por el murmullo de sus vendedores

> ambulantes, así yo sé de memoria las orquestaciones de bulevar parisiense sus motivos que cambian según las horas del día. (*Encanto de Buenos Aires*, 23, 25)
>
> Opening my balcony this first morning, strange sensations disturb my soul. Everything I have done since the day that I left Paris disappears immediately like a dream. Cadiz, a dream . . . The ship, a dream . . . Montevideo, a dream . . . And reality appears before my eyes, forcing me to notice that I have not moved, I have not left my house, I have not abandoned my habitual corner. Indeed, I see what I always see: sky, street, people, cars. And even before I get out of bed, the noise that rises to my room from the street surprised me with its familiar notes. Because, as Cairo's blind know each neighborhood by its rustling peddlers, I know the orchestrations of the Parisian boulevard by heart, with its motifs that change with the time of day.[10]

Saigon, Shanghai, Buenos Aires: it could be argued that the dislocation of Parisian phantasmagorias to produce a Paris abroad needs to be inscribed within an economy of colonial representations; at the turn of the century, all three places had links to Parisian urban culture that were notably overdetermined by different articulations of formal and informal, material and symbolic, colonialism. Saigon was the first major city that the French colonial army conquered on the Indochinese peninsula in 1859, and it remained the cultural capital of their presence in Southeast Asia for the next century. Shanghai had been an international port with autonomous British, French, and US colonial enclaves since 1849; the French concession in particular was designed with tree-lined streets to resemble a Parisian neighborhood (thus its nickname, "The Paris of the East"). In the case of Buenos Aires, the dramatic redesign of the city's center that was carried out from 1880 to 1920 was inspired by Baron Haussmann's renovation of Paris between 1853 and 1870. Reinforcing this connection, the construction of *goût grec* (Greek taste) neoclassical public buildings and art nouveau commercial buildings and private mansions satisfied the French aspirations of the Argentine elite.

The fact that Gómez Carrillo sees Paris in Saigon, Shanghai, and Buenos Aires could be read as an effect of French colonial domination, and in this sense the fact that he feels at home there could be seen as a reproduction of colonial mappings and relations of power. After all, his trip would have been impossible without the transoceanic and intercontinental infrastructure that the French and British empires had developed in North Africa and Asia. And yet, a critical interpretation of his representation of peripheral locations as displaced "pequeños Parises" ("little Parises") should look beyond colonial determinations (which are by all means present in his narrative) and pay attention to the underlying deexoticizing, cosmopolitan drive to produce the world as an undifferentiated totality of Parisian modernism. But to posit such a global formation, Gómez Carrillo needs a figure invested with an unmistakable universality that can serve as grounds to identify such disparate cities and cultures. Naturally, for Gómez Carrillo, as it was for Darío, that figure of universality is a Paris stripped of its particularly French content. In contrast to the particularistic ideologies then prevalent in Europe (nationalistic views of France's superiority, or Orientalist views of Asia's irreducible exoticism) that reinscribed Saigon, Shanghai, or Buenos Aires in global mappings that essentialized cultural difference, Gómez Carrillo imagines them as dislocated Parises whose spatial distribution traces the contours of a unified modernist world that follows the shape of his desire.

I have suggested that some of these instances in *De Marsella a Tokio* where Gómez Carrillo sees sameness and continuity, rather than ontological difference, between the capital of Western aesthetics and the Eastern world can be read as cosmopolitan disruptions in the discourse of Orientalism. But Gómez Carrillo's cosmopolitanism needs to be addressed in all its complexity. Why would representing the world as a homogeneous totality where cultural difference is seen as a sign of backwardness be a cosmopolitan stance rather than a celebration of hegemonic forms of universalism? Because this universalist discursive maneuver has the clearly progressive and democratic effect of neutralizing the ethnic hierarchies of the Orientalist construction of the East/West gap. And also because of its Latin American/peripheral specificity: for a writer who thought of Latin America's cultural particularity as a backward, premodern stigma, the representation of the world as a flat and undifferentiated global space makes it possible to imagine the end of exclusion. From the point of view of marginally cosmopolitan Latin Americans, the production of universality as the negation of difference is an emancipatory, equalizing strategic move, for when Saigon, Shanghai, and Buenos Aires are distant and yet organic parts of Paris, Latin American *modernistas* can inscribe their own aesthetic subjectivity in those imagined cities and thus transcend the Latin American identity that bears the marks of exclusion and belatedness.

Upon his arrival in Japan, Gómez Carrillo articulates the most radical instance of representation of an Asian world whose cosmopolitanism is defined by having overcome its cultural difference:

> Por mi parte, este Yokohama me aparece tal cual me lo había figurado. Es un puerto cosmopolita, y no una ciudad japonesa. Su arquitectura es la misma de Amsterdam y del Havre. Su vida es de negocio y no de placer. Los edificios grandes, los que tienen torres, miradores, galerías, los que dominan las calles y humillan a las casas en general, no son ni templos, ni universidades, ni bibliotecas, ni museos. Son oficinas. Aquel que parece un teatro es el depósito de los petróleos de la Compañía Standard de Nueva York; el otro, muy grande, muy blanco, que se enseñora en un inmenso espacio vacío y que los extranjeros toman por Casa Consistorial, es la Specie Bank; el de más allá, tan noble en su aspecto con fachadas del Renacimiento, es la agencia de los vapores alemanes; el de enfrente, algo bajo pero muy vasto, que parece un circo o un teatro popular, es el despacho de la Compañía Nipón Yusen Kaisa. . . . Así es y así tiene que ser. . . .
>
> Pero mis compañeros de viaje no quieren pensar de esta manera. El Japón, para ellos, tiene que ser japonés. Y se preguntan, inquietos, en dónde están las puertecillas correderas de papel, las musmés seguidas de tocadores de chamisen, los hombres desnudos y los árboles de tres pulgadas de altura. . . . ¡Y encontrarse ahora con una ciudad que lo mismo podría ser holandesa que canandiense, o alemana, o escandinava! Porque aquí ni siquiera tienen los enamoradas de lo exótico letreros misteriosos en caracteres increíbles, cual en Shanghai o en Hong-Kong. Todo está en ingles. (*De Marsella* 139–42)

> To me, this Yokohama appears exactly as I imagined it. It is a cosmopolitan port, not a Japanese city. Its architecture is the same as Amsterdam's and Le Havre's. Its life is based on business, not pleasure. The large buildings with towers, lookouts, galleries, that dominate the streets and generally

> dwarf the houses, are not temples, or universities, or libraries, or museums. They are office buildings. That building that looks like a theater is the warehouse of the Standard Company of New York; the other building, very large, very white, taking over an immense space, that foreigners think is the city council building, is Specie Bank; the one that is further away, so noble in appearance with its Renaissance facade, is the German steamship agency; the building in front, rather short but huge, looking like a circus or a popular theater, is the offices of the Nipón Yusen Kaisa Company. . . . That is how it is and how it must be. . . .
>
> But my travel companions do not want to think this way. Japan, to them, must be Japanese. And they ask, restless, where are the little sliding paper gates, the young girls followed by shamisen players, the naked men, and the trees three inches high. . . . And now to find themselves in a city that could be Dutch or Canadian, or German, or Scandinavian! Because here, lovers of the exotic do not even have mysterious signs in incredible characters, as in Shanghai or Hong Kong. Everything is in English.

In establishing Yokohama's cosmopolitanism, Gómez Carrillo does not resort to a figure of Parisian universality. As one of the Asian centers of global capitalism, Yokohama can be depicted as a space defined by the utter absence of signs of cultural particularity, and the concrete content of its cosmopolitanism is the presence of global capital and the city's architecture, wardrobe, and language. (If, at the turn of the century, French is the global language of civilization, English is already the language of business.) To stress the point, he contrasts his normative agreement with the city's modern and antitraditional design ("Así es, y así tiene que ser") with the disappointed exoticist expectations of his travel companions—a clever rhetorical device to allude to his split self. I insist on this constitutive contradiction of the eastbound traveler that can be traced throughout *De Marsella a Tokio:* "¡Singular y lamentable alma del viajero! En vez de alimentarse de realidades lógicas, vive de fantasmagóricas esperanzas y sufre de inevitables desilusiones. Lo que no corresponde a su egoísmo sentimental, le causa tristezas incurables" (147–48) ("Strange and pitiful soul of the traveler! Instead of nourishing itself with logical realities, it lives on illusory hopes. Whatever does not correspond to its sentimental egoism makes it incurably sad").

Gómez Carrillo's Japanese sojourn illuminates a larger point, through a condition that Yokohama shares with the other Asian cities that Gómez Carrillo visits. What makes it possible to produce universal spaces out of Yokohama, Saigon, and Shanghai is that they cease to be Japanese, Vietnamese, or Chinese—that is, Oriental and therefore exotic—to instead become instances (*momente* in the language of Hegel's system) of the global totality of cultural modernism/capitalism.

WHAT OTHER? ORIENTALISM, COSMOPOLITANISM, AND THE JEWISH QUESTION

Gómez Carrillo populated the world that he opened up for the Spanish and Latin American reading publics with a familiar cast of Oriental characters, presenting them as mere surfaces, devoid in their typicality of concrete traces of human affect: eroticized exotic women; charming premodern natives whose behavior is expressive of an entire culture; mysterious, inscrutable, and deceitful men; and government officials, soldiers, merchants, figures of religiosity, and others that signify the colonial landscape.[11] The Oriental Otherness of these characters is defined by their status as oppositional moments in a process of identity formation whose theoretical narrative can be traced in Hegel's master/slave dialectics, Lacan's mirror stage theory, and Said's idea of the differential rise of Western culture as a function of the discourse of Orientalism.

Following the idea that I put forth in the first section of this chapter about the tension between Orientalism and cosmopolitanism in Gómez Carrillo's construction of his many eastbound trajectories, I want to interrogate the complex, interstitial place occupied by Jews in Gómez Carrillo's mappings of sameness and otherness from France to Algeria ("Sensaciones de Argelia" ["Sensations of Algeria"]), from Egypt, Sri Lanka, and Vietnam to China and Japan (*De Marsella a Tokio* and *La sonrisa de la esfinge* [*The Smile of the Sphinx*]), from Greece to Turkey (*La Grecia eterna* [*Eternal Greece*] and *Romerías*), from Paris to Russia (*La Rusia actual*), from Lebanon to Palestine (*Jerusalén y la Tierra Santa*), and from Madrid to Morocco (*Fez, la Andaluza* [*Fez, the Andalusian*]). The irruption of the Jew as victim of injustice and figure of universal suffering ("los más lamentable seres del mundo" [*De Marsella* 11] ["the most pitiful beings in the world"], "Esta raza que tantas virtudes tiene, es odiada universalmente" [*Jerusalén* 189] ["This race that has so many virtues, is universally despised"]) places the Orientalist traveler in a new, convoluted subject position. It reinforces Gómez Carrillo's Orientalist construction of the world east of Paris, identifying it as a cultural space that victimizes and inflicts pain on the Jews. But at the same time, it undermines the self-assuredness and aplomb of the Orientalist traveler and allows him to reimagine his cosmopolitanism as a form of ethical interpellation. The potential and limitations of this ethical moment need to be specified in relation to Gómez Carrillo's witnessing of one of the most important global intellectual debates of the turn of the century, around the false and prejudicial accusations of espionage against the French-Jewish army captain Alfred Dreyfus.

Within the larger argument of this book, Gómez Carrillo's overlooked concern with the figure of the Jew should be understood as a nodal point in modernity's global politics of identity formation, hegemonic relations, and the articulation of particular cultural formations with universalizing desires and discursive projects. This section can therefore be read as a Latin American episode of this problem as Aamir Mufti frames it in *Enlightenment in the Colony: The Jewish Question and the Crisis of Postcolonial Culture*: "the question of the Jews' status in modern culture and society as it first came to be formulated in the late eighteenth century" as defining "the problematic of secularization and minority in post-Enlightenment liberal culture as a whole . . . which are then disseminated globally in the emergence, under colonial and semicolonial conditions, of the forms of modern social, political, and cultural life" (2).

Gómez Carrillo's Jews bear all the external marks of their Oriental difference, but unlike other Oriental characters that express their culture Jews are represented as victims of the Orient. They are liminal subjects, distinguished by their unbelonging, at once included in and excluded from Western civilization and the Otherized East. In Jerusalem, Gómez Carrillo attentively observes prayer at the Western Wall with distanced fascination:

> Nada en ellos me choca. La fealdad de rostros de que hablan los libros europeos, no la noto. Al contrario. Entre los ancianos, descubro a cada paso tipos ideales de belleza bíblica, y muy a menudo los adolescentes me conmueven con sus grandes ojos tímidos. Esos mismos rizos que llevan sobre las sienes para obedecer el precepto levítico, no me parecen, después de todo más ridículos que el peinado de los

> cristianos o de los árabes; y en cuanto a sus túnicas de terciopelo de colores brillantes, de forma noble cuánto más armoniosas son, si bien se ve, que nuestros pantalones modernos. Pero esto del aspecto exterior es lo que menos debe importarnos. Aun ridículos de facha, los hombres que así conservan, a través de la tragedia perpetua su historia, una fe inquebrantable en sí mismos y en su misión providencial, merecen ser admirados como seres superiores. (*Jerusalén* 185–86)
>
> Nothing about them disgusts me. The ugliness of their faces that the European books mention, I do not see. To the contrary. Among the elderly, with every step I discover ideal figures of biblical beauty, and the adolescents move me with their large shy eyes. Those same curls that they wear over their temples out of obedience to the Levitical precept do not strike me, after all, as any more ridiculous than Christian or Arab hairstyles; and their brightly colored velvet tunics, noble in form, are so much more harmonious, if one looks closely, than our modern pants. But this external aspect should concern us the least. Even if ridiculous in appearance, the men that thus preserve, through the perpetual tragedy of their history, an unbreakable faith in themselves and their providential mission deserve to be admired as superior beings.

Gómez Carrillo makes a deliberate effort to express admiration for these Orthodox Jews in spite of their prominent markers of Oriental strangeness. His ambivalence toward them is apparent in his initial description of the scene: "I am not disgusted by them" ("Nada en ellos me choca"). Rather than bridge a gap between self and Other, the effect of this admission is quite the opposite, and the rest of the description is articulated around the distance between the Western identity that results from Gómez Carrillo's self-representation of his own traveling subjectivity, and the Oriental nature of the Jerusalem Jews. In other words, the actual meaning of his opening statement about the appearance of Orthodox Jews is shock and disgust. On his earlier trip to the Middle East, in an Istanbul street market, he repeats the same verb of shock and disgust, "me choca," to construct a scene of Orientalist difference:

> Me choca la gente también. Me chocan las bicicletas que pasan, exponiéndose a resbalar en las cortezas de naranjas; me chocan los conductores de los minúsculos tranvías, que apalean sin piedad a sus caballitos apocalípticos. . . Y me chocan los vendedores ambulantes como seres de cuento fantástico; esos vendedores de cosas misteriosas y brillantes, esos lánguidos vendedores, que llevan a cuestas tinajas plateadas, tablas multicolores, cestos colosales, sacos henchidos, y que pasan por las aceras lentamente, muy lentamente, recitando sus melopeas, incompresibles para mí. Me choca toda la gente, en fin: esta gente venida de todas partes, esta gente que habla todas las lenguas, esta gente que se atropella, que se roza, que se interpela. (*Romerías* 89–90)
>
> The people disgust me, too. The bicycles that pass, at the risk of slipping on orange peels, disgust me; the drivers of the tiny carts, who beat their little apocalyptic horses without mercy, disgust me. And the peddlers disgust me like beings out of a fantasy story; those sellers of mysterious and shiny things, those languid sellers, who carry silver pitchers, multicolored boards, colossal baskets, full sacks, on their backs, and pass slowly, very slowly, on the sidewalks, reciting their monotonous songs, incomprehensible to me. In any event, all of these people disgust me: these people from all over, these people that speak all languages, these people who collide into each other, who brush past each other, who call out to each other.

Readers of Said will recognize Gómez Carrillo's disgust at the physical proximity of Oriental bodies in Istanbul's urban chaos as the flip side of the enchanted fascination of proximity to, say, an exotic Indian dancer.[12] The Orient "choca": it shocks and disturbs, but also collides with and runs into Gómez Carrillo, upsetting and destabilizing him. Upon returning from this trip to Rhodes and Turkey, he will find "este Paris pálido bajo el inmenso cristal ahumado de su cielo," to be a source of "una sensación infinita de congoja" (*Romerías* 107) precisely because it is predictable, understandable, and transparent. In Istanbul, however, he explains his irritation as the result of his inability to comprehend the urban music and movement of a city whose markedly Oriental chaos bewilders and annoys him. If the traveler is unable to read and understand the configuration of human bodies in Istanbul, the structural discourse of Orientalism is at work when, back in Paris, he idealizes and feels nostalgic about that very feeling of befuddlement.

Back in Jerusalem, the same reversal that keeps the Other at a distance can be seen in Gómez Carrillo's articulation of the Orientalist intelligibility that codifies the figure of the Orthodox Jew. The Jews' idiosyncratic physical features are Orientalized by their biblical nature; their attire and ritual hairstyle may be as "ridiculous" as *ours*, but their difference is nevertheless underscored explicitly. The key is not Gómez Carrillo's reaction to ridiculous but harmonious robes and *payot* (sidelocks) but rather their difference from "nuestros pantalones." What interests me is their inscription in an Eastern/Western and premodern/modern matrix of differential signification. "All aspects of the Jew, whether real or invented, are the locus of difference" (Gilman 2); whether, for Gómez Carrillo, Oriental Jews are to be admired and vindicated comes second to an operation of Orientalism that equates them, in their formal difference, to the Oriental subjects that disgust him. Doris Sommer has lucidly read Jewishness as the signifier of the social, political, and racial difference constitutive of the dramatic plot of Jorge Isaacs's *María*, "Jewishness is a Protean stigma that damns the characters one way or another: as an enfeebled inbreeding 'aristocracy' like the planters *and* as a racially different disturbance among the whites. . . . Being 'Jewish' [is] a double-bind that becomes Isaacs' vehicle for representing a dead-end for the planter class" (*Foundational Fictions* 173). In *The Wandering Signifier*, a remarkable book that builds upon these and other insights to postulate Jewishness as a privileged rhetoric of difference in the *longue durée* of Latin American literature, Erin Graff Zivin points out that "anxiety, desire, paranoia, attraction and repulsion towards 'Jewishness' are always in tension with (or representative of) larger attitudes towards otherness, whether racial, sexual, religious, national, economic, or even metaphysical. This is particularly significant in Latin American countries, in which ethnic others are more often of indigenous or African descent, and . . . raises the question of representing 'other others' through the figure of the Jew" (2–3).

But aside from this Orientalist *Otherizing* of the Orthodox Jerusalem Jew, Gómez Carrillo posits a different Jewish figure in his travels to Russia and en route to East Asia. This Jew is no longer the signifier of ethnic difference and irreducible particularity "slavishly bound to external Law and tradition, ritualistic and irrational" (Mufti 38), but

a victim of Oriental culture and social relations that he converts into a rare site of cosmopolitan redemption and ethical interpellation that "raises questions about deracination, homelessness, abstraction, supranational identifications, and divided loyalties" (Mufti 38).

The first of these cosmopolitan denunciations of injustice takes place in Russia, where Gómez Carrillo spent the winter of 1905. He went to cover the political reverberations of the January 22 Bloody Sunday massacre for the newspapers *El Liberal* (Madrid) and *La Nación* (Buenos Aires). On Bloody Sunday, forty unarmed strikers, protesting working conditions and the Russo-Japanese war, were assassinated by the Imperial Guard as they marched toward the Winter Palace to present a petition to Tsar Nikolay II. The repercussions of this brutal repression were felt across Europe (and would trigger the process that led to the October 1905 socialist revolution). Besides his weekly dispatches, Gómez Carrillo wrote two very different books about this journey, which were published almost consecutively.

Sensaciones de Rusia: Paisajes de Alemania (1905) is a traditional *modernista* travel narrative that focuses on the itinerary from Paris to Russia, with special attention to a landscape viewed from train windows. The keyword that summarizes the rhetoric of the entire book is *sensaciones*, which he took from Loti's rhetoric of travel (whether in travel books or novels), defined by the will to "decrier le reel qu'il décrète fugitive et donc insaisissable à l'image du temps qui passé. Chaque paysage, chaque décor, filter par le prisme de ses sentiments perd une partie de sa réalité et se décompose en un kaléidoscope du couleurs et d'impressions vagues" (Gagnière iv) ("censure the real, which he decreed fugitive and, therefore, impossible to apprehend in images of times passed. Each landscape, each décor, filtered by the prism of these sentiments loses some of its reality and is decomposed in a kaleidoscope of colors and vague impressions"). And in travel narratives that bear titles like *Sensaciones de arte* (*Sensations of Art*), *Sensaciones de París y Madrid* (*Sensations of Paris and Madrid*), *Sensaciones de Egipto, la India, la China y el Japón*, and "Sensaciones de Argelia," among others, Gómez Carrillo echoes the above description of Loti's discourse. As he explains in "La psicología del viajero": "Yo no busco nunca en los libros de viaje el alma de los países que me interesan. Lo que busco es algo más frívolo, más sutil, más pintoresco y más positivo: la sensación. Todo viajero artista, en efecto, podría titular su libro: Sensaciones. . . . Comparando descripciones de un mismo sitio hechas por autores diferentes, se ve la diversidad de las retinas" (129) ("I never

look for the soul of the countries that interest me in travel books. I look for something more frivolous, more subtle, more picturesque and more positive: sensation. Indeed, every artist-traveler could title his book: Sensations. . . . By comparing descriptions of the same place by different authors, we see the diversity of retinas").[13] Accordingly, in *Sensaciones de Rusia: Paisajes de Alemania*, all the reader gets is a cultural and social landscape sieved through the traveler's modernist subjectivity.

La Rusia actual (1906) is completely different. There, a journalistic protocol of representation is at work in the encounter with Saint Petersburg; the *crónicas* bear the marks of their original purpose and circulation. The term *actual* in the title is key: this is the really existing and contemporary Russia, as opposed to what attracts the eye on a voyage organized around a narrative of "sensaciones." This idea of travel narrative as reporting (what the newspapers that financed his trip expected from him, given the sense of urgency that political events in Russia generated throughout the world) led him to write extensively on the workers' struggles and sacrifices in furtherance of their revolutionary goals. More important than the representation of the Other in pain, however, is the traveler's encounter, or rather, avoidance of the face-to-face encounter, with the suffering Other: "Hoy he consagrado el día al más lamentable de los estudios: a la cuestión obrera. ¡Cuánta miseria y cuánta injusticia! ¡Cuántas lágrimas! ¡Cuánto rencor concentrado! Y eso que yo no he ido hasta el fondo del asunto viendo con mis propios ojos los dolores y oyendo con mis oídos las quejas sino que me contentado con leer algo de lo mucho que en estos días se ha publicado sobre la vida del obrero y sobre la legislación del trabajo" (81) ("I spent today on the most miserable of studies: labor issues. So much misery and so much injustice! So many tears! So much concentrated rancor! And this is without even going to the root of the issue and seeing the pain with my own eyes and hearing the complaints with my ears, as I have been satisfied to read some of the many recent publications on the life of the worker and labor legislation"). The political situation in Saint Petersburg during Gómez Carrillo's sojourn is so explosive that he rarely leaves his hotel, basing his reporting on second- and thirdhand sources that include books, French-language Russian newspapers, and interviews with experts that come to the hotel to discuss the social, political, and cultural situation. The narrative of *La Rusia actual* is doubly mediated, by the discourse of journalism that articulates the relation between Gómez Carrillo and his readership, but also by his relationship to the materiality of the Other's suffering.[14] It is under these discursive conditions that Jews make their appearance in the text, as the object of Tsarist and popular anti-Semitism, active persecution and legal discrimination, and forced migration:

> Todo les está vedado: creer, comerciar, amar, vivir. . . . En 1891 la sinagoga de Moscú fue cerrada. Y si para orar tienen que esconderse, para vivir tienen que someterse a la humillante costumbre del "ghetto." En las grandes ciudades les está prohibido hablar. Tampoco pueden radicarse en el campo. . . . Luego las restricciones han ido creciendo hasta llegar a los terribles decretos del gran duque Sergio, que determinaron el éxodo doloroso de todos los israelitas de Moscú. No pudiendo vivir en el campo, ni poseer inmuebles, el judío se ha visto reducido al comercio y a la industria. Pero tampoco como artesano tiene libertad de trabajo. Según las leyes, está excluido de todas las fábricas del Estado y de muchas fábricas particulares que existen en pequeñas ciudades donde los judíos no pueden habitar. (158–60)

> They are prohibited everything: believing, conducting business, loving, living. . . . In 1891 the Moscow synagogue was closed. And if they must hide to pray, they must endure the humiliating custom of the "ghetto" to live. In large cities they are prohibited from speaking. They cannot settle in the countryside either. . . . The restrictions increased until the terrible decrees of Grand Duke Sergei, which led to the painful exodus of all the Israelites of Moscow. Unable to live in the countryside or own property, the Jew has been reduced to business and industry. But he cannot work freely as a craftsman either. According to the law, he is excluded from all state factories and many private factories in small cities where Jews cannot live.

Gómez Carrillo's analysis of Russian Jews as victims of a double persecution, as workers and as ethnic subjects, has two apparent effects. On the one hand, because he compares them to the Jerusalem Jews, religion is neither the source of their discrimination nor the basis of his argument that they are treated unjustly. In the context of his Russian reporting, Jews are modern, historical subjects, whose oppression must be explainable by strictly sociopolitical and contingent forms of agency in the state and civil society. In this sense, Jerusalem could not be further from Russia. On the other hand, Gómez Carrillo defines the sorrow of the Jews largely in terms of their inability to actualize their social subjectivity through labor, a description that is very much in sync with Marx's early humanistic notion of productive work as "man's spiritual essence, his human essence" ("Economic and Philosophical Manuscripts" 328–29):

> En épocas florecientes para la minería, los israelitas encontraban ocupación, pero pronto vinieron nuevos reglamentos a hacerles abandonar ese trabajo. . . . Por otra parte, las fábricas de azúcar están situadas fuera de las ciudades y de los grandes centros de población, por lo que se da el caso de que en ellas sólo se encuentran empleados 25 ó 30.000 judíos, de los cuales el 40% son mujeres y niños. Casi la mitad de la población judía, es decir 2.500.000 se compone de artesanos, la mayoría zapateros, sastres, cerrajeros, carpinteros. . . . [Pero] la mayoría de ellos carece de trabajo. Si a esto se le agrega la competencia que les hace la gran industria, generalmente inaccesible para ellos, se comprende que los obreros judíos perezcan de hambre y busquen a todo trance el medio de escaparse del "ghetto" y de emigrar. (160–61)

> In eras when mining flourished, the Israelites found employment, but new rules soon made them abandon that work. . . . In addition, the sugar factories are located outside the cities and large population centers, which means that they employ only twenty-five thousand or thirty thousand Jews, 40 percent of whom are women and children. Almost half of the Jewish population, that is to say, 2.5 million, are craftsmen, mainly shoemakers, tailors, locksmiths, carpenters. . . . But the majority are without work. If to this we add the competition from big industry, generally closed to them, we understand why Jewish workers die of hunger and seek at all costs a way to escape the "ghetto" and emigrate.

Considering that the purpose of his trip was to report on the oppression of workers and their demands for political and economic justice, the fact that Gómez Carrillo dedicates an entire chapter to the situation of the Russian Jewry could be understood as a cosmopolitan demand for justice for subjects doubly victimized as workers *and* as Jews, or rather as workers whose material conditions are determined by a double exclusion because of their Jewish condition. But if Gómez Carrillo's representation of Jews in *La Rusia actual* is a cosmopolitan demand for justice, he keeps his distance from the actuality of Jewish misery in Moscow, a city he never visited. The same is true of the large and bloody pogroms in Kishinev (Bessarabia), Gomel (Belarus), and Irkutsk (Siberia) which he describes and denounces through second- and third-hand sources: "Estos datos los encuentro en la obra de Leroy Beaulieu sobre Rusia, pero hay otros que los completa y los corona. Oíd . . ." (161) ("I find these facts in Leroy Beaulieu's work on Russia, but others complete and finish them. Listen . . ."). The entire book is a collage of quotations and a compendium of references. He asks questions ("¿Cuál es la verdadera significación política del Semski Sobor [asamblea legislativa]?" [170] ["What is the true political significance of the Semski Sobor legislative assembly?"]), and bibliographic sources, rather than eyewitness reporting, provide tentative answers ("Los historiadores no dan a estas preguntas sino respuestas vagas" [171] ["Historians give only vague answers to these questions"]). Regardless of whether it is possible to articulate a cosmopolitan call for justice without any direct experience of Tsarist Russia's political unraveling or firsthand interaction with the victims of this historical process, the sensibility that Gómez Carrillo developed regarding the situation of eastern European Jews is quite remarkable, particularly given that he is significantly less inclined to show similar empathy toward almost any other Oriental subject that he encounters in his excursions beyond Paris and western Europe.

The imagination of Jewishness in Latin American literature is abundant. In *The Wandering Signifier*, Graff Zivin has identified some of their most relevant articulations. Regarding the turn of the century in particular, she explores scenes where Jewishness is seen as a pathological agent that threatens to infect or destabilize the unity of the social body, or the social space of cultural transactions structured around financial signifiers. As to the *modernista* formation, she analyzes several representations of the Franco-Hungarian physician, writer, and Zionist Max Nordau (*née* Simon Maximilian Südfeld), author of *Entartung* (*Degeneration*), an influential pathologico-moralistic, taxonomic, and deterministic exercise in social and cultural criticism. The

French translation of the German original circulated widely among Latin American intellectual elites and was reviewed and discussed extensively by Darío, Asunción Silva, and José Ingenieros, among others.[15] Gómez Carrillo wrote, "Notas sobre la enfermedad de la sensación desde el punto de vista de la literatura" ("Notes on an Illness of the Sensations from the Point of View of Literature") (1892), a long essay inspired by Nordau's *Degeneration*, and "Una visita a Max Nordau" ("A Visit to Max Nordau") (1893), an interview with the author. In both texts, which were later collected in *Almas y cerebros*, Gómez Carrillo appears completely indifferent to Nordau's Jewishness and his Zionist activism.

If not from this *modernista* trope, where does Gómez Carrillo's ethical engagement with the discrimination of eastern European Jews (which was certainly unique in the context of *modernismo*) come from? My hypothesis is that his representation of Jews' exceptional status in the context of a diverse cast of marginalized Oriental characters, and his cosmopolitan empathy for them, derive from having lived through the Dreyfus Affair in France. He was the only *modernista* in Paris for the entire duration of the case that tore apart and redefined France's political and intellectual elites between 1894 and 1906.

In November 1894, Captain Alfred Dreyfus, a young Jewish officer in the French army, was convicted of leaking artillery information to the German Embassy in Paris and was sent to Devil's Island in French Guiana to serve his sentence of life imprisonment. But when new evidence emerged in 1896 that identified a major named Ferdinand Esterhazy as the perpetrator, documents were forged to accuse Dreyfus of new charges and confirm his conviction. Esterhazy was expediently acquitted, and word quickly spread of a conspiracy against Dreyfus based on deeply rooted anti-Semitic prejudice in the French army. Émile Zola wrote a letter denouncing the intrigue and the unlawful deeds of the army, the judiciary, and different members of the government. Addressed to French president Félix Faure and titled "J'accuse," the letter was published in the liberal-socialist newspaper *L'Aurore* (edited by Georges Clemenceau) on January 13, 1898. Dreyfus was tried and reconvicted in 1899, only to be pardoned without rehabilitation by President Émile Loubet. He was finally cleared and reinstituted in the army as a major in 1906 (Drake; Harris).

The legal, political, and cultural consequences of the Dreyfus Affair had a potent and lasting effect in France and throughout the world, influencing, for example, the formal separation of church and state in France, and Theodor Herzl's and Nordau's institutionalization of Zionism. In the cultural field, the constitution of a binary discursive domain of Dreyfusards and anti-Dreyfusards not only provided a matrix for contingent ethico-political identifications but is believed to have given rise to the category of the intellectual (a term Clemenceau coined in 1898 in reference to Zola's "J'accuse") as a learned class defined by their position in the public sphere with respect to political issues of general concern (Sirinelli 17–18).[16] Interestingly, most Latin American intellectuals identified, not with one side or the other in relation to the events in France, but rather with their translation into local politics. In Mexico, for instance, pro- and anti-Dreyfus alignments were structured by the debates over the roles of the church and the military (institutions crucial to the Dreyfus Affair in France) in the process of modernization in Mexican society that took place between the Catholic/conservative intellectual bloc and the positivist/liberal reformers known as *científicos*, over the last decade of Porfirio Díaz's thirty-five-year government.[17]

No Latin American intellectual experienced the impact of the Dreyfus Affair on everyday life in French culture and society like Gómez Carrillo. Identifying with the Republican and antiecclesiastic camp, he was a passive but convinced Dreyfusard who phrased his belief in Dreyfus's innocence as a lack of confidence in the judicial system that decreed "su problemática culpabilidad" ("Sensaciones de París" 310) ("his problematic guilt"). Between 1898 and 1900, at the height of social tensions caused by Dreyfus's imprisonment and second trial in Rennes, he wrote a great deal about the Affair and its social consequences in the column "Sensaciones de París" ("Sensations of Paris"), which was published in the newspaper *El Liberal* (Madrid) and the magazine *El Cojo Ilustrado* (*The Illustrated Cripple*, Caracas) but was also frequently and selectively reproduced in local and regional publications in Spain (like *El Diario de Murcia* [*The Murcia Daily*]), and Argentine national dailies like *La Nación* and *La Prensa* (*The Press*, Buenos Aires). Gómez Carrillo rewrote and reorganized these columns into *crónicas de novedad* and *crónicas de boulevard*, the genres he felt most comfortable with, and published them as a textual continuum without chapters or subtitles in *Sensaciones de París y Madrid* (1900). These columns alternated between social commentary, literary and art criticism, interviews with renowned cultural figures, and gossip and current events. The most significant current event, of course, was the political question at the center of the French agenda since at least 1896–97, when evidence of anti-Semitic bias began to surface.

Gómez Carrillo never concealed his position ("¡Dreyfus, siempre Dreyfus! Sin saber a punto fijo lo que hay, todos estamos seguros de que en el alma francesa hay algo muy grave" (*Sensaciones de París* 305) ("Dreyfus, always Dreyfus! Without knowing for sure what it is, we are all certain that there is something very dangerous in the French soul") and was quick to denounce the anti-Dreyfusard position. When Maurice Barrès published his nationalistic novel *Les déracinés* (1897) and became openly anti-Semitic, Gómez Carrillo described his disenchantment with him and Jules Lemaître: "Barrès y Lemaître han dejado ya de ser los librepensadores de otro tiempo, para converstirse en patrioteros idólatras del militarismo y enemigos de todos los pueblos que no son el suyo" (21) ("Barrès and Lemaître have now ceased to be freethinkers from another time, turning into chauvinistic idolaters of militarism and enemies of all people other than their own"). And, as much as he could, he denounced and undermined the anti-Semitic nature of the anti-Dreyfusards' arguments: "Drumont acaba de decir a Dreyfus: 'No habría más que un medio de que usted fuese inocente, y es que usted no fuera judío.'. . . ¿Os parece ridículo ese modo de discutir? A mi me parece siniestro y macabro" (242–43) ("Drumont just said to Dreyfus: 'There is only one way for you to be innocent, and that is for you not to be Jewish.'. . . Does not that way of debating seem ridiculous to you? I find it sinister and appalling").

In September 1899, when Dreyfus was about to be tried for the second time, Gómez Carrillo sought to record the public dimensions of the social trauma he observed in the French capital: "Aquí en París los teatros han apagado ya sus luces. Allá en Rennes la sala del consejo de guerra en que va a representarse la tragedia de Dreyfus, no ha abierto sus puertas aún. Y Francia está inquieta y el boulevard está nervioso" (235) ("Here in Paris the theaters are dark. There in Rennes the office of the court-martial where the tragedy of Dreyfus will take place has not yet opened its doors. And France is anxious and the boulevard is nervous"). Besides his awareness of a collective sense of anticipation, one of the most noteworthy insights of Gómez Carrillo's writings was his reproduction of the politics of the case on the local and intimate scales of social life: "A medida que la fecha del proceso de Rennes se aproxima, los ánimos parecen exacerbarse cada día más. Ayer una lucha entre militares y paisanos ensangrentó la terraza de un café de Montmartre. Hoy, un oficial judío llamado Klein ha sido muerto por un oficial cristiano en un duelo a sable. Mañana, cuando los testigos principien a decir solemnemente grandes verdades que Francia espera, Dios

sabe qué sucederá" (292) ("As the proceedings in Rennes approach, the mood is more irritable every day. Yesterday a struggle between military personnel and civilians bloodied the terrace of a café in Montmartre. Today, a Jewish official named Klein was killed by a Christian official in a duel of swords. Tomorrow, when the witnesses begin to solemnly tell the great truths that France is waiting for, God only knows what will happen"). And: "Nuestra época, con sus procesos en curso, sus luchas antisemíticas, sus anhelos sociales y sus campañas de prensa, ha llegado ya a formarse una atmósfera sanguinaria" (306–07) ("Our era, with the proceedings currently under way, with its anti-Semitic struggles, social longing, and press campaigns, has already come to create a cruel atmosphere").

As I mentioned above, Gómez Carrillo's experience and account of the Dreyfus Affair was unique in the context of the *modernista* cultural formation. Not only was he the only writer in this loose transatlantic network to live in France for the duration of the Affair, but he was the only one to explore in a sustained way the traumatic events that caught the attention of the French public opinion and cultural field for over a decade. Aside from passing references, *modernistas* wrote about the Affair indirectly and almost exclusively in relation to Zola's death in September 1902, celebrating his contribution to it.[18] Darío, who had been living in Paris since April of 1900, wrote "El ejemplo de Zola" ("Zola's Example"), published in *La Nación* on November 13, 1902. Although his praise of Zola as a committed intellectual ("puso su nombre ante la iniquidad" [17] ["he stood up against evil"]; "no tuvo vacilaciones frente a ningún peligro" [19] ["he did not vacillate when faced with danger"]) does not differ from other eulogies of the naturalist novelist, his relation to the anti-Semitic arguments of those who would condemn Dreyfus is more complicated: "No es aún, ciertamente, convincentemente sabido que el capitán haya sido un traidor. Él ha asistido al entierro del héroe. Me informan—y hay que averiguar esto bien—que ha dado para el monumento que se levantará a Zola trescientos francos. . . . ¡Trescientos francos! Si esto es verdad, ese rico israelita, me atrevería a jurarlo, ha sido culpable del crimen que le llevó a la Isla del Diablo" (17) ("It is still not certainly or convincingly known that the captain was a traitor. He attended the hero's burial. They tell me—and this must be confirmed—that he gave three hundred francs to the construction of a monument to Zola. . . . Three hundred francs! If this is true, that rich Israelite, I would dare say, was guilty of the crime that led him to Devil's Island"). As opposed to Gómez Carrillo's unwavering repudiation of the anti-Dreyfusards, Darío reproduces a prejudiced cliché about the rich and financially corrupt Jew that his much-admired Barrès (whom he later praises in his *Autobiografía*; 98) had articulated a few months before when the military tribunal had acknowledged after several appeals that the evidence against Dreyfus had been fabricated: "Je n'ai pas besoin qu'on me dise pourquoi Dreyfus a trahi. . . . Que Dreyfus est capable de trahir, je le conclus de sa race. . . . Les Juifs sont de la patrie où ils trouvent leur plus grand intérêt" ("Ce que j'ai vu" 153) ("I do not need to be told why Dreyfus has betrayed. . . . The fact that Dreyfus is capable of betrayal is a conclusion I draw from his race. . . . Jews make their homeland where they benefit the most").[19]

Toward the end of his decade-long engagement with the Affair, in 1905, Gómez Carrillo took the trips discussed above, traveling to Russia during the winter of 1905 and to Japan during the summer and fall of the same year. It is my contention that his reaction to the pain of the eastern European Jews that he sees or learns of on these journeys cannot be understood apart from his relation to the Affair and his proximity to the Dreyfusard camp. If in Russia he denounces Jewish suffering from a distance, appealing to second- and thirdhand narratives and statistics, in Marseille, before boarding the ocean liner that will take him to Egypt, Sri Lanka, Singapore, Vietnam, Hong Kong, Korea, China, and Japan, he represents a face-to-face encounter with embodied hardship. In the passage, which bears quoting extensively, he labors to articulate the materiality of misery; I want to focus on the strengths and weaknesses, the ethical potentialities and moralistic limits, of Gómez Carrillo's cosmopolitan ethics when confronted with an oppressed, wretched Other:

> El Puerto Viejo está lleno de gente. ¡Cuánta alegría en el aire! ¡Cuánto ruido! ¡Cuánta animación! Pero ¡ay! de pronto entre la multitud gesticuladora y vocinglera de mercaderes ambulantes, surge, andando despacio, sin hacer un ademán ni pronunciar media palabra, un grupo de miserables que parecen escapados del infierno del Dante. Son los judíos rusos que emigran. Pero no evoquéis, para formaros una idea de la realidad, las visiones de miseria vistas que guardáis en la memoria.
>
> Los más lamentables seres del mundo: los que muertos de hambre, recorren las calles de Constantinopla pidiendo

limosna; los que, en Londres, en los inviernos crudos, se caen de inanición en las calles de White Chapel; los armenios que huyen despavoridos por las rutas de Oriente, no son tan impresionantes cual estos israelitas que vienen a bordo de buques carboneros, amontonados en la proa del puente, comiendo Jehová sabe qué y durmiendo a la intemperie. Sus rostros no sólo dicen el hambre y el dolor, sino también el miedo y la desesperanza. En la tierra en que nacieron se les trata peor mil veces que a las más feroces bestias. Se les encierra en barrios hediondos y se les prohíbe trabajar para comer. Y de vez en cuando, para que no puedan acostumbrarse a la paz dolorosa de la miseria, se organizan cacerías, en las cuales ellos sirven de piezas humanas. . . . Un marino políglota pregunta a estos pobres seres de dónde vienen.

—De Kichinef—contestan.

Kichinef es una de la ciudades rusas en donde con más frecuencia se organizan matanzas de judíos.

Luego el mismo marino hace otra pregunta:

—¿Adónde vais?

Esta vez nadie responde. Una mueca dolorosa crispa los labios marchitos de los más jóvenes, de los menos acostumbrados al dolor. Los ancianos permanecen como petrificados bajo el sol que les carcome los rostros morenos. ¡Qué saben ellos adónde los lleva la suerte! Y mientras la mano de la Providencia no los lance más lejos, allí permanecerán, sentados en el puerto, silenciosos, dolorosos, famélicos, rumiando la amargura de sus recuerdos. . . . Apenas parecerían vivos, a no ser porque de vez en cuando una llama obscura se enciende en sus pupilas y algo que puede ser hambre y que puede ser odio, algo muy rápido y muy expresivo, se asoma a sus labios sin color. Los niños que pululan en este barrio miserable les arrojan, como a perros, mendrugos de pan duro. . . . Es la hora del amuerzo . . . no queda un alma. Durante una hora, toda la existencia del puerto estará suspendida. Y solos entonces los miserables judíos emigrantes, solos con sus penas, solos con sus dolores, se vuelven hacia el horizonte y contemplan en silencio la alegría de la luz de oro que, cabrilleando sobre la superficie del mar, hace surgir del fondo misterioso. (*De Marsella a Tokio* 10–13)

The Old Port is full of people. So much joy in the air! So much noise! So much activity! But oh! suddenly among the gesturing, chattering multitude of peddlers, a wretched group appears, walking slowly, not making a gesture or pronouncing even half a word, seeming as if they have escaped Dante's hell. They are Russian Jews who are emigrating. But make no mistake, so that you might imagine the reality, the miserable visions to keep in your memory.

The most pitiful beings in the world: those who, dying of hunger, roam the streets of Constantinople begging for alms; those who, in London, in the harsh winter, fall from starvation in the streets of White Chapel; those Armenians who flee in terror along the routes of the Orient, are not as shocking as these Israelites who board the coal ships, heaped on the prow of the bridge, eating Jehovah only knows what and sleeping in the open air. Their faces tell not only of hunger and pain but also of fear and hopelessness. In the land of their birth they are treated a thousand times worse than the most savage beasts. They are confined to filthy neighborhoods and forbidden from working to eat. And every so often, so that they cannot get used to the painful peace of poverty, hunts are organized in which they serve as human game. . . . A polyglot sailor asks these poor beings where they are coming from.

—From Kishinev—they answer.

Kishinev is one of the Russian cities where Jews are most often slaughtered.

Later the same sailor asks another question:

—Where are you going?

This time no one answers. A painful expression contracts the withered lips of the youngest, those least accustomed to pain. The elderly remain as if petrified beneath the sun that eats away at their brown faces. What do they know where chance will lead them! And while the hand of Providence does not move them any further, there they remain, sitting in the port, silent, in pain, starving, ruminating on the bitterness of their memories. . . . They would barely seem alive, if not for the dark flame that now and then flickers in their pupils and something that could be hunger and could be hatred, something very quick and very expressive, comes

> out of their colorless lips. The children who overrun this squalid neighborhood throw them, as if to dogs, crusts of hard bread. . . . It is lunchtime . . . not a soul is around. For an hour, the entire existence of the port will be suspended. And for that time, the wretched Jewish emigrants, alone with their sorrows, turn toward the horizon and silently contemplate the joy of the golden light that, glistening on the ocean's surface, comes from the mysterious depths.

The attempt to move his readers is evident in the way Gómez Carrillo constructs the scene. The structure of the passage, as well as the lexical selection (the poetic phrasing of hopelessness is a striking change from the journalistic and statistical discourse he employed in Russia) points to an affective interpellation that could be considered a force to generate an ethical response to these bodies in pain. It begins with the contrast between the vivid and cheerful atmosphere of the port of Marseille and the ghostly vision of a contingent of miserable Jewish migrants escaping the pogroms that he denounced from Saint Petersburg a few months earlier. It is as if these figures of Jewish suffering are haunting him: the same Jews that he avoided in Russia catch up to him in Marseilles. The second meaning of the passage is that of the Jew as a figure of universal suffering ("los más lamentables seres del mundo") whose universality—a rhetorical figure devoid of particular content, intent, or direction can represent anyone's suffering—is reduplicated in its global inscriptions, from Constantinople and London to the Armenian diaspora across Asia and Europe.[20] Meaningfully, Gómez Carrillo, who so intently studied the Jerusalem Jews' clothes, hairstyle, and ritualistic prostheses, now reads desperate silence, hunger, and fear in facial features and expressions ("Sus rostros no sólo dicen el hambre y el dolor, sino también el miedo y la desesperanza"; "Una mueca dolorosa crispa los labios marchitos"). The facial communication conveys a sense of intimacy that was notably absent from his account of Jewish suffering in *La Rusia actual*. That intimacy is produced in the moment when Gómez Carrillo represents himself as the receiver of an ethical call, the efficacy of which can be determined only by his response to it.

He could have had this ethical experience at numerous junctures as he traveled across a world of colonial exploitation, abysmal inequality, and material and symbolic subjugation, but this is the only example of his own involvement in a scene of ethical interpellation. I intend to conceptualize Gómez Carrillo's reaction as a form of empathic cosmopolitanism, a concept that interrogates the narrow potentiality of an ethics of the Other in the context of *modernismo*, wherein only some Others (and not other Others) are invested with a form of humanity capable of arousing empathic feelings that are grounded in an ideological discourse of redemption.

In reading the ethical forms of agency that this encounter in Marseille opens, as well as those it forecloses, I take the notion of empathy from the discursive tradition of moral philosophy and social psychology as seen in the work of David Hume and Adam Smith as well as in very recent developments in interdisciplinary cognitive sciences. Within this intersection of speculative and empirical disciplines, *empathy* refers to "the subject's awareness in imagination of the emotions of another person" (Wispé 316); "a form of receptivity to the other. . . . One is open experientially to the affects, sensations, emotions that the other experiences" (Agosta 4).[21] The discursive articulation of awareness of an Other in pain that stops short of its translation into ethical forms of agency is in fact a perfect account of the restricted scope of an empathic cosmopolitanism that does not transform the traveler's subjectivity after departing the scene and encountering other suffering and dispossessed Others that he fails to notice.[22] Indeed, for all its rhetorical efficacy and the display of sensitivity to "los más lamentables seres del mundo" (the wretched of the earth, to borrow Frantz Fanon's title), the ethical force of this cosmopolitan interruption is not potent enough to undo the safe distance from which Gómez Carrillo looks at them, to reconfigure his subjectivity, or to undo the Orientalism that he will revert to later in the same travel book. The notion of empathy, in fact, marks the moralistic limit of a *modernista* cosmopolitan ethics that presents itself as the other side of the Orientalist coin. If the discourse of Orientalism produced objectified others, representing them in terms of absolute, irredeemable difference, empathy instrumentalizes the pain of others, in a self-referential process of "narcissistic identification" (Freud, "Mourning" 587) that cancels the transcendental individuality of the other, the nonidentity that constitutes the condition of possibility of ethical agency: "The alterity of the Other does not depend on any quality that would distinguish him from me, for a distinction of this nature would precisely imply between us that [empathetic] community of genus which already nullifies alterity" (Levinas, *Totality* 194).

Whatever the potential and limitations of Gómez Carrillo's empathic engagement with the migrating Jews in pain, it is but a self-contained moment in his eastbound travels, an interpellation confined to a port space inherently defined by the liminal exceptionality that seems to affect Gómez Carrillo's perception of the Jews' own liminality. But once onboard the ocean liner, on his way to the Suez Canal and Sri Lanka, he will reconstruct the barrier that separates *us* and *them*, only to undermine it again in the oscillating dynamic that constitutes the map of his Eastern worlds, an oscillation between universalist equalizing drives that erase difference and Orientalist reinscriptions of otherness. These productive tensions (ethical empathy and Orientalism; Paris and its peripheral avatars; traveling imaginaries of relational modernities and landlocked urban phantasmagorias) shape the broader cultural geographies of *modernismo*, whose global scale would be unthinkable without Gómez Carrillo's aesthetic contributions.

Notes

INTRODUCTION

1. Here and subsequently, all translations are my own unless otherwise indicated.

2. There are, of course, exceptions. Sánchez Prado's edited volume *América Latina en la "literatura mundial"* (*Latin America in "World Literature"*) contains his introduction "'Hijos de Metapa': Un recorrido conceptual de la literatura mundial (a manera de introducción)" ("'Sons of Metapa': A Conceptual Journey through World Literature (by Way of Introduction)"), as well as essays by Efraín Kristal, Hugo Achúgar, Graciela Montaldo, Abril Trigo, and Mabel Moraña, all of which explore the possibility of inscribing Latin American critical problems and paradigms in these debates. Recently, Guillermina de Ferrari edited a special issue of *1616: Anuario de Literatura Comparada* (*1616: Comparative Literature Yearbook*) entitled *Utopías críticas: La literatura mundial según América Latina* (*Critical Utopias: World Literature According to Latin America*), as did César Domínguez for *Insula*, the issue *Literatura mundial: Una mirada panhispánica* (*World Literature: A Pan-Hispanic View*). Both compile relevant contemporary interventions that attempt to inscribe Latin American literature in recent discussions of world literature in US academia. The introduction to each volume productively illuminates the current state of a world literary criticism of Latin American literature today.

3. In the United States and the United Kingdom, this transcultural turn in modern literary studies has reached a point of stability. It is the center of the Modernist Studies Association, founded in 1999, and its journals *Modernism/Modernity* and *Modernist Cultures*. Susan Stanford Friedman, Bruce

Robbins, Rebecca Walkowitz, Douglas Mao, Laura Doyle, Laura Winkiel, Michelle Clayton, Eric Hayot, Christopher Bush, Jing Tsu, Melba Cuddy-Keane, Jessica Berman, and Jeffrey Schnapp, among others, have all been consistent proponents of this expansion of the field of modernism. For a history of these developments, see Mao and Walkowitz.

4. Both the writers whose work I analyze and their imagined subject of aesthetic universality were male. For that reason, I use masculine pronouns in referring to this "cosmopolitan intellectual hero."

5. Along these same lines, Alonso identifies Latin American culture as a desiring formation and characterizes the modernist suture that constitutes the region's cultural identity as a quotation: "A formulation of resistance that is relevant to the Spanish American context must also be able to account for the quite explicit desire of appropriation and quotation of metropolitan discourses that is intrinsic to it; in other words, it has to be a reformulation capable of incorporating the passionate commitment to a modernity articulated in hegemonic terms" (*Burden* 27).

6. Another possible formulation for these ideas, following Chakrabarty's seminal *Provincializing Europe*, would affirm that this Lacanian (and Laclauian) approach to the imaginary making of the universal is a way of provincializing the supposedly universal underpinnings of the world.

7. I developed this idea of the world as an imaginary, utopian space of reconciliation and freedom in difference, which Latin American intellectuals imagine as the basis for a cosmopolitan aesthetic practice liberated from a confining and monolingual cultural particularity, under the shadow of Arendt's notion of world:

> The world . . . is not identical with the earth or with nature, as the limited space for the movement of men and the general condition of organic life. It is related, rather, to the human artifact, the fabrication of human hands, as well as to affairs which go on among those who inhabit the man-made world together. To live together in the world means essentially that a world of things is between those who have it in common, as a table is located between those who sit around it; the world, like every in-between, relates and separates men at the same time. (52)

8. Rosenberg has written about the need for a more complex understanding of the tension between cosmopolitanism and those aesthetics defined by their commitment to an autochthonous historical problematic by bracketing "the question of the origins (native or foreign) and the mimicking of cultural production to emphasize a remarkable simultaneity that cannot be explained away by any account of the specific influences and European journeys of individual artists. In the flow of transnational and transatlantic vanguard of creative forces, I intend to highlight a grammar in which the artistic expressions of the periphery issued statements about global positionality" (14). I believe that my conceptualization of the cosmopolitan desires of *modernismo* in Part Two of the book shares a great deal with Rosenberg's approach to the cosmopolitan nature of the avant-garde.

9. Aguilar explains that Rama developed this opposition (transculturation/cosmopolitanism) while analyzing the polemic between José María Arguedas and Julio Cortázar. From 1967 to 1969, the two writers debated in the pages of the magazines *Casa de las Américas* (*House of the Americas*) (Cuba), *Amaru* (Peru), and *Life en español* (United States) and in Arguedas's unfinished novel, *El zorro de arriba y el zorro de abajo* (*The Fox from Up Above and the Fox from Down Below*) (*Episodios cosmopolitas* 9).

10. Jean-Luc Nancy imprints this ethical meaning in the concept of *mondialisation*, which he understands as the creation of a world of human relations and radical immanence (37); he critiques the homogenizing effects of the neoliberal aspects of the globalization of corporate capitalism and the prospect of "an unprecedented geopolitical, economic and ecological catastrophe" (50).

11. D'haen has recently added two northern European precursors of world literature to this list: August Ludwig von Schlözer, who referred to the concept in his 1773 *Isländischen Literatur und Geschichte* (*Icelandic Literature and History*), and Christoph Martin Wieland, who addressed world literature in a note to his early nineteenth-century translations of Horace (5).

12. In *Modernity at Large*, toward the end of the chapter "Disjuncture and Difference in the Global Cultural Economy," Appadurai movingly characterizes the tension between homogenizing and heterogenizing exchanges that, for him, define the cultural experience and political practices of globalization as a process impregnated with suffering and exclusion but also the hope for global justice:

> Thus the central feature of global culture today is the politics of the mutual effort of sameness and difference to cannibalize one another and thus to proclaim their successful hijacking of the twin Enlightenment ideas of the triumphantly universal and the resiliently particular. This mutual cannibalization shows its ugly face in riots, in refugee-flows, in state-sponsored torture and ethnocide (with or without state support). Its brighter side is in the expansion of many individual horizons of hope and fantasy, in the global spread of oral rehydration therapy and other low-tech instruments of well-being, in the susceptibility even of South Africa to the force of global opinion, in the inability of the Polish state to repress its own working-classes, and in the growth of a wide range of progressive, transnational alliances. (47)

13. Other texts crucial to this return of world literature include Reiss's *Against Autonomy*; Cooppan, "World Literature and Global Theory"; Apter, *Translation Zone*; Thomsen; and Prendergast's edited volume.

14. Robbins asserts that world literature is "an ethical project because, like the larger project of cosmopolitanism to which it belongs, it asks us to imagine or act out an ethical relation to the world as a whole" ("Uses of World Literature" 391). Robbins's challenge to world literary critics can be read to propose a localized ethical agency capable of intervening in the world from a concrete position in it, in spite (or, perhaps, because) of its recognition of the imaginary nature of the representation of the world as a cosmopolitan

totality. As Robbins has written elsewhere: "No one actually is or ever can be a cosmopolitan in the sense of belonging nowhere. . . . The interest of the term cosmopolitanism is located, then, not in its full theoretical extension, where it becomes a paranoid fantasy of ubiquity and omniscience, but rather (paradoxically) in its local applications" ("Comparative Cosmopolitanisms" 260).

15. I find Dharwadker's use of moving maps as a way to preserve the notion of a large world literary field very appealing. He proposes thinking about the world in world literature and cosmopolitan imaginaries, not as one system and one world, but as "a montage of overlapping maps in motion" (3). In the same vein, Cooppan points out that Moretti and Casanova's proposals do not see the world in its plurality: "There is no singular 'world' per se but only a changing assemblage of localities that coalesce into globalities of many kinds, each striated by the transverse networks of language, region, area, and moment that simultaneously shape a single text and link it to others" ("World Literature between History and Theory" 194).

16. Spivak has articulated one of the most cogent critiques of these paradigms. For her, the notion of the world in world literature is a homogenizing concept that effectively flattens the globe. She instead writes of the planet, a figure that Spivak uses to designate a political project that overwrites globalization, understood as the universalization of capital. The planet, then, is the site of an ethical community to come; it does not yet exist in the context of the hegemony of the discourses of globalization, but "as presumed collectivities cross borders under the auspices of a Comparative Literature supplemented by Area Studies, they might attempt to figure themselves—imagine themselves—as planetary rather than continental, global, or worldly" (*Death* 72). She underscores the ethico-political nature of the rhetorical figure of the planet as "a catachresis for inscribing collective responsibility as right" (102).

17. In "Rhetoric of Particularism," Sommer proposes a reading of Latin American minoritarian texts that recognizes the particularism of objects, especially where a text resists universal interpretation. I take her insight to be the contribution of wide, potential uses and applications to making sense of the particular determinations of a given object. This is especially important in the case of the abstract universalism of the universalist rhetorics that I work with here (for instance, the discourse of world literature), because of their constitutive and programmatic attempt to veil the local, concrete, marginal determinations that constitute their particularism and their intervention in the hegemonic formation of the global mappings of aesthetic modernism.

18. For an exemplary study of the presence of world literary anxieties and drives in Latin American culture (in spite of the absence of the concept of *Weltliteratur*) in the early modern context, see Kadir, "World Literature."

1. THE GLOBALIZATION OF THE NOVEL AND THE NOVELIZATION OF THE GLOBAL

1. Eleven years after Kant prescribed the notion of a world-republic in "Idea for a Universal History," he opted for a federation of nations (*Völkerbund*) in "Perpetual Peace" (1795), balancing the sovereignty of each nation with the

ultimate and transcendental location of power in the federation as the universal and cosmopolitan determination of the global system of international treaties and agreements.

2. It has been pointed out to me that I am reading Kant literally here and that Kant was referring, not to the novel as a genre, but to the imaginative constructedness of a discourse clearly opposed to philosophy conceived as a scientific disciplinary discourse. In response, I would note that Kant did choose to refer to "the novel" as that which lies at the other end of the spectrum from philosophy and that, in any case, he invokes the workings of imagination embodied in the novelistic form as the space where the type of universal history he imagines might take place.

3. This is a dimension of the novel mostly overlooked in classical materialist genre theories, which view the novel as the aesthetic product of the rise of the bourgeoisie and the consolidation of the national state. This critical perspective is historically determined by a concern about the specificity of national cultures and hegemonic struggles within the context of the nation-state (see, for example, Ian Watt or Raymond Williams). Unfortunately, the explanatory power of these theories has blurred the global dimension of the novel, as well as the possibility of a history of the novel that could account for the ways in which the process of globalization has been shaping the world for the past two hundred years.

4. See Lucio Vicente López's *La gran aldea* (*The Great Village*) (1884), a *costumbrista* novel about Buenos Aires in the 1860s and '70s, the period immediately after the civil war and before the modernizing explosion of the mid-1880s and '90s. That is the Buenos Aires of Holmberg's novels.

5. I am referring here to the novel as the aesthetic form historically determined by the rise of the bourgeoisie and its need to represent its own worldview and place in modern societies. Watt's *Rise of the Novel* (1957) is still the most convincing description of the historical genesis of the novel form (*stricto sensu*) in Europe and in its peripheries. Moretti's *The Novel*, through the inclusion of essays such as Thomas Hagg's "The Ancient Greek Novel: A Single Model or a Plurality of Forms?" and Andrew H. Plaks's "The Novel in Premodern China," criticizes this concept of "the rise of the novel" in favor of a longer history that extends back to medieval chivalric and courtly narratives. Although I subscribe to Watt's view of the novel as a cultural artifact determined by bourgeois worldviews, he considers the novel as an institution at work only on a national stage. The point of this chapter is to think about the novel's role on a global scale.

6. There are many instances in Sarmiento's narrative of his stay in Paris in which he destabilizes the notion of France as the privileged location of the universal. He even depicts most French political leaders as excessively provincial. However, Sarmiento always restores France's place as the model to imitate in the global order of modernity. Thus Sarmiento arrogantly plays with the idea of his own superiority to particular French intellectuals or officials, but in the end France remains the center and origin of the modern world.

7. Although Sarmiento never wrote a novel himself, he used the compositional strategies of the novel to write *Facundo:* "We do not read *Facundo* as

a novel (which it is not) but rather as a political use of the genre. (*Facundo* is a proto-novel, a novel machine, a museum of the future of the novel)" (Piglia 135). See also Sorensen, *Facundo*, particularly her work on the generic instability of Sarmiento's book: "*Facundo* does not allow the reader to keep to a constant generic program. . . . The reader is forced to change programs from one part of the text to another" (42).

8. Laera notes that from 1880 to 1890, one hundred novels were published in Buenos Aires alone; in the previous decade, there had been fewer than two dozen (19).

9. Franco Moretti even goes so far as to deduce "a law of literary evolution" from this process of global expansion of the novel form ("Conjectures" 58). Such a law would state that "in cultures that belong to the periphery of the literary system (which means: almost all cultures, inside and outside Europe), the modern novel first arises not as an autonomous development but as a compromise between a Western formal influence (usually French or English) and local materials" (58).

10. This cultural mediation complements Moretti's "law of literary evolution" (see note 9) by contextualizing the idea that the novel of the periphery results from a compromise between Western form and local materials within a cultural-political (rather than aesthetic) discursive frame.

11. See Hegel's *Elements of the Philosophy of Right*, §§ 246, 247, 324, 347, and 376.

12. As is the case with many canonical Marxian texts, the *Communist Manifesto* establishes a palimpsestic relation with Hegel's *Elements of the Philosophy of Right.* The following renowned passage echoes Hegel: "The bourgeoisie, by the rapid improvement of all instruments of production, by the immensely facilitated means of communication, draws all, even the most barbarian nations into civilization. . . . It compels all nations, on pain of extinction, to adopt the bourgeois mode of production; it compels them to introduce what it calls civilisation into their midst, i.e., to become bourgeois themselves" (Marx and Engels 477).

13. Cook's declaration of impossibility was taken as irrefutable: "The importance of this voyage is enormous. . . . No longer could cogent arguments be made for a populous and fertile southern continent. Cook had demonstrated that tempestuous seas, ice and snow were the elements of high austral regions and had revealed that this part of the earth was uninhabitable. . . . His findings on it were so conclusive that there was no hope of its resurrection" (Simpson-Housley 7).

14. Charles Taylor explains that Hegel's "world-historical individuals" are those agents who participate directly in the construction of the state and that his notion that "reason realizes itself," or that reason expands its territory, "does not come about by some men seeing the blueprint of reason and building a state on the basis of it. That reason realizes itself means that the outcome arises out of human action which is not really conscious of what it is doing, which acts while seeing through a glass very darkly, but which is guided by the cunning of reason" (123).

15. To this day, Antarctica conserves a place that is radically exterior to and exceptional in the globalization of modernity, particularly regarding the question of national sovereignty: it is the only territory on the planet open to universal scientific exploration and closed to the exploitation of natural resources. This cosmopolitan preservation of Antarctica has been achieved in spite of more than two centuries of attempts to take advantage of it in material and symbolic ways. The following is a brief history of Antarctica's exceptionality in the history of modernity. Cook's observations of a superabundance of seals in Antarctica and the neighboring islands were publicized throughout Europe and generated a "sealer wave" that lasted until 1822. During this time, missions usually had a double commercial and scientific motivation. Enthusiasm arose again in the 1890s when the whaling/scientific race began. In 1895, the Sixth International Geographical Congress decided to devote more attention to Antarctica. From 1895 to 1917, the British, Scots, Norwegians, Germans, Belgians, Swedes, French, Argentines, Chileans, New Zealanders, and Australians competed to discover the most and bring the greatest glory to their homelands. The main aim was no longer the South Magnetic Pole, as it had been for early explorers, but the actual geographical South Pole at 90°00' S, the bottom of the world. This Heroic Era of Antarctic exploration features notable characters such as Roald Amundsen and Robert F. Scott (who in 1911 threw themselves into a world-famous race to be the first man to reach the South Geographic Pole), and Ernest Shackleton and Douglas Mawson. From the end of the First World War to the present, a stretch that might be called the Scientific Era, any interested nation was able to conduct scientific observation in Antarctica, so long as it avoided economic exploitation, according to the Antarctic Treaty that was signed in 1959. The treaty suspended any determination of the overlapping claims of sovereignty over Antarctica and the ways in which the White Continent might be used or exploited until 2011. However, in 1991, ten years before the treaty's scheduled expiration, the Protocol on Environmental Protection signed in Madrid extended the treaty's terms for another fifty years. This parenthesis on economic, commercial, and territorial disputes, in effect until 2041, has been called the "Pax Antarctica." The facts in this summary of Antarctica's modern history have been taken from Baughman, Mill, and Stewart.

16. Given the symbolic power that literary discourse held in western Europe during the nineteenth century, the power of Verne's narratives to promote and reinforce the discourse of globalization must have been huge. Indeed, the importance of the role of literature and, more generally, the world of the "arts and entertainment" of the Second Empire cannot be exaggerated: there was a very specific need in France to produce and consume images of a colonial world beyond the borders of the familiar, not only because of the expansive dynamics of bourgeois-modern society, but also—and most importantly—because of boredom with the economic stability and solidification of (recently instituted) traditions of the middle class (see Girardet; Blanchard and Lemaire; Compère).

17. Another important strategy of appropriation is the familiarization of the strange, uncanny, or sublime by means of analogy: the Orinoco is like

the Loire (*Le superbe Orénoque*) (*The Mighty Orinoco*); the moon looks to Ardan, Barbicane, and Nicholl like the mountains of Greece, Switzerland, or Norway (*Autour de la Lune*); on his way to the center of the earth, Lidenbrok discovers another "Mediterranean Sea" (*Voyage au centre de la Terre*).

18. This is the point Barthes makes in his reading of *Vingt milles lieues sous les mers* in *Mythologies*: "Verne appartient à la lignée progressiste de la bourgeoisie: son oeuvre affiche que rien ne peut échapper à l'homme, que le monde, même le plus lointain, est comme un objet dans sa main" (80) ("Verne belongs to the progressive line of the bourgeoisie; his work portrays the fact that nothing is strange to Man, that the world, even its most remote corners, is like an object in his hand").

19. Writing from his prison cell, Gramsci addresses the realist nature of Verne's narratives, explaining that their verisimilar construction of reality is assured by the hegemony of bourgeois ideology: "In Verne's books nothing is ever completely impossible. The 'possibilities' that Verne's heroes have are greater [than were available at the time] and above all [are] not 'outside' the line of development of the scientific conquests already made. What is imagined is not entirely 'arbitrary' and is therefore able to excite the reader's fantasy, which has already been won over by the ideology of the inevitability of scientific progress in the domain of the control of natural forces" (*Selections from Cultural Writings* 367).

20. Holmberg was a physician but never practiced. As a naturalist, he wrote important works on flora, fauna, geography, and paleontology, in addition to his literary and travel writings.

21. Although the complete title of the serialized novel at the end of 1875—*El viaje maravilloso del Señor Nic Nac en el que se refieren las prodigiosas aventuras de este señor y se dan a conocer las instituciones, costumbres y preocupaciones de un mundo desconocido* (*The Marvelous Journey of Mr. Nic-Nac in Which Are Told the Miraculous Adventures of This Man and the Institutions, Customs, and Worries of an Unknown World Are Revealed*)—states that the nature of the planet Nic-Nac visits is unknown, he finds Mars to be a mirror image of the changing face of Argentine society at the end of the nineteenth century. As Sandra Gasparini and Claudia Román explain, "La década del 70 está atravesada, en la Argentina, por una gran cantidad de gestos fundacionales. Se crean academias, establecimientos educativos, museos, observatorios: se echan los cimientos de una modernidad, en cuyo marco se construirá la Nación" (191) ("The 1870s is a decade of foundational gestures in Argentina. Academies, educational establishments, museums, observatories are created: the grounds of modernity out of which the nation will be built").

22. Víctor Vich has pointed out to me that a possible reason for the qualitative disparity between European and Latin American novels in the nineteenth century is that in Latin America the novel had a marginal place in the cultural and literary fields. Indeed, as Efraín Kristal explains, "In Spanish America poetry was the dominant literary genre, and the essay or sociological treatise was of far greater significance than the novel until at least the 1920s, if not later. . . . One would be hard-pressed to point to a single literary work, other than *María* (1867) by the Colombian Jorge Isaacs, as an example of a

nineteenth-century Spanish American novel that was widely read within and beyond the national borders in which it was produced" (62–63).

23. Antonio Pagés Larraya has documented the presence of discourses of spiritism in Argentina in the 1870s and 1880s. Specifically he describes the circulation of books by two authors: Allan Kardec (pseudonym of Hyppolite Léon Denizard Rivail), a disciple of the German scientist and pedagogue Pestalozzi, who late in life developed a technique to contact spirits and became famous as a medium; and Camille Flammarion, the author of very popular works on spiritism and astronomy as well as hack science fiction novels (40–46). On the constitutive tension at the core of Holmberg's discourse, see Rodríguez Pérsico (especially 383 and 389), who argues that an ambivalent gaze meets the positivistic preeminence of scientific imaginaries in turn-of-the-century Latin America in Holmberg's novels. In a recent book on Latin American science fiction, Rachel Haywood Ferreyra analyzes the dislocation of the genre in Latin America in relation to its production and circulation in Europe and the United States. In the first chapter, she presents an interesting analysis of the national determinations of Holmberg's narratives as a function of this binary that nonetheless, in my opinion, disregards the global politics of the genre in favor of a view of science fiction as primarily responsive to local anxieties.

24. Angela Dellepiane makes this connection by tracing the publication of Verne's novels in Buenos Aires between 1872 and 1875 in *El Nacional*, the same newspaper that published *Nic-Nac* in 1875 (220).

25. Even though the widespread polemic about the refashioning of world literature in the United States was reignited by the publication of Moretti's "Conjectures on World Literature" in 2000, Jameson's "Third-World Literature" (1986) anticipated many of the key themes of the debate almost two decades later.

26. For a full account of the debate around Nussbaum's piece, especially in relation to her goals of cosmopolitanism and patriotism, see Nussbaum, *For Love of Country*? For a very cogent critique of Nussbaum's position, see Bhabha, "Unsatisfied."

27. There are exceptions, of course. For example, in two fairly recent and very interesting texts, Cooppan ("Ghosts") and Trumpener give detailed accounts of the creation of world literature and culture courses at Yale. However, I believe that the MLA series "Approaches to Teaching World Literature" overwhelms with its institutional weight any individual attempt to create a world literature syllabus that challenges reified notions of the world and the hegemonic forces that shape it.

28. In spite of her Franco-centrism, Casanova's use of Bourdieu's theory of social spaces organized in (only) relatively autonomous fields structured by specific institutions and practices reveals the asymmetric symbolic power relations that form an uneven global literary and cultural field. At the same time, because her understanding of Bourdieu is overly rigid, her division of a world into a single core (Paris) and several peripheries, where the periphery's structural function is to produce innovation and the core's role is to recognize and consecrate that innovation, is another way of essentializing the periphery.

In fact, the idea that the Third World produces aesthetic innovation and revolutionary ideas seems to be a common fantasy (in the Lacanian sense) of metropolitan cultures.

29. It is important to note that the political economy of transnational publishing (what sells, what does not) determines what gets translated and thus what is read in world literature courses. In other words, European and North American publishing houses more often than not translate works that respond to the expectations of northern readers about what, for instance, Latin American or African literature is and should be. *Cien años de soledad*, as a global best seller, has in particular come to represent what a large portion of the world literary public sphere assumes to be the essence of Latin American culture and social history. See Denning.

30. For commentary on the recent inclusion of García Márquez and Chinua Achebe in world literature anthologies as a result of the globalization of the canon of world literature, see English (306–07).

31. Between 2009 and June 2013 the series added thirty new titles, among them six in Spanish: *Lazarillo de Tormes and the Picaresque Tradition*, Bartolomé de las Casas's *Writings*, poetry by Teresa de Avila and the Spanish mystics, works by Sor Juana Inés de la Cruz, Manuel Puig's *The Kiss of the Spider Woman*, and *The Works of Carmen Martín Gaite*. These additions put Spanish as the third language represented in the series (after English and French, and before Italian and German), and even though the logic that determined these particular inclusions over other potential choices remains the same, it may signal a significant change in the balance of the canon in the years to come. The cosmopolitan openness that the emerging field of world literature is showing in the earlier stages of its institutionalization allows one to be confident about new changes in this series and in the MLA in general in coming years.

32. The MLA boasts thirty thousand members in more than one hundred countries; hosts the largest annual conference in literary critical studies; publishes some of the most important journals in the field, including the *Publication of the Modern Language Association of America* or *PMLA*, as well as several book series (including "Approaches to Teaching World Literature"); and is involved in countless other aspects of academic professional life in literary studies. In terms of its institutional weight, no other organization can even come close to the MLA. For more information, see "About the MLA," www.MLA.org/about.

33. I take the idea of a critical differentiation between *the literatures of the world* and *world literature* from Kadir, "Comparative Literature," although Kadir uses the concept to indict all proponents of world literature, Moretti included.

34. The two volumes of *The Novel*, Moretti's gigantically ambitious attempt to rethink the history and theory of the novel—a project he undertook after "Conjectures on World Literature"—can be read as the practical application of the ideas Moretti proposed in his famous article. Moretti attempts to establish the novel as a site where a community of critics can produce a concrete and well-grounded discourse on world literature. Damrosch, on the other hand,

sees in this infinite and absolute expansion of the horizons of world literature not the elimination of world literature's worst stigma but the dissolution of the discipline's specificity and value: "If the scope of world literature now extends from Akkadian epics to Aztec incantations, the question of what is world literature could almost be put in opposite terms: What isn't world literature? A category from which nothing can be excluded is essentially useless" (*What Is World Literature?* 110).

35. *Planetarity*, as Spivak defines it, would be a possible specific content for the new comparative literature she envisions, a comparative literature based on a form of reading that recognizes the contingency of each particular dis-figuration in the opacity and the undecidability of the figure, never giving in to the hegemonic demand of transparency and full comprehensibility. Planetarity is the figure that must be dis-figured, that is ethically and politically deciphered. The planet, then, is the site where, perhaps, we will be able to inscribe a form of community ethically different from that figured by the globe in globalization. "When I invoke the planet I think of the effort required to figure the (im) possibility of this underived intuition" (*Death* 72). This is the first challenge that the category of planetarity presents: that the planet does not yet exist in the hegemony of the discourses of globalization. World literature, then, could be thought of as the comparative critical study of the symbolic that would deliver the planet to us.

36. One of the most effective critiques of this totalizing paradigm is Apter's idea of a globalization of difference. In "Global *Translatio*," she traces Leo Spitzer's construction, during his exile in Turkey, of discourses of comparative and world literature based on "untranslatable affective gaps" (108): "Spitzer's explicit desire to disturb monolingual complacency" (105) produces "a paradigm of *translatio* . . . that emphasizes the critical role of multilingualism within transnational humanism . . . a policy of *non-translation* adopted without apology" (104).

37. As I was revising the galleys of this book in May 2013, Apter published her very important and polemical *Against World Literature*, a book that articulates a critique of *actually existing* world literature that coincides with my criticism of some of the constitutive tenets of the ways in which world literature has been institutionalized in the US academic field. Apter commends "world literature's deprovincialization of the canon and the way in which, at its best, it draws on translation to deliver surprising cognitive landscapes." However, she expresses "serious reservations about tendencies in world literature toward reflexive endorsement of cultural equivalence and substitutability, or toward the celebration of nationally and ethnically branded 'differences' that have been niche-marketed as commercialized 'identities'" (2). She invokes "untranslatability as a deflationary gesture toward the expansionism and gargantuan scale of world-literary endeavors." She argues that "many recent efforts to revive World Literature rely on a translatability assumption. As a result, incommensurability and what has been called the Untranslatable are insufficiently built into the literary heuristic" (3).

38. See in this regard Sorensen's *Turbulent Decade Remembered* and Santana's *Foreigners in the Homeland*, two remarkable studies of the institutions

and the material circuits and practices that made up the materiality of the 1960s Boom in Latin American literature. Both of them represent possible ways of inscribing Latin America in world literature with attention to the importance of material exchanges, hegemonic relations, and transcultural determinations.

39. Commenting on this proposal to read the universality of García Márquez's novel in cosmopolitan terms rather than in relation to its capacity to express Latin American culture in a global market of commodified cultural particularities, an anonymous reviewer of this chapter noted that "*Cien años*, and magical realism more generally, can make us critical of such universalizing moves (the United Fruit Company is nothing if not cosmopolitan) but only if we read it figurally as a planetary novel." This approach to the novel at the level of plot and rhetorical construction adds another dimension to my argument and, I believe, complements my attempt to reject a globality based on the politics of cultural expression.

40. Roberto Schwarz has written, along these same lines, that if the intention behind unearthing the idea of world literature "is to question the universality of the universal and the localism of the local, then it could be a good starting point for further discussion" (98).

2. THE GLOBAL LIFE OF GENRES AND THE MATERIAL TRAVELS OF MAGICAL REALISM

1. When discussing this idea of what magical realism as a world literary genre does (rather than what it is or what it means), I have the following passage from Deleuze and Guattari's *A Thousand Plateaus* in mind: "We will never ask what a book means, as signified or signifier: we will not look for anything to understand in it. We will ask what it functions with, in connection with what other things it does or does not transmit intensities, in which other multiplicities its own are inserted and metamorphosed" (4).

2. On the historical chronology of magical realism and its versions and mix-ups, see Menton's *Historia verdadera del realismo mágico*, in particular the appendix "Una cronología internacional comentada del término realismo mágico," with special attention to the section "¿1924 o 1925 o 1923 o 1922?" (209–12).

3. In 1943, the Dutch-Flemish writer Johan Daisne (the pseudonym of Herman Thiery, 1912–78) adopted the concept *Magische-Realisme* to describe "a truth behind the reality of life and dream" (qtd. in Guenther 61).

4. During the early 1920s, when Reynaud was working on his scholarly translation of the *Popol Vuh*, he relied on the one that the historian and archaeologist Étienne Brasseur de Bourbourg had published in 1861, and when Asturias and González Mendoza wrote theirs in Spanish between 1925 and 1927, they used both French versions, and to a lesser extent, the Quiché original. In 1927 Asturias published, in Madrid, *Leyendas de Guatemala*, based on his intimate knowledge of the Mayan cosmogony of the sacred book, and soon after it was translated in France by Francis de Miomandre with a laudatory preface by Paul Valéry. To a certain extent this translation's network

serves the purpose of illustrating the transcultural and collective production of Latin American cultural difference as well as of magical realism.

5. The first critic to think of this short story as a paradigmatic exponent of a new magical realist Latin American narrative is the Argentine Enrique Anderson Imbert, who includes it in his *Veinte cuentos hispanoamericanos del siglo XX* (*Twenty Hispanic American Short Stories of the Twentieth Century*) (1956). Anderson Imbert writes that in "Rain" we appreciate "the originality of his 'magical realism,' to use the term coined by the German critic Franz Roh in his study of one phase of contemporary art. Everyday objects appear enveloped in such a strange atmosphere that, although recognizable, they shock us as if they were fantastic" (148).

6. One needs to proceed with caution when writing about postcolonial discourses in Latin America. The exercise can risk losing perspective of the very particular colonial and, eventually, postcolonial nature of culture in Latin America, where formal independence from Spain was achieved during the first two decades of the nineteenth century. Brazil's case is different, since it became the center of the Portuguese court in 1825 and became a truly independent republic only in 1889. The Caribbean and Central America (with the exception of Mexico) is the Latin American region most in sync with the historical temporality of what is commonly known as the postcolonial world.

7. Roberto González Echevarría analyzes Carpentier's first novel as an Afro-Cuban bildungsroman (*Alejo Carpentier: El peregrino* 113), which adds an interesting critical layer to Carpentier's novelistic body, seeing it as structured around the idea that Latin American culture emerges from the antagonism of elite and popular subject positions.

8. For an excellent study of the relations between magical realism and primitivist aesthetics and ideologies, see Camayd-Freixas. He explains that 1920s Paris was "the Mecca of a new international cult of 'the primitive,' and the center of an intense traffic of *l'art negre*, with public and private exhibitions, exchanges, auctions and borrowings between artists and collectors" (33).

9. In those years in Paris, Uslar Pietri participated with Carpentier in weekly surrealist gatherings at Café La Coupole. There he became close with Massimo Bontempelli, who had written about *realismo magico* in his journal *900* (Camayd-Freixas 34). There is no record of Uslar Pietri having discussed magical realism with the Italian critic, but their closeness makes it very likely that the Spanish translation of Roh's piece and those conversations are the sources of that first Latin American appropriation in 1948.

10. This crucial article was published on April 8, 1948, in the Caracas newspaper *El Nacional*, shortly after Uslar Pietri had delivered the lectures where he referred to magical realism. There is no evidence whether Carpentier was aware of Uslar Pietri's talks. Carpentier's seminal essay had several reincarnations between 1948 and 1975: first, as explained, it was included as the preface to *El reino de este mundo*; in 1964 he rewrote it to deliver it at a conference with the same title, a version that was later published in his book *Tientos y diferencias (Touches and Differences)*; finally in 1975 he gave another lecture, "Lo barroco y lo real maravilloso" ("The Baroque and the Marvelous Real"), later included in the collection *Razón de ser* (*Raison d'être*) (1976). In each of

these three rewritings Carpentier added and subtracted examples, cases, and arguments, but the core idea of the marvelous real remained.

11. Carpentier's fascination with Haiti can easily be traced to the exoticist roots of the ethnographic dimension of the avant-gardes, a dimension that Carpentier believed he had left back in Paris when he returned to Cuba in 1939.

12. Even though Carpentier explicitly differentiates his concept from the surrealist *merveilleux*, it bears traces of the influence of Pierre Mabille, the French physician and friend of Carpentier, whose book *Le miroir du merveilleux* (*Mirror of the Marvelous*) was based on his research on Cuban *ñañiguismo* and Haitian *voodoo*. On the influence of Mabille's postsurrealist concept of the *merveilleux Haïtien* (Haitian marvelous) on Carpentier's marvelous real, see Chiampi, "Surrealismo"; Chanady, "Territorialization"; and Scarano.

13. "They all knew that the green lizard, the night moth, the strange dog, the incredible gannet, were nothing but disguises. As he had the power to take the shape of hoofed animal, bird, fish, or insect, Macandal continually visited the plantations of the Plaine to watch over his faithful and find out if they still had faith in his return" (*Kingdom* 30).

14. The timing of the publication of *El reino de este mundo* and *Hombres de maíz* recalled the situation of the early 1930s, when Carpentier and Asturias published *Ecué-Yamba-ó* and *Leyendas of Guatemala* within a few years of each other, anticipating many of the marvelous and magical lines of what would come to be conceptualized as the marvelous real and magical realism.

15. Camayd-Freixas reads *Hombres de maíz* as a mixture of Lautréamont and the *Popol Vuh* (176).

16. Along the same lines, Gerald Martin describes the division of the plot into three parts, "expressed schematically as tribal, feudal-colonial, and capitalist neo-colonial—an Indian protagonist loses his woman and, cut off from the earth and the *milpa* (maizefield), turns to drink and despair. Each is more alienated and distanced than his predecessor. The three phases based on modes of production are aligned, in mythological fashion, to the three-part Mayan cosmic design—underworld, earth, sky (past, present, future)—which is the trajectory of Quetzalcoatl, the plumed serpent and Mesoamerican culture hero for whom, as for Asturias, the irruption from 'prehistory' is the model for all cognitive processes" (Introduction xi).

17. Christopher Warnes notes that "Asturias's capacity to translate the worldview of the indigenous population of Guatemala into fiction should not be overestimated. He spoke no Indian languages, and, as he said to Luis Harss and Barbara Dohmann of his knowledge of the Indian world, 'I heard a lot, assumed a bit more, and invented the rest'" (Warnes, *Magical Realism* 49).

18. The lecture was later published in *Presence Africaine*. In addition to his criticism of magical realist fiction, Alexis also wrote magical realist novels. *Compère Général Soleil* (*General Sun, My Brother*) (1955) is the most important of them; *Les arbres musiciens* (*The Musician Trees*) (1957) deals with the voodoo rites at the core of Haitian culture.

19. Alexis, too, is careful to separate his proposal from surrealism. He does so by foregrounding the political, indeed the revolutionary, potential of the *réalisme merveilleux* that he proposes (Ashcroft, Griffiths, and Tiffin, *Empire Writes Back* 148). On Alexis's *réalisme merveilleux* as a form of opposition and antagonism to *negritude*, see Dash.

20. The inclusion of Borges in some lists of magical realist writers derives from the previously criticized formalist and broad (un)definition of a magical realist aesthetic that would encompass the fantastic. The first to criticize Ángel Flores's formalist and universalist redefinition of the concept of magical realism was Luis Leal, who in a 1967 essay circumscribed and gave the first working definition of magical realism to follow Carpentier's concept of *lo real maravilloso:* "In magical realism key events have no logical or psychological explanation. The magical realist does not try to copy the surrounding reality (as realists did) or to wound it (as the surrealists did) but to seize the mystery that breathes behind things" (123). Even though he does not explicitly circumscribe magical realism within Latin American culture, all of his examples are extracted from the literature of the region. Chanady (1985) has also criticized Flores for conflating magical realism and the fantastic (*Magical Realism*).

21. If, up to this point, magical realism has been analyzed as an almost exclusively Latin American aesthetic phenomenon, it is because it did not exist as such until after what could be called "the globalization of *One Hundred Years of Solitude*." The emergence of magical realist narratives in other postcolonial locations results from a material and concrete process of global expansion.

22. García Márquez fleshes out the content of Latin America's differential historical experience in his 1982 Nobel Prize lecture. There he gives a detailed account of the "outsized reality" of "that immense territory of delusional men" that is Latin America: "hogs with navels on their haunches, clawless birds whose hens laid eggs on the backs of their mates, and others still, resembling tongueless pelicans, with beaks like spoons . . . a misbegotten creature with the head and ears of a mule, a camel's body, the legs of a deer and the whinny of a horse. . . . Our independence from Spanish domination did not put us beyond the reach of madness. General Antonio López de Santana, three times dictator of Mexico, held a magnificent funeral for the right leg he had lost in the so-called Pastry War. General Gabriel García Moreno ruled Ecuador for sixteen years as an absolute monarch; at his wake, the corpse was seated on the presidential chair, decked out in full-dress uniform and a protective layer of medals. General Maximiliano Hernández Martínez, the theosophical despot of El Salvador who had thirty thousand peasants slaughtered in a savage massacre, invented a pendulum to detect poison in his food, and had streetlamps draped in red paper to defeat an epidemic of scarlet fever" ("Solitude"). García Márquez continues to recount all the way to the present and affirms that "we have not had a moment's rest." Regarding the continuities and discontinuities between the novels of the Boom and the regionalist novels that attempt to assert a Latin American differential identity based on the relation of culture and nature, see Sommer's *Foundational Fictions*, especially "Part I: Irresistible Romance."

23. It is obvious that my interpretation of the political nature of magical realism strongly disagrees with Zamora's abstract universalism: "My argument, then, is that the effectiveness of magical realist political dissent depends upon its prior (unstated, understood) archetypalizing of the subject, and its consequent allegorizing of the human condition" ("Magical Romance" 498).

24. Gerald Martin makes an interesting point when he argues that "since the 1960s many of the most important writers—Italo Calvino, Milan Kundera, Salman Rushdie, Umberto Eco—have had to become 'Latin American' novelists" (*Journeys* 7). Being *Latin American*, in Martin's observation, signals a process of becoming minor, subaltern, and postcolonial, as expressed in magical realist fiction.

25. These criteria to describe the specificity of postcolonial magical realist fictions may exclude works usually considered to be within this tradition. Such is the case of Canadian magical realism. Stephen Slemon admits to being unable to find in Canada the kind of postcolonial cultural situation that gave rise to magical realism in Latin America and produced it in Africa and South Asia (407). His solution to the problem of reading novels such as Jack Hodgins's *The Invention of the World* (1977) and Robert Kroetsch's *What the Crow Said* (1978) as magical realist consists in generalizing a specific formal feature of these novels to make a claim about the genre. He argues that in "the language of narration in a magical realist text, a battle between two oppositional systems takes place, each working toward the creation of a different kind of fictional world from the other. Since the ground rules of these two worlds are incompatible, neither can fully come into being, and each remains suspended" (409). Slemon claims that the sustained contradiction staged by the discourse of the genre resembles the colonial condition: a suspension between two codes, two languages, two cultures. Thus he arrives at the interesting conclusion that the relation between magical realism and postcoloniality is mediated by an allegorical relation. Implicit in this argument is the radical and apparently irreconcilable gap between the magical realisms of the so-called Third and First Worlds: whereas in the periphery magical realism seems to emerge, at specific historical junctures, from postcolonial sociocultural situations, in the core it is the appropriation of the formal remains of postcoloniality that produces an effective aesthetic evocation. This would mean that the only way to include these Canadian fictions within the aesthetic genealogy traced in this chapter is to empty magical realism of the traumatic aspect of the postcolonial/peripheric experience that magical realism would work through.

26. Mia Couto's real name is António Emílio Leite Couto; Mo Yan's is Guan Moye. Mo Yan (meaning "Don't speak") is a pen name the author adopted before publishing his first book.

27. Allende's novel is the perfect case study of the afterlife of magical realism as commodity, especially because of the misguided attention it has received in Anglophone academic circles. It is an evident imitation of *Cien años de soledad*'s genealogical structure, where the most significant change is the historical context: from Colombian civil wars and social unrest, to the Pinochet dictatorship in Chile. Even when it is read as a Chilean rewriting of the García Márquez novel, the postcolonial status of Allende's book is hard to defend

unless the conceptual limits of Latin American postcoloniality are expanded to include the 1970s dictatorships and their genocides, a position that cannot be defended convincingly. On the contrary, Allende's *La casa de los espíritus* seems an *out-of-context*, inorganic (in the Lukacsian sense) attempt to produce magical realist effects as mere aesthetic gimmicks.

28. In 1993, Fuguet and Gómez published in Chile another anthology of young writers titled *Cuentos con Walkman* (*Short Stories with Walkman*) that defined a project very similar to McOndo, but as a break with Chilean literature only. One of the blurbs promoting the book explained that "la moral walkman es una nueva generación literaria que es post-todo: post-modernismo, post-yuppie, postcomunismo, post-baby boom, post-capa de ozono. Aquí no hay realismo mágico, hay realismo virtual" ("the Walkman Doctrine is a new literary generation that is post-everything: post-modernism, post-yuppie, post-communism, post-baby boom, post-ozone layer. Here there is no magical realism, there is virtual realism").

29. This candid and transparent relation with market figures and rhetoric would been unthinkable to the Boom writers, in spite of their intense interactions with all aspects of the publishing industry and their acquisition of a group identity (Boom) through a carefully designed marketing operation (Rama, "Boom en perspectiva").

3. THE RISE OF LATIN AMERICAN WORLD LITERARY DISCOURSES (1882–1925)

1. Octavio Paz's hypothesis about the modernity of *modernismo* agrees with Molloy's and González's: the *modernistas* become modern at the very moment of their critique of the pre- or unmodern state of Latin American culture that precedes the actual beginning of the process of material modernization: "La modernidad es sinónimo de crítica y se identifica con el cambio; no es afirmación de un principio atemporal, sino el despliegue de la razón crítica que sin cesar se interroga, se examina y se destruye para renacer de nuevo" (*Hijos del limo* 48) ("Modernity is synonymous with critique and is identical with change; it is not the affirmation of an atemporal principle but the deployment of critical reason constantly interrogating, examining, and destroying itself in order to be reborn").

2. That *modernismo* is the rather arbitrary denomination of a heterogeneous group of poetic discourses is nothing new. M. Henríquez Ureña's *Breve historia del modernismo* (*A Brief History of Modernism*) acknowledges the artificiality of the label, which includes symbolists, Pre-Raphaelites, and impressionists, and indicates that it was first used by Darío in 1890, who placed himself at the center of this unstable and loose aesthetic network (11). In spite of the differences and tensions within it, *modernismo* still designates a common sensibility that I will trace in relation to cosmopolitan imaginaries; the same sensibility also operated to specify a cultural particularity and the desire to break with the past and establish a new aesthetic tradition for the region.

3. See, for instance, Echeverría's romantic take on world literature, which he understands as the definition of Latin American identity in opposition to

modern European literature: "Cada pueblo o civilización [tiene] su poesía, y por consiguiente, sus formas poéticas características. Las formas de la poesía indostánica son colosales, monstruosas como sus ídolos y pagodas; las de la poesía árabe aéreas y maravillosas como los aéreos y columnas de sus mezquitas; las de la griega regulares y sencillas como sus templos; las de la [europea] moderna, pintorescas, multiformes y confusas como las catedrales góticas, pero profundamente simbólicas" ("Fondo" 76–77) ("Peoples or civilizations have their own poetry, and their idiosyncratic poetic forms. Hindustani poetic forms are colossal monstrosities like its idols and pagodes; those of Arabic poetry, aerial and marvelous like the columns of its mosques; those of Greece, even and simple like its temples; those of modern Europe, quaint, multifarious, and convoluted like gothic cathedrals, but also profoundly symbolic"). He continues this line of thought in another essay: "El espíritu del siglo lleva hoy a todas las naciones a emanciparse, a gozar de la independencia, no sólo política sino también filosófica y literaria. . . . Nosotros tenemos derecho para ambicionar lo mismo y nos hallamos en la mejor condición para hacerlo" ("Clasicismo" 99) ("Today, the spirit of the century drives all nations toward emancipation and the enjoyment of independence, not solely political but also philosophical and literary. . . . We have the right to pursue the same, and we find ourselves in the best possible conditions to achieve it").

4. Argentina, for example, was entirely and radically transformed by the global boom in agricultural exportations that began in the 1880s. The economic historian Carlos Díaz Alejandro explains that "en la historia argentina no existen tres décadas que haya experimentado una expansión económica tan significativa como las que precedieron a la Primera Guerra Mundial . . . [marcadas por] un crecimiento irregular, pero vigoroso, orientado hacia las exportaciones, de un dinamismo inusual aun en aquellos años en los que muchas regiones periféricas del mundo asistían a procesos en los que las exportaciones representaban el motor del crecimiento" (369) ("In all of Argentine history there are not three decades that experienced such a significant economic expansion as those that preceded World War I . . . [marked by] regular but vigorous growth driven by exports, [and] an unusual dynamism, even when compared to years when many peripheral regions witnessed processes where exports drove growth").

5. The characterization of *modernismo* as the foundational moment of modern Latin American culture has to do with two different variables. On the one hand, it is well documented that the extended emergence of effective modern cultural institutions and aesthetic practices took place during this historical period and through the cultural agency of these intellectuals (see Rama, Molloy, Ramos, Gutiérrez Girardot, and Montaldo). On the other, it can be explained by paying attention to the ways in which the *modernistas* represented themselves and their historical task. Martí, Darío, and the other *modernistas* did not believe that modernity preceded them, geographically and/or temporally. What was modern for them, in Latin America at the turn of the century, was their own sensibility and desire for modernity.

In her book about the literary relations between Hispanic America and France, Sylvia Molloy introduces two revealing quotations that anticipate her later description of Darío and his contemporaries seeing a void that needed to be filled. The first is from a letter Darío sent to Miguel de Unamuno: "En el asunto del pensamiento y de la literatura hispanoamericana, creo yo, desde luego, que no hay allí nada, o más bien que hay muy poco" ("Regarding Spanish American thought and literature, I believe, of course, there is nothing there, or very little"). In the second quote, Héctor Murena recharacterizes that "cultural void" as poverty: "El modernismo acepta implícitamente esa indigencia cultural y, al aventurarse a crear con un *Ersatz* de la cultura, transmuta la miseria en riqueza. . . . En el cosmopolitismo modernista se reconoce no ser nada y se logra de tal suerte una cierta forma de ser" (*Diffusion* 17–18) ("Modernism accepts implicitly that cultural poverty and, in venturing to create a cultural *Ersatz*, transforms misery into wealth. . . . In modernist cosmopolitanism one recognizes one's lack of being and thus achieves a certain personality"). *Modernismo* views Latin America as an ontological cultural void that needs to be filled in so that the region might enter an order that, following the Western tradition of metaphysics, has its epicenter in Europe, where Being—the essence of humanity—lies.

6. A year later, Manuel Gutiérrez Nájera condemned the Spanish language in even stronger terms: "El castellano es un idioma infeliz. Fue rico y conquistador. Pero enterró sus tesoros y las monedas que hoy extraemos de entre las piedras y la arena, son monedas de museo que no circulan. No cultivamos sus heredades y hoy el diccionario está lleno de terrenos baldíos. Casi podría decirse que es un idioma empajado" ("Toros" 86) ("Castillian Spanish is an unhappy language. It used to be rich and conquering, but its treasures are buried, and the coins we dig out today from underneath stone and sand are museum pieces out of circulation. We do not cultivate its estates, and today's dictionary is full of wastelands. One could almost say it is an abandoned language").

7. Rama's critical ideology changed significantly between the early 1970s and the 1980s. His premature death in 1983 interrupted the transformation of his critical practice from a rather mechanical Marxist matrix characterized by the economical determinism of his approach to literature and culture to a culturalist view of literary phenomena, and from a sociological *Latin Americanism* to a philosophical universalist view of Latin American cultural history. Because of his continuing interest in Martí and Darío, these ideological changes can be traced in his different approaches to *modernismo*, from *Rubén Darío y el modernismo* (1970) and "La dialéctica de la modernidad en José Martí" (1971) to "José Martí en el eje de la modernización poética" (1983) and *Las máscaras democráticas del modernismo* (1985). For example, a deterministic analysis of the *modernistas*' relation to European modern aesthetics in *Rubén Darío y el modernismo* gave way to a conceptualization of the universality of modernity as a horizon for a modernist aesthetic practice in *Las mascaras democráticas del modernismo*. In 1970 he proposed the incorporation of Latin America into a world capitalistic market: "Este movimiento se reproduce de modo paralelo en el campo de la cultura. No sólo en la apreciación primaria, porque los escritores hispanoamericanos se dediquen a la imitación de la poesía francesa, sino porque se sienten llamados a hacerlo en

la medida en que viven, servicialmente, experiencias emparentadas a los centros industriales y culturales" (*Rubén Darío* 24) ("This movement is mirrored in the cultural field, not only, at first appraisal, because Spanish American writers dedicate themselves to imitate French poetry, but also because they feel compelled to do so by the slavish way in which they feel close to what is experienced in such industrial and cultural capitals"). In 1985, Rama sees that "para poder insertar su peculiaridad cultural en la pluralidad de textos europeos, debían transformar su poética y la lengua que le servía de vehículo, o sea los instrumentos del arte, a lo cual debemos el afán técnico que se posesionó de la mayoría de los poetas" (*Máscaras democráticas* 154) ("in order to insert their cultural peculiarity in the plurality of European texts, they had to transform the poetics and language that had served them as a vehicle, that is, their aesthetic instruments, which explains the enthusiasm for technique in a majority of these poets"). I am grateful to Alejandra Josiowicz for bringing Rama's "José Martí en el eje de la modernización poética" to my attention. In her essay "Cosmopolitismo y decadentismo," Josiowicz provides an interesting account of Rama's concept of "internationalism" (an undertheorized notion that does not quite address the transcultural, or rather transnational, dimension at stake in *modernismo*) from his first texts to those published after his death.

8. In *Máscaras democráticas*, Rama explicitly claims that the *modernistas*' achievements can be appreciated only in the larger context of the world field of aesthetic commerce: "Alcanzan su valor . . . sólo en la medida en que se incorporan a un sistema, como partes integrantes, igualmente dignas y equiparables" (109) ("Their value can be appreciated only when incorporated into a system, as integral, worthy, and equivalent parts of it"). For a detailed historization and the most interesting hypothesis on the shifts of Rama's critical discourse since the end of the 1970s, see very lucid essays by Aguilar ("Costuras"), De la Campa, and Spitta.

9. In a brilliant essay on "Nuestra América," Aching argues that Martí's seminal essay should be read not only as an attempt to define a Latin American cultural particularity that results from the reconciliation of opposites as a way of differentiating the new cultural formation from Europe but also as a project of inscribing Latin America "into an international community." Aching reads in "Nuestra América" the desire of being part of a larger modern world that I identify in "Oscar Wilde." What is interesting and crucial here is that Aching's reading places "Nuestra América" much closer to "Oscar Wilde" than I have been willing to acknowledge. The crucial difference remains that while in "Oscar Wilde" Martí's cosmopolitan universalism is at its highest point because he is concerned with the aesthetic shape of the world, postponing identitarian questions, Aching contends that in "Nuestra América" the Cuban "advocates a racially inclusive Spanish Americanism, a *mestizo* America," a racial specificity that will constitute the region's identity within the "international community" ("Against 'Library-Shelf Races'" 151).

10. In fact, Alonso argues that "the Spanish American nineteenth century has become a novel and fertile ground of research . . . result[ing] from the backwards glance away from the 'Boom'" ("Rama" 283).

11. For a much more sophisticated, careful, and complex reading of "Nuestra América" along these same ideological lines, see Saldívar. Among many differences between Saldívar's and Fernández Retamar's vindications of Martí's anti-imperialism is Saldívar's construction of Martí as the founder of an intellectual progeny that shapes a Pan-American identity. Saldívar still works within the discourse of identity, but he appropriates Martí's cultural-political heritage from a transcultural tradition that transcends the reified *Latin Americanist* inscription of Martí in an *exclusively* Latin American heroic tradition.

12. I am not trying to paint a totalizing portrait of Rama's critical ideology regarding *modernismo*. Rather than being invested solely in shaping the figures of autonomy, he also interrogates the dialectical relation between universalism and particularism, and the tension between popular cultural subjects and educated elites. He renovated the critical interpretation of *modernismo* in ways that still dominate the field.

13. Ramos's *Divergent Modernities* (written during the 1980s and published in Spanish in 1989) is one of the most brilliant offspring of Rama's double conceptualization of cultural autonomy. Ramos forcefully articulates both notions of autonomy in his description of the new preeminent place of literature in the nineteenth century regarding both the production of a Latin American cultural identity and "literature's authority as a new place for a moral judgment," which grounded such cultural identity while other social discourses like education and politics were "now oriented toward the realization of practical ends" (51).

14. The Cuban anthropologist Fernando Ortiz originally developed the notion of *transculturación* in the 1940s, but Rama reconceptualizes it in the context of literary criticism as "transculturación narrativa" in the essay "Los procesos de transculturación en la narrativa latinoamericana," published in 1974 in *Revista de Literatura Iberoamericana*. He later rewrote this essay for the book-length study *Transculturación narrativa en América Latina* (*Narrative Transculturation in Latin America*).

15. Perhaps the most important precedent in this tradition of dialectical interpretation of the contradiction between cosmopolitanism and criollism was José Carlos Mariátegui's interpretation of *modernismo* and the avant-garde. In his historical analysis of the formation of Peru's national literature, he traces a succession of oppositions between colonial and colonialist moments of technical virtuosity but shows a disregard for Peru's indigenous cultural specificity and periods of independent self-affirming *indigenismo* without formal sophistication. Mariátegui believes that national literature emerges only when that contradiction is overcome in the work of César Vallejo, which reconciles modernist style with particularly Peruvian content: "En *Los Heraldos Negros* principia acaso la poesía peruana (peruana, en el sentido de indígena)" (*Siete ensayos* 259) ("These lines of *Los Heraldos Negros* probably mark the beginning of Peruvian, in the sense of indigenous, poetry"; *Seven Interpretive Essays* 251). According to Mariátegui, "En Vallejo se encuentra, por primera vez en nuestra literatura, sentimiento indígena virginalmente expresado. . . . [Vallejo] logra en su poesía un estilo nuevo. . . . Al poeta no le basta traer un mensaje nuevo. Necesita traer una técnica y un lenguaje

nuevos también" (259) ("In Vallejo, for the first time in our history, indigenous sentiment is given pristine expression. . . . [Vallejo] creates a new style in his poetry. . . . The poet, not satisfied with conveying a new message, also brings a new technique and language"; 250). For a more contemporary exponent of this tradition, see, for instance, Gustavo Pérez Firmat, who does not see a contradiction between cosmopolitan goals and *literaturas criollistas* (*Creole Literatures*); to the contrary, he considers it necessary to illuminate the fact that Latin American identity (or "American feeling," in his terms) results from the *criollistas*' dialectical reconciliation: "Foreign books are not incompatible with American feeling; indeed, American feeling is nothing other than a certain way of reading foreign books" (8).

16. In this sense, I agree with John Beverley when he writes that "the idea of transculturation expresses both in Ortiz and Rama, the fantasy of class, gender and racial reconciliation" (47).

17. Very few critics have resisted the temptation to explain away the contradictions at the core of the *modernista* project. Carlos Real de Azúa is one of these exceptions. For him *modernismo* is an inherently contradictory moment of Latin American culture: "No creo que pueda hablarse de una 'ideología del 900' sino, y sólo, de un ambiente intelectual caracterizado, como pocos, en la vida de la cultura, por el signo de lo controversial y lo caótico" (15) ("I do not think one can talk about an ideology of the turn of the twentieth century, only of an intellectual atmosphere marked, like few others in cultural history, by the sign of controversy and chaos"). The same is true of Iván Schulman: "El artista modernista absorbe estas fuerzas, algunas de las cuales son de patente dirección antitética. Y éstas se traducen en las estructuras polares que tan relevante función tienen en la escritura modernista. . . . La tensión y la distensión de estos factores en conflicto produjeron una estética acrática, una mentalidad confusa, y una literatura polifacética y contradictoria en sus tendencias" (*Nuevos asedios* 30) ("The modernist artist absorbs these forces, some of which are of clearly antithetical orientation, and they are translated into the polarized structures that fulfill such a relevant function in modernist writing. . . . These conflicting factors' tensions and distensions produced an anarchic aesthetic, a confused mentality, and a multifaceted and contradictory literature").

18. Recent attempts to conceptualize the cosmopolitan nature of *modernismo* have similarly underscored the particularistic determinations of the totality of its discursive enterprise. Cathy Jrade affirms that, while the cosmopolitan attitude of *modernistas* "has been identified with escapism . . . it is actually the manifestation of a complex and profound search, a search that led *modernista* writers to embrace diverse aspects of high culture from all corners of the world with heady enthusiasm in the expectation of achieving—in apparent contradiction—a sense of identity that is clearly Latin American. . . . *Modernista* writers turned their attention from the most-up-to-date European trends toward home and resurrected, through flights of fancy as much as through historical fact, a Spanish American past that included ancient civilizations, indigenous peoples, and Spanish American consciousness" (14). See also Camilla Fojas, who affirms that "Latin American [modernist] cosmopolitanism was part of an overall aim to create a national cultural identity that

was completely modern and completely opposed to a colonial heritage" (3–4), and that "cosmopolitanism meant making use of international culture to set a national cultural agenda" (26). National and regional epistemological scales often constitute the internal boundary of a critical tradition of *modernismo* that finds it very difficult to think beyond the mind-set of cultural particularity and identity-formation processes.

19. Besides the obvious anti-Spanish motivation, Rama detects in Martí a certain rancor toward French culture: "Por ese entonces Martí comprende que el imperialismo de la cultura francesa no puede combatirse encerrándose en las estrechas y arcaicas fronteras nacionales, como reclamaban rezagados románticos o los conservadores, y mucho menos prolongando la dependencia de la cultura española, sino avanzando aún más en el internacionalismo de la hora mediante una audaz ampliación del horizonte universal de la cultura" ("José Martí" 97) "It is then [after arriving in New York City] that Martí understands that one can combat the imperialism of French culture, not by shutting oneself up within the restrictive and archaic borders of nationality as regressive romantics and conservatives have demanded, and even less by prolonging dependence on Spanish culture, but by advancing further on the path of today's internationalism through a bold enlargement of the universal horizon of culture").

20. These thoughts on the concepts of "difference" and "diversity" draw extensively from Bhabha's foundational discussion on the opposition between the two. See *Location* 49–50.

21. Martí writes twice in the essay about the desire to escape oneself, "salirse de sí." The first time is in the opening paragraph that I refer to extensively; the second is later in the essay. Interestingly, this second mention invokes a different meaning of "salirse de sí." If the first is clearly related to the universal desire to be part of something larger than one's particular cultural community, the second alludes to literature as a tool for spiritual subjects to leave behind their social world and realize their longing to be citizens of the world republic of letters: "Embellecer la vida es darle objeto. Salir de sí es indomable anhelo humano, y hace bien a los hombres quien procura hermosear su existencia, de modo que vengan a vivir contentos con estar en sí" ("Oscar Wilde" 288) "Beautify life and you give it meaning. The desire to rise above oneself is an unrelenting human longing, and he who beautifies man's existence serves him well" ("Oscar Wilde" 260). Literature, and its aestheticist embrace, is the path to a universal existence, not necessarily because of our attention to the literatures of the world (rather than our own), but because Literature (with a capital L) is a universal realm, patrimony, and reading practice. This conception of literature (which Martí shared with the rest of the *modernistas*, and with modernists throughout the world) is as essential to the structure of world literary discourses as the cosmopolitan negation of the local, particular inscription of the legibility of literary texts.

22. A few years later, in the poem "Cosmopolitanismo," included in *Minúsculas* (1901), González Prada imagines the vague contours of a cosmopolitan geography defined by the negation of "here" and "now"—cosmopolitanism as

the search for an elsewhere that promises the renewal and the modernization that can be had "here":

> ¡Cómo fatiga y cansa, cómo abruma,
> el suspirar mirando eternamente
> los mismos campos y la misma gente,
> los mismos cielos y la misma bruma!
> Huir quisiera por la blanca espuma
> y al sol lejano calentar mi frente.
> ¡Oh, si me diera el río su corriente!
> ¡Oh, si me diera el águila su pluma!
> Yo no seré viajero arrepentido
> . . . .
> Donde me estrechen generosas manos,
> donde me arrullen tibias primaveras,
> allí veré mi patria y mis hermanos.
>
> How fatiguing, tiresome, and overwhelming
> sighing while eternally staring
> at the same fields and the same people
> the same skies and the same mist!
> I'd like to escape through the white foam
> to the distant sun to warm my brow
> Oh, if the river could give me its currents!
> Oh, if the eagle could give me its feathers!
> I would not be a repentant traveler
> . . . .
> Where generous hands will greet me,
> where tepid springs will lull me,
> there will I see my homeland and my brothers.

23. By "Occidentalist ideology," I am alluding to the notion of Occidentalism as the symbolic construction of the West by peripheral intellectual elites as a function of their cultural, political, and economic interest in the global scene. The concept was first developed by Couze Venn in 2000 and later by Ian Buruma and Avishai Margalit in 2004 as a direct inversion of Edward Said's notion of Orientalism, which accounted for the symbolic construction of the East by European colonial writers. While in East Asia at the turn of the century this discourse had the form of a repudiation of the materialist West as a reaction to sociocultural modernization, in Latin America Occidentalism tended to mimic the Occidentalist discourse that European intellectuals were articulating about their own hegemonic position within the world's uneven relation of forces. Venn defines Occidentalism as the attempt, on the part of European intellectuals, to universalize their modern, capitalist conception of the social. "Occidentalism thus directs attention to the becoming-modern of the world and the becoming-West of Europe such that Western modernity gradually became established as the privileged, if not hegemonic, form of sociality, tied to a universalizing and totalizing ambition" (19). The discourse on European literature

produced by *modernista* writers tended to reinforce this unevenness between the West and its Latin American periphery.

Conscious of the unevenness on top of which Occidentalist discourses are enunciated, Graciela Montaldo offers a more complex view on its place within *modernismo*, underscoring its modernizing effects:

> Toda exageración es poca cuando se trata de describir y pensar el gusto 'europeizante' de los artistas e intelectuales del fin de siglo latinoamericano. Como ha señalado Edward W. Said, el europeísmo se había constituido en el siglo XIX en una ideología que había penetrado todo (desde la clase obrera al feminismo) y un paradigma homogéneo que regía las identidades culturales de los modernos occidentales. Los intelectuales y artistas "esteticistas" latinoamericanos jugaron un rol central en la difusión de los gustos modernos de la cultura occidental poniendo al alcance de sectores cada vez mayores el gusto de las tradiciones estéticas modernas, homogeneizándolos y tratando de borrar, por captura, las diferencias. Al hacerlo, les dieron también a esos sectores acceso a sus mismas prácticas culturales. En la cultura mundializada, sin embargo, esa homogeneidad es para los latinoamericanos el despliegue de todas las diferencias posibles. (*Ficciones culturales* 87)
>
> The Europeanizing taste of turn-of-the-century Latin American writers and intellectuals cannot be exaggerated. As Edward W. Said has explained, Europeanism was during the nineteenth century an ideology that permeated everything (from the working class to feminism) and a homogeneous paradigm that ruled cultural identities throughout the Western world. Latin American aestheticist intellectuals and artists played a central role in the diffusion of the modern tastes of Western culture, making available to ever-growing sectors the taste for modern aesthetic traditions, homogenizing them and trying to erase their differences. In doing so, they gave those sectors access to their own cultural practices. In the context of a globalized culture, however, that homogeneity was for Latin Americans the deployment of all possible differences.

24. It is not only that I disagree with the prevalent approach to modernist universalism in Latin American criticism; it is also that I see a constitutive contradiction within *modernismo* between universalism and particularism, the noncoincidence of *modernismo* with itself. As I have stated before, it is important to acknowledge these contradictions in Martí and *modernismo* more broadly. Regarding world literature, for instance, even though Martí made the most forceful case for a world literary redefinition of Latin American literature and its relations with the universal premises of modernity, before and after his chronicle on Oscar Wilde, he wrote several particularistic invectives against what I define here as a world literary relation with the literatures of the world. In 1878, for instance, Martí wrote, in a letter to José Joaquín Palma, about European literature in terms similar to those he would use years

later in "Nuestra América": "Dormir sobre Musset; apegarse a las alas de Víctor Hugo; herirse con el cilicio de Gustavo Bécquer; arrojarse en las cimas de Manfredo; abrazarse a las ninfas del Danubio; ser propio y querer ser ajeno; desdeñar el sol patrio, y calentarse al viejo sol de Europa; trocar las palmas por los fresnos, los lirios del Cautillo por la amapola pálida del Darro. . . . Así comprometeremos sus destinos [de la patria], torciéndola a ser copia de historia y pueblos extraños" ("A José Joaquín Palma" 94) ("To sleep next to Musset, to fly with Victor Hugo's wings, to torment oneself with Gustavo Bécquer's hair shirt, to hurl oneself down among Manfred's peaks, to embrace the Danube's nymphs, to be one's own and to be a stranger, to disdain the native sun to be warm under Europe's old sun, to change palms for ash trees, Cautillo's lilies for Darro's pale poppies. . . . This way we compromise our homeland's destiny, damning it to be a mere copy of the history of foreign peoples").

And in 1881, in Venezuela, months before arriving in New York, he explains that the *Revista Venezolana* "encamina sus esfuerzos a elaborar, con los restos del derrumbe, la grande América nueva, sólida, batallante, trabajadora y asombrosa" ("is striving to create, from the wreckage of our collapse, a great, new America, solid, bold, industrious, and amazing") and then goes on to ask, "¿Será alimento suficiente a un pueblo fuerte, digno de su alta cuna y magníficos rimadores, la aplicación cómoda y perniciosa de indagaciones de otros mundos. . . ?—No: no es ésa la obra. . . . Es fuerza convidar a las letras a que vengan a andar la vía patriótica, del brazo de la historia" ("Carácter" 209–10) ("Will it be sufficient nourishment for a strong people, worthy of its noble birth and magnificent bards, the comfortable and pernicious activity of investigating other worlds?—No, that is not our task. . . . We must invite the world of letters to travel the patriotic road, hand in hand with history"). One could claim that these essays were written before Martí's arrival in New York, a moment that supposedly reorganized his ideas about Latin America and the non–Latin American (Europe and *Their* America), thus opening the possibility of a universalist drive where before there had been room only for the particularistic struggle for Latin American identity. This is, in fact, an argument Rama puts forth: "Con su llegada a Nueva York toma contacto con la cultura masiva y cosmopolita que, a su vez, lo pone en relación directa con las corrientes de la renovación francesa, inglesa y norteamericana" ("José Martí" 97) ("After arriving in New York, he encounters a cosmopolitan mass culture that, in turn, introduces him to French, English, and North American attempts to renew literary culture"). However, "Nuestra América" was written in 1891, almost ten years after "Oscar Wilde"—clearly, the idea of linear progression in Martí, from particularism to universalism, does not hold. I believe that these contradictions must be interpreted in the context of the tension between *modernismo*'s Latin American particularism and its Occidentalist universalism: world literature represented one of most striking instances of *modernismo*'s noncoincidence with itself.

25. Molloy underlines this asymmetry when she describes Martí's first encounter with Wilde: "Encounter is too generous a word, of course, since the two men never met and since Wilde was totally unaware of Martí's existence. What interests me here, to begin with, is precisely that imbalance

which affords Martí a particularly interesting vantage point" ("Too Wilde" 188).

26. It is interesting to contrast Martí's discomfort with Wilde's queerness and Gómez Carrillo's ease with the Irish writer's erotic appeal: "Cuando en mis visitas matinales a su deliciosa habitación del Boulevard des Capucines, suelo encontrarle, vestido apenas con una camiseta descotada de lana roja, su robusto torso de luchador me hace pensar en las figuras inmortales de Rubens. . . . Su nariz es recta, su boca es sensual, su cuello es firme. Y con todo esto, cierto amaneramiento que constituye su encanto propio y verdadero" ("Visita" 149–50) ("During my morning visits to his delightful quarters at the Boulevard des Capucines, I often find him barely dressed in an open red-wool dressing gown; his robust chest, like that of a wrestler, makes me think of the immortal figures of Rubens. . . . His nose is straight, his mouth sensuous, his neck firm. And together with all this, the mannerisms that constitute his personal and honest charm"). For a complete analysis of Gómez Carrillo's construction of the figure of *his* Oscar Wilde, see Fojas (40–42).

27. Gutiérrez Nájera and Martí were friends. They met during Martí's brief stay in Mexico between 1875 and 1876 and shared an editorial space at the Mexican paper *El Partido Liberal* (*The Liberal Party*). They later corresponded frequently between New York and Mexico. Therefore it is not surprising that, a few years after "Oscar Wilde," Gutiérrez Nájera would accept Martí's challenge. According to Schulman, "De Gutiérrez Nájera, Martí estimaba la obra y la persona. Nájera alabó al escritor cubano de 'alas recias' y 'estilo mágico'" ("José Martí" 111) ("Martí held in high esteem Gutiérrez Nájera's work and literary persona. Nájera praised the Cuban writer's 'powerful wings' and 'magical style'").

28. In "Escritor argentino" Borges writes: "No podemos concretarnos a lo argentino para ser argentinos" (274) ("We cannot confine ourselves to what is Argentine in order to be Argentine"; "Argentine Writer" 427). This essay begins from the same question as Gutiérrez Nájera's and reaches a conclusion along the same lines (albeit more radical because Borges represents the apex of the world literary tradition that the *modernistas* inaugurated). For more on "Escritor argentino," see the Introduction.

29. Most specialists consider Gutiérrez Nájera an organic intellectual of the Porfiriato (see José María Martínez's "Un duque en la corte del Rey Burgués," and "Entre la lámpara y el espejo"). Critics used to identify him, perhaps rather summarily after reading his most famous poem, "La duquesa de Job," with the Francophilia usually attributed to nineteenth-century Latin American elites and especially *modernista* poets. But this passage shows a universal desire that takes the whole world of modernity as its object, and not just an essentialist, passive adoration of France and everything French.

30. Justo Sierra, in the preface to the first published anthology of Gutiérrez Nájera's poems (1896), foregrounds the poet's "individualismo poético" and ascribes it to his romantic inclination (17). Schulman criticized Sierra for this, explaining that Gutiérrez Nájera's individualism has to be understood in relation to the liberal hegemony in nineteenth-century discourses on modernity ("Más allá" 132).

31. I am alluding here to Thomas Friedman's *The World Is Flat*, an apology for capitalistic, neoliberal globalization, which, unlike Gutiérrez Nájera's optimistic cosmopolitan outlook, does not have the benefit of having been written from the historical perspective of the modernizing, progressive moment of the rise of the Latin American bourgeoisie.

32. In the first issue of *Cosmópolis*, Dominici wrote: "¡Pertenecemos a una región estéril, según el vaticinio del profeta moderno! Sin embargo, lucharé con vosotros, pero eso sí, me convertiré en un joven pálido, de frente sudorosa, viviré entre las sombras, esperando siempre la agonía de nuestro hijo enfermo, pensando en las flores mustias que colocaré sobre su cuerpo cuando lo arrojemos desde las rocas del Taigete, esa hecatombe de los niños débiles" (*Cosmópolis* 1 [1894]) ("We belong to a barren region, according to the modern poet's prophecy! I will battle with you, but I will have to become a pale young man with a perspiring brow, I will live in the shadows, constantly awaiting the death of our ill son, thinking of the withered flowers that I will strew over his body when we cast it down from the mountain of Taygetos, that hecatomb of feeble children").

33. Later, Urbaneja Achelpohl published two essays in *Cosmópolis* that are considered foundational to Venezuelan realist regionalism: "Sobre literatura nacional" ("On National Literature") and "Más sobre literatura nacional" ("More on National Literature"). In the second, he writes: "Nada más hermoso que el objeto del americanismo: ser la representación sincera de nuestros usos, costumbres, modos de pensar y sentir" (49) "Nothing is more beautiful than the object of Americanism: the sincere representation of our purpose, customs, and modes of thought and sentiment").

34. In a very interesting essay, Beauregard analyzes the constant self-figuration of the writer as a reader of European literature in Coll's writing. She views it as literary staging ("una espectacularización de la escena de lectura") and foregrounds Coll's first book, *Palabras* (1896), which opens with an epigraph from Hamlet where the Danish prince tells Polonius that he is reading "words, words, words." This, she argues, together with the gallery of authors featured in the book, is meant to be read as a self-portrait of the writer as reader. Moreover, Silva Beauregard argues that the overwhelming presence, in Coll's writings, of "la literatura francesa, a través de citas y escenas de lectura en las que aparece el escritor siempre con libros en la mano, nos coloca de lleno en la espectacularización de la apropiación de la cultura europea" (81) ("French literature, through quotations and scenes of reading where the writer always appears with books in his hands, places us squarely in a spectacularized appropriation of European culture").

35. In the final issue, Coll writes a farewell editorial that narrates the end of the journal in nostalgic and anecdotal terms, rather than underscoring the internal differences between him and Urbaneja Achelpohl: "Hoy no hay en nuestra redacción las bulliciosas discusiones, las alegres charlas de antaño, muchos amigos se han cansado de serlo, otros se han ido lejos" ("Notas" 143) ("Today at our magazine we no longer have the boisterous discussions, the jolly conversations of former days; many friends have stopped being friends, and others have gone away").

36. Molloy explains that at the turn of the twentieth century,

> pour la première fois dans l'histoire des échanges culturels entre la France et l'Amérique hispanique, on peut parler d'une veritable colonie littéraire établie à Paris qui présente, pour ansi dire, un front unique, celui du *modernismo:* Enrique Gómez Carrillo, Rubèn Darío, Amado Nervo, les frères García Calderón, Rufino Blanco Fombona, Enrrique Larreta ne sont que quelques-uns des écrivains quie la composent. Il s'agit de una colonie stable, dont les members s'installent d'une manière quasi définitive à Paris: Darío, lors de son second voyage en France, déclare qu'il y vient s'installer 'por toujours' et il ne survit guère à son depart, en 1914; Gòmez Carrillo y fixe son residence en 1891 et ne quitte Paris—où il mourra en 1927—-que lorsqu'il entreprend ses voyages exotiques; les García Calderón s'installent définitivement à Paris ainsi que le Chilien Francisco Contreras. (*Diffusion* 18–19)

> for the first time in the history of the cultural exchanges between France and Spanish America, it is possible to talk about a true literary colony established in Paris that presents, so to speak, a united front of *modernismo*: Enrique Gómez Carrillo, Rubén Darío, Amado Nervo, the García Calderón brothers, Rufino Blanco Fombona, Enrique Larreta are only some of the writers who were part of it. It is a stable colony where members are established in a quasi-permanent fashion in Paris: Darío, during his second visit to France, declares that he is staying for good and survives only a short while after his departure in 1914; Gómez Carrillo establishes his residence there in 1891 and leaves Paris—where he will die in 1927—only when he travels to exotic destinations; the García Calderón brothers establish their permanent residence in Paris, as do the Chilean Francisco Contreras.

37. Beginning in the 1980s, in lectures and classes, Molloy revised her position on Gómez Carrillo. In conversation, she told me that she regretted not having appreciated the productive and demystifying dimensions of some of Gómez Carrillo's lighthearted writing.

38. Bastos states that the goal of her essay "La crónica modernista de Enrique Gómez Carrillo o la función de la trivialidad" is to "reivindicar su trivialidad . . . rescatar por medio de ella una imagen de la fugacidad del modernismo, de todos los modernismos" (64) "to reclaim his triviality . . . and through it to rescue the image of *modernismo*'s transience, of all modernisms' transience."

39. Jacinto Octavio Picón, a disciple of Spanish novelist and critic Leopoldo Alas "Clarín," does not hesitate to admit the strangeness of Gómez Carrillo's choices in his preface to *Literatura extranjera:* "Hoy por hoy, nos preocupa muy poco lo que se escribe fuera de España, sin que casi nadie se cuide de estudiarlo. . . . Estos escritores y otros que se les parecen sólo son conocidos

en España por muy limitado número de lectores" (v) ("Today we are barely concerned with what is written outside of Spain, and nobody takes the trouble to inquire into this. . . . These and other similar writers are known in Spain only by a very small group of readers"). He even confesses to not knowing some of the French writers Carrillo writes about, "varios de ellos desconocidos hasta para los que seguimos con asiduidad el movimiento literario de esa gran República" (vi) ("many of them unknown even to those of us who follow assiduously the literary scene in that great Republic"). And when writing about Scandinavian artists, he acknowledges that they are completely strange to the Latin *spirit:* "novelistas y poetas cuyas aptitudes y facultades artísticas se hallan en terrible contradicción con el espíritu y el carácter de lo que me rodea, de lo que estoy acostumbrado a comprender, de lo que puedo sentir y de cuanto vive en torno mío" (vi) ("novelists and poets whose artistic aptitudes and faculties are in stark contradiction with the spirit and character of what surrounds me, what I am used to understanding, what I feel and what lives around me").

40. Even though Gómez Carrillo was younger than Darío and always referred to the Nicaraguan poet as his master, his essays on French writers (Verlaine and Huysmans, among others) from *Esquisses* and *Almas y cerebros* (written between 1890 and 1896) are exactly contemporaneous with the original publication of the profiles that would become *Los raros* in 1896. On the relation between Gómez Carrillo's essays and *Los raros*, see chapter 4 below.

41. Gómez Carrillo's peers immediately recognized him for his role as a promoter of French literature. The Mexican poet Amado Nervo wrote in "Entrevista con Gómez Carrillo: Una condecoración de la legión de honor" in 1906: "Gómez Carrillo ha divulgado en América y en España la belleza y el poder prestigioso de la moderna literatura francesa. . . . El ha llevado a nuestros nervios todas las vibraciones, todos los estremecimientos, todas las angustias del viejo mundo intelectual. Fue él nuestro primer guía en este laberinto del pensamiento literario moderno" (1206) ("Gómez Carrillo has revealed to America and Spain the beauty and famous power of modern French literature. . . . He has conveyed to us the vibrations, the thrills, and all the anxieties of the old intellectual world. He was our first guide in this labyrinth of modern literary thought"). French writers have a prominent place in *Esquisses*, *Sensaciones de arte*, and *Almas y cerebros* and in his second book of memoirs, *En plena bohemia*, where Gómez Carrillo tells the story of his relationship to Verlaine and others. He writes of Louis Le Cardonnel that "durante seis meses no dejamos de vernos un solo día" ("Poetas jóvenes" 198) ("over six months not a day went by without our seeing each other"); I quote this line as one example among many of the way that introducing new artists also authorized Gómez Carrillo to be the guide and disseminator of modern aesthetics, as Nervo saw him.

42. It is not rare for Gómez Carrillo to express frustration with Ibero-American audiences' lack of interest in, familiarity with, and knowledge of writers that, he assumed, were within reach for them:

> Gabriel D'Annunzio, cuyas obras sólo eran conocidas hace algunos años en los círculos literarios de las ciudades italianas,

> comienza hoy a ser uno de los escritores jóvenes más universalmente admirados. Alemania, Rusia e Inglaterra han traducido en sus lenguas: *Canto nuovo*, *Terra vergine*, *Il Piacere*, *Invincible*, *La Chimera*, etc.; y hasta el gran país de Francia, que tan poco hospitalario suele mostrarse con las obras extranjeras, empieza ya a leer *L'Innocente* y *Poema paradisíaco* en las elegantes versiones de George Herel. Sólo nuestro público sigue desconociendo casi por completo al autor de tales libros. Los que en España hablan de él, efectivamente, son muy raros, y aún esos suelen hacerlo con poco acierto. ("Gabriel D'Annunzio" 253)

> Gabriel D'Annunzio, whose works, just a few years ago, were known only in the literary circles of Italian cities, is today becoming one of the most universally admired young writers. Germany, Russia, and England have translated *Canto nuovo*, *Terra vergine*, *Il piacere*, *L'invincibile*, *La chimera*, etc., and even the great country of France, so unhospitable toward foreign works, is beginning to read *L'innocente* and *Poema paradisíaco* in the elegant versions of George Herel. Only our reading public continues to ignore almost entirely the author of these books. Those who speak of him in Spain are quite rare, and even they often do so with little competence.

The exclusion of Spain and Latin America from a globalization of D'Annunzio points to the radical backwardness that Gómez Carrillo saw there and foregrounds the role he intends to play in the process of aesthetic modernization to change that situation.

43. During his time as a university professor in the 1920s in England and Scotland, Sanín Cano published many essays that clearly belong in the academic field of comparative philology. A quick review of these titles reveals his affinity for the disciplinary rigors of this prominent group of Spanish scholars: "Porvenir del castellano" ("The Future of Spanish"), "El castellano en la Argentina" ("Spanish in Argentina"), "De cómo se modifican las lenguas" ("On How Languages Are Transformed"), "Nociones y vocabularios" ("Notions and Vocabularies"), "La enseñanza del idioma" ("Teaching Languages"), "El cristianismo, la lengua y el sentido de posesión" ("Christianity, Language and the Sense of Possession"), "Correcciones del lenguaje" ("Language Corrections"), "Lenguas literarias, lenguas populares y francas" ("Literary Languages, Popular Languages, and Lingua Francas"), "Del género en las lenguas escandinavas" ("On Genre in Scandinavian Languages"), "Origen de una palabra internacional" ("Origin of an International Word"), "Un hispanista británico" ("A British Hispanist"), and "Un hispanista dinamarqués" ("A Danish Hispanist"), among others. All of these essays were published in the volume *Divagaciones* (1934).

Although his critical practice relies heavily on close contact with the linguistic original, he does not reject translation when necessary to explore a text or an entire literature written in a language that he has not mastered. For example: "No conozco ni el ruso ni el griego; sé que tienen semejanzas

perceptibles en la superficie y en el fondo; pero no puedo juzgar el mérito literario de obras escritas en esas lenguas. Sin embargo, he leído traducciones de *La Ilíada* en más de una lengua europea, y enriquecido mi sensibilidad leyendo en traducciones más o menos completas, *Los hermanos Karamazov*, de Dostoievski" ("Bajo el signo" 120–21) ("I don't speak Russian or Greek; I know they have perceptible similarities on the surface and underneath it as well, but I cannot judge the literary worth of works written in those languages. However, I have read translations of the *Iliad* in more than one European language and have expanded my sensibility reading, in translations more or less complete, Dostoevsky's *The Brothers Karamazov*"). His Germanic-inflected world literary mapping is structured around the desire to work with originals when possible.

44. Once again, Rama was the only critic outside Colombia to pay attention to the cosmopolitan nature of Sanín Caro's denunciation of the backward tendencies of Latin American critics with respect to the literatures of the world: "Su libertaria defensa del derecho americano a la cultura universal, habría de ser la vía fructífera por la cual se trazaría el perfil cultural de la región" ("José Martí" 98) ("His libertarian defense of America's right to universal culture would mark the productive way to trace the region's cultural profile").

45. Sanín Cano considered himself a Goethe specialist. He frequently quoted him (as in "De lo exótico" ["On The Exotic"]), gave several lectures on his work, and published two long essays about his place in world literature: "Algunos aspectos de la vida y obra de Goethe" (1932) ("Some Aspects of Goethe's Life and Work"), to commemorate the centenary of Goethe's death, and "Segundo centenario de Johann Wolfgang Goethe" (1949) ("Second centenary of Johann Wolfang Goethe"). Already in 1893, in "De lo exótico," he intertwines his reading of *Faust* with the concept of *Weltliteratur*, in order to argue the inexistence of national literatures and the inherent universality of all great works: "El *Fausto* es un microcosmos, como lo fue su autor, el que vaticinó el advenimiento de la literatura universal y la preparó con su ejemplo" (340) ("*Faust* is a microcosm, as was its author, who anticipated the advent of universal literature and prepared the way for it by his example").

46. The contrast between Sanín Cano's preference for the exotic and the nationalistic tendencies of Colombian politics is even more striking when one considers that "el comienzo de su carrera de escritor y un gran período de los años de mayor producción coincide con la tendencia hispanista de la cultura colombiana que había impulsado Miguel Antonio Caro" (R. Sierra 79) ("The beginning of his career as writer and a great part of his most productive years coincide with the period of a Hispanic tendency in Colombian culture that Miguel Antonio Caro fostered"). José María Rodríguez García has described Catholicism's influence at the highest levels of the Colombian government: "Caro and Núñez declared their allegiance—at times even the subordination of their state offices—to Pius IX's antimodernist agenda on the argument that the country's religious, linguistic, and political unity had long been under siege, but could be restored providentially in the form of a peaceful counterrevolution. . . . The reactionaries' restoration of Catholic institutions [was]

expressed more succinctly in the ancient theo-political concept of *regeneration*, which Caro and Núñez adapted as 'La Regeneración'" (3).

47. In European and Latin American Christian and nationalistic circles in the second half of the nineteenth century, *cosmopolitan* was an anti-Semitic code word that was supposed to incriminate anyone perceived as foreign or seemingly different from a normalized notion of national culture and politics. "The cosmopolitan Jew" was a privileged trope in this kind of discourse, seen in modern appropriations of the medieval myth of the wandering Jew who ridiculed Jesus on his way to the cross and was cursed to walk the earth without laying down roots, as well as in Edouard Drumont's *La France juive* (*Jewish France*) (1886) and the Argentine Julián Martel's *La bolsa* (*The Stock Market*) (1891), among many other examples.

48. Svend Erik Larsen has noted the influence of Hegelian thought on Brandes's master work: "Brandes was also well acquainted with German philosophy, and in particular with Hegel, whose philosophy at that time was central to the university curriculum in Denmark and left its mark in *Main Currents*" (22).

4. DARÍO'S FRENCH UNIVERSAL AND THE WORLD MAPPINGS OF MODERNISMO

1. In Darío's fragmentary narrative of the genesis of *modernismo*, his own role is a heroic one. He writes: "Tuvimos que ser políglotas y cosmopolitas y nos comenzó a venir un rayo de luz de todos los pueblos del mundo" (qtd. in Phillips 132) ("We had to be polyglots and cosmopolitans, and a ray of light from all the people of the world began to shine on us").

2. Even though the universalist poet in Darío has eclipsed the particularistic one, the two cultural subjectivities coexisted in his work, sometimes in striking contradiction, between 1888, the year of *Azul*'s publication, and 1916, the year of his death. This coexistence was most evident from 1898 to 1905, the years of Darío's commitment to the Pan-Hispanic cause and opposition to the colonial presence of the United States in the Caribbean. Between the beginning of the Spanish-American War in Cuba, Puerto Rico, and the Philippines and the establishment of the US military base in Guantánamo Bay in 1903, Darío wrote crucial texts that denounced US imperialism and its materialist culture in order to affirm the spiritual core of Latin culture, including "El triunfo de Calibán" ("The Triumph of Caliban") (1898); "A Roosevelt" ("To Roosevelt") (1904); the preface to *Cantos de vida y esperanza* (*Songs of Life and Hope*) (1905) (where he wrote, in reference to the inclusion of "A Roosevelt" in the book, "Si encontráis versos a un presidente, es porque son un clamor continental. Mañana podemos ser yanquis (y es lo más probable); de todas maneras mi protesta queda escrita sobre las alas de los inmaculados cisnes" [230] ["If you find verses to a president, it is because they are a continental clamor. Tomorrow we may all become Yankees [and this is most likely]; my protest stands anyhow, written on the wings of immaculate swans"; *Selected Poems* 161]); and his ode to Pan-Hispanism and the rebirth of Hispanic culture, "Salutación del optimista" ("Salutation of the Optimist") (1905) (which

begins with the often cited "Ínclitas razas ubérrimas, sangre de Hispania fecunda, / espíritus fraternos, luminosas almas, ¡salve!" ["Renowned, fertile clans, prolific blood of Hispania / fraternal spirits, luminous souls, hail!"; *Stories and Poems*, 141]). Before 1888 and after 1905, Darío published many localist, particularistic poems affirming the autonomy of Latin American culture, cities, and state-apparatuses: "Colombia," "Montevideo," "A Bolivia" ("To Bolivia"), "A la República Dominicana" ("To the Dominican Republic"), "Unión Centroamericana" ("Central American Union"), "Canto épico a las glorias de Chile" ("Epic Song to the Glories of Chile"), "Desde la Pampa" ("From the Pampas"), "Himno de guerra" ("War Hymn," about Nicaragua), and "Canto a la Argentina" ("Song to Argentina"), among others.

3. In *Cosmopolitanism in the Americas*, Camilla Fojas insightfully points out the close relation between discourses on cosmopolitanism and queerness in the context of *modernismo*, evident in Darío's identification with the strangeness in the world.

4. In *Historia de mis libros* (*The History of My Books*), Darío describes the kind of particularistic literature that dominated the Latin American literary field before *modernismo:* "Pues no se tenía en toda la América española como fin y objeto poéticos más que la celebración de las glorias criollas, los hechos de la Independencia y la naturaleza americana: un eterno *Canto a Junín*, una inacabable *Oda a la agricultura de la zona tórrida* y *Décimas patrióticas*. No negaba yo que hubiese un gran tesoro de poesía en *nuestra* épica prehistórica, en la conquista y aún en la colonia; más con nuestro estado social y político posterior llegó la chatura intelectual y períodos históricos más a propósito para el folletín sangriento que para el noble canto" (60–61) ("In all of Spanish America there was no end or object other than to celebrate Creole glory, the facts of Independence and American nature: an eternal *Song to Junín*, a never-ending *Ode to the Agriculture of the Torrid Zone* and *Patriotic Decimas*. I did not deny that there was a great treasure of poetry in *our* prehistoric era, in the conquest, and even in the colony; but with our later social and political state came intellectual flatness and historical periods better suited to bloody serials than noble songs"). While Darío recognizes the historical importance of the poetry that preceded him, he is obviously critical of its narrowness and particularism.

5. Darío's manipulation of the rhetoric of indigenous cultures in order to make aesthetic-political points in his poetry, essays, and prefaces changed over time. In "Palabras liminares" (1896), he uses the indigenous that is neither denied or affirmed ("¿Hay en mi sangre alguna gota de sangre de África, o de indio chorotega o nagrandano? Pudiera ser . . . mas . . ." [187] ["Is there in my blood a drop of blood from Africa or of Chorotega or Nagrandan Indian? It may well be . . . yet . . ."; *Selected Poems* 113]) as a counterpoint for a modernist cosmopolitan discourse. By 1905, having experienced US neocolonial policies in the region, he is more prone to affirm a Latin American identity, and he characterizes his new book of poems, *Cantos de vida y esperanza*, as the expression of "un clamor continental" (230) ("a continental clamor"; *Selected Poems* 161); this is the same book that opens with Darío's revision of his previous aesthetic subjectivity: "Yo soy aquel que ayer no más decía/ el

verso azul y la canción profana" (231) ("I am the one who just yesterday spoke / the blue verse and the profane song"; *Selected Poems* 161). Darío includes in this volume the renowned poem "A Roosevelt" (originally published in 1904), which affirms Latin American spiritual superiority in the face of US militaristic and imperialistic attitudes and resorts to indigenous references to depict the region's cultural particularity:

> Eres los Estados Unidos,
> eres el futuro invasor
> de la América ingenua que tiene sangre indígena,
> que aún reza a Jesucristo y aún habla en español.
> . . . .
> . . . la América nuestra, que tenía poetas
> desde los viejos tiempos de Netzahualcoyotl,
> que ha guardado las huellas de los pies del gran Baco,
> . . . .
> la América del gran Moctezuma, del Inca. (240)
>
> You're the United States,
> you're the future invader
> of the guileless America of indigenous blood
> that still prays to Jesus Christ and still speaks in Spanish.
> . . . .
> . . . this America of ours, which has had poets
> since the olden days of Netzahualcoyotl,
> which preserves the footprints of the great Bacchus,
> . . . .
> the America of the great Moctezuma, of the Inca.
> (*Selected Poems* 167–69)

It would be a mistake to place Darío in an indigenist tradition because of this and other poems. The references to a Nahua poet, Moctezuma, and the Inca must be read as functions of an antagonism with the United States that is elaborated through the affirmation of Latin America's indigenous past. In Darío's case, this *indigenista* rhetoric has to be understood contextually as a cultural-political strategy within an anticolonial discourse.

The same can be said about the conspicuous indigenous references in "A Colón" ("To Columbus"). The poem, written in 1892 and performed that same year in the Ateneo de Madrid to commemorate the four-hundredth anniversary of Columbus, was published fifteen years later in *El canto errante*. In it, Darío invokes an "india virgen" ("Indian virgin") and "la tribu unida" ("united tribes") before Columbus's discovery, and laments, "Al ídolo de piedra reemplaza ahora / el ídolo de carne que se entroniza" ("Now the pagan idols of stone have been replaced / by idols of flesh that have taken their throne"), and "¡Ojalá hubieran sido los hombres blancos / como los Atahualpas y Moctezumas!" (280–81) ("If only white people could have had the same ways / as Atahualpa, Moctezuma, and other great kings!"; *Selected Writings* 109–11). The indigenous signifiers are less an affirmation of a regional culture than a denouncement and rejection of Spanish colonization. In fact, in that same poem, Darío equates "the indigenous" and "the French" as signifiers with the potential to resist the injurious Spanish presence in Latin America:

> Bebiendo la esparcida savia francesa
> con nuestra boca indígena semi-española,
> día a día cantamos la Marsellesa
> para acabar danzando la Caramañola. (280)
>
> It's droplets of refined French sap we're drinking,
> that our half-Spanish, half-indigenous mouth sips.
> Day after day it's the "Marseillaise" we sing,
> though we end with the Caramañola on our lips.
> (*Selected Writings* 109)

For different analyses of indigenous cultures in Darío's work, see Monguió, "Origen"; Arrom.

6. For example, Darío uses premodern aesthetic forms and formations, such as those of classical Greek literature, as artifacts that contribute to a very modern sensibility that rejects social modernization's lack of humanity. To Darío, French symbolism becomes the lens through which the classical world can be revised in order to establish the modern classicism of symbolist heroes, as in "Divagación" ("Digression"):

> Amo más que la Grecia de los griegos
> la Grecia de la Francia, porque en Francia
> el eco de las Risas y los Juegos,
> su más dulce licor Venus escancia.
> . . . .
> Verlaine es más que Sócrates, y Arsenio
> Houssaye supera al viejo Anacreonte. (190)
>
> More than the Greece of the Greeks I love
> the Greece of France, because in France
> Venus serves her sweetest beverage,
> the echo of laughter and jollity.
> . . . .
> Verlaine is more than Socrates; and Asène
> Houssaye is superior to ancient Anacreon.
> (*Stories and Poems* 95)

7. The notion of style I have in mind here is the one proposed by Rebecca Walkowitz, in which style is conceived "as attitude, stance, posture, and consciousness" (*Cosmopolitan Style* 2), which constitute the necessary materiality of cosmopolitanism as a critical form of consciousness and affect and in which style reconfigures "the relationship between idiosyncratic expressions of culture and the conditions of international sympathy and reparation."

8. Darío is fascinated with the construction and symbolic appropriations of Japan in French culture; he dedicates an entire chronicle, "Japoneses en París"

("The Japanese in Paris," published in October 1904 in *La Nación*), to one aspect of the subject:

> Fueron primeramente los objetos raros, que traían del Extremo Oriente los navegantes de Saint-Main, los marineros comerciales holandeses; los curiosos artefactos nipones del hotel Pontalba, los servicios china . . . inéditos objetos pintorescos, lacas, sedas y marfiles del Imperio del Medio. Hasta que llegó la exposición del 78, que trajo la popularización de lo antes reservado, la invasión de la pacotilla oriental en el Bon Marché y el Louvre, los biombos baratos, los sables, los abanicos, las *fukusas* y los *kakemonos*. La terminología se hizo conocida. *Tsibultsi* y *shakudo, neizke* y *samisen* aparecía en crónicas de diario y en cuentos exóticos. La hija de Gautier y la esposa divorciada de Méndes, publicó sus *Poemas de Libélula* e introdujo una estrofa japonesa a la métrica de Francia, la *uta*. Y luego dio a la escena su *Marchand de sourires*, en que expresaba la vida de las cortesanas de ojos circunflejos. Los Goncourt daban sus lecciones inolvidables. Gonse coleccionaba e informaba. Y el hombre del *Art Nouveau*, Bing, fue entonces el mayor importador de tantas chucherías exóticas y caras. Y llegó Loti, trayendo su muñequita decorativa, su antisentimental crisantemo. *Sus japonerías se expandieron por todos los rincones de la literatura*. En las letras pasó lo que es la vida, y en todas partes hubo importación de bonitas cosas amarillas. Con las obras de Goncourt, de Gonse, de otros, se tuvo un almacén de provisiones niponas para niponizar por largo espacio de tiempo. (211)
>
> At first, the seafarers of Saint-Main and the Dutch commercial sailors brought rare objects from the Extreme Orient; the Pontalba Hotel's curious Nipponese artifacts and porcelain tea services . . . unheard-of picturesque objects, lacquers, silks and marbles from the Middle Empire. Then came the exposition of '78, bringing with it the popularization of what had been reserved, the invasion of Oriental junk in the Bon Marché and the Louvre, cheap folding screens, cutlasses, fans, *fukusas* and *kakemonos*. The terminology was learned. *Tsibultsi* and *shakudo*, *neizke* and *samisen* appeared in newspaper chronicles and exotic stories. Gautier's daughter, who was also Méndes's ex-wife, published her *Dragonfly Poems* and introduced a Japanese stanza, the *uta*, into the French metric. And then her *Marchand de sourires* came out, telling the lives of courtesans with circumflex eyes. The Goncourts gave their unforgettable lessons. Gonse collected and reported. And Bing, Mister *Art Nouveau*, was the largest importer of so many exotic and expensive trinkets. And Loti arrived, bringing his decorative doll, his antisentimental chrysanthemum. Their Japonaiseries expanded to every corner of literature. What happened in letters happened in life, and beautiful yellow things were imported everywhere. The works of Goncourt, of Gonse, of

others, filled a warehouse with Nipponese provisions to Nipponize for a long time.

9. Darío was able to separate "the idea of Verlaine" from the actual poet, whom he met when he traveled to Paris for the first time in 1893. There Gómez Carrillo (a distant acquaintance of Darío's hero) introduced him to the author of *Fêtes galantes*. Darío could not have been more disappointed and heartbroken. He recounted the encounter in his autobiography:

> Uno de mis grandes deseos era poder hablar con Verlaine. Cierta noche, en el café D'Harcourt, encontramos al Fauno, rodeado de equívocos acólitos. Estaba igual al simulacro en que ha perpetuado su figura el arte maravilloso de Carriére. Se conocía que había bebido harto. Respondía de cuando en cuando, a las preguntas que le hacían sus acompañantes, golpeando intermitentemente el mármol de la mesa. Nos acercamos con [Alejandro] Sawa, me presentó: "Poeta americano, admirador, etc." Yo murmuré en mal francés toda la devoción que me fue posible, concluí con la palabra gloria. . . . Quién sabe qué habría pasado esta tarde al desventurado maestro; el caso es que, volviéndose a mí, y sin cesar de golpear la mesa, me dijo en voz baja y pectoral: "¡La gloire! . . . ¡La gloire! . . . ¡M . . . M . . . encore!" Creí prudente retirarme, y esperar verle de nuevo una ocasión más propicia. Esto no lo pude lograr nunca, porque las noches que volví a encontrarle, se hallaba más o menos en el mismo estado; a aquello, en verdad, era triste, doloroso, grotesco y trágico. (*Autobiografía* 119–20)

> One of my greatest desires was to talk to Verlaine. One night, in D'Harcourt Café, we ran into the Faun, surrounded by equivocal acolytes. He was identical to the image of him that endures in Carrière's marvelous art. It was evident that he had been drinking heavily. From time to time, he answered his companions' questions, pounding the marble table intermittently. We approached with [Alejandro] Sawa, who introduced me: "American poet, an admirer, etc." I murmured in bad French all of the affection that I possibly could, ending with the word *glory*. . . . Who knows what had happened to the wretched master that afternoon; the fact is that, turning towards me, and without ceasing to pound the table, he said in a low and grainy voice: "La gloire! . . . La gloire! . . . M . . . M . . . encore!" I thought it best to remove myself, and hoped to see him again on a more favorable occasion. I was never able to do so, because on the other nights that I saw him, he was more or less in the same condition; it was, honestly, sad, painful, grotesque and tragic.

10. For an excellent analysis of *Los raros* in its historical and cultural context, see Colombi's "En torno."

11. The poet and critic Pedro Salinas, for example, has characterized the poem and all of *Prosas profanas* as a text where "lo amoroso predomina sin disputas" (55) ("love clearly predominates"). He goes on to describe the role of

the woman who goes along on the erotic journey as "simplemente la pareja, la figurante que necesita para representar el dijo de amor itinerante que se inicia" (128) ("just the other person, an extra that he needs in order to embark on his tour of love"). "Divagación" upsets Salinas, and he criticizes Darío for being more interested in the cosmopolitan aestheticist journey than in the portrayal of the woman being wooed: "A fuerza de ser tantas figuraciones, la francesa, la española, la india, etc., todas con sus atributos y trajes nacionales, como una hilera de muñecas, ¿no se perderá la realidad de la mujer verdadera?" (132–33) ("When she is imagined so many ways, French, Spanish, Indian, etc., always with national attributes and costumes, like a row of dolls, is not the reality of the true woman lost?").

12. Darío borrows the opening "¿Vienes?" from a long tradition in French poetry, reinforcing the French inscriptions of his invitation to world literature. Alberto Carlos suggests three possible sources. First, Théodore de Banville, one of Darío's favorite poets, published a collection of poems *Les stalactites* (1846) that includes a famous untitled poem beginning with the verse: "Viens. Sur tes cheveux noirs jette un chapeau de paille" (17) ("Come. A straw hat thrown on your dark hair"). Second, the sonnet "Les bergers" (1893), by the French-Cuban Parnassian poet José María de Heredia, begins with a command/invitation: "Viens. Le sentier s'enfonce aux gorges du Cyllene" (63) ("Come. The trail sinks into Cyllene's gorges"). What is interesting about either Banville or Heredia as a source for "Divagación" is that both French poems conjugate the verb *venir* in the imperative, as a command, "Follow me," rather than "Are you coming?" (In French, the second-person present indicative and second-person imperative are identical, *viens*, but the lack of a question mark denotes the imperative). Darío rewrites the imperative as an interrogation, which may suggest a less assertive, less confident attitude toward the journey through the world of literature. Third and finally, Carlos suggests the presence of Charles Baudelaire's "L'invitation au voyage" ("Invitation to the Voyage") in the opening line of "Divagación."

13. In the tradition of Sarmiento, Groussac's intellectual life, literature, cultural critique, and state politics were very difficult to separate from one another. In 1884, on his return from a short stay in France, Groussac, together with Carlos Pellegrini, Lucio V. López, Delfín Gallo, and Roque Sáenz Peña (all were prominent politicians; Pellegrini would be vice president and Sáenz Peña president), founded the newspaper *Sudamérica* (*South America*) to counteract the Catholic influence of *La Unión* (*The Union*). Groussac wrote literary and cultural criticism for the newspaper but was also a central figure in the debate on the secularity of the state. He resigned from the newspaper in 1885 (and later wrote a fascinating account of his year at the newspaper, *Los que pasaban* [*Those Who Passed*]) to accept the position of director of the National Public Library, a post he occupied for forty-four years until his death in 1929. In this role, he published the state-funded journal *La Biblioteca*, where his articles criticizing Darío and *modernismo* appeared.

Regarding Darío, it is important to consider the complexity of the problem of autonomy of the cultural sphere and to view it as a desire for autonomy that was only barely actualized. This is a classic topic of Latin American criticism

that, as I discussed in chapter 3, has been the subject of much discussion and is largely solved in Ramos's book *Divergent Modernities:* "En respuesta a esta problemática, nuestra lectura se propone articular un doble movimiento; por un lado, la exploración de la literatura como un discurso que intenta autonomizarse, es decir, precisar su campo de autoridad social; y por otro, el análisis de las condiciones de imposibilidad de su institucionalización. Dicho de otro modo, exploraremos la *modernización desigual* de la literatura latinoamericana en el período de su emergencia" (12) ("In response to this problematic, *Divergent Modernities* articulates a double movement: on the one hand, the exploration of literature as a discourse that seeks autonomization or the specification of its field of social authority, and on the other, an analysis of the conditions that made the institutionalization of literature *impossible.* To put it another way, this book will explore the *uneven modernization* of Latin American literature during the period of its emergence"; xli). Ramos returns to the topic later in his study: "las condiciones que llevan a la literatura a depender del periódico, y cómo este limita así su autonomía; la crónica será así un lugar privilegiado para precisar la heterogeneidad del sujeto literario" (84) ("the conditions that led to the dependence of literature on the newspaper, and how such a dependence limited literature's autonomy. The chronicle, in this regard, will become a privileged site for scrutinizing the condition of heterogeneity of the literary subject"; 79). See also Montaldo, *Sensibilidad amenazada.*

14. In her intellectual biography of Groussac, Bruno argues that Groussac is best understood as "un articulador del espacio cultural argentino," that is, a founding figure of the modern Argentine intellectual field.

15. For an analysis of Groussac's exceptionality, particularly in relation to the phenomenon of alloglossia (a writer's decision to switch to an acquired language, leaving his or her native tongue behind), see Siskind.

16. For the idea of origin, see Derrida, "Structure" and *Of Grammatology.*

17. Records reveal only one instance when Groussac's French origin was invoked as a limitation and a handicap. When he was named director of the National Library, Sarmiento, Calixto Oyuela, and Manuel Láinez opposed his designation on the grounds of his foreign nationality. See Bruno and Tesler.

18. It is interesting to note that Groussac's French identity is bound to the specific context of Argentina (which could legitimately be extended to all of Latin America). He traveled to the United States to give a lecture on Argentina's *gauchos* and the *gauchesca* tradition at the World's Folklore Congress in Chicago, on July 14, 1893. In front of an international but predominantly American audience, Groussac—who was going to read his lecture in English—presented himself, not as the European imparting civilized knowledge to a raw, uncultivated American audience, but as a marginal and peripheral subject who, charmingly, could not hide the inferiority complex of the particular in the face of the universal: "Tanto se ha ponderado vuestra indulgencia para con los extranjeros que procuran expresarse en vuestra lengua concise y fuerte, que he sentido cierta curiosidad de correr el albur. Acaso la tentativa sea un tanto atrevida. . . . Me esforzaré por ser claro, si no correcto: vuestra benevolencia suplirá mis faltas" ("Gaucho" 116) ("Your indulgence of foreigners who try to express themselves in your concise and strong language has been praised

so much that I felt a certain curiosity about taking the risk myself. The attempt may be a bit bold. . . . I have tried to be clear, if not correct: your benevolence will compensate for my errors"). If Groussac had effectively constructed the position of authority of the European (French!) intellectual in the Argentine cultural field, in front of this American audience he willingly assumed the marginal subject position of native informant: "A pesar de la carencia de notas auxiliaries, acepté en seguida la invitación que me fue dirigida para disertar en este Congreso sobre un tema familiar. He elegido el presente, por parecerme que viene a llenar una laguna de vuestro interesante y variado programa. Se trata de la vida rústica y aventurera, de las costumbres y creencias de nuestro gaucho argentino" (116) ("Notwithstanding the lack of auxiliary notes, I immediately accepted the invitation extended to me to speak on a familiar subject at this Congress. I have chosen the present topic, because I think that it fills a gap in your interesting and varied program. It is the rustic and adventurous life, the customs and beliefs, of our Argentine *gaucho*"). He did the same thing when in Paris to visit his admired Alphonse Daudet: "Por cierto que no me detenía la aprensión de ser recibido como un simple *rastaquoère*, visitador de monumentos y celebridades . . . [sino porque] me tocaría contemplar de cerca la dolorosa ruina de aquel ser privilegiado" ("Alphonse Daudet" 145–46) ("I was not held up by the fear that I would be received as a simple *rastaquoère*, a visitor of monuments and celebrities . . . but rather that I would have to consider the painful ruin of that privileged person up close"). In the same article, he notes: "Cuando llegué a París, sentíame tan extraño y desterrado como en este Nuevo Mundo [Estados Unidos] que acababa de recorrer" (149) ("When I arrived in Paris, I felt as strange and exiled as I had in this New World [the United States] that I had just traveled through").

19. Alejandro Eujanian sees *La Biblioteca* as an enterprise of imparting civilization within a genealogy that goes all the way back to Sarmiento: "La apelación a la ciencia . . . expresará la pretendida soberanía de la razón de la cual estos intelectuales se creían portadores. . . . En dicho marco, la revista *La Biblioteca* será el último eslabón de un proceso que se inicia a mediados del siglo XIX, ofreciendo un espacio propicio para la difusión de un ideario reformista, planteándose como función principal la de llevar a cabo a través de sus páginas una 'empresa civilizadora,' respecto de la cultura argentina de fin de siglo" ("The appeal to science . . . will express the supposed sovereignty of reason; these intellectuals believed themselves the bearers of this message. . . . Within this framework, *La Biblioteca* magazine will be the last link in a process that began in the mid-nineteenth century, offering a favorable space for the diffusion of a reformist ideology, suggesting that its principal function was to carry out a 'civilizing enterprise' with respect to Argentine culture at the end of the century in its pages"). Groussac wanted to "convertir a la revista en una 'empresa civilizadora,' tendiente al progreso cultural de un país cuyo desarrollo cultural consideraba inferior a esa civilización europea de la cual se sentía su máximo representante, mereciendo, en este sentido, el reconocimiento por parte de sus contemporaneos" (27–30) ("convert the magazine into a 'civilizing enterprise,' tending toward the cultural progress of a country whose cultural development he considered inferior to European civilization,

which he believed that he represented best, deserving, in this sense, the recognition of his contemporaries").

20. To Groussac, there is no difference between Latin America and North America; every writer on the continent is doomed to imitation: "En principio, la tentativa del señor Darío—puesto que de él se trata—no difiere esencialmente, no digamos de las de Echeverría o Gutiérrez, románticos de segunda o tercera mano, sino de la de todos los *yankees*, desde Cooper, reflejo de Walter Scott, hasta Emerson, luna de Carlyle" ("Prosas profanas" 158) ("In principle, Mister Darío's effort—since it is about him—does not essentially differ from those of the second- or third-hand romantics Echeverría or Gutiérrez, but neither does it differ from the efforts of all Yankees, from Cooper emulating Walter Scott, to Emerson emulating Carlyle").

21. The February 1916 issue of the influential magazine *Nosotros: Revista de Letras, Arte, Historia, Filosofía y Ciencias Sociales* (*Us: Review of Letters, Art, History, Philosophy and Social Sciences*) was dedicated to Darío, who had just died. Asked to contribute an original piece to the issue, Groussac sent a letter excusing himself:

> En las circunstancias presentes, me sería imposible escribir una página de arte puro. Por lo demás, en los años a que usted se refiere, expresé, sobre Darío y su talento juvenil, en mi Biblioteca (números Noviembre 96 y Enero 97), lo que sinceramente sentía, y por falta de lecturas posteriores, no sabría modificar. Puede usted reproducir de dichos artículos—sin gran valor—lo que convenga a sus propósitos, si es que algo le conviene. Darío contestó a mi primer artículo en La Nación del 27 de noviembre de 1896. Creo que nunca reprodujo dicho artículo en sus volúmenes de crítica, por haberle pedido yo que no lo precediera del mío—por su escasa importancia. ("Dos juicios" 150)

> Under the present circumstances, it would be impossible for me to write a page of pure art. Moreover, in the years that you refer to, I expressed in my *Biblioteca* [the November '96 and January '97 issues] what I sincerely felt about Darío and his youthful talent, and because I have not read his work since then, I am not able to modify that opinion. You can reproduce from those articles—of little worth—whatever might serve your purposes, if anything should serve you at all. Darío responded to my first article in *La Nación* on November 27, 1896. I do not think that he ever reproduced that article in his volumes of criticism, because I asked him not to reproduce mine before it—for its minimal importance.

The condescending tone of Groussac's letter shows that, even though twenty years had passed since his exchange with Darío, he still believed that *modernismo* was a lamentable waste of time. *Nosotros* published the exchange in its entirety, providing the first and only opportunity for readers to look at the counterposing arguments side by side (no book or journal has republished it in this way).

22. Groussac is quoting Molière's *Le médecin malgré lui* (*The Doctor in Spite of Himself*) 2.4. This line became a famous shorthand conclusion to an explanatory statement in the second half of the nineteenth century.

23. Both reviews insist on Groussac's rejection of Darío's choice of models: "Dado el resultado mediocre del decadentismo francés, es permitido preguntarse: ¿qué podría valer su brusca inoculación a la literatura española" ("Raros" 480) ("Given the mediocre results of French decadentism, it is valid to ask: What value could there be in its sudden inoculation of Spanish literature?"). He later calls the French symbolists "novadores franceses—*fruits secs* universitarios en su mayoría" (478) ("French innovators—mainly university *dried fruits*").

24. Walt Whitman occupies a unique place in the minds of Latin American *modernistas*. French Parnassians and symbolists like Hugo and Verlaine are their über-modern model, but the *modernistas* are conscious of the gap that separates them from them. Whitman, on the other hand, is both ours (*Americanly ours*) and an *other*, and his name preserves echoes of what the Latin Americans could become. Sylvia Molloy has analyzed this ambiguity, finding in Martí's reading of Whitman both a model for community formation based on male bonding and a marked anxiety about the homosexual potential of the political link. "In Whitman's communal masculinity Martí recognizes his own all-male affiliative model, the revolutionary family of sons and fathers confounded in a continuum of natural masculine emotion, and also recognizes the continental, political potential of the model, which he elaborates in later essays (I think, of course, of the discussion on 'natural man' in 'Our America'). Whitman, for Martí, is the precursor. . . . That the intensity of this continental masculine adhesiveness not only rivals 'amative love,' as in Whitman, but precludes it may well account for both the fear and the passion with which Martí reads *Calamus*" ("His America" 379).

25. In fact, almost every critic to pay attention to this exchange misattributes the phrase from Coppée's play to Darío, which shows how grossly Groussac's contributions to this debate have been overlooked.

26. Darío and an important portion of the modern critical tradition understand creative imitation to mean appropriation and articulate it as a heroic conquest undertaken by Darío as the solitary modernizer. In the long passage from "Los colores del estandarte" cited above, Darío declares that, having learned to think in French, he has "conquered" French cultural citizenship: "Él me esneñó a pensar en francés: después, mi alma gozosa y joven conquistó la ciudadanía de Galia" (162) ("He taught me to *think in French;* after that, my young, happy heart claimed Gallic citizenship"; *Selected Writings* 484). Darío's "conquest of Paris" is a repeated trope in his writing: "Desde el día siguiente tenía el carruaje a todas horas en la puerta y comencé mi conquista de París" (*Autobiografía* 69) ("From the next day forward I had the carriage at the door all the time and I began my conquest of Paris"). Another possibility is to understand these creative appropriations in terms of the politico-cultural function of *modernismo*'s cosmopolitanism. As Montaldo has pointed out: "El cosmopolitanismo de los modernistas, cierta avidez por apropiarse de lo exótico y las formaciones culturales de otros pueblos, puede ser entendido como abigarramiento cultural pero también como un afán de resignificar la

propia cultura" (*Sensibilidad amenazada* 113) ("The cosmopolitanism of the *modernistas*, a certain eagerness to appropriate the exotic and the cultural formations of other peoples, can be understood as cultural variegation but also as an urge to resignify their own culture").

27. Octavio Paz had already criticized the interpretation of *modernismo* as an escapist, ivory tower aesthetic: "Se ha dicho que el modernismo fue una evasión de la realidad americana. Más cierto sería decir que fue una fuga de la actualidad local—que era, a sus ojos un anacronismo—en busca de una actualidad universal, la única y verdadera actualidad" (*Cuadrivio* 9) ("It has been said that *modernismo* was an evasion of the American reality. It would be more accurate to say that it was a flight from the local present reality—which was, to their eyes, an anachronism—in search of a universal present reality, the only and true reality").

28. Paz has made this point most cogently: "El amor a la modernidad no es culto a la moda es voluntad de participación en una plenitud histórica hasta entonces vedada a los hispanoamericanos" (*Cuadrivio* 21) ("The love of modernity is not the worship of fashion: it is the will to participate in a historical plenitude that Latin Americans had been forbidden until then"). And Jrade identifies the desire for modernity with an explicit desire for France: "*los modernistas*' desire to be modern, that is, to become contemporaneous with all of Europe but most especially with its intellectual center, the city of Paris" (14).

29. For an excellent, detailed, and thorough analysis of Darío's dispatches for *La Nación* from the Universal Exhibition, see Colombi's "Peregrinaciones parisinas." This essay is unique in its attention to the positioning of Darío's chronicles in the pages of *La Nación;* they shared page 3 with news from international wars in China and South Africa. Colombi notes that the juxtaposition was all too meaningful because "la exposición como la guerra giran en torno a los mismos ejes: la hegemonía de occidente, las etnias, los nacionalismos y las posesiones coloniales" (2) ("exhibition and war revolve around the same axes: the hegemony of the West, ethnicities, nationalisms, and colonial possessions").

30. Zanetti explains that these operations of differentiation are typical of the aristocratic imaginaries of modernist intellectuals: "Responde a los modos en los que los modernistas visibilizan una singularidad que se planta frente a la vulgaridad y el filisteísmo" (530) ("It responds to the *modernistas*' ways of highlighting their singularity by opposing it to vulgarity and Philistinism").

31. During the first months after his April 1900 arrival in Paris, Darío refers to Paris and his presence there as a dream, a *rêverie*, which highlights his idealized perception of the city. This rhetorical shorthand is not limited to this brief but significant period, however; he resorts to it almost every time he evokes whatever is left of his romanticized vision of Paris. See the already cited "Yo soñaba con París desde niño" (*Autobiografía* 69) and "En París," where he describes the city as a place that inspires "dulce(s) *rêverie(s)*" (33), or among many other passages, the chronicle "Algunas notas sobre Jean Moréas" ("Notes on Jean Moréas"), written in 1903 and recalling his first trip to Paris in 1893: "En este *soñado* París había recogido las impresiones espirituales que más tarde fueron *Los raros*. Iba con cosecha de *ilusiones* y

de amables locuras. . . . *Mi sueño*, ver París, sentir París, se había cumplido, y mi iniciación estética en el seno del simbolismo me enorgullecía y entusiasmaba. . . . Juraba por los dioses del nuevo parnaso; había visto al viejo fauno Verlaine; sabía del misterio de Mallarmé, y era amigo de Moréas" (73, emphasis mine) ("In this *imagined* Paris I collected the spiritual impressions that later became *The Strange Ones*. I harvested *illusions* and kind insanities. . . . I had achieved *my dream*, to see Paris, to feel Paris, and my aesthetic initiation into the heart of symbolism filled me with pride and excitement. . . . I had sworn by the gods of the new Parnassus; I had seen the old faun Verlaine; I knew the mystery of Mallarmé, and I was a friend of Moréas").

32. Darío complains about the living conditions of the Latin American writer in Paris in several *crónicas*. See, for example, "El deseo de París" ("The Desire for Paris"), first published in *La Nación*, October 6, 1912:

> Ir a París sin apoyo económico ninguno, sin dinero, sin base. ¿Conoce usted siquiera el francés? ¿No? Pues mil veces peor. . . . Tendrá que pasar penurias horribles. Andará usted detrás de las gentes que hablan español, por los hoteles de tercer orden para conseguir, un día sí y treinta días no, algo con lo que no morir de hambre. . . . Y tendrá que irse al Barrio Latino a fastidiar a los pobres estudiantes compatriotas suyos, a los artistas becados, y aún a los no becados, a los que viven de algo. Luego, su pobre indumentaria se irá marchitando, si es que no ha llegado marchita y tendrá usted que reponerla, porque si no la repone, los *concierges* tendrán orden de decir a usted cuando aparezca: "Monsieur est sorti!" ¿Y para reponer la indumentaria deteriorada, cómo va usted a hacer? (265–66)
>
> Going to Paris without any economic support, without money, without any foundation. Do you even know French? No? A thousand times worse, then. . . . You will suffer horrible poverty. You will chase after those who speak Spanish, in third-rate hotels, in order to get, one day yes and thirty days no, something to keep you from starving to death. . . . And you will go to the Latin Quarter to annoy the poor students from your country, the artists with scholarships, and even those without scholarships, those who have something to live on. Then your shabby attire will start fading, if it was not faded when you arrived, and you will have to buy new clothes, because if you do not, the *concierges* will exclaim when they see you: "The gentleman has left!" And just how are you going to buy new clothes?

33. In "La evolución del rastacuerismo," Darío relates the philological history of the term: "Permitidme una explicación etimológica: los hombres que manipulan las pieles de los animales desollados y que, además, no son destazadores artistas, constituyen una categoría de obreros llamados 'arrastracueros' de donde viene por corrupción la palabra *Rastaquoère*" (133) ("Allow me an etymological explanation: men who work with animal skins but are not skilled butchers constitute a category of workers known as 'dragging-leathers,' which

has been corrupted into *Rastaquoère*"). For over a century, critics have taken Darío's etymological argument at face value; however, the Argentine-Venezuelan linguist Angel Rosenblatt argues that the term comes from Venezuela's *llanos* and explains that it refers to the expression "arrastrar cueros" ("to drag leathers"), which means "echar pompa, alardear de rico o de valiente" (qtd. in Aubrun 433n1) ("to show off, to boast of wealth or bravery").

34. The *rastaquoère* appears briefly in an earlier novel by Aurélien Scholl, *Mémoirs du trottoir* (1882): "Pouah! Des rastaquoères en quête de expositions. . . . Ils cherchent de l'or dans leur pays et de truffe à Paris" (qtd. in Aubrun 433n29) ("Ugh! The *rastaquoères* in these exhibitions. . . . They look for gold in their countries and truffles in Paris").

35. Darío lived in Paris from April 1900 to November 1914, when he left to give a series of lectures in New York. Quite sick, he returned to Nicaragua from the United States to die. During the fifteen years that Paris was his principal residence, he made several trips to Latin America and other places in western Europe and lived in Madrid between 1908 and 1909 as Nicaragua's official state representative at the court of Alfonso XIII.

5. GÓMEZ CARRILLO EASTBOUND

1. Literary critics often read the relation of *modernista* travel writing to the Orientalist French library between the poles of mimesis and rejection. If Fombona sees the modernist traveler as a "lector de textos europeos que se mueve en sus espacios, traduciendo y encontrando" (60) ("reader of European texts who moves in their spaces, translating and finding"), Tinajero takes the opposite view: "lejos de ser una 'reescritura' y una 'repetición' de un texto original, los relatos modernistas amplían los horizontes del imaginario oriental y elucida el afán de los escritores de interpretar a sus lectores diferencias culturales en la moderna Asia desde su propio punto de vista y no desde un punto de vista europeo" (34) ("far from being a 'rewriting' and a 'repetition' of an original text, the modernist stories broaden the horizons of the Oriental imaginary and elucidate the writers' affinity for interpreting modern Asian cultural differences for their readers from their own point of view and not from a European point of view"). If, according to Fombona, the process of signification depends on a particularly French mode of reading ("El viaje al oriente, y en realidad cualquier viaje según Gómez Carrillo, se articula desde París" [97] ["The journey to the Orient, and really any trip that Gómez Carrillo takes, is articulated from Paris"]), Tinajero considers Gómez Carrillo to have a preeminently postcolonial outlook and believes that his eastbound travels produce a South-South, "la representación de un sujeto 'exótico' por otro sujeto 'exótico'" (9) ("the representation of an 'exotic' subject by another 'exotic' subject"). Francisco Morán, in a seminal essay on *modernismo*'s Orientalist discourses, takes a very different approach, inscribing the Guatemalan's eastbound travels in the context of his familiarity with a European library of travel books: "Carrillo va a en busca de un topos en el que Occidente ya ha envasado su Mirada. . . . Su búsqueda de lo 'específicamente' oriental desemboca en el descubrimiento de la repetitividad de lo europeo" (394) ("Carrillo goes in search of a *topos* that

contains the West's Gaze, already packaged. . . . His search for the 'specifically' Oriental leads to the discovery of the repetitiveness of the European"). My goal in this chapter is closer to Morán's framing, but besides pointing out Gómez Carrillo's complex relationship to the French Orientalist archive, I identify un-Orientalist and cosmopolitan moments that destabilize his own markedly Orientalist perception of North Africa, the Middle East, and South and East Asia. For a reading that echoes some of these discussions from a French perspective, see Philippe Meunier's *De l'Espagne aux représentations ibériques et ibéro-americaines de l'exotisme.*

2. In *A Thousand Plateaus*, Gilles Deleuze and Félix Guattari conceptualize different forms of inhabiting and traveling through space: "striated space," which corresponds to a modern experience of geography (teleological, determined by scientific forms of quantifiable knowledge, an economy of gains and losses), and the "smooth space" of the nomad (the desert and sea that resist being captured and instrumentalized). This distinction (the authors rush to clarify that "the two spaces in fact exist only in mixture"; 474) is quite useful in thinking about the ways the *modernistas* create a modern world for Latin American audiences. If "in striated space, lines or trajectories tend to be subordinated to points: one goes *from* one *to* another," and "in the smooth, it is the opposite: the points are subordinated to the trajectory" (478), the space of *modernismo* is one of striae, where itineraries and destinations are marked by a modernizing finality.

3. The first Latin American books on travels to China and Japan, which preceded the journeys and aestheticized accounts of the *modernistas*, were immediately linked to the Meiji reforms and the interest of Latin American nations in establishing diplomatic and commercial relations with both the rapidly modernizing Japanese state and Europe's colonial outposts in Shanghai. Some of these early travel accounts are Nicolás Tanco Armero's *Viaje de la Nueva Granada a China y de China a Francia* (*Journey from New Granada to China and from China to France*) (1861) and *Recuerdos de mis últimos viajes a Japón* (*Memories of My Last Journeys to Japan*) (1888), Henrique Lisboa's *A china e os chins* (*China and the Chinese*) (1888), Eduardo Wilde's *Por mares i por tierras* (*By Seas and by Land*) (1899), Aluísio Azevedo's *O Japão* (*Japan*) (written in 1898 and published in 1910), and Manoel de Oliveira Lima's *No Japão: Impressões da terra e da gente* (*In Japan: Impressions of the Land and the People*) (1903). I owe these references to Rosario Hubert, whose unpublished dissertation "Disorientations: Latin American Diversions of East Asia" makes the most important contribution to date regarding these travel narratives.

4. José Juan Tablada was the first *modernista* to travel to Japan, doing so in 1900. Funded by the patron of the *Revista Moderna*, Tablada wrote chronicles on Japanese cultural life; from Mexico, Japan seemed to be the strangest, most exotic society, but also a nation experiencing a process of modernization akin to what was taking place in Mexico under Porfirio Díaz (Mata 8). In *En el país del sol* (1919) he collected some of his chronicles plus other essays he had written for *Revista Azul* (*Blue Review*), *Revista de Revistas* (*Review of Reviews*), and *El mundo ilustrado* (*The Illustrated World*). He also published a brief study on

Japanese art, *Hiroshigué: El pintor de la nieve y de la lluvia, de la noche y de la luna* (*Hiroshigué: Painter of Snow and Rain, Night and the Moon*) (1914). Efrén Rebolledo's trip to Japan followed the more traditional diplomatic path, and his short novels *Hojas de bambú* (*Bamboo Leaves*) (1907) and *Nikko* (1910), as well as the book of poems *Rimas Japonesas* (*Japanese Rhymes*), were all written—as was often the case—in the abundant spare time that his position as Mexican vice-consul in Yokohama afforded him. The Salvadorean Arturo Ambrogi used family money to fund an eastbound journey of initiation when he was very young, as a result of which he wrote *Sensaciones del Japón y de la China* (*Sensations of Japan and China*) (1915), before embarking on a diplomatic career that took him through more predictable transatlantic routes. The most complete and compelling analysis of this corpus of *modernista* travel narratives to Asia can be found in Tinajero's *Orientalismo*.

5. In his classic book *Travel as Metaphor*, Georges Van den Abbeele defines travel as an economy that "requires an *oikos* (the Greek word for 'home' from which is derived economy) in relation to which any wandering can be comprehended. . . . In other words, a home(land) must be posited from which one leaves on the journey and to which one hopes to return—whether one actually makes it back home changes nothing, from this perspective. The positing of an *oikos* . . . is what domesticates the voyage by ascribing certain limits to it" (xviii).

6. For an excellent and detailed analysis of "La psicología del viajero," see González (*Crónica* 168–75). On the question of the return to Paris, González characterizes the manner in which Gómez Carrillo ends the essay with "un gesto falsamente despreocupado, pero en el fondo profundamente desalentado. . . . El retorno a París es el retorno al centro, al eje vital, pero también es un retorno al interior, al viejo interior, a ese espacio donde el 'yo' aún puede subsistir tranquilamente, libre de los azares de 'la vida errante'" (174–75) ("a falsely carefree gesture, but deep down profoundly discouraged. . . . The return to Paris is the return to the center, the vital axis, but it is also the return to the interior, to the old interior, to that space where the 'I' can still peacefully subsist, free of the whims of 'the wandering life'"). Luis Fernández Cifuentes has insightfully analyzed the meaning of Paris in this essay as the result of a binary opposition between the French capital and Madrid as the elided differential whose exclusion renders it all the more significant:

> La propuesta de Gómez Carrillo (en realidad, toda su reflexión sobre los viajes e incluso, podríamos decir, todas las reflexiones de los viajeros hispanoamericanos) comporta una dicotomía exclusiva, una polarización que lo distingue de todos los otros viajeros finiseculares: en un polo de la geografía—un polo sagrado y siempre explícito—se encuentra París, la metrópoli magistral de la *diferencia*, el paraíso "encantador" que se alcanza al "morir un peu" y que le permite abandonarse a la otredad; en el otro polo—a veces sólo implícito y, en algún caso, vergonzante—se encuentra Madrid, la "madre patria," destino de un retorno a una presunta identidad originaria pero ya distante, problemática, singularmente turbadora. (121)

> Gómez Carrillo's proposal (really, all his reflections on travel and even, we could say, the reflections of all Hispanic-American travelers) involves an exclusive dichotomy, a polarization that distinguishes it from those of other travelers at the end of the century: at one geographic extreme—a sacred and always explicit extreme—is Paris, the magisterial metropolis of *difference*, the "enchanting" paradise that is reached by "dying a little" and that allows one to succumb to otherness; at the other extreme—only implicit and, in some cases, shameful—is Madrid, the "mother country," destination of a return to a presumed identity, originary but now distant, problematic, uniquely disturbing.

Finally, a clarification: Gómez Carrillo's essay has been reprinted many times, even during his lifetime, and in many different contexts, which has led to a variation in the title, which alternately appears as "La psicología del viajero" and "La psicología del viaje" ("The Psychology of the Traveler" and "The Psychology of Travel").

7. In similar terms, Arturo Ambrogi, in *Sensaciones del Japón y de la China* (1915), dreads returning from Japan and China to European cities where technical modernity endangers his newly discovered poetic existence: "Mis días de vida japonesa transcurran, íntegros, en su medio pintoresco, en su propio ambiente, lejos de los barrios europeos, de la vida cosmopolita, en donde un conato de rasca-cielo, un hediondo automóvil, un estruendoso 'tram' eléctrico, puede arrebatarme a mi profundo ensueño exótico, a la estupenda embriaguez de rareza y de refinamiento arcano, que de tan lejos, he venido a buscar a estos rincones asiáticos" (43) ("My days of Japanese life pass, whole, in their picturesque environment, in their own environment, far from the European neighborhoods, from the cosmopolitan life, where the beginnings of a skyscraper, a filthy automobile, a clamorous electric 'tram,' can snatch me out of my deep exotic dream, the stupendous intoxication of strangeness and arcane refinement, that I have come from so far away to search for in these Asian corners").

8. For an excellent survey of the presence of Japonaiseries and Chinoiseries in *modernismo*, see Tinajero's *Orientalismo*.

9. This sense of familiarity can be accompanied by anti-Orientalist disappointment, as Gómez Carrillo experiences at several points on his trip to Egypt as he follows the course of the Nile from Cairo to Memphis, prompting him to reflect on the clichéd expectations of travelers who leave Europe for the Orient:

> La primera impresión en las grandes ciudades Orientales, es casi siempre desilusionante. Llega uno con el alma llena de ensueños maravillosos, con la memoria poblada de recuerdos encantados. Llega uno buscando el visir de las mil y una noches que va a abrirle las puertas de un alcázar. Llega uno sediento de perfumes misteriosos . . . la decepción es cruel. Las guías, sin embargo nos han prevenido. Sabemos antes de ir a Constantinopla, que Pera es una villa *a l'instar* de París, que en Damasco las calles principales están llenas de tiendas alemanas, que Argel es una

prefectura francesa. . . . Así, yo me hallo ahora en mi ventana del Hotel Continental triste cual engañado. Eso que aparece ante mis ojos, no obstante, es lo que el señor Baedecker tuvo la gentileza de anunciarme. Ahí está la vasta avenida con sus palacios, con sus almacenes, con sus cafés. Ahí va el tranvía eléctrico, lleno de gente vestida lo mismo que en Roma o en Viena. Ahí pasan los policemans con sus trajes londinenses. ¡Qué pena, Díos mío! Y no es porque sea feo, ni triste, no. Nada hay tan alegre como esta Charia Bulak cosmopolita. Pero, a mi pesar, siento que mi alma, incurablemente ilusa, aguardaba otra cosa. Anoche, al oír desde mi estancia el murmullo que sube del fondo de las enramadas negras de enfrente, tuve visiones de jardines árabes con terrazas de mirtos, y boscajes de jazmineros, y laberintos caprichosos. La brisa traíame aromas de flores tropicales, ecos de surtidores juguetones. (*Sonrisa* 13–14)

The first impression of large Oriental cities is almost always disappointing. One arrives with a soul full of marvelous dreams, with a memory populated by enchanting recollections. One arrives searching for the vizier of the one thousand and one nights who will open the door to a fortress. One arrives thirsty for mysterious perfumes . . . deception is cruel. The guides, nonetheless, have warned us. We know before we arrive in Constantinople that Pera is a small town in the style of Paris, that the main streets in Damask are full of German stores, that Algiers is a French prefecture. . . . So, I now find myself at my window in the Continental Hotel, sad and deceived. Appearing before my eyes, however, is just what Mister Baedecker had the kindness to advertise. There is the wide avenue with its palaces, its warehouses, its cafés. There goes the electric tram, full of people dressed as they dress in Rome or Vienna. There go the policemen in their London-style suits. What a shame, my God! And not because it is ugly, or sad, no. There is nothing so joyful as this cosmopolitan Sharia Bulak. But, regretfully, I feel that my incurably deluded soul expected something else. Last night, as I heard the rustle that rises from the depths of the black branches in front of my room, I had visions of Arab gardens with terraces of myrtle trees, and jasmine groves, and capricious labyrinths. The breeze brought me the smells of tropical flowers and echoes of playful fountains.

While these reflections are nostalgic, there is also a willingness to account for the complex material reality of North African and Middle Eastern cities in the context of the globalization of modernity.

10. *La Grecia eterna* (1908), narrating his trip to the Attic Peninsula in 1907, features the same scene. Gómez Carrillo arrives in Athens after having traversed the Greek countryside from the port of Piraeus. The modernist teleology that organizes his map of the world indicates that he is traveling to a country

in ruins, culturally dead, out of sync with western Europe. In his mind he is traveling both temporally (to a premodern past, dehistoricized by the adjective *eternal*) and spatially (eastward, to the Orient, to a culture Orientalized by its Ottoman past). This explains his first impression of the Greek capital:

> Atenas, la nueva Atenas que ha resucitado de una muerte milenaria, la Atenas libre, fuerte y docta soñada por Byron, hela aquí. En verdad, yo nunca me la figuré tal vual hoy me aparece en mis primeras peregrinaciones callejeras. A fuerza de oír hablar de su esclavitud, la creí vestida a la oriental, con trapos violentos y joyas vistosas. . . . En cambio, tiene el aspecto de una gran capital. Aquí la llaman un "pequeño París." Los "pequeños Parises" son infinitos e infinitamente variados. Pero, en realidad, es una ciudad elegante, animada, lujosa, limpia, rica y digna. Por ninguna parte un mendigo, ni una tienda sórdida, ni un grupo andrajoso. . . . Atenas es occidental, como una ciudad de Francia, como una ciudad de España. (43, 46)

> Athens, the new Athens that has risen from an ancient death, the free, strong, and learned Athens that Byron dreamed of, here it is. I honestly did not imagine it as it appears today on my first pilgrimages into the street. Because I had heard of its slavery, I imagined the city dressed in an Oriental style, with vibrant clothes and showy jewels. . . . Instead, it has the appearance of a great capital. Here they call it a "little Paris." The "little Parises" are infinite and infinitely varied. But it is really an elegant, lively, luxurious, clean, rich and worthy city. There are no beggars, or sordid stores, or ragged groups. . . . Athens is Western, like a city in France, like a city in Spain.

11. Even though the representation of women as erotic seductresses is at the center of Gómez Carrillo's eastbound travels, the fetishization of feminine sexuality is a constant in his intellectual itinerary, traceable in the titles of his books and *crónicas*. *Entre encajes* (*Between Lace*) (1905) is a gallery of feminine types: "Las Geishas" ("The Geishas"), "La Parisiense del pueblo" ("The Parisienne of the People"), "Las mujeres de Londres" ("The Women of London"), "Bailarinas cosmopolitas" ("Cosmopolitan Dancers"), "Bailadoras orientales" ("Oriental Dancers"), "¡Vienesa, rubia vienesa!" ("Viennese, Blond Viennese!"), "El comercio de las sonrisas" ("The Commerce of Smiles"), and "Una extraña Salomé" ("A Strange Salome"), among others. *El libro de las mujeres* (*The Book of Women*) (1909, reissued in 1919) compiles essays that feature women as mere objects of lust, fascination, and danger (especially in the section titled "Mis ídolas" ("My Idols"), a category that includes Raquel Meller, Loie Fuller, Sadda Yakko, Georgette Leblanc, Marta Brandés, Suzane Després, Berthe Bady, and Emma Calvé). Books like *La psicología de la moda femenina* (*The Psychology of Feminine Style*) (1907) or *Las sibilas de París* (*The Sibyls of Paris*) (1917), among others, rehash the same subjects and themes in similar ways.

12. In *Orientalism*, Said explains that this translation of lust and fascination into disgust, anxiety, and feeling threatened was a staple of Orientalist discourse from its inception in the eighteenth century:

> Many of the earliest Oriental amateurs [like Schlegel] began by welcoming the Orient as a salutary derangement of their European habits of mind and spirit. The Orient was overvalued for its Pantheism, its spirituality, its stability, its longevity, its primitivity, and so forth. . . . Yet almost without exception such overesteem was followed by a counterresponse: the Orient suddenly appeared lamentably underhumanized, antidemocratic, backward, barbaric, and so forth. A swing of the pendulum in one direction caused an equal and opposite swing back. . . . Orientalism as a profession grew out of these opposites, of compensations and corrections based on inequality. (150)

13. Aníbal González has analyzed the Guatemalan's philosophy of travel writing: "Gómez Carrillo posits that the modern travel writer should simply aspire to transcribe the sights, smells, sounds, and experiences of the foreign lands he visits as they affect his consciousness. . . . [He is] a kind of voyageur/voyeur, or better yet, a sort of medium who receives and transmits the experiences of travel for the benefit of readers, who may never be able to travel" (*Companion* 49).

14. This is also apparent in his transcription of abstract and disembodied statistical reports provided by Russian informants and foreign embassies in Saint Petersburg: "La renta nacional de Francia puede calcularse de 35 a 40 mil millones de Francos pero el presupuesto de la tercera república no consume más del 10% de la renta que fue de 3.572 millones en 1904. En cambio la renta nacional del imperio ruso no pasaba en 1890 de 12.000 millones y hoy no debe ser superior de 16.000 millones" (128–29) ("The national income of France can be calculated between 35 and 40 billion francs, but the Third Republic's budget, which was 3.572 billion in 1904, does not consume more than 10 percent of the income. On the other hand, the national income of the Russian Empire did not exceed 12 billion in 1890 and today cannot be more than 16 billion"). He admits openly that his analysis comes from interviews with experts: "Todo el mundo en San Petersburgo me había dicho: 'Si quiere usted estudiar a fondo la organización de los partidos socialistas rusos, visite usted a Rubanovich'" (115) ("Everyone in Saint Petersburg told me: 'If you want to thoroughly study the organization of the Russian socialist parties, go and see Rubanovich'").

15. For an excellent account of this circulation and especially Darío's reading of Nordau, see B. Trigo, "*Raros* de Darío."

16. In Latin America, the notion of the intellectual is first used by Rodó, González Prada, and Ingenieros between 1900 and 1905 (Altamirano 21).

17. Claudio Lomnitz has described the reaction of the Mexican intellectual field to the Dreyfus Affair:

> Los escritores más elocuentes entre los *científicos*—en especial Justo Sierra y Francisco Bulnes—adoptaron el bando dreyfusiano,

> y los periódicos dominados por los *científicos*, *El Mundo* y *El Imparcial*, adoptaron de manera predominante la línea pro-Dreyfus que fue también una posición en contra de la iglesia del militarismo, y de la alianza "latina" impulsada por el papa León XIII, por Francia, España y numerosos gobiernos latinoamericanos. Los periódicos católicos, por su parte, se sirvieron del caso Dreyfus no sólo para "defender a Francia"—y de paso a todas las naciones "latinas"—de los traidores judíos y sus aliados estadounidenses y británicos, sino también para asociar a los *científicos* y a toda la prensa porfiriana, al judaísmo. Mediante la defensa del honor del Ejército, abrieron una brecha entre el poder civil burgués de los *científicos* y los militares, representados por el general Díaz, el general Reyes y otros. (450–51)

> The most eloquent writers among the *científicos*—especially Justo Sierra and Francisco Bulnes—took the side of the Dreyfusards, and the newspapers dominated by the *científicos*, *El Mundo* and *El Imparcial*, tended to adopt the pro-Dreyfus line, a position also opposed to the church of militarism and the "Latin" alliance of Pope Leo XIII, France, Spain, and numerous Latin American governments. As for the Catholic newspapers, they used the Dreyfus case not only to "defend France"—and while they were at it, all of the "Latin" nations—from Jewish traitors and their allies in the United States and Britain but also to connect the *científicos* and the Porfirian press to Judaism. By defending the army's honor, they opened a gap between the *científicos*' bourgeois civil power and the military, represented by General Díaz, General Reyes, and others.

18. See, for example, Blanco Fombona's "Viajes sentimentales" ("Sentimental Journeys"), which describes Zola as "el hombre que, movido por el amor de la justicia, abandonó su tranquilidad, se expuso a las iras del populacho y desafió al Ejército, la Magistratura, el Clero, la Francia toda, en defensa de un inocente, en defensa de un prisionero, en defensa de un desvalido, en defensa de Alfredo Dreyfus" (175) ("the man who, moved by the love of justice, abandoned his peace, exposed himself to the anger of the masses, and challenged the army, the tribunal, the clergy, all of France, in defense of an innocent, in defense of a prisoner, in defense of a helpless man, in defense of Alfred Dreyfus"). Darío, in *España contemporánea*, complains about the lack of coverage of the Affair in Spanish newspapers: "El asunto Dreyfus, de lo que hay ahora de más sonoro en el periodismo universal se publican [aquí] unas pocas líneas telegráficas" (30) ("The Dreyfus Affair currently resonates throughout universal journalism, here they publish a few telegraphic lines"). However, the most meaningful and insightful account of the Affair was Manuel Ugarte's *crónica* on the Universal Exhibition of 1900, in which he took notice of the overwhelming presence of the Affair ("Todo cuanto ocurre ahora en Francia está subordinado al asunto Dreyfus que es el eje de la política, de la literatura y hasta de la vida social" [*Crónicas* 106] ["Everything that happens in France right now is less important than the Dreyfus Affair, which is the axis

of politics, literature, and even social life"]) as the city tried to lose itself in the Exhibition. Nonetheless, Ugarte maintains a distanced and exterior point of view regarding the Affair, as opposed to Gómez Carrillo's proximity to its collective experience as a social trauma and his clear commitment to the Dreyfusard camp.

19. Darío admired many anti-Dreyfusard, nationalist, and militant Catholic artists, from Barrès and Hughes Rebell to Verlaine and Coppée. For a detailed and well-researched account of Darío's connection to the Dreyfus Affair, see Pailler, "Rubén Darío."

20. The question of the Jew as signifier of universal suffering has an important history in Western culture and political thought. Particularly relevant is Marx's "On the Jewish Question" (1843), a critical review of Bruno Bauer's essay *Die Judenfrage* (*The Jewish Question*) published that same year. Bauer uses Jewish marginalization as a point of departure to discuss the nature of the universal emancipation implied in the process of capitalist secular modernization; Marx points out that Bauer's proposal of universal civil rights is insufficient to achieve the goal of universal emancipation and argues instead that only economic emancipation can bring true universal freedom and do away with fragmentary and regressive particularistic demands in favor of an egalitarian transformation of the social body.

21. Several authors insist on a subtle distinction between empathy and sympathy, while others find the definitional differences between them to be a matter of disciplinary perspective (Eisenberg and Strayer 6). In fact, the concept of empathy is a rather new invention of the German psychologist Theodor Lipps, who developed the notion of *Einfühlung* (a neologism that can be translated as *feeling-into*) in 1903. Lipps was reelaborating a notion of sympathy that Hume had vaguely conceptualized in *A Treatise of Human Nature* (1739) and that Adam Smith, taking Hume's cue, had defined in *The Theory of Moral Sentiments* (1759) as "an impulse in Man to concern himself with "the fortunes of others, and render their happiness necessary to him, although he derives nothing from it except the pleasure of seeing it" (47). For Smith, what makes us moral beings is our ability to "become in some measure the same person with him, and thence form some idea of his sensations, and even feel something which, though weaker in degree, is not altogether unlike them" (12). I take this abbreviated genealogy of the relationship between sympathy and empathy from Wispé (314).

22. It would be a mistake to use the references to the face of the Jews in this passage to read its ethical nature in terms of Emmanuel Levinas's *Totality and Infinity* (1961), in which he proposes the face of the Other as an incomprehensible and "infinitely foreign" (94) manifestation of an Other in pain that makes a demand of us, radically reconstituting us as ethical subjects by setting a transcendental limit to our narcissistic self-involvement. As Seàn Hand explains, in Levinas the face of the Other is not "the face in a biological, ethnic or even social sense. The face evoked is rather the concrete idea of [the Other's] infinity that exists within me" (42). In other words, the face of the Other is the transcendental, infinite, and ahistorical moment of the foundation of the subject as obligated to a necessarily unspecified Other that is in fact the

constitutive core of the ethical subject: "I am he who finds the resources to respond to the call" (qtd. in Graff Zivin 21). But Levinas's radical ethics could not be further from Gómez Carrillo's empathic cosmopolitanism, which, as I have shown, does not reconfigure his intellectual and traveling subjectivity. For Levinas, empathy is in fact a "reduction of the other to the same by interposition of a middle and neutral term" such as "cognition of [transient] identity" (43), that is, an attempt to domesticate the Other's absolute otherness, a totalization of self and Other. I have to thank Erin Graff Zivin for her feedback on this last section of the chapter. It was thanks to a conversation with her (after having read her brilliant *The Wandering Signifier*) that I came to terms with the impossibility of framing Gómez Carrillo's *modernista* ethics of the Other with Levinas's philosophical argument in *Totality and Infinity*.

Works Cited

Aching, Gerard. "Against 'Library-Shelf Races': José Martí's Critique of Excessive Imitation." *Geomodernisms: Race, Modernism, Modernity.* Ed. Laura Doyle and Laura Winkiel. Bloomington: Indiana University Press, 2005. 151–69.

———. *The Politics of Spanish American "Modernismo": By Exquisite Design.* Cambridge: Cambridge University Press, 1997.

Achúgar, Hugo. "Apuntes sobre la 'literatura mundial,' o acerca de la imposible universalidad de la 'literatura universal.'" Sánchez Prado, *América Latina* 197–212.

Agosta, Lou. *Empathy in the Context of Philosophy.* New York: Palgrave Macmillan, 2011.

Aguilar, Gonzalo M. "Las costuras de la letra." *Prismas: Revista de historia intelectual* 10 (2006): 173–76.

———. *Episodios cosmopolitas de la cultura argentina.* Buenos Aires: Santiago Arcos Editor, 2009.

Alexis, Jacques Stéphen. "Du réalisme merveilleux des Haïtiens." *Presence Africaine* 8–10 (8 Oct. 1956): 25–26.

Allende, Isabel. *The House of the Spirits.* New York: Knopf, 1985.

Alonso, Carlos J. *The Burden of Modernity: The Rhetoric of Cultural Discourse in Spanish America.* Oxford: Oxford University Press, 1998.

———. "Rama y sus retoños: Figuring the Nineteenth Century in Spanish America." *Revista de Estudios Hispánicos* 28 (1994): 283–92.

Altamirano, Carlos. "Introducción general." *La ciudad letrada de la conquista al modernismo.* Ed. Carlos Altamirano and Jorge Myers. Buenos Aires: Katz Editores, 2008. Vol. 1 of *Historia de los intelectuales en América Latina.*

Altamirano, Carlos, and Beatriz Sarlo. "Vanguardia y criollismo: La aventura de *Martín Fierro.*" *Ensayos argentinos: De Sarmiento a la vanguardia.* Buenos Aires: Ariel, 1997. 211–55.

———. "Una vida ejemplar: La estrategia de *Recuerdos de Provincia.*" *Ensayos argentinos: De Sarmiento a la vanguardia.* Buenos Aires: Ariel, 1997. 103–55.

Ambrogi, Arturo. *Sensaciones del Japón y de la China.* San Salvador: Dirección General del Ministerio de Educación, 1963.

Anderson Imbert, Enrique. *El realismo mágico y otros ensayos.* Caracas: Monte Avila Editores, 1976.

———. *Veinte cuentos hispanoamericanos del siglo XX.* New York: Appelton Century Crofts, 1956.

Andrade, Oswald de. "Anthropophagite Manifesto." *The Oxford Book of Latin American Essays.* Ed. Ilan Stavans. Oxford: Oxford University Press, 1997. 96–99.

———. "Manifesto antropófago." *Revista de Antropofagia* 1.1 (May 1928): 3–7.

Appadurai, Arjun. *Modernity at Large: Cultural Dimensions of Globalization.* Minneapolis: University of Minnesota Press, 1996.

Appiah, Kwame Anthony. *Cosmopolitanism: Ethics in a World of Strangers.* New York: W. W. Norton, 2006.

———. "Cosmopolitan Patriots." *Cosmopolitics: Thinking and Feeling beyond the Nation.* Ed. Pheng Cheah and Bruce Robbins. Minneapolis: University of Minnesota Press, 1998.

———. *The Ethics of Identity.* Princeton: Princeton University Press, 2005.

Apter, Emily. *Against World Literature: On the Politics of Untranslatability.* London: Verso, 2013.

———. "Global *Translatio*: The 'Invention' of Comparative Literature, Istanbul, 1933." *Debating World Literature.* Ed. Christopher Prendergast. London: Verso, 2004. 76–109.

———. *The Translation Zone: A New Comparative Literature.* Princeton: Princeton University Press, 2005.

Arendt, Hannah. *The Human Condition.* Chicago: University of Chicago Press, 1958.

Arguedas, Jose María. *El zorro de arriba y el zorro de abajo.* Buenos Aires: Losada, 1971.

Arias, Salvador, ed. *Recopilación de textos sobre Alejo Carpentier.* La Habana: Casa de las Américas, 1977.

Arrom, José Juan. "El oro, la pluma y la piedra preciosa: El trasfondo indígena en la poesía de Rubén Darío." *Hispania* 50.4 (Dec. 1967): 971–81.

Ashcroft, Bill, Gareth Griffiths, and Helen Tiffin. *The Empire Writes Back: Theory and Practices in Post-colonial Literatures.* London: Routledge, 2002.

———. *Post-colonial Studies: The Key Concepts.* London: Routledge, 2007.

Asturias, Miguel Ángel. *Hombres de maíz.* Buenos Aires: Losada, 1949.

———. *Leyendas de Guatemala. Tres obras: Leyendas de Guatemala. El alhajadito. El señor presidente.* Caracas: Biblioteca Ayacucho, 1977.

———. *Men of Maize*. Trans. Gerald Martin. New York: Delacorte Express / S. Lawrence, 1975.

———. *Mr. President*. Trans. Frances Partridge. New York: Atheneum, 1964.

———. *El señor presidente*. Buenos Aires: Losada, 1955.

Aubrun, Charles V. "Rastaquoère et rasta." *Bulletin Hispanique* 57.4 (1955): 430–39.

Azevedo, Aluísio. *O Japão*. Sao Paulo: Roswitha Kempf, 1910.

Balderston, Daniel. "Borges: The Argentine Writer and the (Western) Tradition." *Borges and Europe Revisited*. Ed. Evelyn Fishburn. London: Institute of Latin American Studies, University of London, 1999. 37–48.

Banville, Théodore de. *Les stalactites*. Paris: Honoré Champion Éditeur, 1996. Vol. 2 of *Oeuvres poétiques completes*.

Barrès, Maurice. "Ce que j'ai vu à Rennes." *Scènes et doctrines du nationalisme*. Paris: F. Juven, 1902.

Barthes, Roland. *Mythologies*. Paris: Editions du Seuil, 1957.

Bastos, María Luisa. "La crónica modernista de Enrique Gómez Carrillo o la función de la trivialidad." *Relecturas: Estudios de textos hispanoamericanos*. Buenos Aires: Hachette, 1989.

Baughman, T. H. *Before the Heroes Came: Antarctica in the 1890s*. Lincoln: University of Nebraska Press, 1994.

Beckman, Ericka. *Capital Fictions: The Literature of Latin America's Export Age*. Minneapolis: University of Minnesota Press, 2013.

Behdad, Ali. *Belated Travelers: Orientalism in the Age of Colonial Dissolution*. Durham: Duke University Press, 1994.

Benjamin, Walter. "Paris, die Hauptstadt des XIX. Jahrhunderts." *Illuminationen*. Frankfurt: Suhrkamp, 1977.

———. "Paris, the Capital of the Nineteenth Century." *The Arcades Project*. Trans. Howard Eiland and Kevin McLaughlin. Cambridge, MA: Harvard University Press, 1999.

Beverley, John. *Subalternity and Representation: Arguments in Cultural Theory*. Durham: Duke University Press, 1999.

Bhabha, Homi K. "Introduction: Narrating the Nation." *Nation and Narration*. Ed. Homi K. Bhabha. London: Routledge, 1990.

———. *The Location of Culture*. London: Routledge, 1994.

———. "Unsatisfied: Notes on Vernacular Cosmopolitanism." *Postcolonial Discourses: An Anthology*. Ed. Gregory Castle. Malden, MA: Blackwell, 2001.

Blanchard, Pascal, and Sandrine Lemaire. "Exhibitions, Expositions, Médiatisation et Colonies." *Culture colonial: La France conquise par son empire, 1871–1931*. Ed. Pascal Blanchard and Sandrine Lemaire. Paris: Éditions Autrement, 2003.

Blanco Fombona, Rufino. "Viajes sentimentales." *Más allá de los horizontes*. Madrid: Casa Editorial de la Viuda de Rodríguez Serra, 1903.

Bontempelli, Massimo. *Opere scelte*. Ed. Luigi Baldacci. Milan: Mondadori, 1978.

Borges, Jorge Luis. "The Argentine Writer and Tradition." *Selected Non-fictions*. Ed. Eliot Weinberger. Trans. Esther Allen. New York: Viking, 1999.

———. "El escritor argentino y la tradición." *Obras completas*. Buenos Aires: Emecé, 1974.

———. "Kafka y sus precursores." *Obras completas*. Buenos Aires: Emecé, 1974.

———. "Paul Groussac." *Obras completas*. Buenos Aires: Emecé, 1974.

Bourdieu, Pierre. *Distinction: A Social Critique of the Judgement of Taste*. Trans. Richard Nice. London: Routledge and Kegan Paul, 1986.

Bowers, Maggie Ann. *Magic(al) Realism*. London: Routledge, 2004.

Brandes, George. *The Emigrant Literature*. London: William Heinemann, 1906. Vol. 1 of *Main Currents in Nineteenth-Century Literature*.

———. "World Literature." Trans. Mads Rosendahl Thomsen. *Mapping World Literature: International Canonization and Transnational Literatures*. By Mads Rosendahl Thomsen. London: Continuum, 2008.

———. *Young Germany*. London: William Heinemann, 1901. Vol. 6 of *Main Currents in Nineteenth-Century Literature*.

Brennan, Timothy. "Cosmo-Theory." *South Atlantic Quarterly* 100.3 (Summer 2001): 659–91.

Breton, André. *Manifestes du surréalisme*. Paris: Gallimard, 1966.

———. *Manifestoes of Surrealism*. Trans. Richard Seaver and Helen Lane. Ann Arbor: University of Michigan Press, 1972.

Bruno, Paula. *Paul Groussac: Un estratega intelectual*. Buenos Aires: Fondo de Cultura Económica, 2005.

Buruma, Ian, and Avishai Margalit. *Occidentalism: The West in the Eyes of Its Enemies*. New York: Penguin, 2004.

Bush, Christopher. *Ideographic Modernism: China, Writing, Media*. New York: Oxford University Press, 2010.

———. Introduction to *Stèles/古今碑錄*. Ed., trans., and annot. Timothy Billings and Christopher Bush. Middletown, CT: Wesleyan University Press, 2007.

Butler, Judith. *Subjects of Desire*. New York: Columbia University Press, 1999.

Camayd-Freixas, Erik. *Realismo mágico y primitivismo: Relecturas de Carpentier, Asturias, Rulfo y García Márquez*. Lanham, MD: University Press of America, 1995.

Candido, Antonio. "Para una crítica latinoamericana: Entrevista de Beatriz Sarlo a Antonio Candido." *Punto de Vista* 3.8 (Mar. 1980).

Carlos, Alberto J. "'Divagación': La geografía erótica de Rubén Darío." *Revista Iberoamericana* 33.64 (July–Dec. 1967): 293–313.

Carpentier, Alejo. *The Kingdom of This World*. Trans. Harriet de Onís. New York: Penguin Books, 1980.

———. "The Marvelous Real in America." Zamora and Faris, *Magical Realism* 75–88.

———. "Prólogo." *El reino de este mundo* Mexico: Compañía General de Ediciones, 1967, 4–6.

———. *Razón de ser: Conferencias*. Caracas: Universidad Central de Venezuela, 1976.

———. *El reino de este mundo*. Mexico: Compañía General de Ediciones, 1967.

———. *Tientos y diferencias: Ensayos*. México: UNAM, 1964.

Casanova, Pascale. *The World Republic of Letters.* Trans. M. B. DeBevoise. Cambridge, MA: Harvard University Press, 2004.

Chakrabarty, Dipesh. *Provincializing Europe: Postcolonial Thought and Historical Difference.* Princeton: Princeton University Press, 2000.

Chanady, Amaryll. *Entre inclusion et exclusion: La symbolisation de l'autre dans les Amériques.* Paris: Champion, 1999.

———. *Magical Realism and the Fantastic: Resolved versus Unresolved Antinomy.* New York: Garland, 1985.

———. "The Territorialization of the Imaginary in Latin America: Self-Affirmation and Resistance to Metropolitan Paradigms." Zamora and Faris, *Magical Realism* 125–44.

Chapman, Walker. *The Loneliest Continent.* London: Jarrolds, 1964.

Cheah, Pheng, and Bruce Robbins, eds. *Cosmopolitics: Thinking and Feeling beyond the Nation.* Minneapolis: University of Minnesota Press, 1998.

Chiampi, Irlemar. *O realismo maravilhoso: Forma e ideologia no romance hispanoamericano.* Sao Paulo: Editora Perspectiva, 1980.

———. "El surrealismo, lo real maravilloso y el vodú en la encrucijada del Caribe." *Alejo Carpentier: Acá y allá.* Ed. Luisa Campuzano. Pittsburgh, PA: Institution Internacional de Literatura Iberoamericana, 2007.

Clifford, James. *The Predicament of Culture: Twentieth Century Ethnography, Literature and Art.* Cambridge, MA: Harvard University Press, 1988.

Cohen, Margaret. "Literary Studies on the Terraqueous Globe." *PMLA* 125.3 (May 2010): 657–62.

Coll, Pedro Emilio. "Decadentismo y Americanismo." *El castillo de Elsinor.* Caracas: Herrera Irigoyen, 1901.

———. "Notas." *Cosmópolis* 12 (July 1895): 141–44.

———. *Pedro-Emilio Coll.* Ed. Rafael Angel Insausti. Caracas: Italgráfica, Colección Clásicos Venezolanos, 1966.

———. "A propósito de *Cosmópolis.*" *Pedro-Emilio Coll.* Ed. Rafael Angel Insausti. Caracas: Italgráfica, Colección Clásicos Venezolanos, 1966.

Colombi, Beatriz. "En torno de *Los raros*: Darío y su campaña intelectual en Buenos Aires." *Rubén Darío en la nación de Buenos Aires.* Ed. Susana Zanetti. Buenos Aires: Eudeba, 2004.

———. "Peregrinaciones parisinas: Rubén Darío." *Orbis Tertius* 2.4 (1997): 1–9.

———. *El viaje intelectual: Migraciones y desplazamientos en América Latina (1880–1915).* Rosario: Beatriz Viterbo Editora, 2004.

Compère, Daniel. *Jules Verne: Écrivain.* Geneva: Libraire Droz, 1991.

Cook, James. *The Journals of Captain Cook.* Ed. Philip Edwards. London: Penguin, 1999.

Cooppan, Vilashini. "Ghosts in the Disciplinary Machine." *Comparative Literature Studies* 41.1 (2004).

———. "World Literature and Global Theory: Comparative Literature for the New Millenium." *Symploké* 9.1–2 (2001): 15–44.

———. "World Literature between History and Theory." D'haen, Damrosch, and Kadir 194–203.

Couto, Mia. *Sleepwalking Land*. Trans. David Brookshaw. London: Serpent's Tail, 2006.

Damrosch, David. *How to Read World Literature*. Oxford: Wiley-Blackwell, 2009.

———, ed. *The Longman Anthology of World Literature*. 6 vols. New York: Longman, 2004–09.

———. *What Is World Literature?* Princeton: Princeton University Press, 2003.

———. "World Literature in a Postcanonical, Hypercanonical Age." *Comparative Literature in an Age of Globalization*. Ed. Haun Saussy. Baltimore: Johns Hopkins, 2006.

Danticat, Edwidge. "The Real Worlds." *PEN America 6, Metamorphoses* (Oct. 2003). www.pen.org/nonfiction-transcript/real-worlds.

Darío, Rubén. "A Colón." *Obras completas*. Buenos Aires: Ediciones Anaconda, 1948. 280.

———. "Algunas notas sobre Jean Moréas." *Opiniones. Obras completas*. Vol. 10. Madrid: Mundo Latino, 1920. 69–76.

———. "A Roosevelt." *Obras completas*. Buenos Aires: Ediciones Anaconda, 1948. 239–42.

———. *Autobiografía: Oro de Mallorca*. Madrid: Mondadori, 1990.

———. *Cantos de vida y esperanza. Obras completas*. Buenos Aires: Ediciones Anaconda, 1948. 230–69.

———. "Los colores del estandarte." *Nosotros: Revista de letras, arte, historia, filosofía y ciencias sociales*, Feb. 1916.

———. "El deseo de París." *Escritos dispersos de Rubén Darío (Recogidos en periódicos de Buenos Aires)*. Vol. 2. Ed. Pedro Luis Barcia. La Plata: Universidad Nacional de La Plata, Facultad de Humanidades y Ciencias de la Educación, 1968.

———. "Dilucidaciones." *Obras completas*. Buenos Aires: Ediciones Anaconda, 1948. 274.

———. "El Dios Hugo y la América Latina." *Escritos dispersos de Rubén Darío (Recogidos en periódicos de Buenos Aires)*. Vol. 2. Ed. Pedro Luis Barcia. La Plata: Universidad Nacional de La Plata, Facultad de Humanidades y Ciencias de la Educación, 1968. 116–20.

———. "Divagación." *Obras completas*. Buenos Aires: Ediciones Anaconda, 1948. 189–92.

———. "El ejemplo de Zola." *Opiniones*. Madrid: Fernando Fé, 1906.

———. "En París." *Peregrinaciones*. Madrid: Editorial Mundo Latino, 1918. 11–140. Vol. 12 of *Obras completas*.

———. *Epistolario 1*. Ed. Alberto Ghiraldo and Andrés González-Blanco. Madrid: Biblioteca Rubén Darío, 1926. Vol. 13 of *Obras completas*.

———. *España contemporánea*. Paris: Garnier, 1901.

———. "La evolución del rastacuerismo." *Opiniones*. Madrid: Editorial Mundo Latino, 1906. 133–39. Vol. 10 of *Obras completas*.

———. "La fiesta de Francia." *Prosa dispersa*. Madrid: Editorial Mundo Latino, 1919. 123–32. Vol. 20 of *Obras completas*.

———. "France-Amérique." *Obras completas*. Buenos Aires: Ediciones Anaconda, 1948.

———. "Los Hispano-Americanos: Notas y anécdotas." *Escritos dispersos de Rubén Darío (Recogidos en periódicos de Buenos Aires).* Vol. 2. Ed. Pedro Luis Barcia. La Plata: Universidad Nacional de La Plata, Facultad de Humanidades y Ciencias de la Educación, 1968.

———. *Historia de mis libros.* Caracas: Biblioteca Ayacucho, 1991.

———. "Impresiones de Salón." *Parisiana.* Madrid: Editorial Mundo Latino, 1918 181–202. Vol. 5 of *Obras completas.*

———. "Japoneses en París." *Escritos dispersos de Rubén Darío (Recogidos en periódicos de Buenos Aires).* Vol. 2. Ed. Pedro Luis Barcia. La Plata: Universidad Nacional de La Plata, Facultad de Humanidades y Ciencias de la Educación, 1968.

———. *Obras completas.* Buenos Aires: Ediciones Anaconda, 1948.

———. "Palabras liminares." *Obras completas.* Buenos Aires: Ediciones Anaconda, 1948. 186–87.

———. "París y los escritores extranjeros." *Obras completas.* Vol. 1. Ed. M. Sanmiguel Raimúndez. Madrid: Afrodisio Aguado, 1959.

———. "Prólogo." *De Marsella a Tokio: Sensaciones de Egipto, la India, la China y el Japón,* by Enrique Gómez Carrillo. Paris: Garnier Hermanos, 1906.

———. *Los raros.* Madrid: Editorial Pliegos, 2002.

———. "El reino interior." *Prosas profanas y otros poemas.* J.O. Jiménez, ed. Madrid: Alianza, 1992.

———. "Salutación del optimista." *Obras completas.* Buenos Aires: Ediciones Anaconda, 1948. 233–34.

———. *Selected Poems of Rubén Darío. A Bilingual Anthology.* Ed. and trans. Alberto Acereda and Will Derusha. Lewisburg: Bucknell University Press; London: Associated University Press, 2001.

———. *Selected Writings.* Ed. Ilan Stavans. Trans. Andrew Hurley, Greg Simon, and Stephen F. White. New York: Penguin, 2005.

———. *Stories and Poems / Cuentos y poesías. A Dual-Language Book.* Ed. and trans. Stanley Appelbaum. New York: Dover Publications, 2002.

———. *La vida de Rubén Darío escrita por él mismo.* Caracas: Biblioteca Ayacucho, 1991.

———. "Walt Whitman." *Obras completas.* Buenos Aires: Ediciones Anaconda, 1948.

———. "Yo soy aquel que ayer nomás decía." *Cantos de vida y esperanza.* Barcelona: F. Granada, 1907.

Dash, J. Michael. "Marvelous Realism: The Way out of Négritude." *Caribbean Studies* 13 (1974): 57–70.

De Ferrari, Guillermina, ed. *Utopías críticas: La literatura mundial según América Latina.* 1616. Spec. issue of *Anuario de literatura comparada* 2 (2012).

De la Campa, Román. "El desafío inesperado de *La ciudad letrada.*" *Angel Rama y los estudios latinoamericanos.* Ed. Mabel Moraña. Pittsburgh, PA: IILI, 2006.

Deleuze, Gilles. *Bergsonism.* Trans. Hugh Tomlinson and Barbara Habberjam. New York: Zone Books, 1988.

Deleuze, Gilles, and Félix Guattari. *A Thousand Plateaus: Capitalism and Schizophrenia*. Trans. Brian Masumi. Minneapolis: University of Minnesota Press, 1987.

Dellepiane, Angela B. "Narrativa argentina de ciencia ficción: Tentativas liminares y desarrollo posterior." *Actas del IX Congreso de la Asociación Internacional de Hispanistas*. Frankfurt: Vervuert, 1989. 515–25.

Denning, Michael. "The Novelists' International." *History, Geography, and Culture*. Ed. Franco Moretti. Princeton: Princeton University Press, 2006. 703–25. Vol. 1 of *The Novel*.

de Oliveira Lima, Manoel. *No Japão: Impressões da terra e da gente*. Rio de Janeiro: Laemmert, 1903.

Derrida, Jacques. "Archive Fever: A Freudian Impression." Trans. Eric Prenowitz. *Diacritics* 25.2 (Summer 1995): 9–63.

———. "Globalization, Peace, and Cosmopolitanism." *Negotiations: Interventions and Interviews 1971–2001*. Ed. and trans. Elizabeth Rottenberg. Stanford: Stanford University Press, 2002.

———. *Of Grammatology*. Trans. Gayatri Chakravorty Spivak. Baltimore: Johns Hopkins University Press, 1976.

———. "Plato's Pharmacy." *Dissemination*. Trans. Barbara Johnson. Chicago: University of Chicago Press, 1981.

———. "Structure, Sign and Play in the Social Sciences." *Writing and Difference*. Trans. Alan Bass. Chicago: University of Chicago Press, 1978.

D'haen, Theo. *The Routledge Concise History of World Literature*. London: Routledge, 2012.

D'haen, Theo, David Damrosch, and Djelal Kadir, eds. *The Routledge Companion to World Literature*. London: Routledge, 2012.

Dharwadker, Vinay, ed. *Cosmopolitan Geographies: New Locations in Literature and Culture*. New York: Routledge, 2001.

Díaz Alejandro, Carlos F. "La economía argentina durante el período 1880–1913." *La Argentina del ochenta al centenario*. Ed. Gustavo Ferrari and Ezequiel Gallo. Buenos Aires: Sudamericana, 1980.

Dimock, Wai Chee. "Deep Time: American Literature and World History." *American Literary History* 13.4 (Winter 2001): 755–75.

———. "Genre and World System: Epic and Novel on Four Continents." *Narrative* 14.1 (2006): 85–101.

———. "Planet and America, Set and Subset." *Shades of the Planet: American Literature as World Literature*. Ed. Wai Chee Dimock and Lawrence Buell. Princeton: Princeton University Press, 2007.

———. "Planetary Time and Global Translation: 'Context' in Literary Studies." *Common Knowledge* 9.3 (Fall 2003): 488–507.

———. *Through Other Continents: American Literature across Deep Time*. Princeton: Princeton University Press, 2006.

Dimock, Wai Chee, and Lawrence Buell, eds. *Shades of the Planet: American Literature as World Literature*. Princeton: Princeton University Press, 2007.

Domínguez, César, ed. *Literatura mundial: Una mirada panhispánica*. Spec. issue of *Insula: Revista de Letras y Ciencias Humanas*, nos. 787–88 (July–Aug. 2012).

Doyle, Laura, and Laura Winkiel. *Geomodernisms: Race, Modernism, Modernity*. Bloomington: Indiana University Press, 2005.

Drake, David. *French Intellectuals from the Dreyfus Affair to the Occupation*. New York: Palgrave/Macmillan, 2005.

Durix, Jean-Pierre. *Mimesis, Genres and Post-Colonial Discourse: Deconstructing Magical Realism*. New York: Palgrave Macmillan, 1998.

Echeverría, Esteban. "Clasicismo y romanticismo." *Escritos en prosa*. Ed. Juan María Gutiérrez. Buenos Aires: C. Casaralle, impr. y libreria de Mayo, 1870–74. Vol. 5 of *Obras completas de Esteban Echeverría*.

———. "Fondo y forma en las obras de imaginación." *Escritos en prosa*. Ed. Juan María Gutiérrez. Buenos Aires: C. Casaralle, impr. y libreria de Mayo, 1870–74. Vol. 5 of *Obras completas de Esteban Echeverría*.

Edwards, Philip. Introduction. *The Journals of Captain Cook*. By James Cook. London: Penguin, 1999.

Eisenberg, Nancy, and Janet Strayer. *Empathy and Its Development*. Cambridge: Cambridge University Press, 1987.

English, James. "Prizes and the Politics of World Culture." *The Economy of Prestige. Prizes, Awards and the Circulation of Cultural Value*. Cambridge, MA: Harvard University Press, 2005.

Erskine, Toni. *Embedded Cosmopolitanism: Duties to Strangers in a World of "Dislocated Communities."* Oxford: Oxford University Press, 2008.

Eujanian, Alejandro. "Estudio preliminar." *Los que pasaban*. By Paul Groussac. Buenos Aires, Taurus, 2001. 9–35.

Faris, Wendy B. *Ordinary Enchantments: Magical Realism and the Remystification of Narrative*. Nashville: Vanderbilt University Press, 2004.

———. "The Question of the Other: Cultural Critiques of Magical Realism." *Janus Head* 5.2 (2002): 101–19.

Fass Emery, Amy. *The Anthropological Imagination in Latin American Literature*. Columbia: University of Missouri Press, 1996.

Fernández Cifuentes, Luis. "Cartografías del 98: Fin de siglo, identidad nacional y diálogo con América." *Anales de la Literatura Española Contemporánea* 23.1 (1998): 117–45.

Fernández Retamar, Roberto. "Caliban: Notes towards a Discussion of Culture in *Our America*." *Caliban and Other Essays*. Trans. Edward Baker. Minneapolis: University of Minnesota Press, 1989.

———. *"Nuestra América": Cien años y otros acercamientos a Martí*. Havana: Editorial Si-Mar, 1995.

———. *Todo Calibán*. Buenos Aires: CLACSO, 2004.

Flores, Ángel. "Magical Realism in Spanish American Fiction." Zamora and Faris, *Magical Realism* 109–17.

Fojas, Camilla. *Cosmopolitanism in the Americas*. West Lafayette: Purdue University Press, 2005.

Fombona, Jacinto. *La Europa necesaria: Textos de viaje de la época modernista*. Rosario: Beatriz Viterbo, 2005.

Foucault, Michel. "What Is an Author?" *The Foucault Reader*. Ed. Paul Rabinow. New York: Pantheon Books, 1984.

Franco, Jean. *The Decline and Fall of the Lettered City: Latin America during the Cold War.* Cambridge, MA: Harvard University Press, 2002.
Freud, Sigmund. *The Ego and the Id.* London: Horgarth Press, 1949.
———. “Mourning and Melancholia.” *The Freud Reader.* Ed. Peter Gay. New York: W. W. Norton, 1989.
Friedman, Susan Stanford. *Mappings: Feminism and the Cultural Geographies of Encounter.* Princeton: Princeton University Press, 1998.
Friedman, Thomas L. *The World Is Flat: A Brief History of the Twentieth-first Century.* New York: Farrar, Strauss and Giroux, 2005.
Fuguet, Alberto. “I Am Not a Magic Realist.” *Salon,* June 11, 2007. www.salon.com/1997/06/11/magicalintro/.
Fuguet, Alberto, and Sergio Gómez, eds. *Cuentos con Walkman.* Santiago: Planeta, 1993.
———, eds. *McOndo.* Barcelona: Grijalbo Mondadori, 1996.
Gagnière, Claude. “Préface.” *Romans d'ailleurs.* By Pierre Loti. Paris: Omnibus, 2011.
García Márquez, Gabriel. *Leaf Storm, and Other Stories.* Trans. Gregory Rabassa. New York: Harper and Row, 1972.
———. *No One Writes to the Colonel, and Other Stories.* Trans. J. S. Bernstein. New York: Harper and Row, 1979.
———. *One Hundred Years of Solitude.* Trans. Gregory Rabassa. New York: Harper Collins, 2004.
———. “The Solitude of Latin America.” Nobel lecture, 8 Dec. 1982. www.nobelprize.org/nobel_prizes/literature/laureates/1982/marquez-lecture.html.
Gasparini, Sandra, and Claudia Román, eds. *El tipo más original y otras páginas.* By Eduardo L. Holmberg. Buenos Aires: Ediciones Simurg, 2001.
Gilman, Sander. *The Jew's Body.* New York: Routledge, 1991.
Girardet, Raoul. *L'idée coloniale en France de 1871 a 1962.* Paris: La table ronde, 1972.
Gómez Carrillo, Enrique. “Alejandro Pouchkine.” *Literatura extranjera.* 71–86.
———. *Almas y cerebros: Historias sentimentales, intimidades parisienses, etc.* Paris: Garnier Hermanos, 1898.
———. “Un cuentista alemán.” *Literatura extranjera.* 31–40.
———. “Cuentos albaneses.” *Literaturas exóticas.* Madrid: Editorial Mundo Latino, 1920.
———. “Del exoticismo.” *Literatura extranjera.* 87–100.
———. *De Marsella a Tokio: Sensaciones de Egipto, la India, la China y el Japón.* Paris: Garnier Hermanos, 1906.
———. “Dos obras japonesas.” *Literaturas exóticas.* Madrid: Editorial Mundo Latino, 1920.
———. *El encanto de Buenos Aires.* Madrid: Mundo Latino, 1919.
———. *Esquisses.* Paris: Garnier Hermanos, 1892.
———. *Fez, la andaluza.* Madrid: Ed. Renacimiento, Imprenta Latina, 1926.
———. “Gabriel D'Annunzio.” *Literatura extranjera.* 253–59.
———. “Gerhardt Hauptmann.” *Literatura extranjera.* 13–30.

———. *La Grecia eterna*. Preface by Jean Moréas. Sevilla: Renacimiento, 2010.
———. "Henrik Ibsen." *Literatura extranjera*. 205–52.
———. *Jerusalén y la Tierra Santa*. Guatemala: Ministerio de Educación, 1965.
———. *Literatura extranjera*. Paris: Garnier Hermanos, 1895.
———. *Literaturas exóticas*. Madrid: Editorial Mundo Latino, 1920.
———. "Notas dispersas sobre los maestros nuevos." *Literatura extranjera*. 317–42.
———. "Notas sobre la enfermedad de la sensación desde el punto de vista de la literatura." *Almas y cerebros: Historias sentimentales, intimidades parisienses, etc.* Paris: Garnier Hermanos, 1898.
———. "La psicología del viajero." *Pequeñas cuestiones palpitantes*. Madrid: Librería de los sucesores de Hernando, 1910.
———. "Los poetas jóvenes de Francia." *Literatura extranjera*. 133–204.
———. *Romerías*. Paris: Garnier Frères, 1912.
———. *La Rusia actual*. Paris: Garnier Hermanos, 1906.
———. "Sensaciones de Argelia." *Cómo se pasa la vida*. Paris: Garnier Hermanos, 1907.
———. *Sensaciones de arte*. Paris: Biblioteca Azul, 1893.
———. *Sensaciones de París y Madrid*. Paris: Garnier Hermanos, 1900.
———. *Sensaciones de Rusia: Paisaje de Alemania*. Barcelona: Ed. Colección Libros Modernos, 1905.
———. "Los siete maestros." *Literatura extranjera*. 309–16.
———. *La sonrisa de la esfinge: Sensaciones de Egipto*. Madrid: Renacimiento, 1913.
———. "El teatro griego moderno." *Literaturas exóticas*. Madrid: Editorial Mundo Latino, 1920.
———. "Una visita a Max Nordau." *Almas y cerebros: Historias sentimentales, intimidades parisienses, etc.* París: Garnier Hermanos, 1898.
———. "Una visita a Oscar Wilde." *Almas y cerebros: Historias sentimentales, intimidades parisienses, etc.* Paris: Garnier Hermanos, 1898.
———. "Walt Whitman." *Literatura extranjera*. 51–58.
González, Aníbal. *A Companion to Spanish American Modernismo*. Woodbridge: Tamesis, 2007.
———. *La crónica modernista hispanoamericana*. Madrid: J. Porrúa Turanzas, 1983.
González Echevarría, Roberto. *Alejo Carpentier: El peregrino en su patria*. 2nd ed. Madrid: Gredos, 2004.
———. *Alejo Carpentier: The Pilgrim at Home*. Ithaca: Cornell University Press, 1977.
González Prada, Manuel. "Conferencia en el Ateneo de Lima." *Páginas libres*. Paris: Tipografía de Paul Dupont, 1894.
———. "Cosmopolitanismo." *Minúsculas*. Lima: Tipográfica de "El Lucero," 1909.
———. "Lecture at the Atheneum in Lima." *Free Pages and Other Essays: Anarchist Musings*. Trans. Frederick H. Fornoff. Oxford: Oxford University Press, 2003.

Graff Zivin, Erin. *The Wandering Signifier: Rhetoric of Jewishness in The Latin American Imaginary*. Durham: Duke University Press, 2008.

Gramsci, Antonio. "Hegemony of Western Culture over the Whole World Culture." *Selections from the Prison Notebooks*. Ed. and trans. Quintin Hoare and Geoffrey Nowell-Smith. New York: International Publishers, 1971.

———. *Selections from Cultural Writings*. Ed. David Forgacs and Geoffrey Nowell-Smith. Trans. William Boelhower. Cambridge, MA: Harvard University Press, 1985.

Groussac, Paul. "Alphonse Daudet." *Jorge Luis Borges Selecciona lo mejor de Paul Groussac*. Ed. Jorge Luis Borges. Buenos Aires: Editorial Fraterna, 1981.

———. "Dos juicios de Groussac y una respuesta de Darío." *Nosotros: Revista de Letras, Arte, Historia, Filosofía y Ciencias Sociales*, Feb. 1916.

———. "El Gaucho." *Jorge Luis Borges selecciona lo mejor de Paul Groussac*. Ed. Jorge Luis Borges. Buenos Aires: Editorial Fraterna, 1981.

———. *Los que pasaban*. Buenos Aires: CEAL, 1980.

———. "Los raros." *La Biblioteca*, Nov. 1896, 474–80.

———. "Prosas profanas." *La Biblioteca*, Jan. 1897, 156–60.

Guenther, Irene. "Magic Realism in the Weimar Republic." Zamora and Faris, *Magical Realism* 33–73.

Gutiérrez Girardot, Rafael. "La literatura colombiana en el siglo XX." *Manual de historia de Colombia*. Vol. 3. Ed. Juan Gustavo Cob-Borda and Santiago Mutis Durán. Bogotá: Instituto Colombiano de Cultura, 1979.

Gutiérrez Nájera, Manuel. "El cruzamiento en literatura." *Crítica literaria*. Ed. E. K. Mapes and Ernesto Mejía Sánchez. Introd. Porfirio MartínezPeñaloza. Mexico City: UNAM, 1959. Vol. 1 of *Obras*.

———. "Literatura propia y literatura nacional." *Crítica literaria*. Ed. E. K. Mapes y Ernesto Mejía Sánchez. Introd. Porfirio Martínez Peñaloza. Mexico City: UNAM, 1959. Vol. 1 of *Obras*.

———. "Los toros de noche." *Cuentos, crónicas y ensayos*. México: Universidad Autónoma Nacional.

Hand, Seàn. *Emmanuel Levinas*. London: Routledge, 2009.

Harootunian, Harry. "The Exotics of Nowhere." *Essay on Exoticism: An Aesthetic of Diversity*. By Victor Segalen. Ed. and trans. Yaël Rachel Schlink. Foreword by Harry Harootunian. Durham: Duke University Press, 2002.

Harris, Ruth. *Dreyfus: Politics, Emotion, and the Scandal of the Century*. New York: Metropolitan Books / Henry Holt, 2010.

Hayot, Eric. *On Literary Worlds*. New York: Oxford University Press, 2012.

Haywood Ferreyra, Rachel. *The Emergence of Latin American Science Fiction*. Middletown: Wesleyan University Press, 2011.

Hegel, G. W. F. *Elements of the Philosophy of Right*. Ed. Allen W. Wood. Trans. H. B. Nisbet. New York: Cambridge University Press, 1991.

———. *Phenomenology of Spirit*. Ed. J. N. Findlay. Trans. A. V. Miller. Oxford: Oxford University Press, 1977.

Henríquez Ureña, Max. *Breve historia del modernismo*. Mexico City: Fondo de Cultura Económica, 1954.

Henríquez Ureña, Pedro. "Literatura contemporánea de la América española." *La utopía de América*. Caracas: Biblioteca Ayacucho, 1978.

———. *Seis ensayos en busca de nuestra expresión*. Buenos Aires: Biblioteca Argentina de Buenas Ediciones Literarias, 1928.

Herder, Johann Gottfried. "Results of the Comparison of Different People's Poetry in Ancient and Modern Times." *Princeton Sourcebook in Comparative Literature*. Ed. David Damrosch, Natalie Melas, and Mbongiseni Buthelezi. Princeton: Princeton University Press, 2009.

Heredia, José María. "Les bergers." *Les trophées*. Paris: Société d'édition "Les Belles Lettres," 1984. Vol. 1 of *Oeuvres poétiques completes de José María Heredia*.

Hervey de Saint-Denys, Marquis d'. *Poésies de l'époque des Thang*. Paris: Amyot, 1862.

Hobsbawm, Eric. *The Age of Empire, 1875–1914*. New York: Vintage Books, 1989.

Hodgins, Jack. *The Invention of the World*. Toronto: Macmillan of Canada, 1977.

Holmberg, Eduardo L. *Viaje maravilloso del señor Nic-Nac al planeta Marte*. Ed. Pablo Crash Solomonoff. Buenos Aires: Colihue, Biblioteca Nacional de la República Argentina, 2006.

Hubert, Rosario. "Disorientations: Latin American Diversions of East Asia." Diss., Harvard University, 2014.

Infante, Angel Gustavo. "Estética de la rebelión: Los manifiestos literarios." *Nación y literatura: Itinerarios de la palabra escrita en la literatura venezolana*. Ed. Carlos Pacheco, Luis Barrera Linares, and Beatriz González Stephan. Caracas: Editorial Equinoccio, 2006.

Jameson, Fredric. "A Brief Response [to Aijaz Ahmad]." *Social Text* 17 (Autumn 1987).

———. "New Literary History after the End of the New." *New Literary History* 39 (2008): 375–87.

———. "On Magic Realism in Film." *Signatures of the Visible*. New York: Routledge, 1990.

———. "Third-World Literature in the Era of Multinational Capitalism." *Social Text* 15 (Autumn 1986): 65–88.

Josiowicz, Alejandra. "Cosmopolitismo y decadentismo en la literatura latinoamericana: Rama (re)lee a Martí junto a Rimbaud." *Nómadas: Revista de Crítica de Ciencias Sociales y Jurídicas* 18.2 (2008): 1–13.

Jrade, Cathy. *Modernismo, Modernity, and the Development of Spanish American Literature*. Austin: University of Texas Press, 1998.

Kadir, Djelal. "Comparative Literature in an Age of Terrorism." *Comparative Literature in an Age of Globalization*. Ed. Haun Saussy. Baltimore: Johns Hopkins University Press, 2006. 68–77.

———. *The Other Writing: Postcolonial Essays in Latin America's Writing Culture*. West Lafayette: Purdue University Press, 1993.

———. "World Literature and Latin American Literature." D'haen, Damrosch, and Kadir 435–43.

Kant, Immanuel. "An Answer to the Question: What Is Enlightenment?" *Political Writings*. Ed. Hans Reiss. Trans. H. B. Nisbet. New York: Cambridge University Press, 1991.

———. "Idea for a Universal History with a Cosmopolitan Purpose." *Political Writings*. Ed. Hans Reiss. Trans. H. B. Nisbet. New York: Cambridge University Press, 1991.

———. "Perpetual Peace: A Philosophical Sketch." *Political Writings*. Ed. Hans Reiss. Trans. H. B. Nisbet. New York: Cambridge University Press, 1991.

Kennedy, William. "Review of *One Hundred Years of Solitude*." *National Review* 20 Apr. 1970.

Kirkpatrick, Gwen. *The Dissonant Legacy of Modernismo: Lugones, Herrera y Reissig, and the Voices of Modern Spanish American Poetry*. Berkeley: University of California Press, 1989.

Kristal, Efraín. "Considering Coldly . . ." *New Left Review* 15 (May–June 2002).

Kroetsch, Robert. *What the Crow Said*. Edmonton: University of Alberta Press, 1988.

Lacan, Jacques. *The Ego in Freud's Theory and In the Technique of Psychoanalysis, 1954–1955*. Ed. Jacque-Alain Miller. Trans. Sylvana Tomaselli. Notes by John Forrester. Cambridge: Cambridge University Press, 1988. Vol. 2 of *The Seminar of Jacques Lacan*.

———. *The Ethics of Psychoanalysis*. Ed. Jacques-Alan Miller. Trans. Dennis Porter. New York: W. W. Norton, 1992. Vol. 7 of *The Seminar of Jacques Lacan*.

———. "The Mirror Stage as Formative of the Function of the I as Revealed in Psychoanalytic Experience." Écrits: A Selection. Trans. Alan Sheridan. New York: Norton, 1977.

———. *The Other Side of Psychoanalysis*. Trans. Russell Grieg. New York: W. W. Norton, 2007. Vol. 17 of *The Seminar of Jacques Lacan*.

Laclau, Ernesto. *Emancipations*. London: Verso, 1998.

Laera, Alejandra. *El tiempo vacío de la ficción: Las novelas argentinas de Eduardo Gutiérrez y Eugenio Cambaceres*. Buenos Aires: Fondo de Cultura Económica, 2004.

Larsen, Svend Erik. "Georg Brandes: The Telescope of Comparative Literature." D'haen, Damrosch, and Kadir 21–31.

Leal, Luis. "Magical Realism in Spanish American." Trans. Wendy B. Faris. Zamora and Faris, *Magical Realism* 119–24.

Levinas, Emmanuel. *Totality and Infinity*. Trans. A. Lingis. Pittsburgh: Duquesne University Press, 1969.

Lionnet, Françoise. "World Literature, Francophonie, and Creole Cosmopolitics." D'haen, Damrosch, and Kadir 325–35.

Lisboa, Henrique. *A china e os chins: Recordações de viagem*. Montevideo: Typográfica a vapor de A. Godel, 1888.

Lomnitz, Claudio. "Los intelectuales y el poder político: La representación de los científicos en México del porfiriato a la revolución." *La ciudad letrada de la conquista al modernismo*. Ed. Carlos Altamirano and Jorge Myers. Buenos Aires: Katz Editores, 2008. Vol. 1 of *Historia de los intelectuales en América Latina*.

Ludmer, Josefina. *Cien años de soledad: Una interpretación*. Buenos Aires: Editorial Tiempo Contemporáneo, 1972.

Mariátegui, José Carlos. *Seven Interpretive Essays on Peruvian Reality*. Trans. Marjory Urquidi. Austin: University of Texas Press, 1974.

———. *Siete ensayos de interpretación de la realidad peruana*. Prologue by Carlos Quijano. Notes by Elizabeth Garrels. Caracas: Fundación Biblioteca Ayacucho, 2007.

Marinello, Juan. *18 ensayos martianos*. Havana: Editora Política, 1980.

Martí, José. "A José Joaquín Palma." *Obras completas*. Vol. 5. Havana: Editorial de Ciencias Sociales, 1963.

———. "El carácter de la *Revista Venezolana*." *Obras completas*. Vol. 7. Havana: Editorial de Ciencias Sociales, 1963.

———. "Nuestra América." *Nuestra América*. Prologue by Juan Marinello. Ed. Hugo Achúgar. Caracas: Biblioteca Ayacucho, 1977.

———. "Oscar Wilde." *Obra literaria*. Ed. Cintio Vitier. Caracas: Biblioteca Ayacucho, 1978.

———. "Oscar Wilde." *The America of José Martí. Selected Writings of José Martí*. Trans. Juan de Onís. New York: Noonday Press, 1953.

———. "Our America." *The America of José Martí. Selected Writings of José Martí*. Trans. Juan de Onís. New York: Noonday Press, 1953.

Martin, Gerald. Introduction. *Men of Maize*. By Miguel Ángel Asturias. Trans. Gerald Martin. London: Verso, 1988.

———. *Journeys through the Labyrinth: Latin American Fiction in the Twentieth Century*. London: Verso, 1989.

Martínez, José María. "Un duque en la corte del Rey Burgués: Positivismo y porfirismo en la narrativa de Gutiérrez Nájera." *Bulletin of Spanish Studies* 84.2 (2007): 207–21.

———. "Entre la lámpara y el espejo: La imaginación modernista de Manuel Gutiérrez Nájera." *Revista Canadiense de Estudios Hispánicos* 32.2 (2008): 247–69.

Marx, Karl. "Economic and Philosophical Manuscripts of 1844." *Early Writings*. Harmondsworth: Penguin, 1975.

———. "On the Jewish Question." *The Marx-Engels Reader*. Ed. Robert C. Tucker. New York: W. W. Norton, 1972.

Marx, Karl, and Friedrich Engels. "The Manifesto of the Communist Party." *The Marx-Engels Reader*. 2nd ed. Edited by Robert C. Tucker. New York: W. W. Norton, 1979.

Mata, Rodolfo. "Prólogo." *En el país del sol*. By Juan José Tabalada. Ed. Rodolfo Mata. Mexico City: UNAM, 2005.

Mejías-López, Alejandro. *The Inverted Conquest. The Myth of Modernity and the Transatlantic Onset of Modernism*. Nashville: Vanderbilt University Press, 2009.

Menton, Seymour. *Historia verdadera del realismo mágico*. Mexico City: Fondo de Cultura Económica, 1998.

Merimée, Prosper. *Carmen*. Paris: Encre, 1984.

Meunier, Philippe. *De l'Espagne aux représentations ibériques et ibéro-americaines de l'exotisme*. Saint-Etienne: Publications de l'Université de Saint-Etienne, 2010.

Mill, H. R. *Siege of the South Pole*. New York: Frederick A. Stokes, 1905.

Molloy, Sylvia. "Conciencia del público y conciencia del yo en el primer Darío." *Revista Iberoamericana* 45.108–9 (July–Aug. 1979): 443–57.

———. *La diffusion de littérature hispano-américaine en France au XXe siècle*. Paris: Presses universitaires de France, 1972.

———. "His America, Our America: José Martí Reads Whitman." *Modern Language Quarterly* 57.2 (1996): 369–79.

———. "Lost in Translation: Borges, the Western Tradition and Fictions of Latin America." *Borges and Europe Revisited*. Ed. Evelyn Fishburn. London: Institute of Latin American Studies, University of London, 1999.

———. "Postcolonial Latin America and the Magical Realist Imperative: A Report to an Academy." *Nation, Language, and the Ethics of Translation*. Ed. Sandra Berman and Michael Wood. Princeton: Princeton University Press, 2005. 370–79.

———. "Too Wilde for Comfort: Desire and Ideology in Fin-de-Siecle Spanish America." *Social Text* 31/32 (1992): 187–201.

———. "Voracidad y solipsismo en la poesía de Darío." *Sin Nombre* 11.3 (1980): 7–15.

Monguió, Luis. "De la problemática del modernismo: La crítica y el 'cosmopolitismo.'" *Revista Iberoamericana* 28.53 (Jan.–June 1962).

———. "El origen de unos versos de 'A Roosevelt.'" *Hispania* 38.4 (Sept. 1955): 424–26.

Montaldo, Graciela. "La expulsión de la república, la deserción del mundo." Sánchez Prado, *América Latina* 255–70.

———. *Ficciones culturales y fábulas de identidad en América Latina*. Rosario: Beatriz Viterbo, 1999.

———. *La sensibilidad amenazada: Fin de siglo y modernismo*. Rosario: Beatriz Viterbo, 1994.

Mora, Luis María. *Los contertulios de la Gruta Simbólica*. Bogotá: Editorial Minerva, 1936.

Morales, Mario Roberto. "Miguel Ángel Asturias: La estética y la política de la interculturalidad." *Cuentos y leyendas*. By Miguel Ángel Asturias. Ed. Mario Roberto Morales. San José: Editorial Universidad de Costa Rica, 2000.

Morán, Francisco. "Volutas del deseo: Hacia una lectura del orientalismo en el modernismo hispanoamericano." *Modern Language Notes* 120.2 (2005): 383–407.

Moraña, Mabel. "'A río revuelto, ganancia de pescadores': América Latina y el *déjà-vu* de la literatura mundial." Sánchez Prado, *América Latina* 319–36.

Morazé, Charles. *Les bourgeois conquérants*. Paris: Librairie Armand Colin, 1957.

Moré, Belford. *Saberes y autoridades: Institución de la literatura venezolana (1890–1910)*. Caracas: Fondo Editorial La Nave Va, 2002.

Moreiras, Alberto. *The Exhaustion of Difference: The Politics of Latin American Cultural Studies*. Durham: Duke University Press, 2001.

Moretti, Franco. "Conjectures on World Literature." *New Left Review* 1 (2000): 55–67.

———. *The Modern Epic: The World-System from Goethe to García Márquez*. Trans. Quintin Hoare. London: Verso, 1996.

———, ed. *The Novel*. 2 vols. Princeton: Princeton University Press, 2006.

Morrison, Toni. *Beloved*. New York: Knopf, 1987.

Mufti, Aamir R. *Enlightenment in the Colony. The Jewish Question and the Crisis of Postcolonial Culture*. Princeton: Princeton University Press, 2007.

Nabuco, Joaquim. *Minha formação*. Paris e Rio de Janeiro: Garnier, 1900.

———. *My Formative Years*. Ed. Leslie Bethell. Trans. Christopher Peterson. Oxford: Signal; Rio de Janeiro: Bem-Te-Vi, 2012.

Nancy, Jean-Luc. *The Creation of the World, or, Globalization*. Trans. François Raffoul and David Pettigrew. Albany: State University of New York Press, 2007.

Nervo, Amado. "Entrevista con Gómez Carrillo: Una condecoración de la legión de honor." *Obras completas*. Vol. 1. Ed. Francisco González Guerrero and Alfonso Méndez Plancarte. Madrid: Aguilar, 1955–56.

Novalis (Friedrich von Hardenbergs). *Schriften*. Vol. 3. Ed. Paul Kluckhohn and Richard Samuel. Stuttgart: W. Kohlhammer, 1960–88.

Nussbaum, Martha. *For Love of Country*? Ed. Joshua Cohen. Boston: Beacon Press, 1996.

———. "Patriotism and Cosmopolitanism." *Boston Review* 19.5 (Oct.–Nov. 1994).

Okri, Ben. *The Famished Road*. New York: Anchor Books, 1993.

Onís, Federico de. "Prólogo." *Antología de la poesía española e hispanoamericana, 1882–1932*. New York: Las Americas, 1961.

Pacheco, José Emilio. "Manuel Gutiérrez Nájera: El sueño de una noche porifiriana." *Letras Libres* 14 (Feb. 2000): 20–23.

Pagés Larraya, Antonio, ed. *Cuentos fantásticos*. By Eduardo L. Holmberg. Buenos Aires: Hachette, 1957.

Pailler, Claire. "Rubén Darío y Dreyfus: Confusión y desencuentro." *Caravalle: Cahiers du Mondo Hispanique et Luso Brésilien* 98 (2012): 203–12.

Palencia-Roth, Michael. *Gabriel García Márquez: La línea, el círculo y las metamorfosis del mito*. Madrid: Gredos, 1983.

Pavie, Théodore. *Choix de contes et nouvelles traduits du Chinois*. Paris: Librairie de Benjamin Duprat, 1839.

Paz, Octavio. *Cuadrivio: Darío, López Velarde, Pessoa, Cernuda*. Mexico City: Joaquín Mórtiz, 1965.

———. *Los hijos del limo: Del romanticismo a las vanguardias*. Barcelona: Seix Barral, 1974.

———. *The Siren and the Seashell and Other Essays on Poets and Poetry*. Trans. Lysander Kemp and Margaret Sayers Peden. Austin: University of Texas Press, 1976.

Pérez Firmat, Gustavo. *The Cuban Condition: Translation and Identity in Modern Cuban Literature*. Cambridge: Cambridge University Press, 1989.

Pérus, Françoise. *Literatura y sociedad en América Latina*. Mexico City: Siglo Veintiuno Editores, 1976.

Phillips, Allen W. "Rubén Darío y sus juicios sobre el modernismo." *Estudios críticos sobre el modernismo*. Ed. Homero Castillo. Gredos: Madrid, 1968.

Picón, Jacinto Octavio. "Prólogo." *Literatura extranjera*. By Enrique Gómez Carrillo. Paris: Garnier Hermanos, 1895.

Piglia, Ricardo. "Sarmiento the Writer." *Sarmiento: Author of a Nation*. Ed. Tulio Halperín Donghi, Iván Jaksic, Gwen Kirkpatrick, and Francine Masiello. Berkeley: University of California Press, 1994.

Pizer, John. "Johann Wolfgang von Goethe: Origins and Relevance of *Weltliteratur*." D'haen, Damrosch, and Kadir 3–11.

Portuondo, José Antonio. *Martí, escritor revolucionario*. Havana: Editora Política, 1982.

Prendergast, Christopher, ed. *Debating World Literature*. London: Verso, 2004.

Prieto, Adolfo. "La generación del ochenta: La imaginación." *Capítulo: La historia de la literatura argentina*. Buenos Aires: CEAL, 1967. 457–80.

Prieto, René. "The literature of *indigenismo*." *Cambridge History of Latin American Literature*. Vol. 2. Ed. Roberto González Echevarría and Enrique Pupo-Walker. Cambridge: Cambridge University Press, 1996.

Puchner, Martin, ed. *The Norton Anthology of World Literature*. 3rd ed. 6 vols. New York: Norton, 2012.

———. *Poetry of the Revolution: Marx, Manifestos and the Avant-Gardes*. Princeton: Princeton University Press, 2006.

Quayson, Ato. "Fecundities of the Unexpected: Magical Realism, Narrative, and History." *History, Geography, and Culture*. Ed. Franco Moretti, 726–56. Princeton: Princeton University Press, 2006. Vol 1 of *The Novel*.

———. *Strategic Transformations of Nigerian Writing: Rev. Samuel Johnson, Amos Tutuola, Wole Soyinka, Ben Okri*. Bloomington: Indiana University Press, 1997.

Rama, Ángel. "El Boom en perspectiva." *Más allá del Boom: Literatura y mercado*. Buenos Aires: Folios, 1984.

———. *Edificación de un arte nacional y popular: La narrativa de Gabriel García Márquez*. Bogotá: Colcultura, 1991.

———. "José Martí en el eje de la modernización poética: Whitman, Lautréamont, Rimbaud." *Nueva Revista de Filología Hispánica* 32 (1983): 96–135.

———. *Las máscaras democráticas del modernismo*. Montevideo: Arca Editorial, 1985.

———. "Los procesos de transculturación en la narrativa latinoamericana." *La novela en América Latina*. Bogotá: Instituto Colombiano de Cultura, 1982.

———. "Processes of Transculturation in Latin American Narrative." Trans. Melissa Meore. *Journal of Latin American Culture Studies* 6.2 (Nov. 1997): 155–71.

———. *Rubén Darío y el modernismo*. Caracas: Ediciones de la Biblioteca de la Universidad Central de Venezuela, 1970.

———. *Transculturación narrativa en América Latina*. Mexico City: Siglo Veintiuno Editores, 1982.

Ramos, Julio. *Divergent Modernities: Culture and Politics in Nineteenth-Century Latin America*. Trans. John D. Blanco. Durham: Duke University Press, 2001.

Real de Azúa, Carlos. "Ambiente espiritual del 900." *Número* 6–8 (Jan.–June 1950).

Rebolledo, Efrén. *Hojas de bambú*. Mexico City: Editorial Nacional, 1910.

———. *Nikko*. Mexico City: Tipográfica Díaz de León, 1910.

Reiss, Timothy J. *Against Autonomy. Global Dialectics of cultural exchange*. Stanford: Stanford University Press, 2002.

Rimbaud, Arthur. *Complete Works. Selected Letters. A Bilingual Edition*. Trans. Wallace Fowlie. Chicago: University of Chicago Press, 2005.

———. "Lettres dittes 'du Voyant.'" *Poesies. Une Saison en enfer. Illuminations*. Ed. Louis Forestier. Paris: Gallimard, 1984.

Rincón, Carlos. "Streams Out of Control: The Latin American Plot." *Streams of Cultural Capital*. Ed. David Palumbo Liu and Sepp Gumbrecht. Palo Alto: Stanford University Press, 1997.

Robbins, Bruce. "Comparative Cosmopolitanisms." *Cosmopolitics: Thinking and Feeling beyond the Nation*. Minneapolis: University of Minnesota Press, 1998.

———. "Uses of World Literature." D'haen, Damrosch, and Kadir 383–92.

Rodó, José Enrique. *Obras completas*. Vol. 2. Ed. José Pedro Segundo and Juan Antonio Zubillaga. Montevideo: Barreiro y Ramos, 1956.

———. *Rubén Darío, su personalidad literaria*. Montevideo: Imprenta de Dornaleche y Reyes, 1899.

Rodríguez García, José María. *The City of Translation: Poetry and Ideology in Nineteenth-Century Colombia*. New York: Palgrave Macmillan, 2010.

Rodríguez Pérsico, Adriana. "'Las reliquias del banquete' darwinista: E. Holmberg, escritor y científico." *Modern Language Notes* 116.2 (2001): 371–91.

Roh, Franz. *German Art in the 20th Century*. With additions by Juliane Roh. Ed. Julia Phelps. Trans. Catherine Hutter. Greenwich, CT: New York Graphic Society, 1968.

———. "Magic Realism: Post-expressionism." Zamora and Faris, *Magical Realism* 15–31.

———. *Nach-expressionismus; magischer Realismus: Probleme der neuesten Europäischen Malerei*. Leipzig: Klinkhardt and Biermann, 1925.

Rosenberg, Fernando J. *The Avant-Garde and Geopolitics in Latin America*. Pittsburgh: Pittsburgh University Press, 2006.

Rosenblatt, Angel. "Rastacueros y arrastracueros (buenas y malas palabras)." *El Nacional* (Caracas, Venezuela) 6 Jan. 1955.

Ruiz, Jorge Eliécer. "Prólogo." *Más arriba del reino; La otra raya del tigre*. By Pedro Gómez Valderrama. Caracas: Biblioteca Ayacucho, 1977.

Rulfo, Juan. *Pedro Páramo*. Trans. Margaret Sayers Peden. New York: Grover Press, 1994.

Rushdie, Salman. "Inverted Realism." *PEN America* 6, *Metamorphoses* (Oct. 2003). www.pen.org/viewmedia.php/prmMID/1153/prmID/1376.
———. *Midnight's Children*. London: Penguin, 1991.
Saavedra Molina, Julio. "Nota a *La oda de Francia*." *Poesías y prosas raras*. By Rubén Darío. Ed. Julio Saavedra Molina. Santiago: Prensas de la Universidad de Chile, 1938.
Saer, Juan José. "La espesa selva de lo real." *El concepto de ficción*. Buenos Aires: Ariel, 1997.
———. "Una literatura sin atributos." *El concepto de ficción*. Buenos Aires: Ariel, 1997.
Said, Edward W. *Orientalism*. New York: Pantheon Books, 1978.
Saldívar, José David. *The Dialectics of Our America: Genealogy, Cultural Critique and Literary History*. Durham: Duke University Press, 1991.
Salinas, Pedro. *La poesía de Rubén Darío: Ensayo sobre el tema y los temas del poeta*. Buenos Aires: Losada, 1948.
Sánchez Prado, Ignacio, ed. *América Latina en la "literatura mundial."* Pittsburgh, PA: Instituto Internacional de Literatura Iberoamericana, 2006.
———. "'Hijos de Metapa': Un recorrido conceptual de la literatura mundial (a manera de introducción)." Sánchez Prado, *América Latina* 7–46.
Sanín Cano, Baldomero. "Bajo el signo de marte." *Escritos*. Ed. J. G. Cobo Borda. Bogota: Instituto Colombiano de Cultura, 1977.
———. "De lo exótico." *Escritos*. Ed. J. G. Cobo Borda. Bogota: Instituto Colombiano de Cultura, 1977.
———. *De mi vida y otras vidas*. Bogotá: Ediciones Revista de América, 1949.
———. *Divagaciones filológicas y apólogos literarios*. Manizales: Casa Editorial Arturo Zapata, 1934.
———. "¿Existe la literatura hispanoamericana?" *Escritos*. Ed. J. G. Cobo Borda. Bogota: Instituto Colombiano de Cultura, 1977.
———. "Influencias de Europa sobre la cultura de la América española." *El oficio del lector*. Ed. J. G. Cobo Borda. Caracas: Biblioteca Ayacucho, 1978.
———. "Jorge Brandes." *Escritos*. Ed. J. G. Cobo Borda. Bogota: Instituto Colombiano de Cultura, 1977.
———. "Jorge Brandes, o el reinado de la inteligencia." *Ensayos*. Bogota: Editorial ABC, 1942.
———. *Letras colombianas*. Mexico: Fondo de Cultura Económica, 1944.
———. "Menéndez Pelayo." *El oficio del lector*. Ed. J. G. Cobo Borda. Caracas: Biblioteca Ayacucho, 1978.
———. "Nietszche y Brandes." *La civilización manual y otros ensayos*. Buenos Aires: Editorial Babel, 1925.
Santaella, Juan Carlos, ed. *Diez manifiestos literarios venezolanos*. Caracas: La Casa de Bello, 1986.
Santana, Mario. *Foreigners in the Homeland: The Spanish American New Novel in Spain, 1962–1974*. Lewisburg: Bucknell University Press, 2000.
Santiago, Silviano. *O cosmopolitismo do pobre*. Belo Horizonte: Editora UFMG, 2004.
Sarlo, Beatriz. *Borges, a Writer on the Edge*. London: Verso, 1993.

———. *Borges, un escritor en las orillas.* Buenos Aires: Ariel, 1995.

———. "Sobre la vanguardia, Borges y el criollismo." *Punto de Vista* 4.11 (1981).

———. *Una modernindad periférica: Buenos Aires, 1920–1930.* Buenos Aires: Nueva Visión, 1988.

Sarmiento, Domingo F. *Viajes.* Buenos Aires: Editorial de Belgrano, 1981.

Saussy, Haun. "Exquisite Cadavers Stitched from Fresh Nightmares: Of Memes, Hives, and Selfish Genes." *Comparative Literature in an Age of Globalization.* Ed. Haun Saussy. Baltimore: John Hopkins University Press, 2006.

Scarano, Tomasso. "Notes on Spanish-American Magical Realism." *Coterminous Worlds: Magical Realism and Contemporary Post-colonial Literature in English.* Ed. Elisa Linguanti, Francesco Casotti, and Carmen Concilio. Amsterdam: Rodopi, 1999.

Schulman, Iván A. "José Martí y las estrategias del discurso (contra)moderno." *El proyecto inconcluso: La vigencia del modernismo.* Mexico City: Siglo Veintiuno, 2002.

———. "Más allá de la gracia: La modernidad de Manuel Gutiérrez Nájera." *El proyecto inconcluso: La vigencia del modernismo.* Mexico: Siglo Veintiuno, 2002.

———. *Nuevos asedios al modernismo.* Madrid: Taurus, 1987.

Schwartz, Jorge. *Vanguardia y cosmopolitismo en la década del veinte: Oliverio Girondo y Oswald de Andrade.* Rosario: Beatriz Viterbo Editora, 1993.

Schwartz, Marcy E. *Writing Paris: Urban Topographies of Desire in Contemporary Latin American Fiction.* Albany: SUNY Press, 1999.

Schwarz, Roberto. "Competing Readings in World Literature." Trans. Nick Caistor. *New Left Review* 48 (Nov.–Dec. 2007): 83–107.

Segalen, Victor. *Essai sur l'exotisme: Une aesthétique du divers.* Montpellier: Éditions Fata Morgana, 1978.

———. *Essay on Exoticism: An Aesthetic of Diversity.* Ed. and trans. Yaël Rachel Schlink. Foreword by Harry Harootunian. Durham: Duke University Press, 2002.

———. *Stèles/古今碑錄.* Ed. and trans. Timothy Billings and Christopher Bush. Foreword by Haun Saussy. Middletown: Wesleyan University Press, 2007.

Shaw, Donald L. *Alejo Carpentier.* Boston: Twayne, 1985.

Shih, Shu-mei. "Global Literature and the Technologies of Recognition." *PMLA* 119.1 (Jan. 2004): 16–30.

Sierra, Justo. "Prólogo." *Poesías de Manuel Gutiérrez Nájera.* By Manuel Gutiérrez Nájera. México: Establecimiento Tipográfico de la Oficina Impresora del Timbre, 1896.

Sierra, Rubén. "Baldomero Sanín Cano." *Pensamiento colombiano del Siglo XX.* Ed. Santiago Castro-Gómez. Bogota: Pontificia Universidad Javeriana, 2007.

Silva Beauregard, Paulette. "La lectura, la pose y el desarraigo: Pedro-Emilio Coll y el 'bovarismo hispanoamericano.'" *Acta Literaria* 37 (2008): 81–95.

Simpson-Housley, Paul. *Antarctica: Exploration, Perception and Metaphor.* New York: Routledge, 1992.

Sirinelli, Jean-Francois. *Intellectuels et passions françaises.* Paris: Fayard, 1990.

Siskind, Mariano. "Paul Groussac: El escritor francés y la tradición (argentina)." *El brote de los géneros.* Ed. Noé Jitrik and Alejandra Laera. Buenos Aires: Emecé, 2010. Vol. 10 of *Historia crítica de la literatura argentina.*

Slemon, Stephen. "Magic Realism as Postcolonial Discourse." Zamora and Faris, *Magical Realism* 407–26.

Smith, Adam. *The Theory of Moral Sentiments.* Edited by Knud Haakonessen. Cambridge: Cambridge University Press, 2002.

Sommer, Doris. *Foundational Fictions: The National Romances of Latin America.* Berkeley: University of California Press, 1991.

———. "A Rhetoric of Particularism." *Proceed with Caution, When Engaged by Minority Writing in the Americas.* Cambridge, MA: Harvard University Press, 1999.

Sommer, Doris, and George Yúdice. "Latin American Literature from the 'Boom' On." *Theory of the Novel: A Historical Approach.* Ed. Michael McKeon. Baltimore: Johns Hopkins University Press, 2000.

Sorensen, Diana. *Facundo and the Construction of Argentine Culture.* Austin: University of Texas Press, 1996.

———. *A Turbulent Decade Remembered: Scenes from the Latin American Sixties.* Palo Alto: Stanford University Press, 2007.

Spitta, Silvia. "Traición y transculturación: Los desgarramientos del pensamiento latinoamericano." *Angel Rama y los estudios latinoamericanos.* Ed. Mabel Moraña. Pittsburgh, PA: IILI, 2006.

Spivak, Gayatri Chakraborty. *Death of a Discipline.* New York: Columbia University Press, 2003.

———. "Post-structuralism, Marginality, Post-coloniality, and Value." *Socio-criticism* 5.2 (1989): 43–81.

Stewart, John. *Antarctica: An Encyclopedia.* 2 vols. Jefferson, NC: McFarland, 1990.

Strich, Fritz. *Goethe and World Literature.* Translated by C. A. M. Sym. London: Routledge and Kegan Paul, 1949.

Suárez Cortina, Manuel. "Laicicismo y anticlericalismo en la España de fin de siglo: Manuel González Prada y las 'dos Españas.'" *Manuel González Prada: Escritor de dos mundos.* Ed. Isabelle Tauzin. Lima: Instituto Francés de Estudios Andinos, 2006. 69–98.

Tablada, José Juan. *En el país del sol.* Edited by Rodolfo Mata. Mexico City: UNAM, 2005.

———. *Hiroshigué: El pintor de la nieve y de la lluvia, de la noche y de la luna.* Mexico City: Monografías Japonesas, 1914.

Tanco Armero, Nicolás. *Recuerdos de mis últimos viajes a Japón.* Madrid: Rivadeneyra, 1888.

———. *Viaje de la Nueva Granada a China y de China a Francia.* London: Historical Collection of the British Library, 2010.

Tanoukhi, Nirvana. "The Scale of World Literature." *Immanuel Wallerstein and the Problem of the World: System, Scale, Culture.* Ed. David Palumbo-Liu, Bruce Robbins, and Nirvana Tanoukhi. Durham: Duke University Press, 2011.

Taussig, Michael T. *Shamanism, Colonialism, and the Wild Man: A Study in Terror and Healing.* Chicago: University of Chicago Press, 1986.

Taylor, Charles. *Hegel and Modern Society.* Cambridge: Cambridge University Press, 1979.

Tekin, Latife. *Dear Shameless Death.* Trans. Saliha Parker and Mel Kenne. New York: Marion Boyar, 2001.

Teng, Wei. "Translating Political Writing into Formal Experiment: Magical Realism and Chinese Literature in 1980s." Unpublished translation, 2011.

Tesler, Mario. *Paul Groussac en la Biblioteca Nacional.* Buenos Aires: Ediciones de la Biblioteca Nacional, 2006.

Thomsen, Mads Rosendahl. *Mapping World Literature: International Canonization and Transnational Literatures.* London: Continuum, 2008.

Tinajero, Araceli. *Orientalismo en el modernismo hispanoamericano.* West Lafayette: Purdue University Press, 2004.

Trigo, Abril. "Algunas reflexiones acerca de la literatura mundial." Sánchez Prado, *América Latina* 89–100.

Trigo, Benigno. "*Los raros* de Darío y el discurso alienista finisecular." *Revista Canadiense de Estudios Hispánicos* 18.2 (1994): 293–307.

Trumpener, Katie. "World Music, World Literature. A Geopolitical View." *Comparative Literature in an Age of Globalization.* Ed. Haun Saussy. Baltimore: Johns Hopkins University Press, 2006.

Tsu, Jing. "World Literature and National Literature(s)." D'haen, Damrosch, and Kadir 158–68.

Ugarte, Manuel. *Crónicas de bulevard.* Paris: Garnier Hermanos, 1903.

———. *Escritores iberoamericanos de 1900.* Santiago de Chile: Editorial Orbe, 1943.

Urbaneja Achelpohl, Luis Manuel. "Más sobre literatura nacional." *Cosmópolis* 11 (June 1895): 49–57.

———. "Sobre literatura nacional." *Cosmópolis* 10 (May 1895): 21–24.

Uslar Pietri, Arturo. "Las lanzas coloradas." *Las lanzas coloradas y cuentos selectos.* Caracas: Biblioteca Ayacucho, 1979.

———. *Letras y hombres de Venezuela.* Caracas: Ediciones EDIME, 1958.

———. "La lluvia." *Las lanzas coloradas y cuentos selectos.* Caracas: Biblioteca Ayacucho, 1979.

———. "The Rain." *Spanish American Short Story: A Critical Anthology.* Ed. Seymour Menton. Berkeley: University of California Press, 1980. 327–41.

———. "Realismo mágico." *Godos, insurgentes y visionarios.* Barcelona: Seix Barral, 1986.

———. *The Red Lances.* Trans. Harriet de Onís. New York: Knopf, 1963.

Valera, Juan. *Cartas americanas: Primera serie.* Madrid: Fuentes y Capdeville, 1889.

Valéry, Paul. "Carta de Paul Valéry a Francis de Miomandre." *Tres obras: Leyendas de Guatemala. El alhajadito. El señor presidente.* By Miguel Ángel Asturias. Caracas: Ayacucho, 1977.

Van den Abbeele, Georges. *Travel as Metaphor: From Montaigne to Rousseau.* Minneapolis: University of Minnesota Press, 1991.

Venn, Couze. *Occidentalism: Modernity and Subjectivity.* London: Sage Publications, 2000.

Verlaine, Paul. *Les poètes maudits.* Paris: León Vanier, 1888.

Verne, Jules. *Autour de la lune.* Paris: Le Livre de Poche, 2001.

———. *Cinq semaines en ballon.* Paris: J. Hetzel, 1865.

———. *De la terre à la lune.* Paris: Le Livre de Poche, 2001.

———. *Five Weeks in a Balloon; or, Journeys and Discoveries in Africa by Three Englishmen.* Trans. William Lackland. Boston: James R. Osgood, 1873.

———. *"From the Earth to Moon," Including the Sequel "Round the Moon."* Trans. Louis Mercier and Eleanor King. New York: Didier, 1947.

———. *Le tour du monde en 80 jours.* Paris: Livre de Poche, 2000.

Viñas, David. *Literatura argentina y realidad política: De Sarmiento a Cortázar.* Buenos Aires: Ediciones Siglo Veinte, 1974.

Walkowitz, Rebecca L. *Cosmopolitan Style: Modernism beyond the Nation.* New York: Columbia University Press, 2006.

Warnes, Christopher. *Magical Realism and the Postcolonial Novel: Between Faith and Irreverence.* London: Palgrave Macmillan, 2009.

———. "Naturalising the Supernatural: Faith, Irreverence and Magical Realism." *Literature Compass* 2 (2005): 1–16.

Watt, Ian. *The Rise of the Novel: Studies in Defoe, Richardson and Fielding.* Berkeley: University of California Press, 1984.

Wellek, René. "The Crisis of Comparative Literature." *Concepts of Criticism.* Ed. Stephen G. Nichols Jr. New Haven: Yale University Press, 1963.

Wilde, Eduardo. *Por mares i por tierras.* Buenos Aires: Jacobo Peuser, 1899.

Wilde, Oscar. "English Renaissance of Art." *Essays and Lectures.* Rockville, MD: Arc Manor, 2008.

Williams, Raymond. *The English Novel from Dickens to Lawrence.* London: Chatto and Windus, 1970.

Wispé, Lauren. "The Distinction between Sympathy and Empathy: To Call Forth a Concept, a Word Is Needed." *Journal of Personality and Social Psychology* 50.2 (1986): 314–21.

Yan, Mo. *Big Breasts and Wide Hips.* Trans. Howard Goldblatt. New York: Arcade Publishing, 2004.

Yepes-Boscán, Guillermo. "Asturias, un pretexto del mito." *Hombres de maíz.* By Miguel Ángel Asturias. Ed. Gerald Martin. Paris: Archivos, 1992.

Young, David, and Keith Holloman, eds. *Magical Realist Fiction: An Anthology.* New York: Longman, 1984.

Zamora, Lois Parkinson. "Magical Romance/Magical Realism: Ghosts in U.S. and Latin American Fiction." Zamora and Faris, *Magical Realism* 497–550.

———. "*One Hundred Years of Solitude* in Comparative Literature Courses." *Approaches to Teaching Garcia Marquez's "One Hundred Years of Solitude."* Ed. Maria Elena Valdes and Mario J. Valves. New York: MLA, 1990.

Zamora, Lois Parkinson, and Wendy B. Faris. "Introduction: Daiquiri Birds and Flaubertian Parrot(ie)s." Zamora and Faris, *Magical Realism* 1–11.

———, eds. *Magical Realism.* Durham: Duke University Press, 1995.

Zanetti, Susana. "El modernismo y el intelectual como artista: Rubén Darío." *La ciudad letrada, de la conquista al modernismo.* Ed. Carlos Altamirano and Jorge Myers. Buenos Aires: Katz Editores, 2008. Vol. 1 of *Historia de los intelectuales en América Latina.*

Index